BRITISH ACADEMY PAPERS
ON
ANGLO-SAXON ENGLAND

BRITISH ACADEMY PAPERS ON ANGLO-SAXON ENGLAND

SELECTED AND INTRODUCED BY
E. G. STANLEY

Published for THE BRITISH ACADEMY
by THE OXFORD UNIVERSITY PRESS

Oxford University Press, Walton Street, Oxford OX2 6DP
Oxford New York Toronto
Delhi Bombay Calcutta Madras Karachi
Petaling Jaya Singapore Hong Kong Tokyo
Nairobi Dar es Salaam Cape Town
Melbourne Auckland

and associated companies in
Berlin Ibadan

Oxford is a trade mark of Oxford University Press

Published in the United States
by Oxford University Press, New York

British Library Cataloguing in Publication Data
British Academy papers on Anglo-Saxon England.
1. Anglo-Saxon civilisation
I. Stanley, E. G. (Eric Gerald) II.
British Academy
942.01

ISBN 0-19-726084-5

CONTENTS

NOTE ON CONTRIBUTORS

Professor Janet Margaret Bately, *Department of English Language and Literature, King's College, London*

Martin Biddle, *Director of the Winchester Research Unit; Fellow of the British Academy*

Professor Raymond Wilson Chambers (1874–1942), *Fellow of the British Academy*

Professor Bruce Dickins (1889–1978), *Fellow of the British Academy*

Professor Angus McIntosh, *Gayre Institute for Medieval English & Scottish Dialectology, University of Edinburgh; Fellow of the British Academy*

Dr Robin Flower (1881–1946), *Fellow of the British Academy*

Dr Kenneth Sisam (1887–1971), *Fellow of the British Academy*

Professor Albert Hugh Smith (1903–1967), *Quain Professor of English Language and Literature, University College, London; Director of the English Place-Name Society*

Professor Eric Gerald Stanley, *Rawlinson and Bosworth Professor of Anglo-Saxon, University of Oxford; Fellow of the British Academy*

Professor Dorothy Whitelock (1901–1982), *Fellow of the British Academy*

Professor Francis Wormald (1904–1972). *Fellow of the British Academy*

LIST OF PLATES

(between pp. 98 and 99)

INTRODUCTION

By E. G. STANLEY

About two dozen of the papers published in the *Proceedings of the British Academy* have some aspect of Anglo-Saxon studies as their subject. Making a volume of reasonable size in which to reprint some of them inevitably involves selection and therefore, regrettably, omission of several papers of interest and value. A few of the papers omitted in the present collection have been reprinted in other collections, sometimes with revisions; but to others that reason does not apply, and the exigencies of space alone are the reason for their absence.

Among papers excluded because in major respects they have not been found persuasive is Henry Bradley's 'The Numbered Sections in Old English Poetical MSS. [*Proceedings*, VII (1915–1916), 165–87], the first of the Academy's papers on a subject of Anglo-Saxon literary scholarship. Its tabulations of the manuscript sections, some of them numbered, some unnumbered but indicated by larger initials, are still useful. His hypothesis, however, which embraced the poems of the *Beowulf* Manuscript, the Junius Manuscript, the Vercelli Book, and in an appendix the Exeter Book, seemed unlikely. He expressed it thus for *Beowulf* in a generalizing conclusion (p. 182) in which are included all poems in unnumbered sections:

> I find that of all the Old English poems (other than *Beowulf*) which are divided into numbered sections there are only two [*Daniel* and *Christ and Satan*] for which it has not been proved that the sections correspond to the separate sheets of the poet's autograph. I therefore conclude that each section of *Beowulf* represents one of the sheets or leaves on which the poem was written by the man to whom it owes its present literary form.

When the table of contents of *Proceedings* VII appeared, the title of Bradley's paper was given as 'The Numbered Lections in Old English Poetical MSS.', and most Anglo-Saxonists would agree with that wording: the sections are of suitable length to serve as lections for reading aloud.

The aim in selecting the ten papers has been to show the range of Anglo-Saxon studies as communicated to the Academy in its papers: history, language and literature, archaeology, history of art, place-name studies, and the history of Anglo-Saxon scholarship. The subject-matter of the selected studies ranges beyond the dates of Anglo-Saxon England, reaching back in time to the archaeology of pre-Roman Winchester, and reaching forward to post-Conquest manuscript illumination with roots in Anglo-Saxon art.

The state of knowledge has, of course, not stood still. Most strikingly perhaps in these papers, our knowledge of Anglo-Saxon Winchester has changed—but also in establishing details of the authorship of the Old English Bede in Dorothy Whitelock's paper, and concerning major parts of the Anglo-Saxon Chronicle in Janet Bately's paper. The brief biography of Laurence Nowell in Robin Flower's paper is made irrelevant by the recognition [first advanced by R. M. Warnicke, 'Note on the Court of Requests Case of 1571', *English Language Notes*, xi (1973–1974), 250–6, and the same author's 'The Laurence Nowell Manuscripts in the British Library', *British Library Journal*, v (1979), 201–12] that Laurence Nowell, the sixteenth-century Saxonist and transcriber of manuscripts, is not the nearly contemporary Dean of Lichfield of the same name.

Flower, though he says, 'I need not compose a eulogy of Laurence Nowell', does so in fact. His important account of the Anglo-Saxon scholarship of the age of Archbishop Matthew Parker, firmly attached to the manuscript evidence that has come down to us in marginalia, glossing and transcriptions, shows for the first time that Nowell deserves praise as pre-eminent among these earliest Saxonists, because he was not merely an interpreter but also a transmitter of material, some of which would otherwise have been lost to us. That account, written over fifty years ago, is unaffected by the question of who Nowell was.

Most Anglo-Saxonists—and probably some others—would accept that Bede is to be numbered among 'master minds'; and perhaps R. W. Chambers spends too much of the little time at his disposal in the Lecture on a Master Mind for 1936, 'Bede', in justifying his choice of subject. He may give too many stories to content his severest readers; but he must have been a delight to hear. The version of the lecture reprinted by R. W. Chambers himself [in *Man's Unconquerable Mind* (London: Jonathan Cape, 1939), 23–52] is a little longer. For the *Proceedings* (as here reprinted) he cut out the account of Bede's death, which, I have been told by one present when he read his paper in May 1936, moved him to tears; but he left out nothing in his paper of what is of scholarly importance for the age of Bede. The Leningrad MS of the *Historia*, for example, is singled out by him as not sufficiently regarded in 1936.

Bruce Dickins's account of 'the life and work of a pioneer of Old English scholarship', J. M. Kemble, 1807–1857, provides a bibliography of Kemble's writings which touched many aspects of Anglo-Saxon literature and history, and included important contributions on *Beowulf, Solomon and Saturn* and related texts, and the poems of the Vercelli Book, especially *The Dream of the Rood* in relation to the Ruthwell Cross inscription. Though in many ways an imperfect basis for the modern study of Anglo-Saxon charters, Kemble's edition of them in *Codex Diplomaticus Aevi Saxonici* was a milestone. The memoirs of Kemble's sister Fanny give us insights into his early life.

Francis Wormald's Aspect of Art Lecture, on 'The Survival of Anglo-Saxon Illumination after the Norman Conquest', suggests a reason for some of the 'exaggerated' mannerisms of Anglo-Saxon illumination, namely, 'the intense love of the Anglo-Saxon artists for expressive line and for the reduction of the object represented to terms of pattern', and he praises that art in absolute terms. At the same time, Wormald fits the achievement in Insular manuscript illumination into the wider context of related continental schools. The centre of Wormald's study is the art of English illumination following that of the Anglo-Saxons and a development of it: 'there was no break with the traditional style, which continued unimpaired both in initial ornament and in outline drawing to about 1120, when new romanesque styles began to influence English artists, but they were not overwhelmed by these new influences.'

Angus McIntosh's analysis of Old English rhythmical prose, specifically that of Archbishop Wulfstan, has enabled readers to understand better some fundamental differences between the rhythm of Wulfstan's prose and Ælfric's, and also between prose rhythms of various kinds and the rhythm of Old English verse, strict and less strict. His analysis of the rhythmic patterns of prose, including Wulfstan's is often borne out by manuscript pointing, much like the pointing of the verse in the Junius Manuscript. On the basis of Wulfstan's rhythm McIntosh directs his attention to the Wulfstan canon.

The early royal Anglo-Saxon genealogies, a unique collection of semi-mythological materials, are discussed by Kenneth Sisam. The basis of the study is the manuscript record, how the name-forms appear in the manuscripts, in what spelling, in what order, with what alliteration if any, and whether they are given in the narrative or in columns. An explanation for the existence of genealogies is perhaps to be sought in the fact that 'great men of the Heroic period took pride in their memory for relationships'.

An appendix deals specifically with the Scylding pedigree in *Beowulf*.

A. Hugh Smith builds on the collections of the English Place-Name Society to emphasize interpretations of the assembled place-name evidence. This is the aspect of the subject in which, as the collecting of materials continues county by county, many interesting conclusions have been reached in the thirty years and more since he read his paper (in February 1956), often along lines adumbrated by him. As Smith points out, the limitations of the evidence, its late date in many cases and the complications of spellings, do not allow conclusions to be reached easily or, in many cases, securely. Nevertheless, already by 1956 much had been achieved.

The starting point of Dorothy Whitelock's study of the Old English Bede is an investigation of why it is right to go against Ælfric's clear statement that King Alfred himself translated the *Historia:* 'It is high time that we looked at the Old English Bede, without prejudging any issues.' We are taught to read Bede's *Historia* with the selecting eye of a careful Anglo-Saxon ecclesiastical historian, and in the process we learn that the spirit in which the translator went to work was at variance with that of Bede himself:

> He [the translator] probably regarded the work as in the first place one of religious edification. Bede's attitude to evidence has sometimes been described as modern; it lay outside the conception of the translator.

The complexities of the compilation of the Anglo-Saxon Chronicle are obvious; and Janet Bately demonstrates its development: 'What happens when an Anglo-Saxon chronicler extends an existing chronicle, and what happens when he reworks earlier material, can both be demonstrated from surviving Chronicle versions.' Syntax, vocabulary and variation by other means of expression are carefully considered over different periods of composition, and significant examples are given. On the problem of how far, if at all, the Anglo-Saxon Chronicle of 890 is connected with King Alfred, and the relationship, if any, between the Chronicle of 890 and the Old English Orosius, she reaches the counclusion that 'there is nothing in the vocabulary to support the theory of a particularly close connection between the compilers [of the 890 Chronicle] and either King Alfred or the author of the Old English Orosius.'

Martin Biddle shows how in 1961 not much was known of

Winchester, 'a preferred location for settlement' through the ages, pre-Roman, Roman *Venta Belgarum,* and Anglo-Saxon Winchester, though of course the importance of Winchester in the Anglo-Saxon period was well understood. The early sixties were a time of great building activity in central Winchester, giving archaeologists a rare opportunity. What emerged in the excavations of 1961–1983, which form the subject of Biddle's report, were details not only of the Old Minster and the New Minster, the royal castle and the bishop's palace, but also 'the demonstration that the street plan of medieval and modern Winchester derived from a deliberate act of urban refoundation in the later ninth century'. The amount of work done in the years under review is enormous, yet it covers little more than two per cent of the walled area of the city, though that two per cent was selected in the knowledge that the results were likely to be of great interest. The paper here republished has been revised substantially by the author, and so has benefited from the most recent work on the archaeology of Winchester.

A very small number of misprints and other minor errors have been corrected, where possible with the help of the authors of the papers or others whom it seemed good to consult. On the whole, however, they appear as they did originally in the *Proceedings of the British Academy*. That has led to some inconsistencies, most obviously in the notes to the papers, appearing as footnotes in some of the papers but as endnotes in others. The index of 'Principal Names and Subjects provided by Sisam for his paper (no. 6) has been subsumed in the index to the volume, with the necessary changes in page numbers.

September 1989

SIR ISRAEL GOLLANCZ MEMORIAL LECTURE

LAURENCE NOWELL AND THE DISCOVERY OF ENGLAND IN TUDOR TIMES

By ROBIN FLOWER

Fellow of the Academy

Read 19 February 1935

IT has sometimes been a matter of dispute among historians at what particular date the medieval changed into the modern world; and there is some uncertainty among linguists as to when Middle English became Early Modern English. These are matters of a gradual and imperceptible evolution. But a librarian cannot doubt at what point of time in his subject the medieval world ended. The dissolution of the monasteries and the consequent dispersal of the monastic libraries draw a definite and disastrous line across the whole field of his studies. The monasteries had by then, no doubt, ceased to be the only or the chief centres for the production of books. But there can be no question that they were still the main centres for the conservation of books. And their destruction threw the manuscripts out upon a world where there were as yet no great public or even stable private libraries to receive them. Certain steps had indeed been taken which might have made the Royal Library the general heir to the monastic collections, though even there they would not have been safe from the Commissioners of Edward VI who raged against any books which they were able to describe as 'superstitious'. John Leland, we know, had a commission from Henry VIII in the year 1533–4, the terms of which, as reported by him in a manner perhaps coloured by later events, betray both the intention and the threat. These instructions were:

to peruse and diligently to serche al the libraries of monasteries and collegies of this yowr noble reaulme, to the intente that the monumentes of auncient writers as welle of other nations as of this yowr owne province mighte be brought owte of deadely darkenes to lyvely lighte, and to receyve like thankes of the posterite, as they hoped for at such tyme as they emploied their long and greate studies to the publique wealthe; yea and farthermore that the holy Scripture of God might bothe be sincerely taughte and lernid, al maner of superstition and craftely coloured doctrine of a rowte of the Romaine bishopes totally expellid oute of this your moste catholique reaulme.

When he came to give an account of his stewardship in his pamphlet, *The Laboryouse Journey and Serche of Johan Leylande for Englandes Antiquitees*, printed in 1546, he wrote thus:

First I have conservid many good autors, the which other wise had beene like to have perischid to no smaul incommodite of good letters, of the whiche parte remayne yn the moste magnificent libraries of yowr royal Palacis. Parte also remayne yn my custodye. Wherby I truste right shortely so to describe your moste noble reaulme, and to publische the Majeste and the excellent actes of your progenitors (hitherto sore obscurid booth for lak of enprinting of such workes as lay secretely yn corners, and also bycause men of eloquence hath not enterprisid to set them forthe yn a florisching style, yn sum tymes paste not communely usid in England of wryters, otherwise welle lernid, and now yn such estimation that except truethe be delicately clothid yn purpure her written verites can scant finde a reader;) that al the worlde shaul evidently perceyve that no particular region may justely be more extollid than yours for trewe nobilite and vertues at al pointes renoumed.

The works here projected to be written in the inkhorn terms with which Leland menaces us never came to fruition. A friend of his, quoted by Bale, suggests that his style was the cause of his downfall: 'I muche do feare it that he was vayneglоryouse and that he had a poetycall wytt, whyche I lament, for I judge it one of the chiefest thynges that caused hym to fall besydes hys ryghte discernynges.' But in his pamphlet he gives a list of these abortive projects. The list begins inevitably with his Antiphilarchia 'concerning the usurpid autorite of the Bishop of Rome and his complices'. Then he proposed to have made a map engraved upon silver so couched that 'it shaul be no mastery after for the graver or painter to make a like by a perfecte exemple'. Next was to follow a book upon the writers of Britain, a work which was executed and lay long in MS. till it was printed in 1709. Then was to come a compilation in fifty books, 'De Antiquitate Britannica', and another in six books on the islands adjacent to Great Britain, and a third on the kings and nobles of all the races that had inhabited the island 'so that al noble mene shaul clerely perceyve theyr lineal parentele'. This scheme, too vast for performance even though Leland should have abated his stylistic ambitions, served as a draft instruction for the labours of all the antiquaries of the Tudor times whose collections form a considerable part of the great Cottonian library. Leland's activities had three main ends: the preservation of the records of the English past, the full exploitation *ad maiorem gloriam Britanniae* of the material thus conserved, and the mapping of the face of that England which he had traversed and lovingly observed in his toilsome journeys.

No student of the antiquarian activities of the second half of the sixteenth century can fail to perceive these ideals at work. The vain attempts of Bale and Sir Robert Cotton and his associates to persuade Queen Mary and Queen Elizabeth to erect a Royal Library for the preservation of England's antiquities, the creation by Archbishop Parker and Cotton of the great libraries which served as a substitute for this defeated design, the histories of Holinshed and others, the publication by Parker and his associates of English chronicles, the *Britannia* of William Camden, and the magnificent development of Elizabethan cartography—all these vigorous enterprises hark back to Leland, and his name is always on the lips of the participants in this great movement for the rediscovery of the records of the English past and the depiction of the physical face of England. But between Leland's death in 1552 and the foundation of the Elizabethan Society of Antiquaries about 1572 a number of scholars of obscurer name were active in the task of keeping his ideals alive. It is of a representative of this intermediate generation that I am to speak to-day.

This is Laurence Nowell, Dean of Lichfield, who since the days of Camden has been frequently and justly described as the restorer of the Anglo-Saxon language and learning. He was more than that, as I hope to show, but that has always been his chief claim to consideration. The evidences for his life are scanty and he has left no personal records behind him. We are forced back upon his surviving MSS. and the signs of his influence upon the work of others, if we would restore any image of his mind and the aims which he proposed to himself. The events of his life may be briefly sketched. He was a Lancashire man, the son of John Nowell of Read Hall in Whalley by Elizabeth Kay, his second wife, and the brother of two men of note, Alexander Nowell, the famous Dean of St. Paul's, and Robert Nowell, attorney-general of the Court of Wards, whose charitable legacy assisted the struggles of the young Edmund Spenser. He was born early in the sixteenth century and entered Brasenose College, Oxford, in 1536, afterwards migrating to Cambridge and graduating there in 1542. He was incorporated B.A. at Oxford and proceeded M.A. there in 1544. Of his studies we have no record. He was a good Latinist, and a minutely annotated copy of the first book of Herodotus, now in the British Museum, proves that he was, according to the standards of his day, an excellent Greek scholar. In 1546 he was appointed master of the grammar school at Sutton Coldfield in Warwickshire. His experience there was unfortunate, for articles were exhibited against him in chancery by the corporation of the town as patrons of the school for neglect of duty, though proceedings were stayed in 1550 by order from the privy council to the warden and fellowship of Sutton that he should not be removed 'unless they have found some notable offences'. It has sometimes been thought that some religious difference was at the bottom of these proceedings, but proof is lacking, and it may well be that there was real neglect of duty occasioned by the linguistic and geographical studies which were already claiming his attention. At any rate his extreme Protestant views made it necessary for him to take shelter at Mary's accession, and he fled, first to Wales where he stayed in the house of Sir John Perrot, King Harry's reputed son and a future Lord Deputy of Ireland, and then to Germany where his brother Alexander had taken refuge. On the Queen's death he returned to England and was made archdeacon of Derby in 1558 and Dean of Lichfield in 1559. He became tutor to the young Earl of Oxford some time before 1563, living in Sir William Cecil's house in the Strand, and accumulated pluralities, being prebendary of Chichester and York and rector of Haughton and Drayton Basset in Staffordshire. We shall see that these years of the sixties, when he was constantly in London with access to the MS. collections which were gathering there, were the period of his greatest activity when most of his significant work was done. In 1570 he was accused by Peter Morwent, prebendary of Lichfield, of having uttered scandal about Queen Elizabeth and the Earl of Leicester, but this was probably a matter of the jealousies of a Cathedral close, based upon some idle word. In 1575 he bought a house and estate at Sheldon and some land at Coleshill, both in Warwickshire. He died about October 1576 and lies buried, it is thought, at Weston in Derbyshire. He left by his wife Mary two sons, Laurence and Thomas, and three daughters.

To these few records of his life may be added a note of his travels. He had been in Italy, for he bought his copy of Stephanus's Greek Lexicon in Padua, and we know that he had observed the characteristic Italian art of mosaic with an appreciative eye and had studied Italian cartography. In 1568 he was in France and there transcribed the history of William of Jumièges from a copy of some antiquity.

It will appear that in London he associated with the circle of Archbishop Parker, the friend and friendly rival in the collection of MSS. of his patron Cecil,[1] being clearly on terms of scholarly intimacy with John Joscelin, Parker's secretary, a fellow student of Old English records. His brother Robert was attorney-general of the Court of Wards of which Cecil was master, and it has been suggested that through him Nowell met the young lawyer, William Lambarde, who was his pupil in Lincoln's Inn, his associate in his studies, and the inheritor of his library. The mind of a scholar of that age may best be discerned in the books he possessed, the books to which he had access, and where, as in this case, he published nothing, by the materials which he gathered in the course of his work. There is ample matter of this nature for Nowell, but before entering on the discussion of these remains I should like to consider his possible relations with Leland, whose inspiration can be observed in the direction of his studies. He may well have known him personally, though there is no direct evidence for their meeting. In Leland's *Collectanea* two papal letters of the tenth century are quoted as from a MS. of the letters of Alcuin. These same two letters are cited by Joscelin in a volume of collections for Anglo-Saxon history, now Cotton MS. Vitellius D. vii, from a MS. in the hands of Master Nowell.[2] This MS. must be the Cotton MS. Tiberius A. xv, which contains the letters of Alcuin and a collection of letters of the tenth century, printed from this MS. by Bishop Stubbs in his *Memorials of St. Dunstan*. An examination of the volume discloses notes in Joscelin's hand, probably made when he was working for Parker on the lives of the archbishops of Canterbury, and on the margins blackened by the fire of 1731 are still to be discerned a number of notes in Leland's script. This was probably one of the books reserved by Leland for himself after his laborious search. And I would venture to suggest that, like other MSS. of Nowell's in the Cottonian Library, it was given to Sir Robert Cotton by Lambarde. If we could assume that Nowell had the book from Leland, the whole history of the manuscript in the sixteenth century would be clear to us.

Our knowledge of Nowell's manuscripts is derived from two main sources. In an appendix to the article on William Lambarde in Nichols's *Bibliotheca Topographica Britannica* there is a list of a collection of transcripts, then in the possession of Multon Lambard, clearly inherited from his famous ancestor. An examination of this list discloses that they were in the main either in Nowell's hand or copied from his original transcripts by Lambarde himself. Most of these manuscripts still survive, and by the generous gift of Lord Howard de Walden eight of them have come in recent years to the British Museum, where they are numbered as Additional MSS. 43703–43710. Others were in the Lambarde sale at Hodgson's rooms in 1924. Another came into the hands of Ralph Thoresby, the historian of Leeds, and is carefully described by him in the account of his Museum appended to his *Ducatus Leodiensis*. The Cottonian Library contains a set of transcripts by Nowell in the MS. Vespasian A. v and a collection of maps and historical texts made by him in Domitian viii, both given to Sir Robert Cotton by Lambarde, and, in Vitellius E. v, a series of copies made from originals in Nowell's hand by Francis Thynne and others in Lambarde's house at Halling in Kent in 1592. The Bodleian Library possesses Nowell's famous Old English Dictionary, which again has passed through Lambarde's hands.[3] It is clear from all this that Lambarde came into possession of his master Nowell's library. It might be assumed that Nowell had bequeathed his books to Lambarde. But this, it will appear, was not the case.

Fortunately a considerable number of Nowell's transcripts are dated, and an examination of these books in the order of their dates will shed a good deal of light upon his method of work, the sources of his materials, and the purpose which all his activity was intended to serve. Significantly enough the first dated book brings us once more into contact with Leland. It is a print of his poem *Cygnea Cantio*, 1545,[4] with its elaborate appendix in which he explains the derivation of the place-names with which that poem is liberally besprinkled. To this Nowell, who acquired the book in 1561, has prefixed a transcript of the similar appendix on place-names printed at the end of Leland's poem *Genethliacon Edwardi*, published in 1543. Notes calling attention to the place-names, some in Nowell's, some in Lambarde's hand, occur in the margins throughout. The intention is clear: to collect all Leland's information upon the Old English and Welsh forms of the place-names of Great Britain. In 1562 Nowell drew up a list of parishes in England, which was in Multon Lambard's library, but has since disappeared. In the same year he made a complete transcript in Sir William Cecil's house of the MS. which was afterwards to be the Cottonian MS. Otho B. xi, containing the Alfredian translation of Bede's *Ecclesiastical History*, the *Anglo-Saxon Chronicle*, a collection of Anglo-Saxon laws, and an Old English poem on the fasts of the church.[5] As this manuscript was almost totally destroyed in the fire of 1731, Nowell's transcript has been the means of preserving it for us. Again in this year he copied the Topography and Itinerary of Wales of Giraldus Cambrensis from different MSS.[6] In the next year, 1763, he wrote a letter to Sir William Cecil, proposing to make a series of maps of English counties, which has been preserved in the Burleigh Papers now in the Lansdowne collection in the British Museum.[7] In 1564 he prepared a volume, now lost, which in the Multon Lambard catalogue is entitled 'Hiberniae Descriptio' and described as incomplete.[8] I think we may spare ourselves conjecture as to the nature of this work, for it is not likely to have differed much from his collections for Irish history and geography which have come down to us in Domitian xviii. The years 1565 and 1566 were clearly given up to the study of English history and antiquities. In 1565 he and Lambarde transcribed the shorter history of Matthew Paris from the MS. now Royal MS. 14 C. vii, then owned by Lord Arundel who lent it to Parker for his edition. In the same year Nowell compiled the volume which Thoresby owned, which has since disappeared. The contents of this latter volume are interesting. They included a copy or abstract of Higden's *Polychronicon*, a series of perambulations of forests in different parts of England in the reigns of Henry III and Edward I, a number of charters of Westminster Abbey, collections for the history of Tewkesbury Abbey, the Old English text excerpted from Alfred's Orosius of Ohthere's account of Northern Europe, excerpts from the Worcester Chartulary, and, finally, a catalogue of the bishops of Chichester. We shall probably not be far wrong in assigning to this same date his abstract of the *Polychronicon* now British Museum Add. MS. 43708 and his extracts from the Worcester Chartulary in Vespasian A. v. This latter MS. also contains excerpts from Symeon of Durham's chronicle and from Sprott's history of Canterbury. In 1566 he excerpted the chronicle of Florence of Worcester,[9] William of Malmesbury's work on the antiquity of Glastonbury and a history of the bishops of Bath and Wells. Two other copies made in this year must be reserved for later discussion. They are the account of the life and death of Edward II, here attributed to Sir Thomas de la More, and an Appendix to Irish History derived from the chronicle of Henry of Marleburgh.[10]

One last copy by this indefatigable transcriber remains to be recorded, the William of Jumièges taken from an old MS. in France in 1568 which appeared in the Lambarde sale at Hodgson's in 1924. So far as my knowledge goes this is the last known writing of his in existence, and the remaining seven years of his life are, for the purpose which we have in view, a blank. This is a curious circumstance and at first sight inexplicable. It is certainly strange that an activity which had seemed to be increasing in range and intensity should come to so sudden a conclusion. Nevertheless, I think that I can offer some explanation of this curious fact, though I cannot profess to have traced the motives which brought it about.

The real end of Nowell's work, it is clear, came in 1566.

The William of Jumièges of 1568 is a kind of epilogue added almost inconsequently in another country. Now we have other evidence of Nowell's journey into France. Lambarde published in 1568 his *'Αρχαιονομία*, the *editio princeps* of the Anglo-Saxon Laws. In the introduction to this book he tells us how, before going to France, Laurence Nowell had given him his transcript of the Laws, bidding him publish them with a translation. In the Old English Dictionary at Oxford, Lambarde records Nowell's gift of that book to him in this same year. The Cotton MS. Domitian xviii, one of the chief monuments of Nowell's cartography, had been for some time in Lambarde's possession in 1574. And I think that it can be proved that the other transcripts which came into his hands had been handed over some years before 1570. But before considering this point, it will be well to discuss the intention which can be read behind all this restless compilation of material.

When Hickes published his *Thesaurus Linguarum Septentrionalium* in 1703–5 he included in it a 'Dissertatio Epistolaris', in which he discussed the tasks which lay before Old English scholarship. Among the chief desiderata in that field he placed the making of a topography of Anglo-Saxon England with the place-names in the Old English form, accompanied by a commentary giving the historical associations of the places so recorded.[11] In the Preface to the three volumes of that great work, written later than the 'Dissertatio', he says that he had since remembered that an attempt had already been made to realize this ideal, partly by Leland in his *Cygnea Cantio*, and more completely by Nowell in his map of Saxon England in Domitian xviii. We have seen that Nowell's work, in the dated transcripts which we possess, began with a collection into one volume in 1561 of all Leland's contributions to the study of Old English place-names. And an examination of his manuscripts reveals that in many cases he treated his originals in a peculiar fashion. His transcripts are often not so much complete reproductions of his sources as a series of excerpts chosen with an eye to the place-names in the text in question, and the place-names so treated are often noted in the margin, sometimes in Nowell's, sometimes in Lambarde's hand. We shall see in the sequel that the *Anglo-Saxon Chronicle* is copied from the Peterborough MS. with collation of all the MSS. accessible to Nowell. This, of course, was a main quarry for the Old English place-names, and their occurrence is noted with especial care in the margin. A study of the Dictionary shows that place-names are there carefully annotated with historical notes. And all this material is set out cartographically in the dissected map of England with Old English place-names which occupies so many pages of Domitian xviii. The intention suggested by the character of these transcripts becomes clear in a passage from the dedication of the first draft of Lambarde's *Perambulation of Kent* to Thomas Wotton, written in 1570:

> To speake playnly, I had somewhile synce gathered out of dyvers ancient histories of this our Contrie sundry notes of suche qualitie, as might serve for the description & stoarie of the moste famous places thorough out this whole Realme: w[ch] Collection bicause it was digested into titles by order of Alphabet, and concerned the description of places I called a Topographicall Dictionary, and out of w[ch] I ment in tyme (if god graunted life and leisure) to drawe (as from a certen stoare howse) fitt matter for eache perticular shire and Contrie. Nowe after that it had pleased god to provide for me in Kent I resolued for sundrie respectes to begynne wth that Shire, and therein (before I wolde move any further) to make estimation and triall, bothe of the thinge it selfe, of myne owne habilitie, and of other mens likinges. [Earlier in this dedication he had written:] I . . . did not onely myselfe digge and rake together whatsoeuer I coulde of that kynde, but procured dyuers of my fryndes also to set to their handes, and doe the like.

Lambarde's *Perambulation* is famous as the first of the great series of county histories which are one of the glories of English antiquarian scholarship. This dedication shows that he had intended to treat the rest of the counties after the same fashion. We have good evidence that he was deterred from this project by the appearance of Camden's *Britannia* in 1586, a book which might well have seemed to contemporaries to have set the final term to the movement initiated by Leland. But the Topographical Dictionary which he had prepared as a quarry for the detailed individual histories of the counties remained in the hands of his family and was put into print in 1730 under the title *Dictionarium Angliae Topographicum et Historicum.* This work was already in existence, we have seen, in 1570, when Lambarde refers to it in his dedication to the *Perambulation.* How long it had been in preparation we cannot certainly say, but much of the material it contains is drawn from transcripts by Nowell made in 1566. Thus there are many references to Thomas de la More, who, we shall see later, was first revealed to Elizabethan historiography by Nowell's abstract from the chronicle of Geoffrey le Baker made in that year. In this same year too Lambarde transcribed into the manuscript, now Cotton MS. Titus A. xiii, another of Nowell's characteristic abbreviations of the chroniclers. This is the work constantly cited in his Topography as the continuator of Prosper of Aquitaine. The title appears to be based upon a misapprehension of the source which he was using. This was a series of abstracts from a form of Higden's *Polychronicon*, resembling, my colleague Mr. Wright informs me, that found in Harley MS. 655, although in the earlier part Henry of Huntingdon and other chroniclers appear to have been drawn upon. Nowell's manuscript is Add. MS. 43708, a squat little book first used by him for the preparation of a manual of French conversation, and phrases in that language run along the tops of the pages. Afterwards on the first page Nowell has entered a note about Prosper the chronicler, and beneath this he has written down a number of moral sentences from other works of that author. This no doubt misled Lambarde into making the very unlikely invention of a continuator of Prosper. We may deduce from this that, when he was making the copy, he was not in direct contact with

Nowell. Lambarde's Topographical Dictionary was thus put together, in all probability, between 1566 and 1570, though there is reason to believe that he made additions to it up to 1577. It was based in large part upon transcripts made by Nowell with some such purpose in view, an intention disclosed as early as 1561 by the addition of the topographical appendix to Leland's *Genethliacon* in Nowell's copy of the *Cygnea Cantio*. Taking these abstracts from the chroniclers in connexion with Nowell's cartographical work, we shall, I think, be justified in claiming that the original scheme was Nowell's, although, no doubt, Lambarde, his pupil, was associated with it from an early stage. We have seen that Nowell had given certain manuscripts indispensable to his studies to Lambarde in 1567. Must we not assume on the basis of these facts that on his departure into France he handed over all his collections to Lambarde, probably with the injunction (for which we have proof in the case of the Anglo-Saxon Laws) to carry on the work which he himself lacked either the opportunity or the humour to continue?

It is difficult to explain this sudden renunciation of a scheme at which he had worked so assiduously and so long. We do not know why he went to France or how long he remained there, or what was the state of his health during the seven years which still remained to him. In the absence of evidence it is idle to conjecture. When Lambarde wrote his dedication in 1570 he evidently regarded the plan as his own and Nowell only figures as one of his anonymous helpers. But I think the evidence of the manuscripts justifies us in claiming for him a larger part in the scheme, although no doubt he had freely given the results of his work to his favourite pupil.

In those busy years between 1561 and 1566 Nowell's mind was set, as his surviving remains show, upon three main objects: the mapping of England, the discovery and the exploitation of the sources for English historical topography, and the restoration of the Old English language and literature. It is not possible in the space at my disposal to deal adequately with the whole range of his performance under these heads, but some attempt may be made to select salient points which will serve to give some hint of his methods and his aims. His ideals in cartography he sets out in a letter to Sir William Cecil in 1563. He had clearly been in Cecil's house for some considerable time at this date, serving in the probably uneasy function of tutor to the turbulent young Earl of Oxford, during whose wardship under Cecil it is recorded that a scullion from the kitchen tactlessly committed suicide by running on the point of the Earl's sword. The Secretary of State, whose unsleeping passion for detail is written all over the state papers of that age, was particularly interested in cartography, and Nowell must have had every opportunity for discussion with the mapmakers whom he encouraged and employed. The letter begins with a reference to Cecil's delight in maps as aids to the better performance of his function in the State. Nowell then expresses his disapproval of the methods of contemporary cartographers who 'lacking any certain rule and all craft to aid their judgement, either placing their reliance upon the reports of certain others or trusting to the wavering conjecture of their own eyes, have huddled into their charts places set down and spaced by guess'. He has often, hoping to do some service to the state and to please his patron, contemplated the making of more accurate maps, both of the country as a whole and of the individual counties. And he asks for Cecil's support in this arduous task, since his work as tutor to the Earl of Oxford is now approaching its conclusion. Whatever answer Cecil made to this letter, the county maps at least were never made, that task being reserved for Saxton, whose county maps recently republished by the British Museum were in hand in 1574. For Nowell's work upon the general maps of England and Ireland we have two main sources, the map now in the possession of Lord Lansdowne and the series of drafts in the Cottonian MS. Domitian xviii. By the kindness of the late Lord Lansdowne I have had the opportunity of studying his map in the original by the side of the Cottonian charts. But I must confess that this study has left me in the face of certain difficult problems which only an expert in Elizabethan cartography could hope to resolve. I must be content here to pose the problem, without attempting any definite answer. The nature of the two documents may be thought to have some part in creating the difficulty. The Lansdowne map is an exquisitely finished production, exactly drawn with a studied care in its configuration and topographical features. The aim of the dissected map in the Cotton MS. is to serve as an outline for the recording of the Old English names of places, and it may well be that we ought not to expect in this hasty draft the minuter accuracy required by a completed composition. In the Cotton volume the map of England is accompanied by three maps of Ireland and a collection of material for Irish history. We know, from the description of the Multon Lambard collection, that Nowell was engaged in 1564 upon a description of Ireland now lost, and this may well suggest a date for the Cottonian volume which is in harmony with the known date of Nowell's letter to Cecil. The Lansdowne map is undated. It is contained in a small volume, the vellum cover of which has a deep fold running perpendicularly down its middle so profoundly impressed that it must be of very long standing indeed. It was probably this feature which suggested to Lord Shelburne the very likely conjecture, which he has recorded on the cover, that this was the pocket map which Cecil carried about with him. It was at any rate intended for him and there is evidence that he used it. In the two bottom corners of the map a little scene is set out with a delicate art that proves Nowell to have been an exquisite draughtsman in that English school which derived its craft from the writing master's art of engrossing initials in manuscripts with human and animal designs. To the left Nowell represents himself seated on a pedestal in an attitude of deep depression, holding an empty purse downwards with its mouth gaping to the ground. A ferocious dog faces him menacingly, barking. We are reminded of the popular song:

> Hark! hark! the dogs do bark,
> The beggars are coming to town,

or more vividly of those words in which King Lear expresses the last agony of his destitution:

> The little dogs and all,
> Tray, Blanch and Sweetheart, see, they bark at me.

On the pedestal Nowell, remembering his Greek and flattering Cecil's scholarship, has inscribed the words from Hesiod's Works and Days describing Pandora's jar:

> In that strong station Hope alone abode
> Neath the jar's rim, nor fluttered thence abroad.

Facing him in the right corner sits Cecil, with arms grimly folded, uneasily poised upon an hour-glass, in which we may imagine the sands are running out, inscribed with Greek words bidding his suppliant hope on and endure.[12]

We might suppose this vivid scene to be the sequel to the rejection of Nowell's proposals in the letter of 1563, and the superiority of the map over the drafts in Domitian xviii would seem to date its execution after 1564. But there are some points which might appear to imply a much earlier date. On one of the pages of the little book are written three descriptions of routes with distances between places carefully indicated, two alternative routes to Augsburg and the way to Edinburgh, with additions by Cecil. This, as the late Lord Lansdowne pointed out to me, might be taken to refer to Cecil's diplomatic journeys in the fifties. And the curious fact that Nowell depicts himself in lay costume might seem to suggest a date before 1550, when he was ordained. Also it would appear to imply a considerable assurance for a dignitary of the church, in the enjoyment of many pluralities to depict himself with an empty purse, though, to be sure, it is not an unusual thing in any age for people very comfortably off to 'cry poor' when circumstances demand that attitude, and we know that the Elizabethans were exceptionally lacking in scruple in these matters. Also the English map is preceded in the volume by a fine map of Sicily, obviously based upon Italian cartography, and this would seem to indicate a later date than the forties. The exact date of the map must, then, be left in suspense, but, whatever its date, it must count as one of the earliest and most accurate maps of the Tudor time. The interest of the Domitian map is indicated by Hickes, that it was the first attempt to give the place-names of Anglo-Saxon England in their geographical setting. It is to be read in connexion with Lambarde's Topographical Dictionary, based upon Nowell's researches, where the Old English names are systematically set out. The maps of Ireland in this volume are very interesting. My colleague, Mr. Lynam, has pointed out to me their close resemblance to John Goghe's map of 1567. But I have given reasons for believing that Nowell was at work on Ireland in 1564, and it may be that Goghe used his map, or that they borrowed from a common source. A map of Scotland in Domitian, remarkably accurate for its period, shows a piece of the opposite coast of Ulster. Ortelius in 1570 included a similar piece of Ulster in his map of Great Britain. Nowell's Scotland, Mr. Lynam points out, is much in advance of Gerard Mercator's 1564 map of the British Isles, and resembles, though it is an improvement upon, the Scotland in Rumold Mercator's map of 1595. It is also a great advance on the Scotland in the Lansdowne map. The volume also originally contained four maps of the world, but these were given by Lambarde in 1574 to Adrian Stokes and seem to have disappeared. I offer these remarks upon Elizabethan cartography with great hesitation, but at least I may claim that they prove Nowell to have been an innovator far in advance of his age in the mapping of the British Isles.

Nowell's attitude to the English chroniclers and other

historical sources was clearly conditioned by his general historico-topographical aim. A consideration of his surviving and recorded transcripts and of the side-notes to Lambarde's Topographical Dictionary will show how wide his range was. But it will be more interesting now to discuss certain cases in which his researches affected the historiography of his own age and, in some cases, of succeeding times. One curious example is the so-called chronicle of Sir Thomas de la More. I should like to put forward the contention that this reputed French chronicle owes its existence solely to Nowell's activity. Camden in 1603 and, following him, Bishop Stubbs in 1883 printed a work under the title of *Vita et Mors Edwardi Secundi*, said to be translated from the French of Sir Thomas de la More. Stubbs, indeed, with his usual acuteness pointed out that this work was no more than an excerpt from the chronicle of Geoffrey le Baker, much compressed in its earlier part, but practically *verbatim* for those passages which dealt with the king's death. Nevertheless he believed that Geoffrey le Baker was here dependent on a lost French original. Sir Edward Maunde Thompson in his edition of Geoffrey le Baker's chronicle took the view that the reference in that work to Sir Thomas only belonged to certain incidents on which he was Geoffrey's informant.[13] This view I think is entirely supported by a consideration of the sources of the independent *Vita et Mors*. The earliest evidence for the existence of this work is in the familiar form of a transcript by Nowell dated 1566 based upon a manuscript then in the possession of William Bowyer, Keeper of the Records in the Tower. This transcript, now in the British Museum (Add. MS. 43707), is a characteristic example of Nowell's method of making historical excerpts, abbreviating the original text, or copying it in full as his interest dictated. All the other MSS. are later and probably dependent upon Nowell. The Pettyt MS. in the Inns of Court belonged to his friend John Foxe, the martyrologist, and the form of the heading there shows that it derives from Nowell. The copy in Harley MS. 310,

f. 92, professedly derived from Nowell's transcript, is in the hand of one of Parker's scribes. There are two copies in the Cottonian MS. Vitellius E. v, one made by Francis Thynne and the other by an unidentified scribe, but both drawn from Nowell's MS., then (1592) in Lambarde's house at Halling in Kent. Camden was a friend of Lambarde and was obviously dependent upon this same transcript. He knew also of some excerpts made by John Stowe from what he called the chronicle of Thomas de la More, but the character of these extracts makes it clear that they were taken from the complete work of Geoffrey le Baker, possibly the same original as Nowell used. This ghost of Thomas de la More haunts Elizabethan historians. He is naturally used as a source in Lambarde's Topographical Dictionary. Holinshed quotes him freely, and Stowe in his *Annales* and Samuel Daniel in his *History of England* have no doubt of his independent value. We have seen that Bishop Stubbs still had a faint hope of him, but I think that, if Maunde Thompson is not considered to have finally disposed of him, the evidence I have here adduced for Nowell's final responsibility for his independent existence may be held to put the last nail in his coffin.

This may seem a small matter, but, when we turn to Irish history, there seems every reason to believe that Nowell was the first scholar of his age to attempt to construct a connected account of the story of that country. For this purpose he probably used the material which Cecil had accumulated. There is good evidence that Cecil had a special interest in Ireland and, after his habitual fashion, took steps to get the best information he could upon all that pertained to that country's history. In the sixties he commissioned Lythe to make a careful and detailed survey of Ireland for the construction of a map, and Lythe's account of his expenses on his journey is still extant in the Lansdowne MSS. Among the Carew MSS. at Lambeth is a large volume of the genealogies of the Irish chiefs in Cecil's own hand. And a MS. of an abridgement of Pembridge's

Annals of Ireland, now in the British Museum, belonged to Cecil, is carefully annotated by him, and can be proved to have been used by Nowell.[14] We have seen that he compiled a Description of Ireland, now lost, in 1564, and that it is probable that the materials for Irish history and geography still extant in Domitian xviii compensate us for that loss. The chief document in this last collection is a chronicle of Ireland in Nowell's hand, drawn from three main sources. It is in the main derived from the Annals of Philip Flattisbury, a servant of the eighth Earl of Kildare, who in his turn based himself upon Pembridge's Annals. This rather jejune record Nowell has supplemented from the works of Giraldus Cambrensis and the chronicle of Henry de Marleburgh. Now these three writers are the chief authorities for the account of Ireland in Holinshed, and for reasons which I am about to give it is not likely that that account is independent of Nowell. The proof depends upon the MS. authority for Henry de Marleburgh, a fifteenth-century vicar of Ballyshaddan, near Dublin, who compiled a copious chronicle of England based in the main upon Higden's *Polychronicon*, but supplemented by Irish entries derived in the latter stages from personal knowledge. This chronicle only exists in a copious series of extracts in Vitellius E. v, copied by the hand which transcribed Nowell's excerpts from Thomas de la More in Lambarde's house, probably in 1592. There can be little doubt that the copyist's original was again a transcript by Nowell. Where did Nowell find his source? I suggest in Cecil's house. From Dr. Greg's valuable account of Cecil as a collector of MSS. in his article on 'Books and Bookmen in Bishop Parker's correspondence' (*The Library* for December 1935) we know that Cecil possessed a MS. called 'Vetus Chronicon Angliae et Hiberniae'. This MS. is not known to exist, but we may believe that it was the original chronicle of Marleburgh and that Nowell excerpted it and used it when he was putting together his history of Ireland in Domitian xviii in 1564.

Of his other historical work I lack room to speak, but it may be noted that the Annals of Gloucester of Gregory of Caergwent, which contain useful information not found elsewhere, survive only in excerpts in his hand in Vespasian A. v, and that, when in 1735 Hearne printed the *Peregrination* of Andrew Boarde, that quaint roving physician of Henry VIII's day, his sole source was again a transcript by Nowell in the Lambarde collection, then at Sevenoaks.[15] It is plain from all this that, though it was not in his immediate intention, we owe a good deal to Nowell's activity in the transcription of materials for history and topography.

We come at last to that subject which has won him the modest reputation which he has always possessed, the fame of being the first restorer of the Anglo-Saxon language and learning. To some extent Leland, Owen, and Talbot had here paved the way for him. But there can be no doubt that the claim, admitted in his own day, is a just one. John Joscelin, working with him on parallel lines, must always dispute some part in this claim, but his interests were limited to history and particularly ecclesiastical history and controversy, and, as we shall see, Nowell had a juster view and a wider range. The attempt to show that he was much more than an Old English scholar has left me little time to illustrate this side of his work, but this is the less to be regretted as no competent opinion will question his services in this matter.

The first document here is, of course, his Dictionary in the Bodleian Library, the first attempt to make a glossary of Old English words. We may expect an edition of this fascinating book from my friend, Professor Marquardt, of the University of Michigan, and this dispenses me from the need of any minute description. But some points, which demonstrate Nowell's originality, I should like to make. First the question arises as to how such a pioneer set out to make a dictionary at all. Mr. Kenneth Sisam has pointed out that an obvious means of learning Old English in those days was the comparison of translations of Latin texts with their originals.[16] Another was, of course, the study of Latin–Old English glossaries such as that which Ælfric appended to his Grammar. It is possible to indicate one such collection of glossed Latin words which Nowell used. He quotes the word 'Bleostaening', glossing it delightfully in words which must reflect his experiences in Italy:

> Mosaicke workes w^{che} is a kinde of ornament in picture made wth litle square stones like dies of all coulours sette together wth certayne fine cyment vpon a walle or floore so that the foormes of thinges be therewth pourtrayed & expressed as though they were paynted & it is more durable than any other kind of paynting by reason that nayther by wearing, wether nor wasshing the coulour can be taken away w^{che} hath the thicknesse of the litle dies wherewth the woorke is made of. This kinde of woorke is litle in England howbeit I haue seen of it especially upon churche floores before altares, as is to be seen before the high altare at Westminster, although it be but grosse. In Italie it is almost everywhere.

Now the only occurrence of this word in Old English books is in the collection of glossaries in the Cotton MS. Cleopatra A. iii, where it is employed to gloss the Latin word in the odd form 'musac', and it may be confidently assumed that Nowell used this MS. One singular feature of his Dictionary is the use of dialect words from his own speech of Lancashire and some northern dialect to explain the Old English words of which they were the survivals. And in connexion with this it may be said that he recognized dialect forms in Old English, for he quotes Northumbrian variants from the gloss to the Lindisfarne Gospels. This is the earliest mention of that famous MS. in Tudor times. It was given later to Sir Robert Cotton by Robert Bowyer, and we may safely assume that it was then in the possession of William Bowyer, to whose MSS. we know that Nowell had access.

His work on the Anglo-Saxon Laws is represented by his copy of the legal part of the burnt Cotton MS. Otho B. xi and by Lambarde's reproduction of the copies handed to him by Nowell in 1567.[17] It may be noted here that Lambarde used Nowell's Dictionary, presented to him at the same time, and has added a number of words, mainly legal, collected no doubt while he was preparing his Ἀρχαιονομία.

For the topographical work which culminated in his Saxon map of England he made a careful study of the *Anglo-Saxon Chronicle.* It is fortunate that by the survival of a list of the then existing MSS. of the *Chronicle* and their owners, compiled before 1566 by Joscelin, we know exactly where all the chief MSS. of that record or series of records which still exist were at the time when Nowell was engaged upon his work.[18] The Parker MS. was in the hands of Nicholas Wotton, Dean of Canterbury, the famous diplomatist; the Laud MS. was in Cecil's collection, and Joscelin records that Master Nowell possessed a transcript of it, which is now in the British Museum; the B MS. (now Tiberius A. v) was owned by John Twyne of Canterbury; the C MS. (now Tiberius B. i) was in William Bowyer's collection; D (now Tiberius B. iv) was still in the library of Worcester Cathedral; and Otho B. xi (doomed to perish almost entirely in the fire of 1731) was in Cecil's house and was there, to our great good fortune, copied in its entirety by Nowell. Nowell's transcript of the Laud MS. was carefully supplemented from C and D and extracts from these two MSS. are added at the end of the book. The place-names throughout are minutely annotated both by Nowell and Lambarde, obviously in preparation for the Topographical Dictionary. Other extracts from these three MSS. are to be found in the MS. Domitian xviii, which, we have seen, there is good reason to believe Nowell had in hand in 1564. To this date, then, we may tentatively assign his work upon the *Chronicle.* It had, at least by Joscelin's account, proceeded some way in 1566. I may add that, while engaged upon this work, he probably came across King Alfred's account of Ohthere's northern journeys, for the translation of Orosius in which that remarkable document appears preceded the *Chronicle* in Bowyer's MS., now Tiberius B. i, and was copied, no doubt from that source, in 1565 by Nowell into the MS. which Thoresby afterwards possessed. The geographical names in this account are explained in the Dictionary at Oxford, and Nowell's translation of this early narrative of exploration was included by Hakluyt in his *Navigations*. Of another direction of his activity I have left myself no time to speak. He was the only man of his time to take an interest in Old English poetry. I was so fortunate as to identify his hand in the sixteenth-century versions of certain passages in the Exeter Book of poetry. And Mr. Sisam has shown that he owned the famous MS. which contains the epic of *Beowulf*.[19] It is fitting, then, that he should have preserved for us the long and interesting poem on the fasts of the church, unique in Old English poetry by the distribution of the alliterative lines into stanzas, which Lord Howard de Walden's gift of his transcript of Otho B. xi to the British Museum has revealed to us.[20] Of his many services to scholarship this is not one of the least, and it is pleasant to be able to end an account of his labours with this addition to the canon of our early poetry.

I need not compose a eulogy of Laurence Nowell. If the story I have had to tell is true, and I am persuaded that it errs only on the side of incompleteness, his works may be left to speak for him. I hope that my description of him as one of those faithful scholars who, inspired by a devoted patriotism, gave themselves in Tudor times to the discovery of the face of England and the rediscovery of the tradition of England may be accepted as just. He published nothing and his fame has suffered in consequence. He is not so much as mentioned in the chapter on the scholars and antiquaries of that age in the *Cambridge History of English Literature*. He did his work and handed over the results to another.

Of what manner of man he was in his personal life, or how he discharged the important ecclesiastical functions committed to his charge, I can find no sufficient evidence. On these matters it must suffice me to quote two verdicts on him from different points of view. The present Dean of Lichfield, to whose kindness I owe a sight of his valuable pamphlet on his predecessors in that office, ends an interesting account of Nowell with these words: 'The primary devotion of his life was to researches of this kind. His absorption in them, and his prolonged absences in London entailed by them, fortunately prevented him from taking an active part in the administration of the Cathedral where his bent would have been to "pull down and destroy" all Catholic tradition.' It is not for us, who are antiquaries, to thrust ourselves between the 'fell incensèd points of mighty opposites', or to take part in the controversies which still rage round the Elizabethan settlement of the church. We may perhaps rather prefer to acquiesce in the milder verdict of Churton, the biographer of Laurence's brother Alexander, the Protestant Dean of St. Paul's, who writes thus upon him: 'The learned works on which the Dean of Lichfield employed his leisure afford a presumptive argument that he was a good man.'

NOTES

1. For the relations between Parker and Cecil see an article by W. W. Greg, 'Books and Bookmen in Archbishop Parker's Correspondence', *The Library*, Dec. 1935.

2. Leland, *Collectanea*, ed. Hearne, ii, p. 404; Joscelin's collections in Vitellius D. vii, f. 143 a, b.

3. MS. Selden, *supra* 63.

4. British Museum, pressmark C. 95. c. 18.

5. Add. MS. 43703. This MS. also contains a copy of the West Saxon Genealogies, apparently taken from a stray leaf of the Abingdon Chronicle (Cotton MS. Tiberius A. vi) in Tiberius A. iii, f. 178; a complete text of the Burghal Hidage, hitherto only known in a fragmentary form; and a collection of Leechdoms. An edition of texts from this MS. is in preparation.

6. The Topography was copied from a MS. of the first edition closely resembling the Cotton MSS. Nero D. viii and Vitellius C. x. The Itinerary was taken from the manuscript now Add. MS. 34762, the only surviving medieval representative of the second edition of this treatise, which was known to Dimock (Rolls Series ed., p. xi) only from

Harley MS. 359, f. 126, a sixteenth-century transcript from the same Additional MS., probably made for Dr. Dee, notes by whom are at the beginning and end.

7. Lansdowne MS. 6, art. 54, printed by Ellis, *Letters of Eminent Literary Men*, Camden Soc., 1843, p. 20.

8. Certain excerpts in Lansdowne MS. 229, f. 73, made by William Camden in 1573 from a MS. of collections for Irish history by Nowell (?then in Lambarde's possession), were perhaps drawn from this source. They were not taken from Domitian xviii.

9. For Florence of Worcester see Add. MS. 43705. A transcript from this MS. of Nowell's in various hands, perhaps made for Dr. Dee (the hand which copied Geraldus's Itinerarium in Harley MS. 359, see note 6 above, is found also in this MS.), is in Harley MS. 556.

10. Malmesbury, Thomas de la More and the 'Appendix Historiae Hiberniae' are in Add. MS. 43707.

11. Hickes, *Thesaurus*, ii, p. 121. In the Preface, p. xxvii, Hickes, by an error or a misprint, attributes the *Cygnea Cantio* to Selden.

12. The two inscriptions are:

> Μούνη δ' αὐτόθι Ἐλπὶς ἐν ἀρρήκτοισι δόμοισιν
> ἔνδον ἔμιμνε πίθου ὑπὸ χείλεσιν οὐδὲ θύραζε
> ἐξέπτη.
>
> Hesiod, Ἔργα καὶ Ἡμέραι, 96–98.

and

> Οἰστέον καὶ ἐλπιστέον.

13. For Thomas de la More see Camden, *Anglica, Normannica*, etc., 1603; Stubbs, *Chronicles of the Reigns of Edw. I and Edw. II*, ii, p. 297; E. Maunde Thompson, *Chronicon Galfridi le Baker*, Oxford, 1889, p. vi.

14. For Lythe see Lansdowne MS. xxii, art. 72, for the Irish genealogies Lambeth MS. 626 (Carew MS. QQ), and for Pembridge's Annals British Museum Add. MS. 40674 and the Irish MSS. Commission's *Analecta Hibernica*, no. 2 (1931), p. 326.

15. A copy of this, made for Lambarde, is now British Museum Add. MS. 43710. It gives the full text of the *Peregrination*, which was abbreviated in Hearne's edition, and shows that the work was put together in 1535 and dedicated to Prince Edward. Certain notes by Lambarde suggest that he circulated the MS. among informants in England and Ireland, no doubt with the intention of securing supplementary information to be used in his *Topographical Dictionary*.

16. See the article in the *Modern Language Review*, xx, p. 253, in which Mr. Sisam claims that certain passages in Lambarde's *Αρχαιονομία,* for which no source is to be found in surviving MSS. of the Anglo-Saxon Laws, were translated into Old English from the Latin Quadripartitus by Nowell. This claim, contested by Liebermann, appears to be justified by the consideration of certain passages added to Nowell's transcript of the Alfredian Bede from Otho B. xi in Add. MS. 43703, ff. 19b–21. These passages, added between the lines and in the margins, represent certain sentences of Bede's Latin which do not appear in the translation in any of the surviving MSS. Nowell makes no attempt elsewhere to collate his text, and the curious character of the language would suggest that he is solely responsible for the translation. As the point is of some interest and Mr. Sisam's contentions have not been universally accepted, the passages in question may be given here. They occur in Bk. I, capp. xv, xvi. References are here given to Miller's edition, Early English Text Society, i (1890). Ed., p. 52, l. 5, after 'oneardað' is added '7 sio þeod þe git to dæge is geata gehaten ongean pight þæm ealond in pestseaxna mægþ'; l. 8, after 'Norðhembra cynn' is added 'þàs þeod þe norþ humbres þas ea eardiað'; l. 11, after 'Hengest 7 Horsa' is added 'pæs se horsa æfter on gefeoght from Brettas ofgeslôgene 7 hafað git to dæge Byrgene on east dæle centrices þurh his noman ḡ . . .'; l. 19, after 'æfter þissum' is added 'semninga' (Bede 'nec mora'); l. 20, after 'adrifan' is added 'Hie ongunnon piþ hiora geferan compian. on fruman hie him geneddon mære corne sellan', and after 'intingan' is added 'geflites' (Bede 'diuortii', a word so glossed in Cleopatra A. iii, a glossary used by Newell, see above, p. 22); l. 29, after 'land' is added 'from east sæ to pest'. Ed., p. 54, l. 14, after 'Romanisces cynnes mon' is added '7 an þæs cyninglic strynd to lafe gepordene'.

17. Since the delivery of this lecture I have found among the Somner MSS. in the Chapter Library at Canterbury Nowell's transcript of the Laws of Canute from Harley MS. 55, prepared for the press by Lambarde.

18. For Joscelin's list see Cotton MS. Nero C. iii, f. 91, printed by Hearne in his *Robert of Avesbury*, p. 267.

19. See Mr. Sisam's article in *Modern Language Review*, xii, p. 335. A solitary gloss on the first page of the *Beowulf*: 'egsode' glossed 'feared', is in Nowell's hand. It may be noted here that Otho B. xi, on the evidence of Wanley in Hickes, *Thesaurus*, ii, p. 219, at least that part of the MS. containing the Alfredian Bede, came, like the first part of Vitellius A. xv from the monastery of Southwick in Hampshire.

20. For this poem see the *British Museum Quarterly*, viii (1934–5), p. 131. It will be published in the forthcoming edition of texts from Add. MS. 43703 in Methuen's Old English Library.

ANNUAL LECTURE ON A MASTER MIND
HENRIETTE HERTZ TRUST

BEDE

By R. W. CHAMBERS
Fellow of the Academy

Read 27 May 1936

OURS is an age in which those who delight in such things delight to take a 'master mind' and to throw him down from his pedestal. My friend and predecessor in this series, Tenney Frank, speaking of Cicero as a master mind, had to vindicate against cavillers his hero's claim to that title. Indeed, said Professor Frank, 'the first poet of Greece is perhaps the only human being who has attained an undisputed place of honour'. Yet even here he was too optimistic. I was brought up on Mahaffy's *History of Greek Literature*, and Mahaffy and Sayce between them taught me that Homer was *not* a human being, but a collection of interpolations, 'fitted together', which is what the name *Homêros* means, so that 'with a closer insight into the structure of the epic poems' we must depose him from his pedestal and give the first place to Aeschylus.[1] All my lifetime Homer has been slowly climbing back on to his pedestal again. But he has not yet been selected for the 'master mind' lecture. He lacks one important qualification for public recognition as a master mind: a fixed date of death, which will ensure his merits being officially brought under the notice of the Academy at least once every century.

Bede is more fortunate. We can say with fair certainty that he died at the hour of Vespers, on Wednesday, 25 May 735, the eve of Ascension Day. Quite certainly he did not die before that date, so we are on the safe side in keeping his celebration a little late. To-day, the 27th of May, is, of course, his day in the Church's calendar.

[1] *History of Classical Greek Literature*, 3rd edit., 1891, I. i. 284, I. ii. 51.

In a broader sense, it is to his date that Bede owes his supreme position. His life was preceded, and it was followed, by a period of great darkness. The seventh century, in which Bede was born, has been called 'the nadir of the human mind'; or at least a great historian of to-day, George Sarton, has censured a great historian of a century ago, Henry Hallam, for so calling it.[1] Sarton has pointed out that, though things were bad in Europe, the early seventh century was a golden age in Arabia, in Tibet, in China, and in Japan. Hallam hardly deserves the censure of his critic, for what he really said was that the seventh century was the nadir of the human mind in Europe. Two pages later on, however, Hallam does so far abandon caution as to say that 'the Venerable Bede may perhaps be reckoned superior to any man *the world* then possessed'. Hallam would have been on safer ground if here also he had said 'Europe'. To-day, as we pass through any great museum, the marvels of the T'ang dynasty warn the most careless of us not to suppose that 'Europe' and 'the world' are synonymous. But of these things Hallam could know nothing; they were hidden in recesses of China and Japan then inaccessible to Westerners.

Amid the European darkness of the seventh and eighth centuries Bede's life 'throws its beams' far; it shines, as Bede's editor, Charles Plummer, has said, like

a good deed in a naughty world.

Or rather, *we* will say, 'like a good deed in a naughty Europe'.

Bede is the most striking example of the truth which Oderisi of Gubbio[2] uttered to Dante, as they paced, crouching together, round the first circle of Purgatory, the circle of the Proud:

Oh vain glory of human powers! How short a time does it remain green upon the top, *if it be not followed by ages of darkness.* Cimabue

[1] George Sarton, *Introduction to the History of Science*, i, p. 460, 1927. Compare Hallam, *Literature of Europe*, i, p. 5, footnote, 1837.

[2] *Purgatorio*, xi.

thought to hold the field in painting; now Giotto has the cry. . . . And for thee, if thou livest to be old, how will thy fame be more than if thou hadst died a babe, ere a thousand years be passed; which yet, to eternity, is a shorter space than the twinkling of an eye.

Which shows, incidentally, how much Dante underestimated his own fame. The six hundred years following Dante's death have been no ages of darkness, yet, so far as anything can be predicted, it seems safe to predict that, a thousand years after his birth, Dante's glory will remain undimmed. Dante tells us how he was burdened by thinking of the heavy load of penance which he would have to carry in Purgatory for his pride.[1] For my part, I find myself amazed at his modesty.

But Bede had a humbler mind than Dante. He was an expert in Chronology, and he knew that he was living in the Sixth, and Last, Age of the World. For the first Five Ages, those before Christ, Bede's reckoning did not differ materially from the results arrived at by Archbishop Usher, which are still in the margins of our bibles. These Ages, according to Bede, together covered 3,952 years, only 52 less than Usher allowed. The last of these five pre-Christian Ages (from the destruction of Solomon's Temple at Jerusalem by Nebuchadnezzar to the Coming of our Lord in the flesh) was the epoch in which, Bede asserted, the world had grown old. The Sixth Age was to stretch from the Incarnation of Christ to the Day of Doom: it was, according to Bede, the age of complete decrepitude, as befitted the epoch which was to end in the destruction of all.[2] Bede deprecated inquiry as to how long this last age of decrepitude would continue; but assuredly he would not, like Dante, have thought in terms of thousands of years. Dante's idea of successive painters, poets, scholars, each surpassing and obscuring the fame of his predecessor, shows how much the

[1] *Purgatorio*, xiii. 136–8.

[2] Mon. Germ. Hist., *Chronica Minora*, ed. Th. Mommsen, iii, p. 248, Berlin, 1898.

outlook of the human spirit had grown since the Dark Age of Bede. The Dark Age continued for many centuries after Bede, and so Bede, as generation followed generation, had few rivals to fear in the West. George Sarton, in the first volume of his mighty *Introduction to the History of Science*, gives the name of one great man to each half-century of his survey, and, with some hesitation, he names the first half of the eighth century after Bede. 'This was my last chance', he says, 'in this volume, of giving a Christian title to a chapter.' Not till the great revival which took place after the year 1100 does the West again begin to take the lead. The two half-centuries before Bede Sarton names after two Chinese travellers. The seven half-centuries after Bede he names from seven sages of the Moslem world. So that, during a period of 500 years, from A.D. 600 to A.D. 1100, Bede is the only master mind of Christendom whom Sarton thinks worthy of a supreme place.

But though Bede lived in what was, so far as Europe was concerned, a dark age, there is nothing dark about *him*. In the words of W. P. Ker:

> He did not, in his reading or writing, go beyond the sources or the models that were commonly accessible. For all that, the impression he leaves is that of something different from his age, an exceptional talent escaping from limitations and hindrances. There is no period in the history of Britain or of the English Church in which Bede is antiquated; in every generation he speaks familiarly. The seventeenth century is less intelligible to the eighteenth, the eighteenth century more in opposition to the nineteenth, than Bede to any one of them; his good sense is everywhere at home. . . . The reputation of Bede seems always to have been exempt from the common rationalist criticism, and this although his books are full of the things a Voltairian student objects to.[1]

Ker goes on to speak of matters where Bede is intolerant. Yet, he says,

> Like Dr. Johnson's refusal to countenance a Presbyterian church in Scotland, the severity of Bede has been taken lightly by the most sensitive, and has failed to make him enemies, even among the

[1] W. P. Ker, *The Dark Ages*, 1904, p. 141.

> fiercest advocates of Christian charity and impartial toleration It appears to be felt that he is a great man. The volume of his book is too much for carpers and cavillers.

Or, if we may translate the classic periods of 'W. P.' into the vulgarisms of to-day, we may say that even Lytton Strachey would have found it difficult to debunk the Venerable Bede. True, there *is* a volume entitled *The Venerable Bede expurgated, expounded, and exposed*, but the satire of that moderately amusing book is aimed, not at Bede, but at Anglican clergy who dare to claim him as their own.

Therefore, when the Academy did me the honour of asking me to give a lecture on the Master Mind Foundation, and chose Bede as the subject, I could only obey, although with many doubts as to my ability to deal with him. There is something which overawes us, in the contemplation of this unchanging reputation, in a world where everything else seems to be open to challenge and dispute, a challenge of which I, at least, am reminded every time I enter the British Museum Reading Room. All my life, when overcome by the atmosphere of that Reading Room, I have been accustomed to get up and walk along the Roman gallery, where the long line of Roman Emperors stood on their polished pedestals, till I finished opposite the bust of Julius Caesar. There, I said to myself, are the features of the foremost man of all this world, fashioned from the life by some master-craftsman of the first century B.C. And I returned refreshed to my work. In accordance with the spirit of our age, the polished pedestals have all been swept away; a sadly diminished line of Emperors now stands, in the Roman gallery, on a shelf reminiscent of a cocktail bar. Julius Caesar has been expelled. He now faces us, as we enter the Reading Room, with an inscription, *Julius Caesar, Ideal portrait of the 18th Century. Rome, bought 1818.*

And so he, who insisted that his wife must be above suspicion, now only serves to warn the unsuspicious Englishman against buying sham antiques abroad. There is change and decay in all the galleries of the Museum. No longer does the Etruscan lady deliver, with uplifted finger, an everlasting curtain-lecture to her recumbent spouse. I believe that after the night watchman has done his rounds, from one monument of Antiquity to another there passes

> A timid voice, that asks in whispers
> 'Who next will drop and disappear?'

Yet there *are* works of art in the Museum which have nothing to fear from any hostile critic; and two supreme ones have a special bearing on the Age of Bede. The Chinese pottery statue of a Buddhist apostle sits in the centre of the King Edward VII Gallery, rather more than life-size. In his grand simplicity, utterly remote from all earthly affairs, the apostle gazes into eternity. If our art-critics are right in their dates, he shows us what the East could do in the Age of Bede. He serves as a symbol to remind us that the darkest period of Western civilization coincides with the glories of the T'ang dynasty in China. Dynasties might have changed, and empires fallen, and the meditations of the Chinese sage, from whom that portrait was modelled (for a portrait it must assuredly be), would have been as little disturbed thereby as have been the features of his porcelain image. Like the sage of Bacon's New Atlantis, he has an aspect as though he pitied men. He belongs, we are told, to an age when inspiration was fresh, and Chinese Buddhist art young and virile.

The other great monument of the Age of Bede in the British Museum we can date exactly. It, again, is a monument of a young and virile art. It is the Lindisfarne Book, made on Holy Island by Bede's friend Eadfirth. The Lindisfarne Book is apparently the first great surviving masterpiece of the school to which it belongs. Its perfection is, at that date, so surprising that at least one eminent Celtic expert[1] has persuaded himself that the book was really

[1] Prof. R. A. S. Macalister, in *Essays and Studies presented to William Ridgeway*, Cambridge, 1913.

written about 120 years later (and, of course, in Ireland), shortly after which it fell into English hands, 'doubtless by some nefarious means'. But the Celtic expert forgot that the Lindisfarne Book is not only a masterpiece of design. It is a text of the Latin gospels, and, as such, has a very definite textual history; it has a liturgical history likewise, and these make it clear that the inscription which the Lindisfarne Book bears is not to be disputed when it says that the book was written by Eadfirth, Bishop of Lindisfarne, in honour of God and St. Cuthbert. Eadfirth also showed his veneration for St. Cuthbert by causing a Latin life to be made by some anonymous writer. Not satisfied with this, he asked Bede to write a second *Life*. Bede did so, and revised it carefully, after conference with those who had known the Saint. He then so far departed from his usual custom of seclusion within his own monasteries of Monkwearmouth and Jarrow, that he took it himself to Lindisfarne, some fifty miles away. There, for two days, it was diligently scrutinized by the brethren. They could find no fault in it, and Bede dedicated it to Eadfirth.

At the time when Bede visited Holy Island, Bishop Eadfirth had probably finished his long task of writing and illuminating the Lindisfarne Book.[1] It seems unlikely that, when Bede brought to Lindisfarne his tribute to St. Cuthbert, the Bishop in return would have failed to show Bede *his* tribute. So we may think that Bede and the Bishop bent their tonsured heads over the leaves of the Lindisfarne Book, and followed the intricate subtleties of the ornamentation, so delicate that the eye can scarcely trace them, and that we wonder how any brain devised them.

The figure of the Buddhist apostle and the designs of the Lindisfarne Book are both, in their way, as near perfection as work of man can be. Compared with the Chinese apostle

[1] In the *De temporum ratione* (725) Bede speaks of having written the prose *Life of St. Cuthbert* recently (*nuper*). This seems to preclude a date much earlier than 720 for Bede's visit to Holy Island. And Eadfirth died in 721.

the Lindisfarne Book belongs to a primitive—almost barbaric—culture. But it is the most beautiful thing the West could do in that age, just as Bede is the greatest product of the West in knowledge. When we think of this meeting, in a humble shack on Holy Island, of the greatest scholar and the greatest artist of the West, we may ask, How did it come that one small English district produced both?

Bede, the scholar, following knowledge, Eadfirth, the craftsman, creating beauty, Cuthbert, the saint, seeking God, were all alive together, pursuing their quest in one remote corner of England.

How did it come, that just when learning and civilization seemed to be dying out on the continent of Western Europe, they flourished among the Celts of Ireland and the Angles, Saxons, and Jutes of England—tribes who had never before known Roman discipline or Greek learning? Whilst Bede as Chronologist was conscious of living in the last, final age of the world, Bede as Geographer was equally conscious of living in the last, uttermost regions. He speaks of Ireland and Britain as the two remotest isles of the ocean.[1] His abbot, Ceolfrid, addressing the Pope, spoke of himself as living 'in the extreme limits'. How did it come that this monastery on the outskirts was the refuge, not only of the English, but also of the European spirit in the eighth century?

Two centuries before, under the magnanimous rule of Theodoric, Italy had still been the centre of Western culture. It was in Italy that Boethius, Cassiodorus, and St. Benedict had planted, amid the ruins of the Roman world, the beginnings of a new world which was to exceed the old in glory. These Italians were the Founders of the Middle Ages. And even in Britain there had been a temporary rally of Christian and Roman civilization; at Mount Badon the harassed Roman-Britons enjoyed that brief taste of victory, the distant reverberations of which have echoed through the

[1] *Ecclesiastical History*, iii. 25. (A speech placed in the mouth of Wilfrid, at the Council of Whitby.)

ages in the stories of King Arthur and his knights. But the sixth century, despite its fair beginning, closed in disaster for the Roman world. Gregory the Great had to watch bands of 'unspeakable' Lombards, as he called them, plundering up to the very walls of Rome. Yet Pope Gregory had such pity for the barbarian world outside those walls that he dispatched St. Augustine on his mission to England. Like Columbus later, Gregory little realized what he was doing. Gregory merely hoped to snatch a few more souls from perdition before the Coming of Antichrist and the Day of Doom ended an unfortunate business which, thanks to Adam and Eve, the Serpent and the apple, had gone wrong from the first. For, as he explained in his letter to King Ethelbert of Kent, the end of the world was approaching, and would shortly be upon us.[1]

Yet, in reality, Pope Gregory was 'calling in a new world to redress the balance of the old'.

For civilization at the moment had little chance in Romanized Western Europe. The conquering barbarians were quarrelling over the loot of the Roman Empire till they lost whatever barbaric virtues they had formerly possessed, when they lived in the more austere surroundings of their native forests and swamps. A good idea of life in Western Europe can be drawn from the two historians who are nearest in date to Bede, Gregory of Tours for the *History of the Franks*, and Paul the Deacon for the *History of the Lombards*.

What the ruling Frankish kings and queens were like we may gather from the way in which Queen Fredegund suppressed her naughty daughter Rigunth. Growing tired of the impertinences of her daughter, Fredegund invited her to share the crown jewels, which were kept in a huge chest. She handed out one after another, and at length, pretending to be tired, she said, 'Take them out for yourself, my dear.' The daughter put her arm into the chest, and the mother brought down the lid with all her might upon the head of

[1] *Ecclesiastical History*, i. 32.

her unruly offspring, and pressed her throat against the edge of the chest, till her daughter's eyes were starting out of her head. The murder was prevented by a handmaid calling for help: 'Her Royal Highness the Queen is suffocating Her Royal Highness the Princess.'[1] This is not an unfair example of the manners and morals of the reigning house in Merovingian France, though there were exceptions like the worthy King Guntram, 'whose memory is stained by only one or two murders'.

Paul's *History of the Lombards* is not as sordid as Gregory's *History of the Franks*. The Lombards had a certain rough chivalry, but they were utterly barbarous. Alboin, their king, slew the king of a rival Teutonic tribe, the Gepids, and made a drinking-cup of his skull. With typical inconsequence he also wedded Rosamund, the daughter of the king he had slain. The queen managed to avert her eyes from the gruesome table ornament, and all went well for a time. But it befell on a day that Alboin sat at the banquet longer than was proper, and filling the cup with wine, bade his cup-bearer carry it to the queen and tell her to drink with her father.[2] That was more than Queen Rosamund could stand, and Alboin's reign ended suddenly in 572 or 573. He was succeeded by other Lombard rulers, equally barbarous and less picturesque.

Even before the barbarians had gained such complete mastery, the Roman world had been oppressed by a sense of its age. A fifth-century historian tells us that 'Rome is falling more from the weakness of age than from external violence'.[3] What must the depression have become when Romans had to flatter masters like Alboin and mistresses like Fredegund? The only way of escape was the way of complete renunciation. Gregory of Tours[4] tells of a recluse who ate nothing but bread (upon which he condescended to put a little salt), who drank only water (which, however,

[1] *History of the Franks*, ix. 34. [2] *History of the Lombards*, ii. 28.
[3] Orosius, ed. Zangemeister, II. vi. 14.
[4] *History of the Franks*, v. 5 (10).

he allowed himself to sweeten with a little honey), who never slept, ceasing from prayer only to read or write, and who perpetually wore a hair shirt. Such a man was likely to get the reputation of working miracles. And, miracles or no, he dominated his surroundings: he was respected, and feared, by Roman and barbarian, by good and bad alike. Yet the path of complete renunciation is too difficult for many men and women to follow, and the barbarians who overran the Roman Empire found that most Christians were not like that. Therefore the mixture of barbarian and Roman within the Roman Empire resulted in that degradation which often follows when two different cultures and languages are violently brought together. Each nation finds that the task of learning from the others their irregular manners is easier than that of learning their irregular verbs, and generations pass before either morality or grammar becomes stabilized again.

That accounts for the superiority, both in its grammar and its subject matter, of Bede's *Ecclesiastical History of the English People* over Gregory's *History of the Franks*. For when Romanized Christians went forth to convert Irish or English in their own homes, they found conditions very different from those within the decaying Roman world. The missionaries found the barbarians living according to the standards which their ancestors had followed for hundreds, perhaps thousands, of years. It is true that there were in England some small remains of Roman civilization, and that those remains were useful to the missionaries. But the point is that the Christian evangelists found the native Teutonic culture intact. And on their side the missionaries who came among the heathen English were chosen men, trained in saintliness or obedience. No others would have undertaken so thankless a task. Also, they were often men of learning. Here, then, Roman, Celt, and Teuton, Christian and Heathen, met, each at his best. And there were things in the new Christian teaching which harmonized with the Germanic heroic traditions.

The essential virtue of the Old Germanic system was loyalty. The chieftain surrounded himself with a band of young companions who were pledged to live and die with him. It was a lifelong disgrace, Tacitus tells us, for the companion to return alive from the field on which his lord had fallen. This loyalty to a person was the bond of Germanic civilization; not the Roman or Greek conception of loyalty to a community: not 'The Republic', but 'My Chief'.

Abstract conceptions of Theology or Philosophy would have been difficult for the primitive English to grasp. But they were ready to listen to the story of 'the young hero, that was God Almighty, strong and stout of heart'. Let us remember the deep words of St. Augustine in the *Confessions*, where he tells how he found certain books of the Platonists, 'and therein I read, not indeed in those words, but with that meaning: "In the beginning was the Word, and the Word was with God, and the Word was God." . . . *But that the Word was made Flesh, and dwelt among us, that I read not there*.'[1]

Whilst all traditions in Western Europe seemed in danger of breaking down, these two traditions of loyalty to Christ and loyalty to the chief fortified each other, whenever the chief became a true Christian convert.

It was the great good fortune of Bede to be born into a society, in the first freshness of its conversion, which understood those two personal loyalties. The glory of it lasted only for a generation—but Bede caught it before it perished, and enshrined it in his *Ecclesiastical History*, to endure as long as the story of England endures. The *Ecclesiastical History* is the greatest, but not the only, expression of it. In the Old English poem, *The Dream of the Rood* (which certainly belongs to the age of Bede), we have a perfect fusion of the loyalty of the Germanic companion to his lord, and the loyalty of the Christian to Christ, and the mystery of a creation groaning and travailing in pain at the foot of the Cross: not the historic cross of Calvary, but a marvel

[1] vii. 9.

beyond man's understanding. And all this in the style, phraseology, and metre of Germanic heathen heroic poetry, familiar to the companions as they drank beer in the lord's hall at night. We know that Bede was skilled in English poetry, and the English verses which he composed on his death-bed have survived. Bede tells in the *Ecclesiastical History* how Cædmon first combined Christian teaching with the style of the old heathen lays; Bede's elder contemporary and fellow scholar, Aldhelm, was doing the same in the south of England; and *Beowulf*, with many another Old English poem, remains as a monument of the fusion.

It was the same combination of loyalties which had led, some years after Bede's birth, to the foundation of the monastery in which he was to work, and without which he would not have been the man he was. There was among the retinue of King Oswy of Bernicia a certain young noble named Biscop. Biscop must have seen a good deal of hard fighting in the early days of his king. When Biscop was twenty-five, Oswy offered him an estate on which he might marry and settle down—just as Hygelac did to Beowulf after he had slain Grendel. It was the usual reward to a young warrior who had proved his worth, and was entitled to pass from the *geoguð*, the young companions, to the *duguð*, the veterans. But, instead, Biscop abandoned the world, went on the pilgrimage to Rome, and set himself to learn all that a monk should know. He sojourned altogether in seventeen monasteries at different times of his life, 'committing to memory whatever he found most profitable in each'. Biscop, who had taken the name Benedict after the founder of the monastic rule which he followed, at length returned to Northumbria, and King Ecgfrid (son of Oswy) gave him a large estate upon which he founded the monastery of Monkwearmouth. The monastery was about five years old when Bede, a boy of seven, entered it. For a dozen years Biscop was Bede's teacher and master. When Ecgfrid gave Biscop a further grant of land, upon which he founded the monastery of Jarrow, the young Bede was transferred there.

Biscop made his monasteries centres of art and learning. He made altogether five journeys from England to Rome, every time bringing back many books and works of art. Biscop brought builders and glaziers from France, but, as any one realizes who examines what is left to-day, his buildings were minute if compared with the great structures of later monasticism. In their simplicity, the remains of Biscop's building remind us of the beginnings of the Franciscan movement. A small church was surrounded by the small huts or cells of the brethren. There were many brethren: by the middle of Bede's life he tells us that there were about six hundred in the two monasteries. The terrible mortality when the plague fell on these communities shows how unhealthy they must have been. But treasures like the Codex Amiatinus and the Lindisfarne Book survive to show that no labour was spared in order to make their equipment beautiful.

All this helps us to understand how, in the seventh century, Christian civilization found a refuge in Northumbria. There was the background of the primitive warrior life, not much altered from what it had been in the days of the *Germania* of Tacitus. That was the soldierly education which men like Biscop or Eostorwine received till they were twenty-four or twenty-five. To these still uncorrupted barbarians came Celtic missionaries of the type of the saintly Aidan. Most important of all, the Roman missionaries brought the ordered life of the Benedictine rule.

And so the tone of Bede's *Ecclesiastical History* is altogether different from that of Gregory's *History of the Franks* or Paul's *History of the Lombards*. The tale of Oswin of Deira, which I am going to read from Bede, is typical of Bede's *History*, just as the tales of Fredegund half-strangling her daughter Rigunth, or Rosamund contriving the death of her husband Alboin, are typical of the continental histories.

King Oswin was of countenance beautiful, of stature high, in talk courteous and gentle, in all points civil and amiable: no less honourable and bountiful to the noble, than free and liberal to persons of low degree. Whereby it happened, that for his outward personage, inward heart, and princely port, he had the love of all men. Especially the nobility of all countries frequented his court, and coveted to be received in his service.

Among other his rare virtues, and princely qualities, his humility and passing lowliness excelled. Whereof we will be contented to recite one most worthy example.

He had given to Bishop Aidan a very fair and proper gelding, which that virtuous bishop (though he used most to travel on foot) might use to pass over waters and ditches, or when any other necessity constrained. I fortuned shortly after, a certain poor weak man met the bishop, and craved an alms of him. The bishop, as he was a passing pitiful man, and a very father to needy persons, lighted off, and gave the poor man the gelding, gorgeously trapped as it was.

The king hearing after hereof, talked of it with the bishop, as they were entering the palace to dinner, and said, 'What meant you, my lord, to give away to the beggar that fair gelding, which we gave you for your own use? Have we no other horses of less price, and other kind of rewards to bestow upon the poor, but that you must give away that princely horse, which we gave you for your own riding?' To whom the bishop answered, 'Why talketh your grace thus? Is that son of a mare dearer in your sight than that son of God?'

Which being said, they entered for to dine. The bishop took his place appointed, but the king, coming then from hunting, would stand a while by the fire to warm him. Where standing, and musing with himself upon the words which the bishop had spoken unto him, suddenly he put off his sword, giving it to his servant, and came in great haste to the bishop: falling down at his feet, and beseeching him not to be displeased with him for the words he had spoken unto him, saying he would never more speak of it, nor measure any more hereafter what or how much the bishop should bestow of his goods upon the sons of God.

At which sight the bishop, being much astonied, arose suddenly and lifted up the king, telling him that he should quickly be pleased, if it would please him to sit down, and cast away all heaviness.

Afterward, the king being at the bishop's request merry, the bishop contrariwise began to be heavy and sorry; in such sort, that the tears trickled down by his cheeks. Of whom, when his chaplain in his mother tongue[1] (which the king and his court understood

[1] They were both, of course, of Irish stock.

not) had demanded why he wept: 'I know,' said he, 'that the king shall not live long. For never before this time have I seen an humble king. Whereby I perceive, that he shall speedily be taken out of this life: for this people is not worthy to have such a prince and governor.'

Shortly after, the bishop's dreadful abodement was fulfilled, with the king's cruel death, as we have before declared. Bishop Aidan himself also was taken away out of this world, and received of God the everlasting rewards of his labours, even on the twelfth day after the king, whom he so much loved, was slain.[1]

Bede's life shows what a fine thing Benedictine monasticism could be in early eighth-century England. But the words which Dante puts into the mouth of St. Benedict in Paradise were to prove true: 'So easily seduced is mortal flesh, that a good beginning on earth lasts not so long, as the time between the first springing up of an oak, and its bearing an acorn.'[2] When Bede was a boy of twelve or thirteen the reckless aggression of King Ecgfrid ruined the Northumbrian kingdom. The anonymous *Life of St. Cuthbert* tells how Ecgfrid was ravaging the land of the Picts in the far north, and his queen, attended by St. Cuthbert, was awaiting the issue of the war in the city of Carlisle. The governor of the city was showing them an old Roman fountain constructed in wondrous wise, when Cuthbert exclaimed, 'Oh, Oh, Oh, I deem that the war is finished, and that judgement has been pronounced against our soldiers in their warfare. Oh my children, consider how beyond scrutiny are the judgements of God.' In a few days came the news of the death of Ecgfrid and all his army at Nechtansmere. From this defeat Bede at a later period dated Northumbrian decay: 'The prowess of the dominion of the English began to decay and go backwards.' The year after the death of Ecgfrid came the visitation of plague, which carried away from the monastery of Jarrow all who could read, or preach, or recite the antiphons, except Ceolfrid the abbot,

[1] From the translation of the *Ecclesiastical History*, by Thomas Stapleton, 1565, Book III, cap. 14, revised.

[2] *Paradiso*, xxii. 85–7.

and one small lad, nourished and taught by him. In the anonymous *History of the Abbots* the moving story is told of how the abbot and the lad carried on the services unaided. The small lad was certainly[1] Bede himself. I mention these anonymous historical works because, with Eddi's *Life of Wilfrid*, they show us that there was already a school of historical writing in Northumbria before Bede produced his masterpiece.

It has been said that, 'some day, scandal mongers and disintegrating critics may become aware that they have produced most accurate autobiographies'.[2] In his *History* and in his *Lives of the Abbots* Bede has, unconsciously, written his own autobiography. But it adds to our understanding of his character when we realize that Bede's world had already begun to decay when he was a boy of thirteen. Although for another twenty years King Aldfrid ruled the defeated Northumbrian realm competently within its narrower boundaries, after his death, which took place when Bede was about thirty-three, the state of Northumbria became deplorable. Bede's enormous labours were carried on amid a general decline of Northumbrian civilization. Yet Bede only occasionally refers to the decadence of his age. It was not till the last year of his life that Bede spoke out. A young man of royal birth, probably a pupil of his own, Egbert, had just been appointed Archbishop of York. In a letter of advice to him, Bede deals fully with the abuses which had grown in the thirty troubled years since the death of Aldfrid. He is particularly shocked at the bogus monasteries which were everywhere springing up, filled by pseudo-monks whose only object was to avoid military duties and to live in idleness. Bede is for drastic remedies.

[1] Bede was nourished and taught at Jarrow by Ceolfrid. If only one trained lad was left there, it can only have been Bede.

[2] Rand, *Founders of the Middle Ages*, p. 73. Prof. Rand's book places under a great debt all who are interested in the continuity of civilization, and more particularly the transition from Classical times to the Dark Ages.

Even monasteries of professed monks ought to be dissolved or converted if the monks do not live according to their vows:

> And because there are very many places of this kind which, as the common saying is, are useful to neither God nor man, because neither is the religious life observed in them, according to the law of God, nor do they have in them soldiers or thanes of the secular powers to defend our people from the barbarians; if any one were to turn such monasteries into bishoprics, he would be doing a virtuous act. Your Holiness, with the help of the devout king of our nation, ought to tear in pieces the unrighteous charters of former princes, and to provide things useful to our country, lest either religion die out in our day, or else the number of our armed men diminishes, so that there are none left to defend our borders from barbarian invasion.

Bede complains that monasteries have grown so numerous that there are no lands upon which time-expired soldiers can be settled. Such soldiers are compelled either to emigrate oversea, leaving their native land unprotected, or else to live idle and unmarried, growing more and more demoralized.

But, even worse than these many monasteries of unworthy monks, says Bede, are the sham monasteries of laymen, who escape their secular duties without even making any attempt to live the monastic life.[1]

The young archbishop was not able to carry through all the reforms which Bede desired; but he founded the Cathedral school at York and taught in it. It was an epoch-making act—for thereby he passed on the learning of his friend and master, Bede, to his friend and scholar, Alcuin, and through him to the Carolingians and the Middle Ages.

Bede was already ill when he wrote the letter to Egbert—it has been called his swan-song. But, as we know, he went on labouring to the day of his death. 'I do not want my boys to read a lie, or to labour in vain after I am gone,' he said on his death-bed.

If the lifetime of Bede was one of downfall and decay

[1] *Epistle to Egbert*, 11, 12.

throughout his own Northumbria, it was even more so throughout Christendom. At the time of Bede's birth, although the Mohammedan power had established itself in Syria and Egypt, nevertheless the Mediterranean was still the central sea of the Christian world. But during Bede's lifetime the whole of Africa, and almost all Spain, was lost to Christendom. When Bede was writing his *History*, the Saracens had reached the centre of France. Then came the turn of the tide. The year after Bede finished his *History* Charles Martel won the great victory over the Saracens which saved France from utter devastation. Bede slipped a reference to it into his *History*. He could not know how epoch-making the victory was to be. Yet we can imagine his satisfaction as he told how, after their terrible devastation of Gaul, the Saracens had incurred the just judgement of God.

There is something very appropriate in this final reference. Bede instructed Egbert, and Egbert taught Alcuin, so we may regard Alcuin as Bede's spiritual grandson. Bede's spiritual grandson was destined to serve Charles the Great, the grandson of Charles Martel, in the re-establishment of learning in Europe. For, contemporary with all this decay within the borders of Christendom had been the amazing missionary efforts of the Englishmen, Willibrord and Boniface and their companions, among the heathen German tribes of the Continent, which first changed the face of Germany, and then had such repercussions upon Gaul as to make possible the Carolingian Renaissance. It is remarkable how constantly the missionaries write back to England for the works of Bede:

> We, labouring to plant the seeds of the Gospel among the wild and ignorant Germans, beg you to send us something of the writings of Bede the monk, who of late was shining among you like a lantern, with knowledge of the Scriptures. And if you could send us a bell also, it would be a great comfort to us in our exile.[1]

[1] Boniface to Huetberht, Abbot of Wearmouth and Jarrow; Jaffé, *Monumenta Moguntina*, 180.

Or

We beg that you will comfort us by doing as you have done before, by sending us some ray from that lantern of the Church enlightened by the Holy Spirit in your land—Bede. And we are sending by the bearer two small vats of wine, that you may have a day of joy with your monks.[1]

Or

I beg that you will send us, for a comfort in our exile, any one of these works, which Bede the priest of blessed memory wrote. [A list follows.] I am asking much, but it will not seem much to your charity.[2]

Or

I am sick, and like to leave this vale of tears. I beg, as a consolation both of my exile and my illness, for the books of Bede of blessed memory on the building of the Temple, or on the Song of Songs, or his epigrams in heroic or elegiac verse—all, if possible, but, if not, the three books on the building of the Temple. Perhaps what I ask is difficult, but I think nothing will be difficult to your charity.[3]

Such is the constant appeal of the missionaries, Boniface, Lull, and the rest, writing home to the abbots of Monkwearmouth and to Egbert at York. The English ecclesiastics do what they can to supply the need—the abbot of Monkwearmouth laments that he cannot send more of Bede's writings: he has put his boys to work, but it has been a horrible winter, with cold and frost and storms, which have numbed the hand of the writer.[4]

It is thanks to the labours of Boniface and Alcuin, and the inspiration of Bede, that discipline and learning were re-established on the Continent. In England the worst time had still to come, when the whole country was harried by

[1] Boniface to Egbert, Archbishop of York; Jaffé, *Mon. Mog.*, 250.

[2] Lull to the Archbishop of York; Jaffé, *Mon. Mog.*, 288.

[3] Lull to Cuthbert, Abbot of Wearmouth and Jarrow; Jaffé, *Mon. Mog.*, 289.

[4] Cuthbert to Lull, Jaffé, *Mon. Mog.*, 300. Cuthbert is, of course, the man who, at an earlier date, had been present at Bede's death, and has left us an account of it.

the Vikings, but on the Continent learning, however depressed, never sank again as low as it had done before Bede and those whom he inspired began their labours.

When, at the end of the ninth century, King Alfred had at last checked the Viking raids in England, one of the works he promoted was the translation of Bede's *History* into English. England, therefore, was the first of the nations of Western Europe to have a great history written in the vernacular. But the book was multiplied much more frequently in Latin, and William of Malmesbury looked back to the *Ecclesiastical History* as a model when, four centuries after Bede's time, he re-established in England Bede's tradition of Latin historiography.

How great had been the popularity of Bede's *History*, during the period which intervenes between Bede and William of Malmesbury, is proved by the large number of early manuscripts which have survived, despite all the destruction wrought by Vikings and others. Two of these earliest manuscripts contain chronological notes, which enable us to date them. The oldest, which was written on the Continent, though it is now at Cambridge, was made within some two years of Bede's death. The second oldest, written within eleven years of Bede's death, was once at Corbie, and is now in Leningrad.[1] It has been generally overlooked, and is not mentioned either by Plummer or by Dr. James. Yet it would seem to be of great importance.

Nowadays the medieval veneration of saints' relics is being revived, and the uncorrupted body of Lenin is worshipped by crowds of pilgrims in Moscow, just as that of Cuthbert was of old revered in Lindisfarne and Durham. Could not the trade in relics also be resuscitated? Our Government might then acquire the Leningrad manuscript for the British Museum, in exchange for the bones of Karl Marx, now resting in Highgate Cemetery.

The Durham library claimed, in the Middle Ages, to have

[1] See O. D. Rojdestvensky in *Speculum*, iii. 314–21; E. A. Lowe, *English Historical Review*, xli. 244–6.

four manuscripts written by the hand of Bede. Three of these are still extant, in whole or in part. They are early, but the writing shows too much variation to permit of their being all from the same hand.[1]

In time, Bede's reputation grew mythical. He was supposed to have visited Rome in order to give the *Curia* the benefit of his scholarship. The University of Paris was convulsed by a dispute between Picard and English students, the Englishmen claiming priority on the ground that Bede had founded the University. Pope Martin V is alleged to have sent a legate to allay the quarrel. The legate is alleged to have allowed the English claim, agreeing that Bede, on his way to Rome, *had* stopped at Paris and founded the University there.[2] The University of Cambridge also claimed Bede, and Fuller, though he obviously did not believe the claim, did not like to contradict it.

> Some report [he says] that Bede never went out of his cell, but lived and died therein. If so, the scholars of Cambridge will be very sorry, because thereby deprived of their honour, by Bede's living once in their University, whose house they still show, between St. John's College and the Round Church or St. Sepulchre's. Surely Bede was not fixed to his cell, as the cockle to his shell.[3]

Dante saw Bede in Heaven;[4] he also reproached the Cardinals for not studying their Bede as they should. When

[1] See article by Dr. Montague R. James in *Bede: Essays in Commemoration, edited by A. Hamilton Thompson*, 1935, p. 235. Dr. James enumerates the following as extant in whole or in part:

(1) *The Gospels*; Durham, A. ii. 16: there is also a small slip in the Pepysian library, Magdalene College, Camb.

(2) *Epistles of Paul, glossed*; Trin. Coll., Camb., B. 10. 5: there is also a fragment in the British Museum, Cotton Vitellius C. viii.

(3) Cassiodorus *On the Psalter*; Durham, B. ii. 33.

Dr. James thinks (2) and (3) better claimants than (1).

[2] César Égasse du Boulay, *Historia Universitatis Parisiensis*, Parisiis, 1665, i. 113. Rashdall has described Du Boulay as 'perhaps the stupidest man who ever wrote a valuable book' (*Universities of Europe*, 1895, i, p. 271).

[3] *Church History*, 1655, Cent. viii, p. 98.

[4] *Paradiso*, xxii. 85.

printing was introduced, the rapidity with which Bede's *History* was printed testifies to its continued popularity. At the Reformation Bede continued in favour with both sides. As an early translator of the Bible, he was applauded by the Wycliffites: and his knowledge of the Scriptures won him the praise of John Foxe, the martyrologist. Bede's characteristic apology for his writings, that at least they had kept him from doing worse things, is reproduced by Foxe:

> As touching the holiness and integrity of his life, it is not to be doubted: for how could it be, that he should attend to any vicious idleness, or had any leisure to the same, who, in reading and digesting so many volumes, consumed all his whole cogitations in writing upon the Scriptures? For so he testifieth of himself in the third book of Samuel, saying in these words: 'If my treatises and expositions', saith he, 'bring with them no other utility to the readers thereof, yet to myself they conduce not a little thus: that while all my study and cogitation was set upon them, in the meanwhile, of slippery enticements and vain cogitations of this world I had little mind.'[1]

On the other hand, Bede, as a strenuous defender of the Roman allegiance and practice, was applauded by the Catholics. Thomas Stapleton, the Roman Catholic controversialist, translated the *Ecclesiastical History* into English, and dedicated it to Elizabeth, in the pathetic hope that it might convert her. Stapleton's translation, revised, is the one I have used in this lecture. It needs revision. Bede, for example, had recorded how Edwin of Northumbria provided for the needs of his subjects: where there were springs by the highway, he planted wooden stakes with metal cups attached to them, for the refreshing of wayfarers. In Stapleton the cups become great brazen basons to bathe in, and the stakes become quick-set bowers, planted around in the interests of propriety.[2]

To be simultaneously applauded by Foxe and Stapleton was a triumph, and is characteristic of Bede's wide appeal. We are driven back to the judgement of W. P. Ker: Bede's good sense is everywhere at home.

[1] *Acts and Monuments*, ed. Townsend and Cattley, i. 364–5.

[2] ii. 16.

Bede is an ascetic, but with good sense: his asceticism was unlike that of the Egyptian hermit of whom St. Jerome tells us, who lived in an old cistern upon five rush-stalks a day.[1] Bede's life of self-denial allowed him to keep a few treasures in his casket—some pepper, some napkins, and some incense. That was all which the greatest scholar of his age had been able to accumulate in a lifetime. But still, he could distribute these things to his friends on his death-bed: 'such gifts as God has given me', in his own words.

Self-denial and heroism are sacred things to Bede—whether in a King Oswald fighting for justice and righteousness, or in a soldier like Lilla throwing his body between his king and the sword of the enemy, or in monks like Cuthbert or Chad.

But it is characteristic of Bede that he, the historian of the earliest English monasticism and its great example, is also the earliest great advocate of the dissolution of monasteries. For those who entered monasteries in order to escape their civil or military duties, yet without submitting to the even more rigorous discipline incumbent upon the good monk, Bede, as we have seen, has complete contempt. 'The result of this', he wrote, 'the next age will see.'[2] The next age *did* see it, amid the complete downfall of Northumbrian civilization. Bede's influence continued, a link between ancient and modern times. But it continued outside the limits of his beloved Northumbria, which lay in ruins.

Yet although Bede's main function was to connect Classical times with the Middle Ages, to help to bridge the gap between the end of the sixth century and the beginning of

[1] Rand, *Founders of the Middle Ages*, p. 122. But *was* it rush-stalks? The text in Migne's *Patrologia*, xxiii. 5, runs *quinque caricis per singulos dies sustentabatur*. This would make it five dried figs per day—a meagre diet, to be sure, but, considering the rations of Egyptian hermits, too nutritious, one would think, to justify Jerome's expressions of extreme amazement. So I think Jerome may have written (or at any rate meant to write) *quinque caricis stipulis*, or something of that sort.

[2] *Ecclesiastical History*, v. 23.

the twelfth, we must remember that what he passed on was not information, but the spirit of freshness in worship, in learning, and in teaching. 'Spending all my life in my monastery,' he says, 'and observing the regular discipline and the daily singing of God's service in the church, the rest of my time I *was delighted* always to learn, to teach, or to write.' Bede placed the *opus Dei* first, as every true monk must; he would not allow either study or sickness to keep him from it. Alcuin, in a letter to the monks of Wearmouth, records the tradition that Bede believed that the angels were present at the canonical hours: 'Will they not say, Where is Bede? Why comes he not to the services with his brethren?' Only the residue of his time was given to learning and teaching, but he did that with gusto and originality. A few examples will suffice.

In the sixth century a certain Scythian monk at Rome, known as Dionysius Exiguus, in compiling his Easter Tables, had reckoned from the Incarnation.[1] The exact measure of Bede's originality here we shall never know: but Bede was certainly the first scholar and historian to make the reckoning by the year of our Lord the standard reckoning. Every time we date a letter we should render homage to the Venerable Bede.

His *Ecclesiastical History* was not only a pattern for all future historians; not only has it been praised by Mommsen for its accuracy, but in many ways it spread through Western Europe a new conception of history, and of other things. I may mention one detail. Bede wrote the *Ecclesiastical History of the English Nation* before there was any English nation in existence. He might have adopted the political unit and have written an Ecclesiastical History of Northumbria; he might have taken the geographical unit and have written an Ecclesiastical History of the British Isles. He did neither. He preferred to consider all the Germanic-speaking inhabitants of the British Isles, despite their different origins, Angles, Saxons, and Jutes, as one nation

[1] Poole, *Chronicles and Annals*, 1926, p. 22.

—English. It was not an individual conception of Bede's: the correspondence of Boniface and his fellow missionaries shows that they think of themselves, and of the people they have left at home, not as Northumbrians, West Saxons, or Mercians, but as English. Yet it was Bede who gave world-wide currency to this conception. It is time we abandoned the fallacy that the Norman Conquest first hammered Englishmen into unity. Bede's *Ecclesiastical History of the English People* was one of the many forces which had made England into a nation, long before Normans and Angevins formed the impossible idea of creating one nation out of England and so much of France as they could hold: an idea which led to the Hundred Years' War, that 'tissue of calamitous follies' which put back the clock in Western Europe for generations.

Yet Bede's title to our gratitude is not that he spread this or that idea, but that he made it his business 'to maintain a standard of learning, and to preserve the continuity of civilization'. The words are those which our President used, in his address last year,[1] to define the objects of this Academy, and of its members, individually or conjointly.

I suppose that it would be possible to demonstrate an apostolic succession, from teacher to pupil, from Bede in his cell at Jarrow to our President in his chair this evening.[2] Don't be alarmed; at this hour I am not going to attempt it. I have pointed out how Bede instructed Egbert, Egbert Alcuin. Alcuin was not so great a master as Bede, but he was master of a greater school. All Europe was his school, and his influence stretched to Fulda, to Tours, to Rheims, to many other places, till the streams came together in the University of Paris, and so flowed on to the University of Oxford.

Omitting intermediate stages, I will pass to three Oxford men of our own day who knew intimately their Dark Ages

[1] Mackail, *Presidential Address*, July 1935, p. 9.

[2] Some earlier stages are given in the *History* of Ademar (Pertz, iv. 119).

and their Bede. W. P. Ker, S. J. Crawford, and Charles Plummer all possessed that 'plain heroic magnitude of mind' which marked Bede himself. If you have followed this lecture carefully, you will have realized that anything of value in it I have learnt from those three men, through whom alone, if at all, I must claim to be in touch with the Venerable Bede.

S. J. Crawford, cut off before his time ('Alas, too little and too lately known'), was a man whose scholarship Ker would have deeply admired. A colleague wrote Crawford's epitaph:

> For him books were no dead things; through their pages
> He passed into a happy country, where
> He held communion with saints and sages,
> Heroes and prophets, spirits wise and rare.
>
> He has left his books now; those great souls he knew
> Called him from this small world of time and space:
> This is not death; he has gone to share the true,
> The glorious life of that immortal race.[1]

Charles Plummer seemed the reincarnation of Bede, if ever one man seemed the reincarnation of another—in his vast learning, his humility, his piety, his care for the young. Elected a Fellow of Corpus at a time when celibacy was still imposed, Plummer never broke his monastic vow, remaining single during the fifty-eight years of his Fellowship. Gibbon spoke scornfully of the 'monks of Magdalen' and their unproductiveness. I wish he had lived to see the production of the monks of Corpus, and above all, Plummer's edition of Bede's *Historical Works*.

Plummer was born within a few miles of the spot where Bede was born, lived, and died; and Plummer was not altogether satisfied with the way in which collieries and furnaces had transformed what in Bede's day had been the wooded banks of the Tyne. I myself remember standing on the roof of the North Eastern Hotel at Newcastle, and thinking that, if Bede could have seen the circles of smoke

[1] In Memoriam S. J. Crawford in *The Invisible Sun*, by V. de S. Pinto.

with which I was surrounded, he would have had no doubt where he was, though he might have wondered what he had done to be put there. When Plummer wrote, forty years ago, it was less common than it is in these days to doubt the value of such industrial over-development; and it is with the words of Charles Plummer, rather than any of my own, that I wish to close this lecture. 'Even rating these things at the very highest value that has ever been put upon them by the most zealous votary of material progress, we have not, it seems to me, amid all our discoveries, invented as yet anything better than the Christian life which Bede lived, and the Christian death which he died.'

SIR ISRAEL GOLLANCZ MEMORIAL LECTURE

JOHN MITCHELL KEMBLE AND OLD ENGLISH SCHOLARSHIP

(WITH A BIBLIOGRAPHY OF HIS WRITINGS)

By BRUCE DICKINS

Read 15 March 1939

IT is almost a hundred years since the first volume of the *Codex Diplomaticus Aevi Saxonici* was published by the English Historical Society; it was completed in 1848 and is still the only comprehensive collection of charters of the pre-Conquest period. When the Council of the British Academy did me the great honour of an invitation to give the Gollancz Memorial Lecture the occasion seemed appropriate for an account—however brief and inadequate—of the life and work of a pioneer in Old English scholarship, of a man called by his Cambridge contemporary Lord Houghton 'as interesting an individual as ever was portrayed by the dramatic genius of his own race'.[1]

For John Mitchell Kemble was of a distinguished family, distinguished not in the study but on the stage.[2] Fanny Kemble was his sister, John Philip Kemble his uncle, the tremendous Sarah Siddons his aunt—to name three only of the most famous family in the history of the English theatre. His father, Charles Kemble, was a finished actor of more than common merit, less mannered than John Philip, but like him—of whom it was said 'Had John Kemble not been the greatest actor of his day, he would most probably have been one of its very foremost philologists'—with more scholarship than is usual in a player, then or now.[3] His mother Maria Theresa de Camp, partly French, partly Swiss, and born in Vienna, had been an actress from early youth;[4] the National Portrait Gallery has A. E. Chalon's caricature (1804) of her (in her own burlesque *Personation*) which gives a better impression of her vivacity than more laboured compositions. But there was nothing Bohemian about her household. Her son's Cambridge friends found her a delightful unaffected hostess,[5] and she was a notable housekeeper, being the 'accomplished lady' to whom Dr. Kitchiner owed several of the recipes in *The Cook's Oracle*.[6] And when the Kembles were offered peers' seats for the Coronation of William IV, and the parents were engaged, John went, but Fanny had to stay at home, an elder brother being an inadequate escort.[7]

Kemble was born on 2 April 1807 and christened John after his uncle, Mitchell, after a London merchant who bore that surname and was his godfather. He was first sent to a school at Clapham kept by Charles Richardson,[8] a disciple of Horne Tooke and compiler of a well-known English Dictionary, which, if in many ways defective, was one of the first to make use of the historical method.[9] Richardson is said to have employed the more intelligent of his boys on the dictionary,[10] and Kemble may have become interested in philology at an early stage. Thence he was sent to King Edward VI Free Grammar School at Bury St. Edmunds, which, under Benjamin Heath Malkin, had a deservedly high reputation, especially among parents of latitudinarian or progressive views in Church or State.[11] Among his contemporaries at Bury were James Spedding, the biographer and editor of Bacon, William Bodham Donne, his lifelong friend and successor in the Examinership of Plays, and Edward FitzGerald, who has left a silhouette of Kemble as a schoolboy: 'I never heard such capital declamation as *his* Hotspur, and Alexander's Feast when we were at Bury together, he about eighteen and then with the profile of Alexander himself, as I have seen it on medals, etc.'[12]

Kemble was admitted as a pensioner of Trinity College, Cambridge, on 26 June 1824,[13] but did not go into residence till the Michaelmas Term of 1825.[14] He held a Hewer Exhibition from his school,[15] and great things were expected of him. He won the first place in the Trinity Declamations in 1827 with an essay, which his tutor[16] wrote 'was as tastefully and modestly delivered as it was well written'; but did not otherwise distinguish himself academically, and all hope of a fellowship vanished before long. He talked hard and played hard, fencing, rowing, and shooting, but when he read it was metaphysics instead of mathematics, Anglo-Saxon instead of Latin and Greek. His sister Fanny, writing in January 1828, was most uneasy about him:

> He is really a highly gifted creature, but I sometimes fear lest the passionate eagerness with which he *pursues his pursuit*, the sort of frenzy he has about politics, and his constant excitement about political questions, may actually injure his health, and the vehemence with which he speaks and writes in support of his peculiar views will perhaps endanger his future prospects.
>
> He is neither tory nor whig, but a radical, a utilitarian, an adorer of Bentham, a worshipper of Mill, an advocate for vote by ballot, an opponent of hereditary aristocracy, the church establishment, the army and navy, which he deems sources of unnecessary national expense; though who is to take care of our souls and bodies, if the three last-named institutions are done away with, I do not quite see. Morning, noon, and night he is writing whole volumes of arguments against them, full of a good deal of careful study and reading, and in a close, concise, forcible style, which is excellent in itself, and the essays are creditable to his laborious industry; but they will not teach him mathematics, or give him a scholarship or his degree.[17]

Kemble's associates at Trinity were the most brilliant group ever in residence at a single college, though few of them were reading for a tripos. Some, like John Sterling, Charles Buller, and Arthur Hallam, died too young to have fulfilled their promise, but Tennyson, FitzGerald, and Thackeray were among his friends. He was prominent among the 'Apostles'—officially the Cambridge Conversazione Society—who were ardently speculative and took nothing for granted.[18] Here he was in his element, and several of his papers were long remembered, though, so far as I know, the only sentence preserved is one recorded by the critical Merivale: 'The style of our lucubrations may be illustrated perhaps by a saying of one of our profound philosophers, Jack Kemble:—"The world is one great thought, and I am thinking it".'[19]

Kemble was also one of the most eloquent and best-prepared speakers of the Union Society—the mother of all Unions. He spoke once as a freshman, more frequently in his second year, when he was Secretary for the Lent Term, no less than seventeen times in his third year, when he was President for the Lent Term of 1828, Charles Buller, John Sterling, and (Sir) Spencer Walpole immediately preceding and Richard Chenevix Trench (later Archbishop of Dublin) succeeding him in the Presidency.[20]

He kept the normal ten terms as an undergraduate and sat for the *Poll* degree. According to Lord Houghton[21] he was 'very ill-treated . . ., nobody knows why, except that in his examination he called Paley a "miserable sophist", and talked of Locke's "loathsome infidelity" which pleased one very much but made the examiners very angry. Some proposed to pluck him, but one said "We will not make him a martyr"'. However, he was put back for his degree, to give him an opportunity for further study of Locke and Paley.

Early in 1829 he spent some time with Trench, and by the summer of that year had given up his original intention of going to the bar and decided to read for the Church, to the relief of his family and friends, who were satisfied of the reality of his vocation.[22] In the Long Vacation he went to Germany with his Trinity friend, Charles Barton, and two sonnets published in *The Athenæum* give his impressions of the castled rock of Rheinfels.[23]

They parted at Heidelberg, and Kemble went on to Munich, thence to the Tyrol, 'gratifying his prejudices with the sight of the glen where ten thousand French fell beneath the rifle-balls of the peasantry. He also ingratiated himself into the good grace of the people by waltzing with certain of the more good-looking girls, and then returned to Munich to read Kant, practise the broad-sword and wage [like Jonathan Oldbuck] an ἀκηρυκτὸν πόλεμον against tea and coffee, which he considers to vie with the doctrines of Helvetius in the mischief done by it to mankind.'[24] He was fascinated by German scholarship and by the variety of subjects studied in the universities. 'The depth of the knowledge of the young men there is something he could hardly have conceived; they study everything, and everything well.'[25] Towards the end of the year he read in a newspaper that his sister Fanny was to appear for the first time as Juliet. To Lord Houghton[26] 'he described the impression as a cold sword run through his heart'; he had squandered time and money, and his sister was being sacrificed to the necessities of Covent Garden. Thus, when early in 1830 his father had the promise of a living from Lord ——, he returned at once to prepare for ordination. He went into residence again in February and took his degree, apparently without further examination, on the 25th, but found that he would have to wait for Divinity lectures till the Michaelmas Term. He kept the rest of the Lent Term and the Easter Term as well, though feeling that he might have been better employed in Germany.[27] He spoke frequently at the Union, and on 19 March took the part of Dogberry:

> Conceive a party of large and logger-headed fellow-commoners playing 'Much Ado About Nothing'. Conceive Milnes doing the elegant and high-minded Beatrice like a languishing trull; also if you can, conceive Hallam and myself setting our faces and taming our eyes into stupidity that we might present some distant resemblance of Verges and Dogberry. I can assure you that if laughing be a criterion, no company ever did better, for from first to last, specially during the tragic scenes, the audience were in a roar.[28]

But when October came Kemble was in Spain, striving to re-establish the constitution in a country where constitutions have never been robust. John Sterling and his friends on *The Athenæum*—mostly old 'Apostles'—were zealous backers of General Torrijos, leader of the Constitutionalists who had left Spain in 1823; Carlyle's description of these exiles in *The Life of John Sterling* is too familiar to bear repetition.[29]

By 1830 Torrijos had persuaded himself that Spain was ready to rise against the absolute government of Ferdinand VII. Sterling's cousin Robert Boyd, a retired officer of the Hon. East India Company's service, provided funds for the purchase of arms and of a ship which was placed under the command of an experienced smuggler. Just as it was about to drop down the Thames to take aboard Torrijos and his followers it was seized at the instance of the Spanish Government.[30] Kemble, along with Trench, who had spent a good deal of time in Spain, had been caught up into the adventure, and Tennyson's 'Sonnet to J. M. K.' was known before 23 June.[31] On 7 July he left for Gibraltar with monitory dispatches;[32] the first thing his sister heard of it was a letter from Algeciras, adjuring her to keep his family in the dark.[33] Boyd, Trench, and the Spaniards made their way to Gibraltar by different routes. There Trench and Kemble 'hired a house which they denominated Constitution Hall, where they passed their time smoking and drinking ale, John holding forth upon German metaphysics, which grew dense in proportion as the tobacco fumes grew thick and his glass grew empty'.[34] The English also vowed to abstain from scissors and razor till the Spanish constitution should be restored, and Kemble, as one would expect, was the latest to give way.[35] They found on arrival that nothing had been arranged by the Junta, who in May had assured Torrijos that nothing was wanting but his arrival—'a rout of the most lying imbeciles that ever formed that most imbecile of all associations, a Spanish Junta', as Trench called them in a letter of 21 October.[36] All had to be begun from the beginning; but on 24 October Torrijos is to strike, in less than twelve hours. He has been promised the co-operation of most of the subaltern officers and soldiers who form the small corps of observation on the opposite coast. They are to arrest their superior officers and join Torrijos immediately on his landing, which will be at midnight. Next day Trench announces the failure, and probably the entire wreck of their hopes.[37] Torrijos and his party—rather more than a hundred men, mostly general officers—were lying aboard a schooner in the bay awaiting the signal from their friends in Algeciras when they were boarded by an English ship and put under arrest. They planned to overpower their guards if the beacons should be lighted, but the beacons never were lighted, and next day the conspirators 'were ignominiously suffered to go quietly on shore again'.[38] A letter of Trench, dated 17 November, says that Kemble has been in the Bay for the last two or three days on business, and goes on 'There no longer remains any hope of effecting a revolution, at least for the present, in Spain. Almost all our friends in the country, who have attempted to fulfil the promises they made to us, are prisoners or fugitives; our own attempts, either to make a lodgment on the other side, or to secure the ships of war in the bay, have been thrice baffled. If we enter the country it is to our sure destruction.' Four days later he says 'A chink of hope is still ours. An officer has devoted himself and has departed for Cadiz to make an appeal to the soldiery there, whose general disposition is said to be excellent. Give us Cadiz, and the contest will then remain to be fairly fought, and I shall not fear for the result.'[39] But the troops in Cadiz did not rise. Torrijos did land near Algeciras on the night of 28 January 1831, but was forced to re-embark. Less fortunate was the attempt of Manzanares on 21 February, of which Sterling speaks in a letter of 31 March 1831 (Trench, i. 86). Convinced that all was hopeless, Trench sailed for England towards the end of February 1831;[40] he used every persuasion to induce Kemble to return with him and had even got him on board the vessel in which they were to sail.[41] Kemble held on for almost three months before he followed Trench's example, which, as he says in a letter of 28 May 1831, 'might have given me courage sooner were I less subject to foolish and false fancies of my own. Thank God, however, the step is taken. I am here in the bosom of my family, and very resolute to shut my ears to the voice even of the wisest charmers that shall tempt me again to leave it. Poor Boyd remains in Gibraltar, and, indeed, I hardly know what he could do were he to leave it. Yet he is, I think, quite as hopeless as myself for the event.'[42] The event was tragic enough. Led into the trap by an old friend, Torrijos landed near Malaga on 1 December 1831, but, finding no support, his men barricaded themselves in a farm-house. They were forced to surrender at discretion and all shot, Boyd included, on the esplanade at Malaga.[43]

Trench, like Sterling, never spoke of his share in the Torrijos adventure, and his family first heard of it nearly forty years later from Fanny Kemble's *Record of a Girlhood*, which the Archbishop read with annoyance, his children with delight.[44] Kemble was less reserved; an anonymous friend, quoted in *The Cambridge 'Apostles'*, said:

> When Jacky Kemble returned from the Torrijos affair in Spain, to College, he had a story of adventure which had three versions. In the first, say in the stage of friendly confidence, he would say—'I once strayed beyond our lines alone and unarmed and suddenly came upon fifteen Spanish Grenadiers, who were closing round me, when I took to my heels, and though pursued by a few shots, escaped with my life and unharmed.' Somewhat later the version began in the same way as the first but proceeded—'I disarmed them—most of 'em—wounded several—and the rest fled with the Devil take the hindmost.' The third, or three o'clock in the morning version, commenced like the others, but continued—'they fell at my feet to a man and implored mercy.' 'Well, what did you do, Jacky? Did you let them go?' 'No, by G—, I *slew them all*!'[45]

I should add in parenthesis that Carlyle[46] is less than just to the 'young democrats of Regent Street', who were prepared to lay down their lives for the cause of liberty in Spain, as young Cambridge men were laying down theirs but yesterday.

Trench was ordained deacon in October 1832, but

Kemble took up again the study of the law. Once more like Jonathan Oldbuck, he made himself master of the whole forms of feudal investitures, but never applied his knowledge to lucrative and practical purposes.[47] He soon turned to philology, and from the Michaelmas Term of 1832 till the summer of 1835 spent most of the academic year in Cambridge, working in the University and college (notably Trinity and Corpus Christi) libraries and acquiring a more intimate knowledge of the manuscript sources for Old English literature and history than any scholar had had since Wanley. A glance at the manuscript notes preserved in C.U.L. Ii. i. 33, will show the care with which he worked. In the vacations he was often seen in the British Museum.[48] His first philological publication was a notice of E. Jäkel's *Der germanische Ursprung der lateinischen Sprache* in the *Foreign Quarterly Review*, x. 365–411. In 1833 he contributed a paper 'On English Præterites' to *The Philological Museum*, ii. 373–88, applying and extending the work of Jacob Grimm, to whom he dedicated his edition of *Beowulf* in the same year. Also in 1833 he wrote a 51-page appreciation of Grimm's *Deutsche Grammatik*, which was set up for the *Foreign Quarterly Review*, but, as too technical or too partial, never published; he had a few copies struck off while it was in type. In 1834 he issued a syllabus of twenty lectures to be delivered in Trinity on the *History of the English Language, First, or Anglo-Saxon, Period*, dealing with language and texts (*Beowulf* and the legend of Locrin by Laȝamon) turn about. According to Donne his first lecture was well received; when congratulated on the size and distinction of his audience, he said 'I'll soon thin them', and so he did.[49] A second course was announced but never given.

For some time Kemble had been preaching the doctrines of Rask and of Jacob Grimm, and in a favourable review of his ally Benjamin Thorpe's *Analecta Anglo-Saxonica*, which appeared in *The Gentleman's Magazine* in 1834, he wrote:

Had it not been for the industry of Danes and Germans, and those who drew from the well-heads of their learning, we might still be where we were, with idle texts, idle grammars, idle dictionaries and the consequences of all these—idle and ignorant scholars. . . Our Saxonists hitherto, with extremely few exceptions, . . have begun by editing books which they could not hope to understand; and though some may have succeeded during the progress of their work in picking up a little of the grammar, the great majority certainly have not. We could mention, were we so inclined, Doctors, yea, Professors of Anglo-Saxon, whose doings in the way of false concords, false etymology, and ignorance of declension, conjugation and syntax would, if perpetrated by a boy in the second form of a public school, have richly merited and been duly repaid by a liberal application of ferula or direr birch.[50]

Oxford possessed the only chair of Anglo-Saxon, endowed by Richard Rawlinson the Non-Juror, an excellent scholar and a man of many prejudices, who expressly barred from election natives of Scotland, Ireland, and the Plantations, and Fellows of the Royal and Antiquaries' Society. It was to be held for five years only, and his own College of St. John Baptist was to have the first and henceforward every fifth turn, 'so that the several colleges do enjoy it one after the other upon every vacancy'.[51] It is not surprising that Anglo-Saxon Professors were defined as 'persons willing to learn Anglo-Saxon',[52] and it is as a species of studentship rather than as a professorship of the normal kind that one must regard the Rawlinsonian Chair down to its reconstitution in 1858. Of the nine occupants from 1795 till 1834 three only—James Ingram, John Josias Conybeare, and Thomas Silver[53]—are to be found in the Bodleian catalogue as having published on the subject, and Kemble's letter to the *Gentleman's Magazine* (N.S. ii. 601–5) makes it clear that he referred to Conybeare's posthumous *Illustrations of Anglo-Saxon Poetry* (1826) and was fully able to substantiate his charges. His bitter words provoked even bitterer replies, which were republished with additions in *The Anglo-Saxon Meteor; or Letters, in Defence of Oxford, treating of the Wonderful Gothic Attainments of John M. Kemble, of Trinity College, Cambridge*, a pamphlet supposed to have been printed abroad in March 1835 under the supervision of Joseph

Bosworth, then English Chaplain in Holland; Bosworth was elected to the reconstituted Oxford Chair in 1858, added to its endowment, and gave £10,000 for the foundation of the Elrington and Bosworth Professorship in Cambridge, having found philology more profitable than Kemble was to do. Kemble had been arrogant, and his assailants were able to score minor hits, but their taunts about his Popish ancestry and *Poll* degree and their hapless references to his paper 'On English Præterites',[54] which in essentials is the now-accepted classification into seven strong and three weak classes, did not make a favourable impression abroad.[55] It was the *Letters of Phalaris* controversy on a smaller scale, with Kemble in the place of Bentley.

By the time *The Anglo-Saxon Meteor* appeared Kemble had met Jacob Grimm. He had written to Grimm on 28 May 1833 telling that Thorpe's *Cædmon* was out, his own *Beowulf* in the press, and that Thorpe and he projected editions of the Anglo-Saxon Gospels and probably of the *Codex Exoniensis*. Grimm was enthusiastic,[56] and again on 8 January 1834 Kemble wrote enclosing copies of *Beowulf*, *Cædmon*, and the unpublished review of *Deutsche Grammatik*,[57] but it was not till August 1834 that he visited Göttingen, where he spent three weeks or more—all his spare time with the Grimms, somewhat to the dismay of Jacob, who was lecturing on the History of German Literature for the first time. Wilhelm Grimm described him as 'the first really loveable Englishman I have seen, young, handsome, lively, *geistreich*, not ceremonious, and very learned in the Anglo-Saxon tongue. . . . He laughed so heartily, and it is very pretty when a man who is learned can laugh heartily.'[58]

It was doubtless on this visit that Kemble met his future wife Natalie Auguste, daughter of Johann Amadeus Wendt, Professor of Philosophy in Göttingen, for before 20 April 1835 Charles Kemble had written to Jacob Grimm inquiring about Fräulein Wendt.[59] Kemble was in Germany again late in 1835, and his marriage—on regrettably short acquaintance—had taken place sometime before 2 September 1836.[60] It was a surprise to Kemble's friends, though a milder shock than if Spedding or H. Romilly had sacrificed himself to the good of posterity. The marriage seems to have been happy at first,[61] and three children were born, Gertrude, who married Charles Santley the singer, Henry Charles, who became Colonel of the 2nd Bengal Cavalry, and Mildred, first wife of the Rev. C. E. Donne (son of her father's friend); but eventually Kemble and his wife parted, not later than 1847.

Before his marriage he had become editor of the new *British and Foreign Review; or European Quarterly Journal*, a post for which he was unusually well qualified and which he held from 1835 till 1844, when it ceased publication.[61a] According to the Prospectus—probably written by Kemble—the Review set out to support the voluntary principle of government and to call the attention of the public to the close connexion between the progress of social and intellectual improvement in England and in other countries. 'The power of steam has thrown a bridge over the channel—a bridge which no storm can scatter. Her liberty can no longer exist alone.' Its conductors did not disguise their anxiety to see the restoration of Poland as an independent power, and throughout its career the *Review* had its eye on the Russian Emperor. Kemble's indictment of Nicholas I in 'The Present Government of Russia' (xi. 543–91) drew an amusing comment from FitzGerald:

'Without losing one single instant, rush off to some Divan, Club, or Bookseller's, and forcibly read the last sentence of an Article called "the Emperor Nicholas" in the British and Foreign Review. It must annihilate the person in question: he will either die, kill himself, or abdicate. It made *me* tremble.'[62] On the other hand, there are letters from Kemble urging discretion on a contributor: 'however just it may be to insist upon matter of right (the British claims in Oregon), it is also a question whether such insisting be always a matter of prudence.'[63]

He was much tied by his duties as editor:

> Prometheus himself was never tighter bound to his bit of the Caucasus than I am to my Review: I have been, and am still, sitting amidst piles of proofsheets, revises, publishers' letters, authors' complaints, articles rejected, and articles accepted, but which the authors (from a modest feeling, perhaps, of their own incompetence to the task) have entrusted it to me to *translate* into respectable and readable English for them.[64]

All this time he was working at his translation of *Beowulf* (1837) and his *Codex Diplomaticus*, which appeared in six volumes between 1839 and 1848. He was also Secretary of the English Historical Society, at any rate from 1844 till it was dissolved in 1849. On 24 February 1840 he succeeded his father as Examiner of Plays[65]—the Devil's archdeacon, as W. B. Donne called himself when Examiner.[66] It involved the unsavoury duty of inspecting theatres as well as censoring the plays to be performed in them. On 10 October 1844 FitzGerald asked if it were true that Kemble and Wentworth Beaumont (the Yorkshire owner of the *British and Foreign Review*) had split,[67] and the review came to an abrupt end with the first number of vol. xviii. Henceforward Kemble was very short of money, and his sister Fanny, writing on 1 February 1849, described him and his children as living in a poor small cottage, on a wild corner of common near Cassiobury (Herts.), which, though sufficient for absolute necessary comfort, was nothing more. He had advertised in *The Times* for a pupil to prepare for the University, and in the meantime was working with characteristic zeal on a history of the English Law; the first volume was completed but could not find a publisher.[68] In 1849 he published the first two volumes of *The Saxons in England*, and was a candidate for the Cambridge chair of Modern History, which fell, however, to Sir James Stephen.[69]

About this time he went to Hanover and, as he told Donne in a letter of 23 October 1850, found there the Leibniz correspondence[70] from which he drew a great part of the material printed in *State Papers and Correspondence illustrative of the . . . state of Europe from the Revolution to the Accession of the House of Hanover* (1857); his knowledge of the Revolution period made him a redoubtable critic of Macaulay's *History*, the third and fourth volumes of which he reviewed for *Fraser's Magazine*.[71] In the meantime Donne was acting as his deputy in the Examinership of Plays,[72] and on 1 January 1852 FitzGerald has heard that unless Kemble returns to his Duties he will probably be dispossessed of his place.[73] But he was still in Hanover in the summer of 1854, when he was entrusted with the excavation of the funeral barrows on the Lüneburg Heath and the adjoining district. He showed uncanny skill in detecting mounds all but obliterated by the plough and in the classification of his finds, and when the Royal Museum, now the Landesmuseum, at Hanover was opened in 1856 he was asked to give the three lectures printed in English translation at pp. 36–70 of the posthumous *Horæ Ferales*.[74] He returned to England in 1855 and contributed some excellent papers and reviews to *Fraser's Magazine*, to *Archaeologia*, and to the *Archaeological Journal*. He had in project the continuation of *The Saxons in England* and a revised and augmented edition of the *Codex Diplomaticus*, which was out of print and already 'scarce'. He had obtained a publisher for a work on his excavations, to be entitled *Horæ Ferales*; the manuscript of this vanished at his death and the book eventually published under that title was something quite different. At the beginning of 1857 Kemble was in good spirits; Henry had done well at Addiscombe, and Gertrude was in high favour with Garcia; his *State Papers* had been well received, and he had been engaged with a salary to superintend the exhibition of Celtic and Anglo-Saxon art at the Manchester Exposition of that year.[75] He had promises of loans from all quarters when he crossed to Dublin to address the Royal Irish Academy.[76] His paper on *The Utility of Antiquarian Collections*[77] was a great success, and he had made many friends in Dublin when he was taken ill with pneumonia[78] and died on 26 March.[79] He was buried in St. Jerome's Cemetery, Dublin, and in 1865 a memorial bust by Thomas Woolner—not a happy choice—was placed in Trinity College Library.[80]

Kemble published much, and, as I have indicated, on a variety of subjects. Here it will not be possible to give more than a brief estimate of his work on Old English language, literature, and history. He was one of the first in this country to grasp the importance of the discoveries of Rask and Grimm. Hitherto the etymology of the native element in English had been little more than a series of guesses; Grimm's 'ironbound' system, expounded by Kemble in the suppressed review, placed it on a scientific basis. Kemble published no grammar of Old English, and nothing came of his projected dictionary, which, like Johnson's cookery-book, was to have been constructed on philosophical principles.[81] Among his few specific contributions to Old English philology are 'On English Præterites' (*The Philological Museum*, ii. 373–88) and 'On the North-Anglian Dialect' (*Proceedings of the Philological Society*, ii. 119–28, 131–42), but his debt to Rask and Grimm is implicit in all his work.

He had seen the dangers of relying on 'idle texts' and 'idle dictionaries' and went to the manuscript sources of Old English literature and history, travelling as far afield as St. Gall, where he found the text of 'Bede's Death-Song' of which he spoke in a letter to Sir Henry Ellis.[82] One can see from the introductory letter and bibliography he supplied to Francisque Michel's *Bibliothèque anglo-saxonne* that his acquaintance with the printed material was no less remarkable. Nor did he neglect the native character of the Germanic peoples. His paper 'On Anglo-Saxon Runes' (*Archaeologia*, xxviii. 327–72) shows him as familiar with the monumental as with the manuscript material; it first placed the study of the English variety of the runic alphabet on a sound basis. He was the first, again, to recognize that the Ruthwell Cross, in Dumfriesshire, bore fragments of an early Northumbrian poem preserved in Late West Saxon in the newly discovered Vercelli Book (*Archaeologia*, xxx. 31–46).

He went to press too early with his *Beowulf*, and it is in some ways a maddening book to use. His marking of quantities for which in general he had no manuscript authority was violently attacked at the time and is in some points, such as the accentuation of *wæs* (here he admitted in his preface he had been misled by Rask), inaccurate. I speak of the first edition of 1833; the second of 1837 was much improved. The glossary in the first edition dealt only with a handful of hard words; in the second it covered the vocabulary fairly enough, though it is sometimes a puzzle to find the form one needs. Thus in 2777 (K. 5551) *ǽr-ge-scod*, taken by Kemble to be a compound meaning 'shod with brass', must be sought under the noun *sceó*. The translation, first published in volume ii of the second edition, has faults—in general of carelessness and affectation; as J. S. Cardale said in a letter to Bosworth inserted in Bodley 3024, f. 1, 'where plain & simple English words would naturally present themselves he frequently prefers unusual, bombastic, and sometimes nonsensical and un-english expressions.' But when all deductions have been made, it remains the first critical edition of *Beowulf*, and Kemble probably did more towards the orientation and interpretation of the poem than any other single scholar, at a time when lexical help was non-existent or unreliable.

Less need be said of the editions of Old English poems printed for the Ælfric Society, to whose publications Thorpe and Kemble were the sole contributors. But his introduction to *Salomon and Saturn*, undertaken as a relief from severer labours and first set up in the thirties, is a wide-ranging study in comparative literature designed as a contribution to the history of fiction.

Old English prose, including the Laws, he left to Thorpe, reserving to himself the charters both in Latin and in the vernacular. Many of these had been published by seventeenth- and eighteenth-century scholars, such as Twysden, Dugdale, Wharton, Hickes, and Hearne, but Kemble's *Codex Diplomaticus Aevi Saxonici* was, and is, the only comprehensive collection covering the whole period from the late seventh century to the Norman Conquest. It included much new material, notably the 180 Winchester charters from the Codex Wintoniensis (now British Museum Add. 15350). Its arrangement leaves a good deal to be desired; the separation of lists of boundaries from the charters to which they are annexed is to be deplored. Also, from no fault of Kemble's, new material kept coming in when the volume to which chronologically it belonged had gone through the press. The fifth and sixth volumes include close on four hundred documents that could not find a place in the first four. In the preface to the sixth volume Kemble states that he has many charters still unprinted, and to the end of his life he was hoping to publish a corrected and enlarged edition of his *Codex*. Many years after his death this was undertaken by W. de Gray Birch, of the British Museum, whose publisher unfortunately got into difficulties and the *Cartularium Saxonicum* stopped short at 975. Similarly Kemble's projected 'lists of Kings, Bishops, Dukes and Abbots, and the general Fasti of the Anglo-Saxon kingdoms' (KCD. VI. xxix) were left to Stubbs, Birch, and Searle.[83]

As Maitland has said, 'Kemble was a great man, but, even according to the standard of his own time, not a very good editor of legal documents'.[84] He was often dependent on a copyist, and he, or his copyist, deliberately or unconsciously made a good many departures from the text of the original; one has only to look at the footnotes in a trustworthy modern edition of an Old English charter, such as those to Leofgifu's will (KCD. 931 of 1035/44) in Miss Dorothy Whitelock's *Anglo-Saxon Wills*, pp. 76 and 78.[85] But it should be emphasized that Kemble's dating is in general pretty accurate and his judgement of the authenticity of a charter surprisingly often correct.[86] No translation, commentary, nor glossary is added, and, as one need not be surprised, many of the place-names in the index are unidentified. In such cases Kemble would have done well to have omitted the hypothetical modern forms he prints in *italic*; he made his intention clear in the introduction to that index, but people will not read long rubrics, and causes of stumbling are best removed.

He claimed, and justly, that

> The extraordinary amount of information to be derived from these documents, renders their publication an era in the studies of Teutonic scholars; for law, language, and history, they are full of data, without which no inquiry in this field, however industrious and conscientious, could possibly be successful; . . . though it belongs immediately to England, it contains many notices which will be valued both north and south of the Elbe.[87]

The *Codex Diplomaticus* brought Kemble recognition from many learned societies in Germany and Scandinavia.[88] It is needless now to stress its importance to the legal and economic historian, and there are many scraps of miscellaneous information to be found. To take a few at random, we learn from a charter of Offa that Harrow-on-the-Hill was the heathen shrine of a family or group known as the *Gumeningas* (KCD. 116 of 767). KCD. 591 of 963/975 provides the first historical reference to London Bridge,[89] where a woman was drowned for practising pin-sticking magic—the first English case recorded. And KCD. 862 tells us that Edward the Confessor was born at Islip, Oxfordshire.

In his own day Kemble was most widely known as the author of *The Saxons in England*, of which two volumes had been published at his death; the third and fourth were still in his head. These are prolegomena to history—not a history of the Old English period; but they touch on almost every aspect of Old English society, and there are few of us who have not something still to learn from them—some fact or inference we have forgotten or overlooked.

Kemble had qualities and qualifications not often found united in a single man. He had first-hand knowledge of the sources, literary, historical, legal, and archaeological, of his period, and his outlook was not bounded by the North Sea or the English Channel. He was absolutely candid, with a horror of the charlatan and the dabbler that had brought him many enemies. His early philosophical reading had cultivated a power of generalization. His gift of historical imagination enabled him to see the past as vividly as the present; and he could write. It is true that the uncompromising Germanism of his outlook has few sympathizers to-day and that his 'Mark-theory', which held the field for more than a generation, is now discredited. More serious perhaps is the complaint of legal historians that Kemble lacked the lawyer's acuteness and precision and was too apt to indulge in very abstract, sometimes ill-founded, theories.[90] Yet the greatest of them, Maitland, thought it well 'to say at once that no one who has felt the difference between genius and industrious good intentions can ever differ with Kemble lightly or without regret. Kemble's work often requires correction; but if Kemble's work had not been, there would have been nothing to correct.'[91] And a man whom Stubbs described as 'my pattern scholar'[92] stands in no need of an apologist.

REFERENCES

ABBREVIATIONS

BCS. = W. de G. Birch, *Cartularium Saxonicum*, London, 1885–93.

BFR. = *British and Foreign Review.*

DNB. = *Dictionary of National Biography.*

Donne = *William Bodham Donne and his Friends*, by Catherine Bodham Johnson, London, 1905.

FitzGerald = *Letters and Literary Remains of Edward FitzGerald*, ed. W. Aldis Wright, 7 vols., London, 1902–3.

Further Records 1848–83, by Frances Anne Kemble, 2 vols., London, 1890.

Houghton = *The Life, Letters, and Friendships of Richard Monckton Milnes, First Lord Houghton*, by T. Wemyss Reid, 2nd ed., 2 vols., London, 1890.

KCD. = J. M. Kemble, *Cartularium Diplomaticum Aevi Saxonici*, English Historical Society, 1839–48.

Merivale = *Autobiography of Dean Merivale*, by Judith Anne Merivale, London, 1899.

Record of a Girlhood, by Frances Anne Kemble, 3 vols., London, 1878.

Records of Later Life, by Frances Anne Kemble, 3 vols., London, 1882.

Trench = *Richard Chenevix Trench, Archbishop: Letters and Memorials*, ed. by the author of 'Charles Lowder' [M. Trench], 2 vols., London, 1888.

1. Houghton, ii. 161.
2. *DNB.* under Kemble. Yvonne ffrench in *Mrs. Siddons: Tragic Actress*, p. 278 (London, 1936), gives a genealogical tree of the Kembles, which could be considerably amplified and in places corrected.
3. *Fraser's Magazine*, l. 616; see also *Record of a Girlhood*, i. 82–3.
4. *Record of a Girlhood*, i. 2 ff.
5. Trench, i. 41.
6. *Record of a Girlhood*, i. 11.
7. Ibid. ii. 305–6.
8. Ibid. i. 65.
9. M. M. Mathews, *A Survey of English Dictionaries*, pp. 62–4 (London, 1933).
10. *Record of a Girlhood*, i. 62.
11. Ibid. i. 136–8; *Biographical List of Boys Educated at King Edward VI. Free Grammar School, Bury St. Edmunds, from 1550 to 1900* (Suffolk Green Books, No. xiii), pp. 217 and 478. School lists for 1823 and 1824 are missing, but Kemble appears as fifth in the Sixth Form in 1825. The compiler of the *Biographical List* evidently believed that J. M. K. stayed on at school till 1827; but the Kemble who appears in the school lists for 1826 and 1827 must be his younger brother Henry.
12. FitzGerald, iv. 37–8; see also i. 2.
13. W. W. Rouse Ball and J. A. Venn, *Admissions to Trinity College, Cambridge*, iv. 241 (Cambridge, 1911).
14. Trinity College Lower Buttery Books, for access to which I have to thank the Vice-Master and the Librarian of the College. *DNB.* gives 1826 as the year in which Kemble went into residence.
15. Suffolk Green Books, No. xiii, p. 217.
16. *Record of a Girlhood*, i. 178–9, 195. Kemble's Tutor at Trinity was George Peacock, 2nd Wrangler in 1813, who became Lowndean Professor of Astronomy in 1837 and Dean of Ely in 1839.
17. Ibid. i. 199; Trench, writing to W. B. Donne on 18 October 1829, said: 'Kemble . . . . . is the only one who upheld for a long space of time the most degrading system of philosophy that ever was framed, without having his mind or heart impoverished or worsened by it. I now regard him as a Mithridates.' (Trench, i. 37.)

18. Frances M. Brookfield, *The Cambridge 'Apostles'* (London, 1906), *passim.*
19. Merivale, p. 81.
20. Information kindly supplied by Mr. Stanley S. Brown, Chief Clerk to the Society.
21. Houghton, i. 60; according to Merivale, p. 59, he took occasion, as he boasted with high glee, 'to crumple up that sciolist Paley'.
22. *Record of a Girlhood*, i. 292–4; Donne, p. 5: 'Kemble has been keeping terms at Cambridge. He wrote me a most affectionate letter to explain his sudden resolution of taking Orders, and his present studies and feelings with them in Prospect. He will be a bright and burning light in God's Church.'
23. *Athenæum*, ii. 630; Trench, i. 46. Other poems by Kemble are two sonnets entitled 'Philosophy' (*Athenæum*, ii. 104; see Trench, i. 22), and 'Love's Dirge', three stanzas of short lines rhyming *abaabaaccb* printed at Donne, pp. 13–14; 'these [stanzas] were written in Spain, in a sad moment enough'. With Trench he translated a 'Sonnet from Calderon' (*Athenæum*, ii. 72; see Trench, i. 17). I do not think there is conclusive evidence that J. M. K. wrote the two poems 'Clouds' and 'The Spirit of the North' signed 'K' and printed in the *Athenæum*, ii. 157 and 679–80.
24. Letter from J. W. Blakesley, later Fellow of Trinity and Dean of Lincoln, dated 24 January 1830 (Trench, i. 49).
25. Houghton, i. 90; yet, later writing anonymously in the *British and Foreign Review*, v. 175, Kemble said: 'We ourselves were one of *four* pupils who followed the philological course of a celebrated professor in Munich [probably Schmeller]. . . . Schlegel read the *Nibelunge Not*, the national epos of Germany, to five students, and Massmann expounded Grimm's German Mythology to seven, one of whom was a foreigner.'
26. Houghton, i. 93.
27. Letter, dated 1 April 1830, in which Kemble says characteristically: 'If I could read mathematics with Blakesley, or sleep on the sofa with Hallam or Donne in the daytime, I might be a happier man. . . .' (Trench i. 59).
28. Letter from Kemble (Donne, pp. 5–6). For other accounts of this production see *The Cambridge 'Apostles'*, pp. 164–6; Stephen Tennant thought Kemble acted excellently, except that he enjoyed it rather too much himself.
29. Thomas Carlyle, *The Life of John Sterling*, c. ix. José María de Torrijos had been Minister of War in the short-lived ministry of the 'Comuneros', which was in office in 1823 when the French invaded Spain and swept away the Constitution of Cadiz.

30. *The Life of John Sterling*, c. x.

31. Trench, i. 72. Tennyson's sonnet was published in *Poems, Chiefly Lyrical*, which appeared in this year: it is here reprinted for its biographical interest:

    My hope and heart is with thee—thou wilt be
    A latter Luther, and a soldier-priest
    To scare church-harpies from the master's feast;
    Our dusted velvets have much need of thee:
    Thou art no Sabbath-drawler of old saws,
    Distill'd from some worm-canker'd homily;
    But spurr'd at heart with fieriest energy
    To embattail and to wall about thy cause
    With iron-worded proof, hating to hark
    The humming of the drowsy pulpit-drone
    Half God's good sabbath, while the worn-out clerk
    Brow-beats his desk below. Thou from a throne
    Mounted in heaven wilt shoot into the dark
    Arrows of lightnings. I will stand and mark.

32. Trench, i. 76; about the same time Arthur Hallam and Tennyson went to the Pyrenees to meet the heads of the conspiracy on the Spanish border, and Tennyson was not too favourably impressed with the chief man Señor Ojeda (*Tennyson, A Memoir*, pp. 43–6).

33. *Record of a Girlhood*, ii. 180.

34. Ibid. ii. 282.

35. *Further Records, 1848–1883*, i. 277.

36. Trench, i. 79.

37. Ibid. i. 81.

38. *Record of a Girlhood*, ii. 281–2.

39. Trench, i. 81–3.

40. Ibid. i. 85.

41. *Record of a Girlhood*, ii. 281.

42. Letter of Kemble, dated 28 May 1830 (Trench, i. 89). He had reached London on 21 May (*Record of a Girlhood*, iii. 25).

43. See Martin Hume, *Modern Spain*, pp. 274–9 (new edition, London, 1906), where A. Gisbert's painting of the execution of Torrijos and his men is reproduced at p. 279. Two portraits and other material relating to Torrijos are reproduced in vol. vii of Antonio Ballesteros y Beretta's *Historia de España* (Barcelona, 1934), which gives the main facts about his attempt (pp. 226–8).

44. *Further Records 1848–1883*, i. 275–6.

45. *The Cambridge 'Apostles'*, p. 171. On his return from Spain Kemble was accustomed to sing a Spanish constitutionalist song, the beginning of which, 'Si un Elio conspiró, alevoso contra el pueblo y su libertad', with the air, is given in FitzGerald, iii. 257–8. Francisco Javier Elio was a Spanish general executed

in 1822 for his earlier cruelties towards the Constitutionalist conspirators in Valencia.

46. *The Life of John Sterling*, c. xiii.

47. *Fraser's Magazine*, lv. 613. 48. Merivale, p. 127.

49. *Fraser's Magazine*, lv. 614. Kemble did not feel that his work had been in vain; in a letter of 4 August 1834 he says to Trench: 'I cut politics, and stick to Teutonics, which progress bravely. I have carried the point of getting people to take an interest in their own language, have shown them the system, and, even more, have created a school which will take up my work when I cease from labour. Who says that this is nothing to have achieved?' (Trench, i. 163). See also W. W. Skeat's Inaugural Lecture printed in *Macmillan's Magazine* for February 1879, pp. 304–13. Yet Thomas Wright claimed to have been the only auditor (Skeat, *A Student's Pastime*, p. lxi).

50. *Gentleman's Magazine*, N.S. i. 391–3.

51. *The Deed of Trust and Will of Richard Rawlinson* (London, 1755), pp. xi, 17, 22, 29.

52. *DNB.*, under 'Robert Meadows White', the editor of the *Ormulum*, Rawlinsonian Professor 1834–9.

53. James Ingram (1803–8), Fellow and later President of Trinity, published his Inaugural Lecture in 1807. It includes some queer etymologies, such as 'The word *barbarian* . . . signifies nothing more than a son of the North, a North-born man, *bor-bairn*! Hence Boreas for the North wind' (p. 15), and 'Conyng-stapel is become by corruption *Constable*, the *staple* or support of the King . . . Mayor (i.e. May-er, the man of superior power; not from *major*, Lat.) . . . &c. are obvious' (p. 21). He also edited the *Anglo-Saxon Chronicle* in 1823; his translation was unfortunately reprinted in Everyman's Library, but is to be replaced in the near future.

Ingram's successor was J. J. Conybeare (1808–12), Student of Christ Church.

Thomas Silver (1817–22), Fellow of St. John's, printed his valedictory lecture in 1822; he took a very sensible view of the functions of the Chair (p. 1) and drew attention to Jacob Grimm's grammar (p. 5). His excursions into *Beowulf*-criticism were less happy (pp. 37–9). Silver's later book, *The Coronation Service, or Consecration of the Anglo-Saxon Kings, as it illustrates the Origin of the Constitution* (London, 1831) is as much a political pamphlet as a contribution to scholarship.

54. *The Anglo-Saxon Meteor*, pp. 11 and 13.

55. Letter of Jacob Grimm, dated 14 July 1837 (*Briefe der Brüder Grimm* gesammelt von Hans Gürtler—Albert Leitzmann, p. 84, Jena, 1923).

56. Letter of Jacob Grimm, dated 13 July 1833 (*Briefe der Brüder Grimm*, pp. 76–8).
57. Letter of Jacob Grimm, dated 26 April 1834 (*Briefe der Brüder Grimm*, pp. 78–9).
58. Letter of Wilhelm Grimm to Friedrich Blume, dated 15 September 1834 (*Briefe der Brüder Grimm*, pp. 185–7). Kemble went on to Switzerland where he worked in the library of St. Gall. In early October Trench met him and his younger sister Adelaide in Paris on their way home (Trench, i. 172). He had been prevented from proceeding to Vercelli by the breaking-up of the passes (letter of 19 Dec. 1834 to C. P. Cooper in the Library of Lincoln's Inn).
59. Letter of Jacob Grimm, dated 20 April 1835 (*Briefe der Brüder Grimm*, p. 82).
60. Donne, pp. 23–4.
61. Ibid., pp. 25–30.
61a. I do not feel perfectly happy about the date 1835. In a letter of 20 Nov. 1836 Merivale (p. 188) writes 'Have you seen the first specimen of Kemble's editorship? I have not, but I hear it is all about Russia and all Kemblegeschrieben.' Yet, if the reference be to Number vi (for December 1836), there are only two papers on Russia and neither of these is quite certainly by Kemble.
62. FitzGerald, i. 94; cf. also 97 and 102.
63. Letters to J. Ward, dated 29 September 1839 and undated (but endorsed November 1843), in Cambridge University Library (6157 D). Ward was the author of *Experiences of a Diplomatist* (London, 1872) and is included in *DNB*.
64. Donne, p. 27.
65. F. Fowell and F. Palmer, *Censorship in England*, p. 184 (London, 1913). This book tells some odd stories of the vagaries of the Censorship under J. M. K.'s control—the refusal to license Shirley Brooks's dramatization of Disraeli's *Coningsby* (pp. 195–6), and the licensing and suppression of J. Stirling Coyne's *Lola Montes*, which was allowed to reappear as *Pas de Fascination* with the substitution of a Russian count for the King of Bavaria. Yet it is only fair to say that the Committee of 1853 reported that the censorship had not been vexatiously exercised and should be maintained; see J. Palmer, *The Censor and the Theatres*, p. 45 (London, 1912).
66. Donne, p. 276.
67. *A FitzGerald Friendship*, ed. N. C. Hannay, p. 8 (London, 1932).
68. *Records of Later Life*, iii. 151.
69. G. O. Trevelyan, *The Life and Letters of Lord Macaulay*, ii. 261.
70. Donne, pp. 183–4.
71. *Fraser's Magazine*, liii. 147–66; for the justice of Kemble's strictures

on Macaulay's neglect of German archives and German histories and striving to exalt William III at the expense of all with whom he came into contact, see Sir Charles Firth, *A Commentary on Macaulay's History of England*, pp. 242–5 (London, 1938).

72. Donne, p. 190.
73. *A FitzGerald Friendship*, ed. N. C. Hannay, p. 45.
74. *Fraser's Magazine*, lv. 615–16.
75. Letters from W. B. Donne to Fanny Kemble dated 18 July 1856 and 20 January 1857 (Donne, pp. 204 and 216).
76. *Fraser's Magazine*, lv. 618.
77. Published separately in 1857 and reprinted in *Horæ Ferales*, pp. 71–82. In it Kemble pleads for a wider outlook in archaeology; 'nothing can be dissociated in History, and . . . nothing must be dissociated in the study of Archæology'.
78. Kemble had been threatened with tuberculosis while still at Cambridge; see a letter (undated but, from its references to Sterling and Trench, clearly of late 1834 or early 1835) to William Whewell, Fellow and afterwards Master of Trinity, now in Trinity College Library, which has two other letters from Kemble to Whewell.
79. Kemble's ill luck pursued him beyond the grave. There were a number of obituary notices, some, like the *Athenæum*'s (1857, pp. 406 and 439), ill-natured and not always well-informed. Worthy of note are those in *Fraser's Magazine*, lv. 612–18, and the *Literary Gazette* for 1857, pp. 303–4 (both by W. B. Donne; see Donne, pp. 340–1), and the *Gentleman's Magazine*, 3rd Series, ii. 620–1.

    In 1861 Longmans intended to reissue *The Saxons in England* with a sketch of the author's life by W. S. W. Vaux of the British Museum, but Donne protested as he purposed writing himself 'a short Life, more than a Sketch', and working into it as much as could be extracted from Kemble's journals and papers; he had, moreover, an unpublished chapter of *The Saxons in England* (Donne, p. 253).

    When W. de G. Birch eventually re-edited the book in 1876, no biographical matter was prefixed. No memoir in fact appeared till 1892 when J. M. K. was included in *DNB.*, where W[illiam] H[unt] made use of material contributed by Kemble's son-in-law the Rev. C. E. Donne. In her chapter on Kemble in *The Cambridge 'Apostles'*, pp. 159–87 (London, 1906) Frances M. Brookfield used matter not to be found in the numerous memoirs of his Cambridge contemporaries quoted in the preceding Notes.
80. As no portrait of J. M. K. is available in the National Portrait Gallery or in the Print Room of the British Museum the following notes on his iconography may be welcome:—

    (1) Drawing by Saville Morton, reproduced on the plate facing

p. 27 of Catherine B. Johnson's *William Bodham Donne and his Friends* (London, 1905).

(2) Drawing reproduced on the plate facing p. 160 of Frances M. Brookfield's *The Cambridge 'Apostles'* (London, 1906).

(3) Marble bust (done after Kemble's death) by Thomas Woolner, in Trinity College Library, Cambridge.

(4) Engraving by Henry Lane of Charles Kemble and his children (mentioned in *DNB.*, but not seen).

Sketch in the possession of Mrs. Charles Kemble in 1831 and mentioned in *Record of a Girlhood*, ii. 293–4—possibly the same as (1).

Rough sketch, made about 1832–3, by Edward FitzGerald or another, sent to Fanny Kemble in 1879 (FitzGerald, iv. 94).

Drawing by Lady Eastlake, according to *DNB.* in the possession of the Rev. C. E. Donne—possibly the same as (2).

Medallion likeness 'of John and his wife together in one sphere' by Henry Lane, mentioned in a letter from Fanny Kemble to Harriet St. Leger dated June 1844, *recte* 1841 (*Records of Later Life*, ii. 94).

81. *The Cambridge 'Apostles'*, p. 178.

82. British Museum MS. Add. 38626, ff. 184–5 (written from Trinity College, Cambridge, and postmarked Cambridge, Jan. 4, 1835).

Other letters from Kemble in the B.M. are:

Egerton 2842, f. 116, [dated in pencil 1 Nov. 1839].

Egerton 2843, ff. 375–6, dated 21 Nov. 1844.

Egerton 2844, f. 394, dated 13 Dec. 1848.

(All three are to Sir F. Madden and deal with Anglo-Saxon charters.)

Add. 37194, f. 564, written from Hanover and dated June 29th, 1851 (to Charles Babbage, F.R.S., the inventor of the calculating machine, introducing a Hanoverian professor).

Mr. N. R. Ker has kindly called my attention to five letters from Kemble in the Charles Purton Cooper correspondence in the Library of Lincoln's Inn—four of 1834 and one of 1836. The first (undated) begs the loan of Rask's notes on Thorkelin's *Beowulf*, the second (postmarked 26 May 1834) acknowledges the receipt of Rask's copy of Thorkelin, the third (again undated) returns the Thorkelin and tells Cooper that Kemble is about to publish 'in a second volume the entire Glossary and the Translation of Beowulf'. The fourth has been quoted above in Note 58. In the fifth (undated, but clearly of the latter part of 1836) Kemble vigorously repudiates the statement (published in REPORT FROM THE SELECT COMMITTEE ON RECORD COMMISSION *ordered by* The House of Commons *to be printed*, 11 *July* 1836, p. 272) that Thorpe and he think the Vercelli Fragments valuable, inasmuch as they illustrate the

Chronicles and Laws of The Saxons. 'I am so far from entertaining any such opinion, as on all occasions openly to have expressed my reprobation of their appearing in any work of the Commission whatever. . . .' They were printed none the less in Appendix B of *Report on Foedera.*

83. W. Stubbs, *Registrum Sacrum Anglicanum*, Oxford, 1858, 2nd ed., Oxford, 1897;
W. de G. Birch, *Fasti Monastici Aevi Saxonici*, London, 1873;
W. G. Searle, *Onomasticon Anglo-Saxonicum*, Cambridge, 1897, and *Anglo-Saxon Bishops, Kings and Nobles*, Cambridge, 1899.

84. G. P. Gooch, *History and Historians of the Nineteenth Century*, p. 289 (London, 1913).

85. See also BCS. I, xiii–xiv.

86. During the last quarter of a century many of Kemble's charters have been well re-edited by Miss F. E. Harmer, *Select English Historical Documents of the Ninth and Tenth Centuries* (Cambridge, 1914), Miss Whitelock, *Anglo-Saxon Wills* (Cambridge, 1930), and Dr. A. J. Robertson, *Anglo-Saxon Charters* (Cambridge, 1939), but a new *Codex Diplomaticus* is one of the desiderata of English scholarship.

Later investigation has naturally modified Kemble's judgement in a good many cases. Thus the authenticity of KCD. 569 and 684 (both starred by Kemble) is maintained by A. S. Napier and W. H. Stevenson, *The Crawford Collection of Early Charters and Documents* (Oxford 1895), pp. 90 and 121, and Professor F. M. Stenton (*Oxoniensia*, i. 105–6) is inclined to accept KCD. 709, of which a better text has come to light since Kemble's day. On the other hand, Miss Harmer in her valuable *Anglo-Saxon Charters and the Historian* (reprinted from vol. xx of the *Bulletin of the John Rylands Library*) points out that Kemble rarely stars a vernacular charter and that 'anachronism' is the only criterion he applies when dealing with such a charter. She suggests some further criteria, to which attention may be called. Yet, when one considers that Kemble had for the most part to forge his own tools, the statement made in the text is not too strong.

87. KCD. VI. v.

88. See the title-page to *Horæ Ferales.*

89. See Gordon Home, *Old London Bridge*, pp. 7–8 (London, 1931).

90. See P. Vinogradoff, *Villainage in England*, pp. 16–21 (Oxford, 1892); H. C. Lodge in *Essays in Anglo-Saxon Law*, p. 96 (Boston, 1876).

91. F. Pollock and F. W. Maitland, *A History of English Law*, i. 4 (Cambridge, 1895). Points, for example, in which Kemble's work needed correction were his opinions that a man lost personal

freedom, or at any rate the ordinary political rights of a freeman, by becoming one of the king's companions (*The Saxons in England*, i. 166 ff.; see Pollock and Maitland, i. 9), and that it is impossible to allow as much as 120 acres to the hide of Domesday or the OE. Charters (*The Saxons in England*, i. 487; see F. W. Maitland, *Domesday Book and Beyond*, pp. 499–500, Cambridge, 1897).

92. Letter to E. A. Freeman dated 8 December [1859] in *Letters of William Stubbs*, ed. W. H. Hutton, p. 77 (London, 1904).

WRITINGS OF JOHN MITCHELL KEMBLE

1832

Review of E. Jäkel's *Der germanische Ursprung der lateinischen Sprache* (*Foreign Quarterly Review*, x. 365–411).[1]

1833

The Anglo-Saxon Poems of Beowulf, the Traveller's Song, and the Battle of Finnes-burh, edited together with a glossary of the more difficult words and an historical preface, pp. xxxii+260; Second Edition, pp. xxxii+263, dated 1835, but not issued till 1837.

On English Præterites (*The Philological Museum*, ii. 373–88, Cambridge).

Review of *Cædmon's Metrical Paraphrase* (*Gentleman's Magazine* CIII, i. 329–31; not signed, but see *Anglo-Saxonica*, ii. 146).

Review of *Deutsche Grammatik*, von Dr. Jacob Grimm, pp. 51 (set up for the *Foreign Quarterly Review*, but never published; presentation copy from the author in Cambridge University Library).

1834

Review of *Analecta Anglo-Saxonica* [by Benjamin Thorpe] (*Gentleman's Magazine*, N.S. i. 391–3).

Letter on 'Oxford Professors of Anglo-Saxon' (*Gentleman's Magazine*, N.S. ii. 601–5).

History of the English Language. First, or Anglo-Saxon, Period. Cambridge, pp. 20+2 tables of Paradigms.

1835

Prospectus and Introduction (*British and Foreign Review; or European Quarterly Journal*, i. 1–16).[2]

Letter 'On Anglo-Saxon Accents' (*Gentleman's Magazine*, N.S. iv. 26–30).

1836

Ueber die Stammtafel der Westsachsen. München, pp. 36.

Anglo-Saxon Proverb (*Gentleman's Magazine*, N.S. v. 611).

[1] The place of publication is London unless otherwise stated. For poems see p. 71.

[2] None of the contributions to the *British and Foreign Review*, of which Kemble was editor, were signed. In view of what has been said on p. 63 it is hazardous perhaps to attempt to identify Kemble's contributions, but it seems likely that the articles listed below are, in whole or part, to be attributed to him.

The Drama (*BFR*. ii. 568–90).
Freidank's Poems (*BFR*. iii. 23–61).

1837

A few historical remarks upon the supposed antiquity of Church Rates, and the three-fold division of Tithes. By a Lay Member of the Church of England. 16mo., pp. 20 [copy in Dr. Williams's Library]; the New [and considerably enlarged] Edition of the same year, pp. 30, is in the British Museum.[1]

A Translation of the Anglo-Saxon Poem of Beowulf, with a copious Glossary, Preface, and philological Notes, pp. viii+lv+127+Glossary, Appendix and Corrigenda unpaged (of pp. 178).

Letter to M. Francisque Michel, printed as pp. 1–63 of *Bibliothèque anglo-saxonne* (Paris and London), the second volume of *Anglo-Saxonica* (by P. de Larenaudière and Francisque Michel).[2]

Report on the Record Commission (*BFR*. iv. 120–68).[3]
Report on the British Museum (*BFR*. iv. 213–54).[3]
British and Foreign Universities: Cambridge (*BFR*. v. 168–209).

1838

British and Foreign Universities: Oxford (*BFR*. vi. 97–122).
The Hanoverian Coup d'État (*BFR*. vi. 269–338).
The English Historical Society (*BFR*. vii. 167–92).

1839–1848

Codex Diplomaticus Aevi Saxonici, opera Johannis M. Kemble, Tomi VI (Sumptibus Societatis, *i.e.* The English Historical Society).

1839. Tomus I, half-title and title-page+pp. 4+cxxix+321+3 plates.
1840. Tomus II, title-page+pp. 4+xxiv+436.
1845. Tomus III, pp. lii+4+468.
1846. Tomus IV, pp. xx+317.

[1] Published anonymously, the authorship being acknowledged in *The Saxons in England*, ii. 559. There Kemble gives the date of publication as 1836, but, as Mr. Stephen K. Jones suggests, there is nothing to lead one to believe that the Dr. Williams's Library copy is not of the original edition. Perhaps that, dated 1837, was actually published late in 1836.

[2] Kemble was also in large part responsible for the bibliography that follows (*Gentleman's Magazine*, N.S. iv. 483).

[3] These two papers are attributed to Kemble in a MS. note in University College, London, Rotton 46, d. 11.

1847. Tomus V, pp. xv+403.
1848. Tomus VI, pp. xxxviii+359.

1840

On Anglo-Saxon Runes (*Archaeologia*, xxviii. 327–72).
The Political Opinions of the Germans (*BFR*. x. 25–49).
Reynard the Fox (*BFR*. x. 399–425).
The Present Government of Russia (*BFR*. xi. 543–91).[1]
Postscript (*BFR*. xi. 655–62).

1841

Anglo-Saxon Laws and Institutes (*BFR*. xii. 46–94).

1842

Further Notes on the Runic Cross at Lancaster (*Archaeologia*, xxix. 76–9).
La Chronique de Rains (*BFR*. xiii. 163–88).

1843

The Poetry of the Codex Vercellensis, with an English Translation. Part I: The Legend of St. Andrew (printed for the Ælfric Society), pp. xvi+100.
Additional Observations on the Runic Obelisk at Ruthwell; the Poem of the Dream of the Holy Rood; and a Runic Copper Dish found at Chertsey (*Archaeologia*, xxx. 31–46).
Retrospect (*BFR*. xvi. 1–4).

1844

Thierry's *Récits des Temps Mérovingiens* (*BFR*. xvii. 270–303).
Salomon and Saturn, pp. 292, without title-page or prelims; never issued, but copies in the British Museum, the Bodleian, and Cambridge University Library.[2]

[1] See p. 62.

[2] Kemble (*The Dialogue of Salomon and Saturnus*, p. iii) says of this item that it was 'first commenced in Cambridge in 1833', and the latest-published work he quotes is of 1834. William Pickering had published the *Beowulf* of 1833 and this too was to have been issued by him. The Chiswick Press Costs Book C (British Museum MS. Add. 41887, ff. 37v and 38r and v) shows that the setting-up, begun on 17 Dec. 1836, was not completed till 2 May 1840. The last corrections were made on 5 Nov. 1844. Most of the 250 copies of sigs. B–O must have been 'wasted', for only 24 copies of pp. 209–92 were printed on 14 Nov. 1844 (Ledger E = B.M. Add. 41927, f. 403v). This item is therefore given under 1844; the British Museum Catalogue dates it '?1845'.

1846

On the North-Anglian Dialect (*Proceedings of the Philological Society*, ii. 119–28, 131–42, but not completed as promised).

The Names, Surnames, and Nicnames of the Anglosaxons (*Proceedings of the Archaeological Institute at Winchester, September* MDCCCXLV, pp. 81–102).

1848

The Dialogue of Salomon and Saturnus with an Historical Introduction (printed for the Ælfric Society), pp. vii+326.

1849

The Saxons in England: a History of the English Commonwealth till the Period of the Norman Conquest, 2 vols., pp. x+535 and iv+562; translated into German by H. B. Chr. Brandes. *Die Sachsen in England*, 2 Bde., Leipzig 1853–4; New Edition of 1876 revised by W. de G. Birch, 2 vols., pp. xii+535 and iv+562.

Certaine considerations upon the Government of England by Sir Roger Twysden, Kt. and Bart. Edited from the unpublished Manuscript (printed for the Camden Society), pp. lxxxv+191, quarto.

Introductory Address (*Archaeological Journal*, vi. 1–3).

1850

On a peculiar use of the Anglo-Saxon Patronymical Termination *ing* (*Proceedings of the Philological Society*, iv. 1–10).

1851

A few Notes respecting the Bishops of East Anglia (*Memoirs illustrative of the History and Antiquities of Norfolk . . . communicated to the Annual Meeting of the Archaeological Institute . . . held at Norwich, July 1847*, pp. 24–56).

1853

Reviews in *Fraser's Magazine* of J. M. Lappenberg's *Urkundliche Geschichte des Hansischen Stahlhofes in London* (xlvii. 699–706) and of E. Vehse's *Geschichte des Preussischen Hofs und Adels, und der Preussischen Diplomatie*, and *Geschichte der Höfe des Hauses Braunschweig in Deutschland und England* (xlviii. 59–70 and 445–51), though unsigned, have all the appearance of Kemble's work.

1854

Surrey Provincialisms (*Transactions of the Philological Society*, 1854, pp. 83–4).

Ausgrabungen im Amte Soltau im Sommer 1853 (*Zeitschrift des historischen Vereins für Niedersachsen* 1851, pp. 183–193).[1]

Beschreibung eines merkwürdigen Thongefässes in der Sammlung des Vereins (*Zeitschrift* . . . 1851, pp. 389–92).

1855

On Mortuary Urns found at Stade-on-the-Elbe, and other parts of North Germany, now in the Museum of the Historical Society of Hanover (*Archaeologia*, xxxvi. 270–83); reprinted in *Horæ Ferales*, pp. 221–32.

On some remarkable Sepulchral Objects from Italy, Styria, and Mecklenburgh (*Archaeologia*, xxxvi. 349–69); reprinted in *Horæ Ferales*, pp. 233–51.

Burial and Cremation (*Archaeological Journal*, xii. 309–37); reprinted in *Horæ Ferales*, pp. 83–106.

Zur Geschichte der Succession des Hauses Hannover in England (*Zeitschrift* . . . 1852, pp. 64–144).

Bericht über Ausgrabungen in Amte Oldenstadt, Nov. 1851 (*Zeitschrift* . . . 1852, pp. 165–98, but not completed as promised).

Review of Dr. Doran's *Lives of the Queens of England of the House of Hanover* (*Fraser's Magazine*, lii. 135–49); signed 'T. M. K.', but certainly by Kemble.

1856

The Poetry of the Codex Vercellensis with an English Translation. Part II: Elene and Minor Poems (printed for the Ælfric Society), pp. x+110.

Review of Macaulay's *History of England*, vols. iii and iv (*Fraser's Magazine*, liii. 147–66).

Review of R. Pauli's *Geschichte von England* (*Fraser's Magazine*, liv. 665–80).

1857

State Papers and Correspondence illustrative of the social and political state of Europe, from the Revolution to the Accession of the House of Hanover. Edited with historical introduction, biographical memoirs, and notes, pp. xlviii+559.

[1] Three of the four papers in *Zeitschrift des historischen Vereins für Niedersachsen* are doubtless the 'notices of the sepulchral antiquities of the Northern nations, published among the *Transactions of the Archaeological Society of Hanover*', to which Donne refers in *Fraser's Magazine*, lv, 617.

The Knights Hospitallers in England: being the Report of Prior Philip de Thame to the Grand Master Elyan de Villanova for A.D. 1338, edited by the Rev. Lambert B. Larking, M.A., with an historical introduction by John Mitchell Kemble, M.A. (printed for the Camden Society), pp. lxxii+301, quarto.

The Utility of Antiquarian Collections, as throwing Light on the Pre-historic Annals of the European Nations: An Address delivered to the President and Members of the Royal Irish Academy at their Meeting, February 9, 1857. With advertisement by James H. Todd, D.D., President of the Royal Irish Academy, Dublin, pp. 32; reprinted in *Horæ Ferales*, pp. 71–82.

Anglo-Saxon Document relating to lands at Send and Sunbury in Middlesex, in the time of Eádgár: and the Writ of Cnut, on the accession of Archbishop Æthelnoth to the See of Canterbury, A.D. 1020 (*Archaeological Journal*, xiv. 58–62).

Notices of Heathen Interment in the Codex Diplomaticus (*Archaeological Journal*, xiv. 119–39); reprinted in *Horæ Ferales*, pp. 107–22.

1858

The Gospel according to St. Matthew in Anglo-Saxon and Northumbrian versions, synoptically arranged: with collations of the best manuscripts [edition completed by Charles Hardwick after Kemble's death]. Cambridge, pp. iv+231, quarto.

1863

Horæ Ferales; or Studies in the Archaeology of the Northern Nations, edited by R. G. Latham and A. W. Franks, pp. xii+251, with 34 plates, quarto; it contains the Dublin address of 1857 and papers from *Archaeologia* (xxxvi. 270–83 and 349–69) and the *Archaeological Journal* (xii. 309–37, and xiv. 119–39), together with a translation (pp. 36–71) of unpublished lectures given at the opening of the Hanover Museum.

THE SURVIVAL OF ANGLO-SAXON ILLUMINATION AFTER THE NORMAN CONQUEST

By F. WORMALD

Read 14 June 1944

WITHIN recent years the study of the Norman Conquest has shown that while much of English life was changed by that invasion of this country, many aspects of English civilization remained comparatively unaffected. One of the most notable studies in this field is the remarkable essay by Professor Chambers on the continuity of English prose where he shows that though the use of English prose died out for official purposes it continued without interruption in works of piety, such as the *Ancren Riwle*.[1] Speaking of the Conquest Chambers says:

> The foreign prelates and abbots whom William imposed upon the conquered English found in their monasteries a tradition of two things without parallel on the Continent, a splendour of manuscript illumination and a tradition of vernacular composition. We might have expected on *a priori* grounds that they would have encouraged the art and discouraged the language. But, in fact, while illumination disappears, manuscripts in the English language continue to be transcribed, not only at Worcester, under Wulfstan, but under Norman rule at many other places.[2]

Dr. Eric Millar also says:

> The Battle of Hastings forms a convenient break in the history of English illumination, if only because for the time being it leaves us in complete darkness. What is at least certain is that Norman monks, including scribes and illuminators, were introduced in large numbers into English religious houses throughout the country and a change of style followed as an almost inevitable result.[3]

Both these opinions imply that the Conquest upset the cultural life of England so much that an important and flourishing aspect of English art was destroyed and that the next important school of English illumination was that centring round the Albani Psalter, now at Hildesheim, whose style is entirely different

[1] R. W. Chambers, *The Continuity of English Prose from Alfred to More*, see Early English Text Society's edition of Nicholas Harpsfield, *The Life and Death of Sir Thomas Moore*, 1932, pp. xc–c.

[2] R. W. Chambers, op. cit., p. xc.

[3] E. G. Millar, *English Illuminated Manuscripts from the Xth to the XIIIth Century*, 1926, p. 25.

from Pre-Conquest illumination. If this is so, then there is indeed a gap of at least thirty years which has got to be bridged, and, if the Albani Psalter, which cannot be before 1119, is to be considered an early example of the first Pre-Conquest style, then this gap is of about fifty years.[1] Now the style of the Albani Psalter is so different from that of the Pre-Conquest illuminators that it would seem at first sight most probable that the Conquest had indeed destroyed the Anglo-Saxon style and left England for at least a generation without anything to replace it. The following remarks will, I hope, serve to show that this was not so, and that the Pre-Conquest style had still a most important role to play in the development of English illumination.

At the Norman Conquest the style of illumination was the direct descendant of the style of the 'Winchester' school which had been evolved a century earlier as a result of the great monastic reform associated with the names of St. Dunstan, St. Ethelwold, and St. Oswald. Its primary origin was Carolingian, some of its elements coming from the school of Metz and some of them from the Franco-Saxon style of the North of France.[2] A less showy element seen in certain initials is undoubtedly a survival from earlier Anglo-Saxon illumination of the eighth and ninth centuries.[3] The chief features of the 'Winchester' school were an abundant leafy scroll ornament and a remarkable outline drawing style which was without contemporary parallel in the rest of Europe.

The leafy scrolls of the border ornaments can be seen in such manuscripts as the Benedictional of St. Ethelwold at Chatsworth and the Benedictional of Archbishop Robert at Rouen. At the corners of the borders are roundels over which the leafwork clambers and on the sides these leaves grow over the frames of the border in the manner of creepers. Very often they

[1] See Adolph Goldschmidt, *Der Albani Psalter in Hildesheim*, 1895, pp. 28–30. It is unfortunately not possible to date precisely the other manuscripts belonging to this style; see handlist of English Illuminated MSS. in E. G. Millar, op. cit., pp. 113, 114, nos. 69, 73–6. B.M. Cotton MS. Titus D. XVI is dated about A.D. 1100, but this may be rather too early.

[2] For the connexions between the 'Winchester' school and its Carolingian predecessors see Otto Homburger, *Die Anfänge der Malschule von Winchester im x. Jahrhundert*, Leipzig, 1912. The connexion with the Franco-Saxon school is most clearly seen in some of the large initials, e.g. London, College of Arms, Arundel MS. XXII, fragment of a late tenth-century Gospel Lectionary with a fine initial and border.

[3] F. Wormald, 'Decorated Initials in English MSS. from A.D. 900–1100', *Archaeologia*, xci. 107–31.

grow out on long stalks ending in a kind of trefoil. Their ends curl over in a crinkled pattern which gives the artist an opportunity to vary the colours. The effect produced is extremely lively and gives the illusion of an endless and scintillating activity. One's eye is carried up and down, in and out, over the whole of the decoration. This device of carrying the eye swiftly over the pattern must surely be the reappearance of the spirit which produced the elaborately interlacing birds and animals of such early manuscripts as the Lindisfarne Gospels. In the beautiful initial 'B' in Harley MS. 2904 in the British Museum, which belongs to the last quarter of the tenth century, this 'Winchester' scroll may be seen in its purest form.[1] The device of the never-ending pattern can be fully appreciated here because, though the ornament is kept within the framework of the initial, it is nevertheless allowed considerable freedom within its border. During the eleventh century the scrolls tend to become more writhing and more stringy in appearance. The effect is more animated than ever. Another initial 'B' from a manuscript in the University Library at Cambridge shows how this is achieved.[2] In the Harley Psalter the leaves have a certain body to them, but in the Cambridge MS. they have become thin and wiry. The stalks have become much longer and thinner and the leaves crinkle and flutter in a much more exaggerated manner. It seems clear, therefore, that during the course of the eleventh century the typical 'Winchester' scroll developed even more rococo habits than it was endowed with originally. What was the reason for this tendency towards exaggerations of this kind? The answer seems to be the intense love of the Anglo-Saxon artists for expressive line and for the reduction of the object represented to terms of pattern. This dependence on the use of line for the achievement of the desired effect is of fundamental importance for the whole development of English medieval art, and the skill displayed by the Anglo-Saxon artists of the tenth and eleventh centuries in the use of it has never been surpassed.

In the tenth century, when the artists were still to some extent adhering faithfully to their Carolingian and earlier archetypes, the figures and draperies have a semblance of solidity. Such a figure as the St. Matthew from the tenth-century Gospels at

[1] B.M. Harley MS. 2904, f. 4; reproduced by E. G. Millar, op. cit., pl. 11.

[2] Cambridge, University Library MS. Ff. 1. 23, f. 1. Reproduced in Wormald, op. cit., pl. 1.

York Minster shows how carefully the artist was trying to follow his original, but the liveliness of the figure is undoubtedly created by the enormous hands and the characteristic fluttering, crinkling folds of the drapery (Plate *2a*).[1] Nothing could be simpler than the drawing of a splendid fish in Harley 2506, but in no contemporary work of art is such intensity of expression achieved with such economy (Plate *2b*).[2] This book is known to be a copy of a much earlier manuscript, yet the English artist has strikingly modified it by the impress of his own personality. The effect is most remarkable and it is achieved by the complete assurance with which the artist has used his line and by the skilful management of the blank space behind the object. This use of the blank vellum behind the figures is most important, since by it the English artists of the tenth and eleventh centuries achieved an illusion of space which was not possible by the use of coloured backgrounds. But outline was not merely used to procure an illusion of vitality. It was also used by the 'Winchester' school artists to express the spiritual content of a scene. The famous miniature of the Crucifixion in a Psalter in the British Museum is not only a superb drawing, but is a moving expression of the artist's feelings. In it the outline is varied from the thick solid lines of the legs of the Christ to the thin suggestive drawing of the muscles of His body or the fluttering draperies of the figure of St. John. By this variation the artist was not only able to represent the dead Saviour with His mother and the Beloved Disciple, but he was also able to express the grief of the Virgin and the eager love of St. John. The whole miniature is given thereby a kind of lyrical mysticism which is not met with in contemporary European art.[3]

The intensity of feeling which these artists could give their works is particularly well illustrated in a miniature of the Crucifixion in a Gospel book which seems to be datable about the second quarter of the eleventh century, now in the Pierpont Morgan Library in New York (Plate 3). This miniature will be referred to as the Weingarten Crucifixion. It is a splendid work of great poignancy, but, what is so extraordinary about it, is a quality which makes one think of late medieval art with the tendency towards violent expression of the sufferings of the Passion. When looking at this miniature one's mind turns

[1] See New Palaeographical Society, *Facsimiles of Ancient MSS.*, 2nd Series, Plates 163–5.

[2] B.M. Harley MS. 2506, f. 40 b.

[3] B.M. Harley MS. 2904, f. 3 b, reproduced by E. G. Millar, op. cit., pl. 10.

involuntarily to that wonderful English fourteenth-century lyric which begins:

Gloryouse Lord, so doolfully dyȝte
So rewfully streyned upryȝt on þe cros;
For þi mykel mekenesse, þi mercy, þi myȝt
þou bete al my bale with bote of þi blood.

This miniature makes use of expressive line and the jagged outline of the high cross serves only to intensify the dramatic aspect of the situation. The contrast between the tall figures of St. Mary and St. John and the kneeling woman at the foot of the cross serve to heighten the expressiveness of the whole scene. What the artist did was to give as it were a calligraphic note of his emotions by endowing his outline with a burning vitality.[1]

By 1060, however, some English artists were experimenting with a style entirely independent of the outline drawing style which has just been discussed. Arundel 60, a Psalter from the New Minster at Winchester, has in it two miniatures of the Crucifixion. One is executed in the old outline style and is not a very good example of it.[2] The other is a work of remarkable power and importance (Plate 4).[3] This miniature is framed by a border of leaf work which is derived from the old 'Winchester' scroll. There are the same long leaves clambering all over the framework of the border and gripping the edges, but whereas in such manuscripts as the Cambridge Psalter these leaves have a hard wiry look about them, in the New Minster Psalter they are more serpentine and fleshy. It is, however, in the figure of the Christ that the difference is most remarkable. In the Weingarten Crucifixion the whole effect was gained by the characteristic management of the outline. In the New Minster Psalter this is achieved by a deliberate attempt to represent the solidity of the human form by exaggeration of the muscles, particularly of the torso. The folds of the loin-cloth instead of being soft and fluttering are divided up into hard geometrical shapes, enriched with heavily jewelled borders. What is the explanation of this? The answer must be that during the Confessor's reign artists in

[1] New York, Pierpont Morgan Library MS. 709, f. 1 b. Gospels, of the second half of the eleventh century, formerly in the Benedictine Abbey of Weingarten.

[2] B.M. Arundel MS. 60, f. 12 b. This miniature shows 'Winchester' outline drawing just before the Norman Conquest. If compared with the Crucifixion in the Weingarten Gospels in New York it will be obvious that the Arundel MS. is much less vigorous in style.

[3] Ibid., f. 52 b, reproduced in E. G. Millar, op. cit., pl. 31.

England were beginning to experiment with means of representing solid form in the same way that the artists on the Continent were experimenting, for there is no doubt that this artist was definitely turning his back on the accepted 'Winchester' style and was interested in the treatment of folds and a representation of the human body which ultimately goes back to archetypes entirely different from the 'Winchester' school. The whole figure looks much less naturalistic than the Weingarten Crucifixion and is much more hieratic. What is more surprising is that the artist does not appear to be copying a continental archetype in a purely mechanical way. The ornament is certainly derived from 'Winchester' manuscripts, but the figures show something quite new in English art.

It is not easy to find contemporary manuscripts from the Channel area which show the same advanced interests, but a Gospel book in the British Museum provides some means of comparison, though it may be slightly later.[1] Unfortunately we do not know where this book comes from. Usually it is called North French. The figures of the Evangelists in this manuscript show something of the same interest in the representation of the muscles as well as the stiff angular treatment of the draperies. What is, however, quite clear is that the New Minster Crucifixion is much closer in spirit to this manuscript than it is to the Weingarten Crucifixion and both are experimenting in something which is moving away from the illusionism of the 'Winchester' manuscripts towards something which will develop into the romanesque.

Arundel 60 is, therefore, of very great importance in the history of English illumination, because it shows that on the eve of the Conquest there were artists in England who were breaking away from the traditional style of the country in favour of the new style which was beginning to stir on the Continent. It is tempting to see the influence of the Confessor's foreign friends here, but the evidence is not forthcoming for the proof.

Having now seen what the position was in England at the Conquest, let us see what was the position in northern France from which any new style would be most likely to come. From the start it is important to remember that from the end of the tenth century the 'Winchester' style had a number of continental

[1] B.M. Add. MS. 11850, f. 91 b. This manuscript is copied from a manuscript illuminated in the 'Winchester' manner, but the treatment of the draperies shows definite tendencies towards the stylizations already found in B.M. Arundel MS. 60, f. 52 b. The manuscript should be dated *circa* 1100.

followers, particularly in large and important North French monastic houses like Saint Bertin at Saint Omer.[1] The work of these foreign followers was remarkably close to 'Winchester' originals, but it can usually be distinguished quite easily from real English work. The splendid Gospels from Saint Bertin in the Pierpont Morgan Library in New York (MS. 333) show how the fluttering 'Winchester' folds become hardened when produced second-hand on just the other side of the Channel. The ornament, too, was hardened, not in the way it was hardened in England, where it is thin and stringy, but it becomes as it were petrified and without liveliness. A Bible from Saint Vaast at Arras, also of the eleventh century, shows the same close borrowing from the 'Winchester' style, both in figure drawing and in ornamental details.[2] In a fine initial, f. 198, the top of the letter is a direct copy of an initial style which was well known in England at the beginning of the eleventh century. This Bible shows also certain borrowings from the other important eleventh-century style derived from the Ottonian MSS. from Trier and Echternach. From what we know, therefore, of the North French style of illumination during the eleventh century there seems to be every indication that the Anglo-Saxon element played an important part in its make-up. When, therefore, the Conqueror put Norman abbots into the English monasteries it is likely that any foreign manuscripts which they brought with them were illuminated in a style which had at any rate in part an old 'Winchester' element in them. From what little evidence we have it seems that in fact the Normans had very little to offer in the way of a style which could be used as an alternative to a vigorous national style which was still flourishing.

The Norman Conquest undoubtedly upset the normal tenor of English monastic life and with it the production of books. There is, however, no evidence to suggest that the Conqueror attempted to interfere with an entirely harmless activity. Indeed the presence of Lanfranc at the head of the Church in England was sufficient to ensure that it was not interfered with.

[1] Particularly the manuscripts executed during the abbacy of Otbert, *circa* 988–1007. See Dom. A. Wilmart, 'Les livres de l'abbé Otbert', in *Bulletin Historique de la Société des Antiquaires de la Morinie*, xiv. 169–88. New York, Pierpont Morgan Library MS. 333, a Gospel Book of this period shows this very well.

[2] Arras, Bibliothèque Municipale MS. 559, a Bible from Saint Vaast, eleventh century, contains initials, particularly f. 198, with ornament derived from initials found in English manuscripts of about 1000, see F. Wormald, op. cit., pp. 121–4.

It is true to say, however, that there are no illuminated books which can safely be dated within the first fifteen years after the Conquest. It may be that when the chronology of the palaeography of this period is more sufficiently established it will be possible to date books within these years.

The first body of decorated books which can be dated in Post-Conquest England are the manuscripts connected with William of Saint Carileff, Bishop of Durham, from 1081–96. At least sixteen books can be ascribed to this group. Their illumination is confined to their very fine and interesting initials, and this fact has perhaps been the reason why they have not received more attention from students of English illumination. There is sometimes a tendency to minimize the importance of initials in favour of full-page miniatures, especially if the initials are primarily of an ornamental nature. The ornament of the initials in the Durham MSS. can be shown to be for the most part derived from Pre-Conquest Anglo-Saxon ornament. In the first place the leafy scroll ornament is certainly derived from the scrolls found in the sumptuous manuscripts of the end of the tenth century, such as Harley MS. 2904. There are the same long and short leaves which spring from a knot-like protuberance on the stalk. This scroll-work is frequently combined with dragons which have wide open jaws and tails ending in a rich crop of 'Winchester' leaf-work. Such dragons may be paralleled in English Pre-Conquest initials from the middle of the tenth century onwards. A third type of initial is a curious construction of small gripping heads, broken interlace with fragments of 'Winchester' scrolls. Initials with an exactly similar construction are found in Anglo-Saxon manuscripts of about 1000.[1]

From this it can be seen that the majority of the ornamental motives in the manuscripts of William of Saint Carileff are derived from Pre-Conquest English initials. There is one modification, however, which is important, and that is the increase of figures amongst the ornament of the initials. Admittedly scrolls inhabited by human beings occur in the New Minster Psalter (Arundel 60), but the style of this manuscript has already been shown to have certain peculiarities.[2] This use of the humanly inhabited scroll is related to another new type of English initial

[1] Particularly R. A. B. Mynors, *Durham Cathedral Manuscripts*, plates 18, 25, and F. Wormald, op. cit., pl. VIII *b*.

[2] See B.M. Arundel MS. 60, f. 13. Figures forming part of initials are found in English manuscripts of the first half of the tenth century, see Oxford, Bodleian MSS. Tanner 10 and Junius 27.

LAURENCE NOWELL: abbreviated transcript, with side-notes by himself and Lambarde, of Offa's grant to Bredon, from the Worcester Chartulary (Cotton MS. Tiberius A. xiii, ff. 11 *b*, 12). Cotton MS. Vespasian A. v, f. 157.

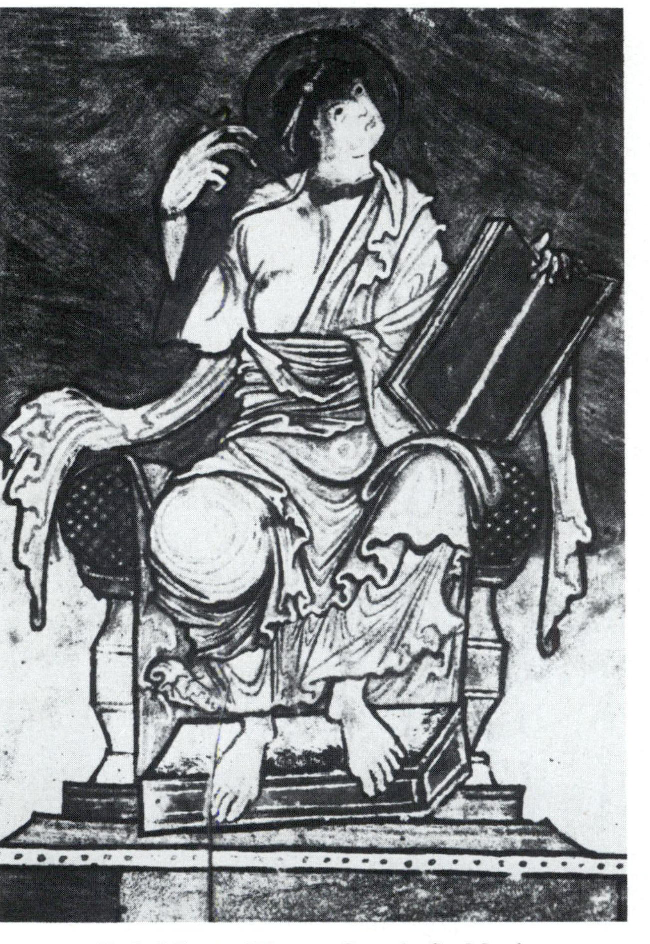

a. York, Minster Library, Gospels, St. Matthew, late 10th cent.

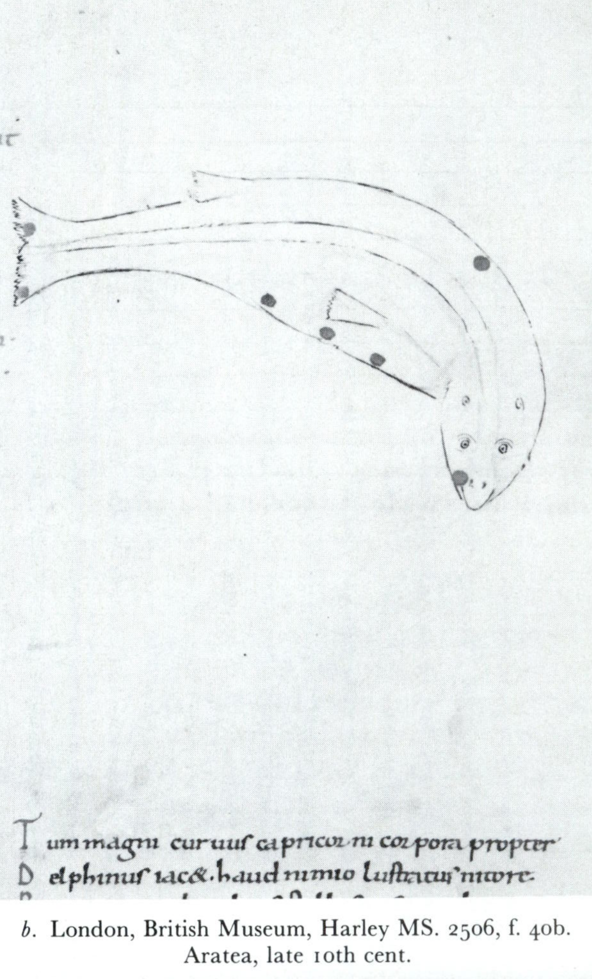

b. London, British Museum, Harley MS. 2506, f. 40b. Aratea, late 10th cent.

New York, Pierpont Morgan Library, Morgan MS. 709, f. 1b. Gospels, *c.* 1050

London, British Museum, Arundel MS. 60, f. 52b. Psalter, from Winchester, *c.* 1060

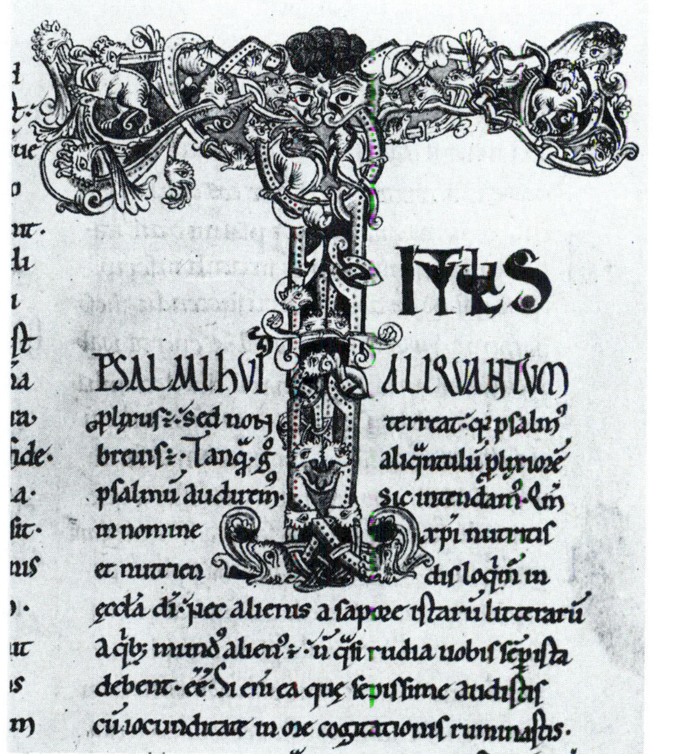

a. Durham Cathedral Library, MS. B II. 13, f. 49r. St. Augustine, from Durham, before A.D. 1088

b. Oxford, Bodleian, MS. Bodl. 569, f. 92b. Lanfranc, etc., early 12th cent.

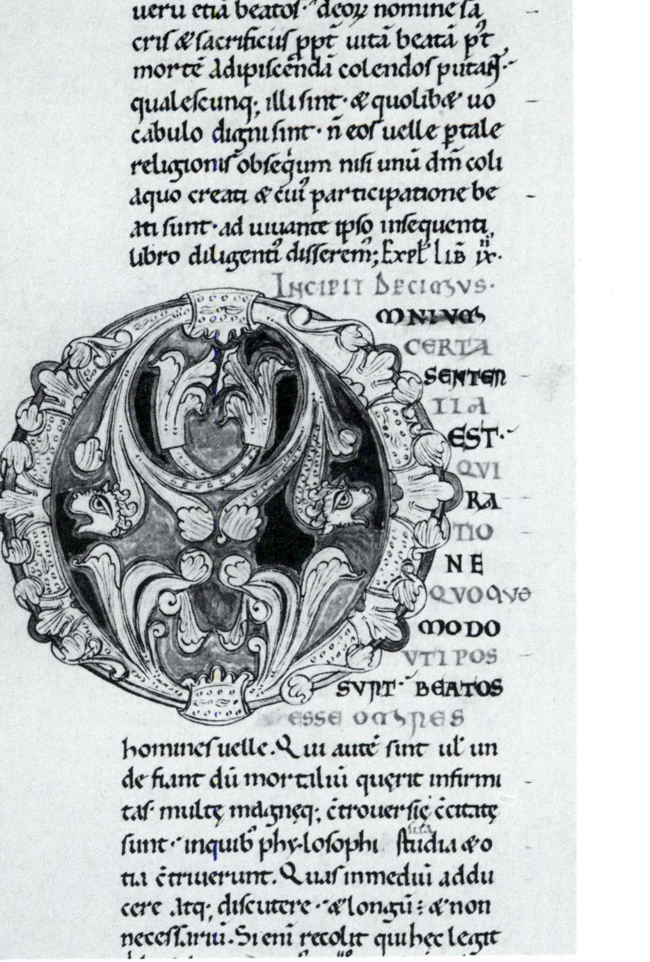

a. Oxford, Bodleian, MS. Bodl. 691, f. 92v. St. Augustine, from Exeter. *c.* 1100

b. London, British Museum, Arundel MS. 91, f. 40b. Passionale, from St. Augustine's, Canterbury, early 12th cent.

London, British Museum, Nero C. IV, f. 15. Psalter, from Winchester, *c.* 1150

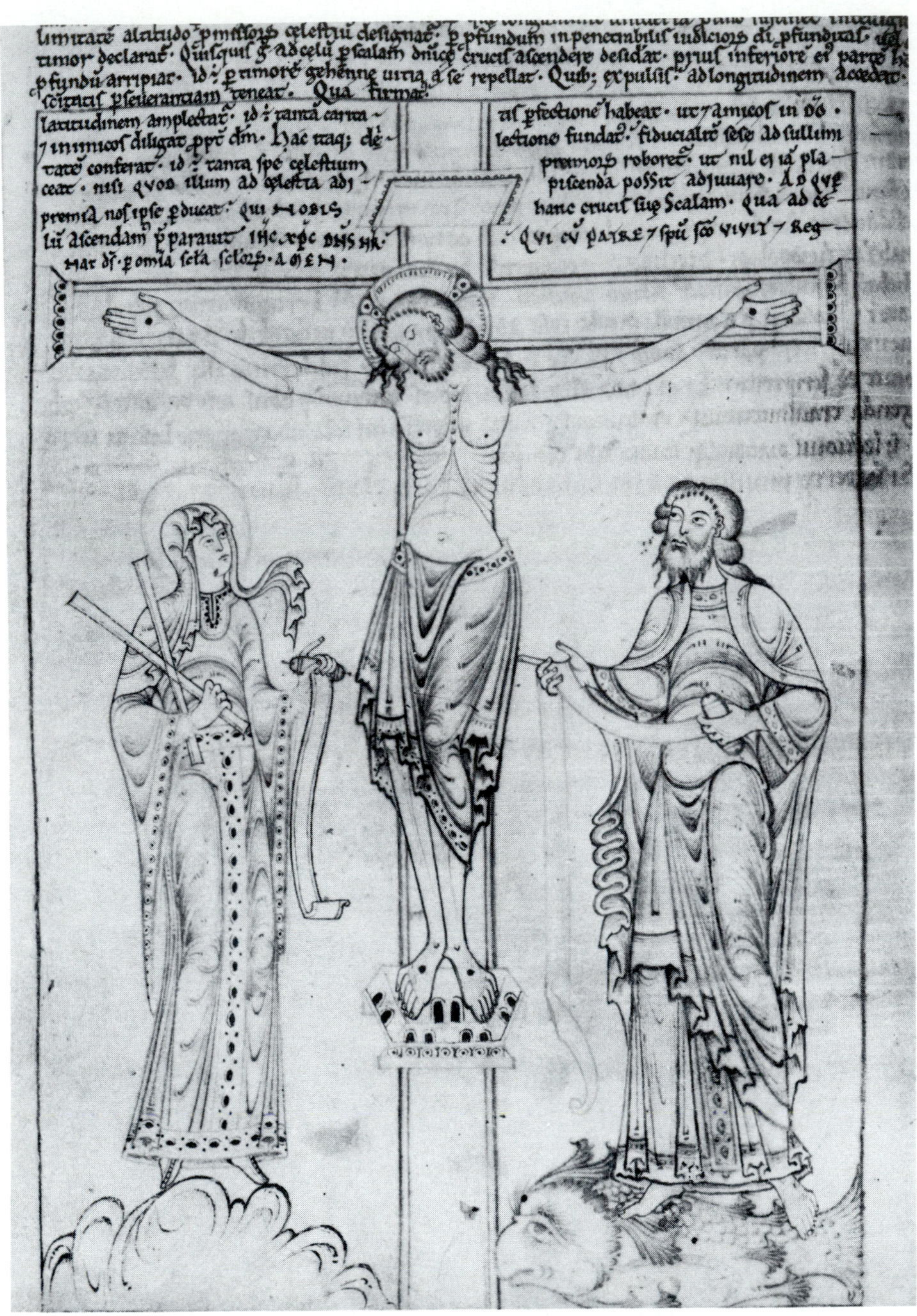

Oxford, Corpus Christi College MS. 157, f. 77v. Chronicles, from Worcester, mid 12th cent.

a. B.M. Harley Roll, Y. 6. The Guthlac Roll, *c.* 1200

b. London, British Museum, Cotton MS. Tiberius C. VI, f. 14, *circa* 1050

Holkham. MS. 666, f. 32. Bible Picture-Book, 14th cent.

Winchester Cathedral and the excavation of Old Minster, 1966.

(*a*) Old Minster: the excavation in 1968 of the northern apse of the double-apsed martyrium built *c*.971–4 around the tomb of St Swithun (d. 862), looking north. Trench XXXIII, discussed on pp. 306–7, occupied the central foreground, around the tomb of Swithun.

(*b*) Lankhills: the excavation in 1972 of the eastern limit of the late Roman cemetery, looking east. See p. 321 and n. 3.

(*a*) Winchester Castle: the excavation in 1968 of the early twelfth-century keep below Castle Yard, looking north-west.

(*b*) Winchester Castle: the excavation in 1971 of the early Norman chapel built *c.* 1070 using the Anglo-Saxon structural technique of long-and-short quoins, looking south-east.

(*a*) Wolvesey from the air, 1966. The bishop's palace lies within the south-east angle of the Roman and medieval city wall, seen to the left. Looking south-west.

(*b*) Wolvesey: the excavation in 1971 of Henry of Blois's east hall, built *c.*1135–8, showing the ditches of an Anglo-Saxon field (meadow?) system running at an angle below it. Looking south-east.

(*a*) Lower Brook Street: the excavation in 1970 of the church of St Mary in Tanner Street, looking west. The church reached this form *c.*1000, but the nave was originally constructed *c.*800 as a domestic structure of stone in an estate of thegn status. (See p. 324.)

(*b*) Lower Brook Street: the excavation in 1969 of House XII, with St Pancras Lane (*centre*) and rows of flint-packed post-holes for tenter-racks on the site of House XI (*left*). Looking west.

South Gate: the excavation in 1971 of the Roman south gate of *Venta Belgarum*, looking north-west. The cambered Roman road (*under the right-hand scale*) has been blocked by the cutting of a ditch *under the left-hand scale*. The blocking was subsequently reinforced by the construction of a stone wall along the inner edge of the ditch. See p. 327.

and that is the so-called 'gymnastic' style, where animals and creatures clamber all over the frame of the initial rather in the manner of acrobats. This type was rare in England before the Conquest, but is found in the Durham MSS. and is an outstanding characteristic of Canterbury illumination of about the year 1100.[1]

Although the Durham MSS. can be shown to have such a respectable Anglo-Saxon ancestry, there is a good deal in the style which shows the artists were not merely slavish imitators of their parents. In some ways the treatment of the scrolls is much more robust than in the later 'Winchester' manuscripts. The dragons, too, are stouter than their somewhat exiguous forebears, and the initials with the dragons' heads are often more animated than the original style which is much drier and more precise. Nevertheless these initials remain fundamentally Anglo-Saxon and show a development rather than a break in the style.

While the Durham MSS. display this very 'Winchester' ornament, the figure style is in some ways much less accomplished than the figure style of the Pre-Conquest manuscripts. There does not seem, however, to be any reason to suppose that there is anything new here, and the use of coloured outline and stripes suggests that this is merely a modification of the 'Winchester' treatment. But it was not only in Durham that the ornament was derived from the Anglo-Saxon manuscripts. The great abbey of Christ Church, Canterbury, used a very effective type of initial which was executed in outline and composed of dragons and scroll ornament. In the same way as the Durham initials, both have become much fatter and fleshier than most of the earlier work.[2] Other places also show similar initials. They are to be found in manuscripts from St. Albans and Exeter as well as from Durham and Canterbury (Plates 5*b*, 6*a*).[3] Thus

[1] A good example is reproduced by M. R. James, *Catalogue of the Western MSS. in the Library of Trinity College Cambridge*, iv, pl. IV *a*.

[2] e.g. Cambridge, Trinity College MS. B. 3. 14.

[3] Oxford, Bodleian MS. Bodl. 569, ff. 28, 42, 58 b, 92 b, a Lanfranc from St. Albans, *circa* 1100; Bodl. 691, ff. 72 b, 84 b, 92 b, St. Augustine from Exeter. Many of the initials in this manuscript have been entirely redrawn in the fourteenth century. Bodl. MS. 717, St. Jerome on Isaiah, also from Exeter, which is reproduced in New Palaeographical Society, 2nd Series, pls. 190–2, should be placed in this group. Its initials should be compared with St. Augustine on the Psalter, Durham Cathedral MS. B. 11. 13, which is dated about 1088, see Mynors, op. cit., pls. 19, 20. Initials in this manuscript have also been compared with Bodl. 301, also from Exeter. The Exeter St. Jerome seems to be dated too late by the editors of the New Palaeographical

we have ample proof that numerous Post-Conquest initials were based on their Anglo-Saxon predecessors. In this connexion it is surely significant that all these places, with the possible exception of Exeter, were closely connected with Lanfranc and his reforms. It is obvious that current views should be revised.

The survival of the famous Anglo-Saxon drawing style can be seen in a number of manuscripts which date from the early years of the twelfth century. What is significant is that here again the survival is to be seen for the most part in historiated initials and not in large miniatures, which are not common at that time. There are three manuscripts which show this survival very well, and it is interesting that two of them should come from St. Augustine's, Canterbury. The first of these is a very fine martyrology with obits which seem to belong to the first decade of the twelfth century.[1] The illuminations are confined to the KL monograms at the beginning of each month and the figures in them are the signs of the zodiac. If we take the figure of Virgo we shall see that while the figure itself is closely related to Anglo-Saxon drawings, the ornament is much less close. The old rich scroll has been modified and several new types of flowers appear. The figure is, however, surprisingly 'Winchester' in style. There is the same flickering of the draperies and the same use of the expressive outline to endow the figure with life.[2] We have here the beginning of the com-

Society. The position of Exeter is very interesting. During the episcopacy of bishop Leofric, who died in 1072, there had been a considerable interest in the library, see Max Förster, *The Exeter Book of Old English Poetry*, 1933, pp. 10–32. It is not, therefore, inconceivable that books were being produced in Exeter at that time. At any rate there are the two manuscripts mentioned above which show that the Pre-Conquest types survived there. Another manuscript, Bodl. 783, St. Gregory, Cura Pastoralis, also shows both in script and decoration considerable affinities to the Exeter manuscripts, and consequently to the Carilef books. The style of this manuscript is also derived from Pre-Conquest illumination.

[1] B.M. Cotton MS. Vitellius C. XII.

[2] Ibid., f. 139, reproduced by F. Wormald, 'The Development of English Illumination in the Twelfth Century' in *The Journal of the British Archaeological Association*, 3rd Series, vol. viii, pl. XIII *b*. The origin of romanesque initial ornament is still to be written, particularly the history of the introduction of new types in the early years of the twelfth century. Special attention should be paid to the appearance of flower motives having a strong family likeness to the 'Blütenblatt' ornament of Byzantine illumination, see Kurt Weitzmann, *Die Byzantinische Buchmalerei des ix. u. x. Jahrhunderts*, 1935, pp. 22–32. In this connexion the Gloucester candlestick in the Victoria and Albert Museum of about 1110 offers some important early evidence on the introduction of new types of ornament.

bination of the Anglo-Saxon drawing style with romanesque ornament.

The second manuscript, a collection of lives of saints, is British Museum, Arundel MS. 91 (Plate 6*b*). Its decoration is also confined to its fine series of decorative and historiated initials. The artist is possibly the same as the artist of the St. Augustine's martyrology. In this manuscript we find the same active combination of the 'Winchester' drawing and romanesque ornament, indicating that we are not dealing with a purely conservative creation, but with artists who were using the Anglo-Saxon style because they found that it answered their requirements.

Probably the most sumptuous manuscript to show the survival of the 'Winchester' outline drawing style is a manuscript of the De Civitate Dei of St. Augustine, now in the Laurenziana at Florence.[1] It is usually dated early in the twelfth century and may be either North French or English in origin. Wherever it was made, it is extremely English in spirit and there is no doubt that its miniatures are derived from Anglo-Saxon figure drawings and romanesque ornament as in the case of the two St. Augustine's books. Thus we can see that in the first years of the twelfth century there were flourishing schools of illumination which owed the greater part of their style to Anglo-Saxon illumination.[2]

Undoubtedly the most important stylistic change during this period was the growth of the historiated and humanly inhabited initial. Before the period of the Carileff books there had been large and magnificent initials like the great 'B's at the beginning of Psalters which had their origin in Carolingian scroll work. In the theological manuscripts, as distinct from the liturgical ones, there was the style which was composed of a number of different elements, but which is most easily recognized by its characteristic interlace and gripping heads. As we saw, the Carileff artists used both these types of initial in great profusion. They also introduced figures into the initials on a much more lavish scale. The idea of a richly inhabited initial was, therefore, already well

[1] Florence, Biblioteca Medicea-Laurenziana MS. XII. 17, St. Augustine, *De Civitate Dei*, late eleventh or early twelfth century, see New Palaeographical Society, 1st Series, pls. 138, 139, and G. Biagi, *Fifty Plates from the MSS. in the R. Laurentian Library*, pls. X–XII.

[2] The St. Thomas bowl in the Department of British and Medieval Antiquities in the British Museum should also be connected with these outline drawings, see O. M. Dalton, 'On Two Medieval Bronze Bowls in the British Museum', *Archaeologia*, lxxii. 133–40.

established before 1100. Nevertheless, both the ornamental motives and the figure style were based upon the Anglo-Saxon manuscripts of the 'Winchester' school. What was new was the scale upon which these initials were done. This growth of the large and elaborate initial must be, I think, considered a manifestation of the romanesque and should be considered in any historical account of romanesque illumination. Whatever the origin it was not English and, therefore, introduced probably from the Continent by the followers of the Conqueror.

On the whole Durham can be called conservative in its development of the ornament of large initial. The Durham artists introduced figures into Pre-Conquest ornament. Canterbury, on the other hand, not only did the same as Durham, but also made use of the entirely new type of initial style, the gymnastic style. These initials are not constructed from leafy scrolls, interlace, and dragons with the occasional introduction of a figure. They are built up by causing a number of miscellaneous creatures and dragons to clamber on top of each other, in and out of the framework. These initials are, I think, a contribution from the Continent. They are found in Continental manuscripts of this period, and appear at a later date in manuscripts from Citeaux. To a certain extent the same principle is found in some early romanesque carvings. At Canterbury this style of initial was extremely popular and is found side by side in the same manuscripts with motives derived from Anglo-Saxon manuscripts. They are often executed in a drawing style which we have seen was derived from the outline drawings of the 'Winchester' school, and are a striking indication of the vigour in which artists working in a purely insular drawing style could modify their traditional initial style and create something new in it.

Probably towards 1120 England produced a style of illumination which was quite different from these radically Anglo-Saxon styles which we have just discussed. This is the style associated with the Albani Psalter. Its characteristics are a complete contrast to the Durham and Canterbury illumination which relied on the expressive outline to give it vitality, and used elegant delicate colours. The effect was pale and ethereal with a marked emphasis on the pattern. In the Albani Psalter the colour is heavy and the draperies, instead of fluttering in a scintillating design, hang in heavy folds about their wearers. The faces, too, which are frequently represented side-face, are heavy, with large staring eyes and rather gloomy expressions. These figures no longer live in a world of mystical excitement like those in the Weingarten Crucifixion. Here one is in the presence of a solemn hieratic art. The spiritual effect is not achieved by an impression of burning personal passion, but by an almost liturgical solemnity.[1] Indeed the contrast bears something of that which exists between the short prayer that pierces unto Heaven and the grandeur and pageantry of a High Mass. In the Albani Psalter we see the English artists abandoning their fundamental love of the continuous pattern for a style which was based upon the art of the Mediterranean with its stress on the representation of the human figure as a corporeal being. In the twelfth century, and indeed all through the Middle Ages, England was to make use of styles deriving from Mediterranean art, but in all cases, having received the style, it is modified in order to maintain the love of expressive outline and of reducing everything to terms of pattern. An exception appears in the case of the Albani Psalter group of manuscripts. Here heavy colours and rich modelling satisfied the twelfth-century artist's desire to clothe his figures with flesh and blood, but there was lacking the vitality which was so expressive in the Anglo-Saxon style. Artists working immediately after the period of the Albani Psalter were attracted by its richness and solidity, but still wanted the Anglo-Saxon vivacity. They, therefore, treated the Albani Psalter style as they were to treat all imported styles. They combined it with the native style and thereby assimilated it. This fusion may be seen in a number of manuscripts of the second quarter of the twelfth century, notably in such manuscripts as the Shaftesbury Psalter in the British Museum which we know was partially copied from the Albani Psalter.[2] A magnificent drawing of the Virgin and Child at Oxford, of the same period as the Shaftesbury Psalter, shows the reduction to pattern very well. The subject is of a most hieratic nature and yet the whole figure is endowed with vitality by a skilful arrangement of the design which is reduced to pure pattern by the heart-shaped

[1] Compare for instance the treatment of the Christ in majesty in a thoroughly Anglo-Saxon manuscript such as B.M. Cotton MS. Tiberius C. VI, f. 126 b, and a miniature of a similar composition in Cambridge, Pembroke College MS. 120, f. 6 b, which is of the school of the Albani Psalter.

[2] B.M. Lansdowne MS. 383, reproduced in E. G. Millar, op. cit., pls. 32, 33. The miniature of the Women at the Sepulchre on f. 13 of this manuscript is a copy of that in the Albani Psalter.

arrangement of the knees and the geometrical treatment of the crown and the veil.[1]

The English artists' adherence to the Anglo-Saxon principles of expressive outline are no more clearly seen than in the Psalter of Henry of Blois, now in the British Museum.[2] This manuscript was made in the early years of the second half of the twelfth century at Winchester. The artist, like others of his time, was certainly influenced by South Italian or Byzantine manuscripts. Indeed, there are copies of Italo-Byzantine paintings in this very manuscript.[3] Yet his style is quite inexplicable unless it can be allowed that he was also influenced by the Anglo-Saxon tradition. The miniature of the Presentation of Christ in the Temple shows this very well (Plate 7).[4] The figure of the ancient Simeon is much closer to the spirit of the Weingarten Crucifixion than to the Albani Psalter. His whole figure, and particularly his beard, is extraordinarily expressive of old age, but there is really no attempt to represent him as the historical Simeon. He is the expression of the artist's conception of old age. The whole miniature is indeed symbolic and this symbolism is produced by a kind of calligraphic convention. This calligraphic convention is exactly what is found in the Weingarten Crucifixion.

In Nero C. IV there also appears a tendency towards violent caricature which was to remain an important element in English illumination.[5] This can be seen not only in the figure of the aged Simeon, but also in the picture, immediately below, of Christ disputing with the doctors in the Temple. The scene is extraordinarily well staged. Christ, small and innocent, sits isolated under the central arch. At the sides are the Jewish doctors, and what a terrifying crew they are with their eager faces and clawing hands ready to confound their victim. One sees here the whole medieval conception of the Old and the New Law. The

[1] Oxford, Bodleian MS. Bodl. 269, see F. Wormald, 'A Romanesque Drawing at Oxford' in *The Antiquaries Journal*, xxii (Jan. 1942), pp. 17–21.

[2] B.M. Cotton MS. Nero C. IV. For a bibliography of this manuscript, see E. G. Millar, op. cit., p. 84.

[3] ff. 29, 30.

[4] f. 15, reproduced in *Journal of the British Archaeological Association*, tom. cit., pl. XVIII.

[5] One of the sources of these caricatures has been suggested to me by Dr. Otto Pächt. It is that they are adaptations by twelfth-century artists of late antique masks such as may be seen in the Terence MSS. copied from late antique manuscripts, see particularly Oxford, Bodleian MS. Auct. F. 2. 13, twelfth century, reproduced by L. W. Jones and C. R. Morey, *The Miniatures of the MSS. of Terence*, 1932, pl. 8.

drama of the situation is accentuated by this careful use of caricature and equally careful stylization of the folds which form a network of pattern over the whole picture, so that one's eye is again hurried over its surface.

The development of the treatment of folds in English twelfth-century manuscript painting affords a most interesting study of the English artists' love of reducing everything to terms of pattern. In many figures the folds divide the body up into zones. Originally this was a device borrowed from Mediterranean art to accentuate the muscles of the human form under the drapery, but in England it was violently stylized and reduced to an intricate pattern system which would infuse into the figures the required vitality. Nowhere is this more clearly seen than in the miniatures of the Lambeth Bible which also can be dated in the second half of the twelfth century.[1] In this manuscript the folds have become a conglomeration of shapes built up into a pattern, which gives the scene a kind of agitated vitality, though fluttering draperies have here been reduced to a kind of frozen formula. What has all this, however, to do with the survival of the Anglo-Saxon style? A good deal, I think. The English illuminator of the twelfth century was very much like his predecessor of a century earlier. He was anxious to be able to put down in terms of a calligraphic pattern something which would express more than a mere representation of the scene. He wished to endow his figures with a life of their own by reducing them to a continuous pattern by means of expressive outline. The result is as fantastic as the conglomeration of animals in the Lindisfarne Gospels. It is inconceivable that this treatment of folds is anything else but a recrudescence of a spirit that had already appeared in Anglo-Saxon art during the eighth century and again during the tenth and eleventh centuries in the 'Winchester' school.

During the twelfth century a knowledge of the Anglo-Saxon style must have been kept very much alive by the copying of manuscripts with 'Winchester' school illuminations. A remarkable example of English twelfth-century artists copying 'Winchester' school miniatures is the drawing of the Crucifixion in the Chronicle of Florence of Worcester, in the library of Corpus Christi College, Oxford (Plate 8).[2] If we compare the treat-

[1] London, Lambeth Palace MS. 3, see E. G. Millar, 'Les Principaux Manuscrits à Peintures du Lambeth Palace à Londres', in *Bulletin de la Société française de reproduction de manuscrits à peintures*, 1924, pls. II–XI.

[2] Oxford, Corpus Christi College MS. 157, Chronicle of Florence of

ment of the loin-cloth of the Christ with that in the great Crucifixion miniature in Harley MS. 2904, it will be seen at once how the twelfth-century artist was capable of reproducing the fluttering folds of the Anglo-Saxon manuscript, as well as changes of emphasis which were so noticeable in a work like the Harley Crucifixion. The Virgin's veil also shows how the twelfth-century artist was able to reproduce the spirit of earlier Anglo-Saxon drawing. The implication, therefore, is that the artist was interested in the 'Winchester' style as a style. This again surely argues against a complete disappearance of Anglo-Saxon influence, since the Florence of Worcester Crucifixion is not earlier than 1130 and may be later.

By 1150, however, England as well as the rest of northern Europe was profoundly influenced by the twelfth-century renaissance and its interest in the Mediterranean style. Throughout the second half of the century there was a continuous influence from Byzantine art, which may be seen in such manuscripts as the Winchester Bible where some of the hands have been quite rightly compared with Sicilian mosaics. But as in the case of the Albani Psalter style the Winchester Bible style was modified in England by contact with the traditional outline drawing. Nowhere can this be more clearly seen than in the Guthlac Roll in the British Museum which was probably made at Croyland about the year 1200 or a little later.[1] It is helpful to compare a drawing in this manuscript of the death of St. Guthlac, with a drawing of the Harrowing of Hell, in a Psalter of about 1050, Cotton MS. Tiberius C. VI, f. 14 (Plate 9*a*, *b*).[2] The composition of the first is an intricate pattern of fluttering draperies with the two angels built up into tall shape, and in the earlier drawing we have the same use of the fluttering folds with their endless pattern to express the tumult of the scene. In the Guthlac Roll the same effect is achieved by the same device. Both artists wished to express the drawing up of the soul to Heaven,

Worcester, see New Palaeographical Society, 2nd Series, pl. 87. Dr. Pächt has pointed out to me that, though the original drawing may have been made as early as 1130, it has been redrawn in the second half of the twelfth century by an artist working in the manner of the Terence MS., Oxford, Bodleian MS. Auct. F. 2. 13. Nevertheless this second hand was equally influenced by Anglo-Saxon drawings.

[1] B.M. Harley Roll Y. 6, see Sir George Warner, *The Guthlac Roll*, Roxburghe Club, 1928.

[2] For a reproduction of the death of St. Guthlac, see Warner, op. cit., pl. XIV. B.M. Tiberius C. VI, f. 14, is reproduced in *The Journal of the British Archaeological Association*, tom. cit., pl. XII.

and in each case this is managed by the use of this tall mass covering the whole picture. In the picture of the death of St. Guthlac the treatment of the border is important. The angel is represented as hovering in front of the border, because both his halo and his wing come over it. The artist undoubtedly devised the angel thus, so that the spectator did not feel that the angel was cramped by the border and consequently the feeling of ascent, which is essential to the whole idea of the picture, lost. This fear of loss of movement is, I think, an essential aspect of Anglo-Saxon drawing, because if it were lost the all-important principle of the expressive and continuous line would be violated.

Throughout the Middle Ages one finds in English manuscripts superb outline drawings which are certainly in the tradition of the drawings of the 'Winchester' school and of their twelfth-century successors. Their most important characteristic is that the drawings are not unfinished sketches for the illuminator to fill in with colour afterwards, but are independent works of art whose principal aesthetic effect was not achieved by colour but by line. This tradition can be traced through such works as the Guthlac Roll, the drawings associated with Matthew Paris, the drawings of Queen Mary's Psalter, and the Holkham Picture-book. Admittedly all reflect the various influences of their age, but all of them achieve their effect by the use of the expressive line, even by having recourse to the most violent kinds of caricature. If one looks at the representation of the Tartar cannibals in the manuscript of the Chronica Majora of Matthew Paris, one sees how successful he was in handling this tradition.[1] What the artist wished to represent was the savagery of their habits and the rapacity of their horses. The whole scene could be merely disgusting, but he has endowed it with a fierce realism which transcends mere savagery. This realism is achieved by the very opposite of realistic representation. The whole thing is a fantastic expression of the artist's views on Tartars and their horrid ways. Everybody is doing something violent, and all this is achieved in the same way that the artist of the Weingarten Crucifixion obtained his effect. Both artists wished to record not only the historic fact of the Crucifixion or the historic existence of cannibals, but also the ideas which lie behind them, whether it be the horror and loneliness of the Cross or the savage terror of the Tartar hordes. Both artists made use of the never-

[1] Cambridge, Corpus Christi College MS. 16, f. 166, see M. R. James, 'The Drawings of Matthew Paris', *Walpole Society*, xiv (1925–6), pl. xvi, no. 86.

ending outline pattern and the exaggeration of the expressive outline.

This tradition is shown very well in the fourteenth century by such manuscripts as the Bible Picture-book belonging to the Earl of Leicester, Holkham MS. 666. Heaven forbid that one should say that all the stylistic elements in this manuscript are attributable to its Anglo-Saxon ancestors. What is true is that the style of this manuscript is inexplicable unless the tradition of Anglo-Saxon drawing is taken into consideration. The miniature of the Crucifixion is typical of fourteenth-century religious piety with its tendency to dwell on the more horrible aspects of the Passion (Plate 10).[1] The whole scene in its fantastic terror reminds one of the picturesque passages in the mystical writings of Richard Rolle, who, when speaking of Christ's wounds, said: 'Thy body is like to a dovehouse. For a dovehouse is ful of holys, so is þy body ful of woundes.' In the Holkham miniature there is the same restless agitation as in Rolle's meditation. The rolling eyes of the thieves and of Christ and the grotesque expression of the executioner once again take one back to the Psalter of Henry of Blois, and ultimately to the eleventh-century drawings. The use of the scrolls is certainly a means whereby the artist heightened the movement and wildness.

> Yet dare I almost be glad, I do not see
> That spectacle of too much weight for mee
> Who sees God's face, that is selfe life, must dye;
> What a death were it then to see God dye?

These scrolls in a sense perform the same function as the fluttering draperies of the 'Winchester' school drawings, carrying the eye ever and again over the whole picture, just as in the Lindisfarne Gospels the animals and birds twist in and out and form a pattern over the surface of the picture.[2] In this miniature we see, therefore, not only the reduction of the scene to a pattern but also the use of the calligraphic line to express the artist's

[1] Holkham Hall MS. 666, see M. R. James, 'An English Bible-Picture Book of the Fourteenth Century', *Walpole Society*, xi (1922–23), pp. 1–27, pls. I–XIX. The miniature of the Crucifixion on f. 32 is reproduced on pl. XV.

[2] The most elaborate use of scrolls in a decorative manner is found in the Tickhill Psalter, an early fourteenth-century manuscript from Worksop Priory, now New York Public Library, Spencer Collection MS. 26, see D. D. Egbert, *The Tickhill Psalter and Related Manuscripts*, 1940, particularly pl. XXV. Another case is the miniature of the benefactors of Croyland Abbey in the Guthlac Roll, see Warner, op. cit., pl. XVIII.

emotions at the sight of the crucified Saviour, and once again one must admit that the artist was in this dependent on Anglo-Saxon tradition.

Now to sum up. We have seen that at the Norman Conquest there was no break with the traditional style, which continued unimpaired both in initial ornament and in outline drawing to about 1120, when new romanesque styles began to influence English artists, but they were not overwhelmed by these new influences. They took them and frequently modified them, ever maintaining their affection for the calligraphic method and expressing their emotions by the reduction of the essentials of a scene to a significant pattern. Both these characteristics belong to Anglo-Saxon art and were its great contribution to English medieval art, endowing it with a power and vividness which are its own. The story is in some ways very close to Chambers's story of the continuity of English prose. English prose survived in devotional treatises made for devout men and women, the Anglo-Saxon style survived in the initial frequently decorating a dry theological treatise, but survived nevertheless with sufficient power to mould much of medieval English art.

My thanks are due to the following for permission to reproduce their MSS.: The Trustees of the British Museum, the Bodleian Library at Oxford, the Pierpont Morgan Library, New York, the Dean and Chapter of York Minster, the Dean and Chapter of Durham Cathedral, the President and Fellows of Corpus Christi College, Oxford, the Right Honourable the Earl of Leicester, and to the Director of the Warburg Institute, the University of London, Dr. Saxl, for permission to use the photograph of the York Gospels.

SIR ISRAEL GOLLANCZ MEMORIAL LECTURE FOR 1948

WULFSTAN'S PROSE

By ANGUS McINTOSH

Read 11 May 1949

WHEN the British Academy honoured me with an invitation to deliver this lecture, I thought at first of speaking about the alliterative measure. It was on the poetry written in the various forms of this measure that Sir Israel Gollancz worked for the greater part of his life, to the advantage of all who have come after him, and it would have been a fitting act of commemoration to consider something with which he was so nearly concerned. But the alliterative measure, though by no means completely understood, has received much attention, and I do not feel that it would be easy to say something new about it, at least of a kind which lends itself to presentation in a lecture. On the other hand, less work has been done on those early English prose writings which have affinities with the alliterative verse, and it so happens that the writings of Wulfstan provide a valuable focal point for any study of this kind. Here, then, is a subject not too far removed from that which I had at first contemplated. It will allow me, I hope, to avoid trespassing too blatantly on the chosen territory of those who are best qualified to speak about Wulfstan, and at the same time to consider some problems about the art of writing in late Old English times which have a wide interest and a considerable importance.

I do not wish to suggest that Wulfstan has been entirely neglected from this point of view; his style has been examined by all those interested in establishing the canon of his works, his fondness for certain words and turns of phrase has been noted, and his avoidance of others. So also his habitual use of rhyming and alliterative phrases, and more broadly, certain general characteristics of his style closely connected with what he chose to say, his exhortatory and prescriptive manner, his avoidance of the straight narrative technique which Ælfric was so fond of, and so forth. Professor Dorothy Bethurum has, I think, written more fully and interestingly on these matters than anyone else, but a study of the literature on Wulfstan problems will show that many others have given serious attention to such things.[1] Yet most of what has been written merely touches the edge of the rhythmical problem, just as it would more obviously if said of *Beowulf*, and it is my purpose here to attempt a more rigid analysis of his rhythmical habits and to show what importance they have not only for Wulfstan scholars but for those interested more generally in the practice of prose and verse in Old and Middle English.

I

I shall begin by attempting to distinguish certain different ways of writing in the Old English period, different ways, that is, from the rhythmical point of view. There is not just verse on the one hand, like *Andreas*, the *Metres of Boethius* or *Maldon*, and prose on the other, such as the works of Alfred or Ælfric or the charters or Byrhtferþ's *Manual*. There are in the late Old English period at least five clearly separable stylistic genres, between which there are important and significant rhythmical distinctions. How many of these five are 'verse' and how many are 'prose' is a terminological problem which I should prefer to avoid. I am anxious merely to distinguish types, not to provide them all with an exactly suitable label, and it might be proper to add two warnings. First, that if I distinguish five types it must not be assumed that there are no more; secondly, that though these types are distinguishable, it is possible to find texts in which characteristics of more than one type are found, where there is, in other words, a mixing. But except in obvious pastiches, such as we may find in some of the homilies in Napier's collection, these are not very numerous; a man normally chose his medium and stuck to it throughout a whole piece of writing.

The first of these five types is what I shall call the 'classical' Old English verse, the verse which obeys the rules of Sievers or Heusler or Pope according to which school of thought you belong to, the verse which descends from early times and yet is still used at the beginning of the twelfth century in the *Description of Durham* much as it was in Cædmon's *Hymn* over four centuries before. One may split this kind of verse on metrical grounds into more than one sub-type, as Heusler does, but in all its forms it is clearly distinct from any of the other four types I shall proceed to describe.

The second is the late 'debased' Old English verse, though I reserve the term for a rather less miscellaneous rag-bag than some who have used it. The kind of verse I have in mind has not survived in any quantity, but there are two notable examples of it in the *Chronicle*. The first is the poem on the death of Eadgar in manuscripts D and E under the year 975, beginning

Her Eadgar gefor   Angla reccend
Westseaxena wine   ⁊ Myrcna mundbora.

The second is the poem about Alfred and Godwine found in manuscript C (and less perfectly in D) under the year 1036.[2] The surviving specimens are not numerous, but the evidence of Early Middle English suggests that this kind of verse was well established towards the end of the Old English period. It has these characteristics. First, that its half-lines are genuinely half lines, being constructed as parts of a whole line the two components of which are welded together. This welding is most commonly achieved by alliteration, but sometimes by end-rhyme instead; sometimes by the use of both. Alliteration, we may note, is not debarred from falling on the last stressed syllable of the line. Secondly, the half-lines of this kind of verse frequently do not conform to the patterns which were obligatory in the classical verse; this is the main ground for the term 'debased' though some would argue that it implies, and *wrongly* implies, that the second kind descends from the first. This is a problem which need not concern us here, though I would note that there is no evidence for the existence of 'debased' verse of this sort except in the latter part of the Old English period. I would also remind you that two years ago, on this same occasion, Professor Wrenn suggested that Cædmon's great achievement was simply to put the popular measure of the time to a new religious use; in other words the popular measure that he found ready to hand was rhythmically the measure used in his *Hymn* or in Bede's *Death Song*.[3]

The third type is the style used by Ælfric in his *Lives of Saints*; it is completely distinct rhythmically from his normal everyday prose, and it is also distinct from either of the two styles hitherto mentioned.[4] It resembles them in that it is made up of whole lines, composed of pairs of half-lines joined by alliteration. But the alliteration differs from that of the classical verse in several particulars. It can fall on the last stressed syllable of the line; it is not associated so strictly with the syllables bearing the main stress; and there are certain new conventional alliterations of sounds which are not phonetically identical with which I propose to deal in another place. We may note also that in contrast with most of the classical verse, the main sense pauses are very rarely allowed to fall in the middle of the whole line. To all this might be added that 'poetical' words are seldom used; the vocabulary is similar to Ælfric's normal prose vocabulary. The *Life of St. Oswald* may be verse, it is hardly poetry.[5] From the metrical point of view, this style resembles that of the debased verse in the failure of its half-lines to fit the accepted classical patterns. But it differs from it in the precise form of the patterns which it does use, and also in using end-rhyme as an alternative or supplement to alliteration only very rarely.

My fourth type is the style used by Wulfstan, with which I shall deal later, my fifth that of ordinary prose. This last is a convenient label for all Old English prose which uses no rhythmical devices comparable to those I have already discussed; the prose of Alfred or that of the greater part of the *Chronicle* will serve as examples. If I also include here such prose as that of most of the *Catholic Homilies*, it is not without being aware that rhythmically as well as in other ways this has a sophistication not found in my other examples. We may subdivide 'ordinary' prose as we might have subdivided the classical verse, but all varieties of it will still be distinguishable without difficulty from a text written in any of the other four styles.

The first question we might ask, since all these five types were in use at the same time, say in the year 1000, is whether they were all generally current. About the first, the classical verse, we may have certain doubts; perhaps in the south it was fast going out of use, for there is something ominous about the way it was being brought together into definitive collections at this very time, often, as it would appear, from manuscripts probably a century older. It may be that it survived only in the north and Midlands to any extent in this period. We may note, however, as a curious fact that there are writings relating to the reign of Eadgar which provide examples of all five styles. There are the two poems in classical verse in manuscripts A, B, and C of the *Chronicle* for the years 973 and 975. Then there is the poem in debased verse in manuscripts D and E under 975. Ælfric produces three panegyrics in the third style in the *Epilogue to the Heptateuch*, in the *Life of St. Swiðun*, and in the *Life of St. Æðelðryð*. In the fourth style we have the two *Chronicle* poems by Wulfstan about the accession and the death of Eadgar.[6] Further references to him in the ordinary prose of the *Chronicle* need not be considered here.

The way in which examples of classical and debased verse are distributed among the various manuscripts of the *Chronicle* is perhaps of some significance. A and B preserve classical verse only. C has all the classical poems that A and B have and one other, and in addition it has one example of debased verse (*sub anno* 1036). D has both kinds, and E is remarkable in recording no poems at all in classical verse. I am not competent to discuss the possible implications of this distribution, but I would remark that, while it suggests that the different styles may have been fashionable in different areas, it also shows that classical verse was still composed in the south.

As to the debased verse of the kind I have discussed, I think it probable that it first began to be used in the tenth century, and had become common during the eleventh. There are prosodic features in the *Bestiary*, in Laȝamon's *Brut*, in the *Proverbs of Alfred*, and in the *Worcester Fragments* which suggest a considerable debt to it; if so, we must conclude that the debased verse came in the end to be familiar over at least a large part of the Midland area. About the general currency of type three, the style of the *Lives of Saints*, I have serious doubts. If Ælfric had a model which he was following closely, it clearly differed, as did his own medium, from both the debased measure (as I have defined it) and from the classical. But one must not rule out the possibility of his having been influenced by some other form of debased verse in which, for example, end-rhyme was not used. And, in fact, embedded in the prose of the Vercelli Homilies and elsewhere there are things of this sort with which Ælfric must have been familiar.[7] But even these are not models which he simply copied, for I know of nothing written before his time which has all the rhythmical and stylistic characteristics of the *Lives of Saints*. There is, indeed, one document which must be mentioned here, because its ostensible date is 970 and because it is written in a manner which I cannot distinguish from that of Ælfric. This is the English version of the charter granted in that year by Eadgar to Ely. But I think there are other good grounds for believing that Ælfric himself was the author, so that this document may well not be an exception after all.[8]

The probability is that Ælfric was not slavishly following any existing pattern. Cædmon, it has been suggested, took over the old music for a new purpose; Ælfric may have deliberately worked out a less fettering medium for the enormous task he envisaged. He was to undertake an immense amount of narrative and expository writing, and was at many points seriously preoccupied with the problem of faithfully recording a Latin original. So even if he knew the traditions of classical verse, there was good reason for his not following them. As for the contemporary debased verse, there is no evidence to suggest that it was highly esteemed or even as yet in common use, and it is not strange that, while perhaps familiar with such deviations from the classical verse as were known at the time, he chose to work out for himself something not identical with any of them.

But I feel it is not desirable to say more about the complex problem of the genesis of Ælfric's alliterative writing till the rhythmical character of his first attempts in this style (for example, occasionally in the *Catholic Homilies*) has been properly investigated. Already in the *Lives of Saints* he has evolved a highly developed system which does not cramp him in his task, and which, if one takes into account its general 'feel' as well as details of technical procedure, is hardly to be paralleled outside of his own work. I do not question that, like Wulfstan, he had a rhythmical influence on his successors, but I doubt whether any of them by accident or design acquired his characteristics so completely that what they wrote cannot be distinguished from what he wrote.[9]

II

This brings us to the prose generally acknowledged to be by Wulfstan, and my reasons for giving it, along with certain other things, the honour of a separate group. What features has it which entitle it to this? If I begin by asserting that Wulfstan's prose consists of a continuous series of two-stress phrases related in structure to the classical half-line, and severely restricted in somewhat the same fashion to certain rhythmical patterns, I shall run the risk of having concocted some fabulous abstraction. So having stated what I believe to be the fact, I should like to present some of the grounds on which what I say is based. In the beginning, my views about the structure of his prose formed themselves simply as a result of reading it aloud, when again and again his sentences (to my ear) divided themselves in this way. Let me try to give two examples of what I mean, the first from a fairly restrained quiet passage at the end of Napier i, the other from a more impassioned part of the *Sermo ad Anglos*:[10]

Ac þá beoð adwéalde
and þurh déofol beswícene
þe þǽs ne gelýfað
ac wénað þæt se mán
scyle déadlice swýltan
éfne swa nýten
and sýþþan ne þóljan
ne ýrmðe ne mýrhðe
ne ænig léan hábban
þǽs ðe he wórhte
on lífes fǽce
þa hwíle þe he méhte

Ac sóþ is þæt ic sécge
of éorþan gewúrdan
ǽrest gewórhte
þá ðe we sýlfe
éalle of cóman
and to éorþan we scýlan
éalle gewéorþan
and sýþþan hábban
swa éce wíte
áa butan énde
swa éce blísse
swa hwǽþer we on lífe
ǽror geéarnodon
Gód ure hélpe
Amen.

Allowing for shortcomings in my pronunciation of individual sounds, and for inevitable uncertainties about tempo, intonation, and the relative weighting of main stress and various kinds of subsidiary stress, this appears to me to be the way Wulfstan's homilies were intended to be delivered. The only special point necessary for such delivery is a recognition of the existence of a continuous chain of phrases of certain permitted rhythmical patterns each containing two main stresses, no more no less.

I confess that it was only later that I turned to the literature on the subject to see what justification there might be for such an interpretation, and found that my views did not differ radically from those propounded by Einenkel sixty-four years ago in the short note in *Anglia* to which he gave the title 'Der Sermo Lupi ein Gedicht'.[11] In the last fifty years little attention has been given to what he said, and his note is vitiated by a number of faults which partly account for this. There is to begin with the rather glib use of the word 'Gedicht,' though one may note that such a description has been accepted implicitly for two compositions of Wulfstan, the *Chronicle* poems of 959 and 975, which do not differ in rhythmical character from the text we are discussing nor exceed it in poetic fire. With this there is the somewhat alarming appearance of Einenkel's printing; the excerpt from the *Sermo* is given a separate line for each phrase, and it must be confessed that it looks more like *Hudibras* or *The Lay of the Last Minstrel* than an Old English sermon. Besides, some of his line divisions, though only a few, are demonstrably false. He makes other errors; he believes in the old theory that each half-line of classical verse has four stresses, and makes the same assumption for the rhythmical phrases of the *Sermo*. He also insists on attempting to explain each unit of the text as an example of a normal classical half-line. He is forced to admit exceptions, but he fails to see the significance of this, that it means in fact that the rules are very different; for not only are some of the classical 'types' absent, but the relative frequency of some of the others bears no relation to that in the classical verse. But perhaps the most serious fault is the absence of any convincing arguments justifying the cutting up of what most regard as prose into a succession of short units of the kind I have described.

I will not pursue the discussion of any of these shortcomings except the last. What in fact is the justification for successively pulling a few consecutive words out of a continuous bit of writing in order to build up a series of what I shall from time to time refer to as two-stress phrases? Apart from the rhythmical satisfaction which I believe comes from the consistent application of this procedure, its first and most obvious justification is that these phrases are always *small syntactic units*. They are not mere metrical motifs torn from the text by wilfully or arbitrarily cutting between two adjacent elements in a sentence which have an intimate syntactic connexion, for example, preposition and noun, or pronoun and verb. Some phrases are more obviously separable than others, as is true of half-lines in the classical verse, but on the whole Wulfstan's prose is easier to split up on the basis of natural speech-pauses which delimit these small syntactic units, than the verse is, and this is saying a good deal. A closely related justification is that the whole of a text can be divided in this way; it is not that embarrassing and untidy islands of one-stress or three-stress phrases are left isolated after we have put in our thumbs and pulled out the more obvious two-stress plums. This at least was clearly seen by Einenkel and carried out with only minor errors.

I have said that the whole of the text *can* be divided in this way, but to this the objection could be made that there may be other equally acceptable ways of splitting it up, that it is possible but arbitrary. Thus it could be argued that given a sentence with six syllables bearing main stress, you may often divide it equally well into two three-stress or three two-stress groups.[12] But this is not possible as often as one might believe, and if due attention is given to stresses and pauses as legitimately required by the sense, it will be found that most such sentences will divide naturally in only one of these two ways. Wulfstan's sentences divide most happily and easily into phrases of two stresses and, as I hope to show, it is clear that he intended them to divide in this way.

I believe that it has always been a common and natural thing for this to happen rather often in ordinary spoken English. There is some peculiar psycho-physical attraction in the two-stress phrase which accounts if not for the origin at least for the persistence of the half-line of Old English poetry. It is seen in most of the titles of modern books, which when pronounced in isolation, have two stresses: *Gone with the Wind*, *Three Men in a Boat*, *The Making of English*, *Wulfstan's Prose*.[13] If books have longer titles, they often readily divide into a pair of two-stress phrases: *The Decline and Fall of the Roman Empire*, *The Growth and Structure of the English Language*. This is not to say that the three-stress phrase has no part in our lives, but both it and that with one stress are less used than the two-stress. On the other hand, a good prose-writer usually avoids too excessive a use of two-stress phrases, though this is not always true of public speakers and I know a canon who employs them almost exclusively in his sermons.

I believe that the half-line of Old English classical verse is a highly stylized embodiment of this predilection, with certain common and rhythmically pleasing patterns selected as the only forms acceptable for verse. Wulfstan, though he made use of a rather different set of patterns, nevertheless chose to compose and orate in a succession of rhythmically rich variations on the basic two-stress theme. A simple analysis of Wulfstan's sentence structure is sufficient to show that he has systematized this procedure, but there are other pieces of evidence. The alliterative and rhyming words which are so characteristic of his work regularly form themselves into a two-stress phrase or into a succession of them. The pattern is illustrated by this short passage:

ac wæs *h*ere and *h*unger
*st*ric and *st*eorfa
*o*rfcwealm and *un*coðu
*h*ol and *h*ete. . . .

This is the way the words are used—in pairs, the two components of which form the backbone of a two-stress phrase; what we do not get is an alliterative or rhyming scheme suggesting phrase units with three stresses, as if we were to find

ac wæs *h*ere and *h*unger and *h*ete
*st*ric and *st*eorfa and *st*alu.

Furthermore, the common tags that Wulfstan uses have this same rhythmical characteristic; they either form a two-stress phrase in themselves (for example, *ealles to gelome*) or else they serve to fill out a phrase which would otherwise be too light rhythmically (for example, *georne* in *and beorgan us georne*). All this strongly reinforces what the sentence structure has suggested, and it becomes very difficult to say that such a splitting as Einenkel made is arbitrary or meaningless or misleading.

There is another more striking and valuable kind of evidence which may be said to clinch the whole matter and this comes from the manuscripts themselves. Here I must beg to be allowed to relapse for a moment into autobiography. I had made my own Hudibrastic transcript of the *Sermo ad Anglos* using the modern printed text of Miss Whitelock's edition. Having discovered that my version agreed in most of its phrase divisions with that of Einenkel's specimen, I turned finally to the manuscripts to see whether the pointing there gave any support to these divisions. I accordingly added to my transcript the punctuation marks of all the manuscripts. Now each of these has some punctuation though not all have the same amount. And although each supplies marks at places where the others have none, what emerged very clearly from an examination of the contributions of all five manuscripts was that there was almost no clashing; nearly all of the marks when entered into my transcript came at the end of my Hudibrastic lines.[14] In other words it became clear that they were used to delimit the phrases I had already isolated on ordinary rhythmical and syntactic grounds, and they offer as I believe final and convincing proof of the reality of these two-stress units.

This function of pointing reminds one of the similar way in which it is used in the Cædmon Manuscript. It also resembles that found in the *Lives of Saints*, which Skeat preserves in his edition, though he has not always assessed it critically. The thorough study of the function of marks of punctuation in late Old English and early Middle English, together with the evidence it provides about rhythmical matters, would be well worth the labour.[15] In the cases I have mentioned there can be little doubt that the main purpose of the marks was to help readers to enunciate the text in the proper manner. In the manuscripts from which Napier prints his texts this system of pointing is, of course, by no means confined to the genuine Wulfstan homilies. But in the others, even where the prose has strong rhythmical features, the phrase units which are delimited by marks of punctuation have patterns which by mere cold analysis can often be shown to differ from those of Wulfstan.

The textual history of the pointing of the *Sermo* is a problem fascinating in itself. For if the original text was provided with marks of punctuation, one would expect the best manuscripts to reproduce them with reasonable fidelity, while those more remote from the original would each present their own clouded picture of its pointing, clouded because of the chance omission at various intermediate stages of some of the marks and the independent (though usually intelligent) insertion of new marks. I will not claim that it would be possible to construct a *Stammbaum* on the basis of the punctuation alone, but in fact the evidence it supplies does confirm the relationship of the various texts as deduced from much wider and more telling evidence.[16] That it does so is sufficient to indicate that many of the marks in the five manuscripts were in the version from which they all ultimately descend, and it is reasonable to assume that Wulfstan had a hand in their insertion.

Another remarkable piece of evidence concerning Wulfstan's intentions is provided by texts which he rewrote. The most instructive are his refurbishings of Ælfric texts. I will merely state here the fact that this evidence strengthens that which has been given already, and reserve a discussion of Wulfstan's methods in these cases till I have described in more detail some of the rhythmical characteristics of his two-stress phrase-unit.

III

Wulfstan's prose resembles that of my first three types in having this two-stress phrase as its base, but it differs from them all in not building pairs of these into a larger unit welded by alliteration or rhyme. Such alliteration and rhyme as Wulfstan has, and there is much of it, serves instead to join more intimately the two important elements within a single phrase, as in the examples I have already given. There is therefore no equivalent in his writing to the whole line of the classical verse; so if you are going to print him as verse there is much more justification for doing it Hudibrastically than for treating *Beowulf* or the *Lives of Saints* in this way.[17] This, then, is sufficient to distinguish the style of Wulfstan from all the other styles I have mentioned. Can we go farther and find any other features within the phrase-units which will connect them with or distinguish them from the half-line units of the other verse types?

We may note first that in overall length and weight they are much closer to the units of the classical verse than to Ælfric's more rambling half-lines. You can assess this roughly by counting syllables. The average length of a half-line of *Beowulf* is something just under 5 syllables, and the usual range only between 4 and 6. In the *Sermo ad Anglos* the average length is a little over 6 syllables, and while the normal range is between 5 and 7, there are something like 8 per cent. of phrases with 8, and 4 per cent. with 4 syllables. In the *Life of St. Oswald* the average length is nearly 7 syllables, and half-lines with only 4 are entirely absent. The difference between 6 and 7 syllables may seem trifling, but in itself it makes a profound difference between the rhythmical texture of the writing of Wulfstan and Ælfric. Wulfstan's phrases have a crispness and firmness which is striking and effective, and the contrast with Ælfric will be of some importance when I come to consider precisely what happened when Wulfstan had done his best and worst with the somewhat looser rhythms of the Abbot of Eynsham.

Despite an obvious resemblance between Wulfstan's phrases and the classical half-line, there are certain quite striking and notable differences. In the first place, though I say this with due reserve, length of syllable appears to be of no functional importance. In the second, the phrases are such that it is not desirable to assess them at all on the basis of the five-type system of Sievers, or any other system designed to account for the classical verse. Some types familiar there are absent here; it is difficult for example to find phrases with the precise rhythmic flavour of D and E half-lines.[18] On the other hand, Wulfstan uses other rhythmical patterns which were not allowed in the classical verse at all, but which we cannot but regard as entirely normal and proper in his writing.[19] Two characteristics may be mentioned here, the frequency of what for want of a better word I shall call anacrusis, and the frequency of phrases ending with the motif /××. Of patterns which are common to Wulfstan and to the verse, it may be noted that the B type (basically ×/×/) which is found on an average once every 5 half-lines in *Beowulf*, accounts for only about 4 per cent. of Wulfstan's phrases. Type A is the commonest of all in the classical verse; in *Beowulf* nearly 45 per cent. of all half-lines have this form. In Wulfstan, if we allow cases with anacrusis of not more than 2 syllables, a pattern of this kind accounts for no less than about 70 per cent. of the phrases. So much for some of the facts about this remarkable kind of prose. May I, having said as much, return to the second of my two passages and read it again, bringing out as well as I can its rhythmical character, but without distorting the normal flow of the words to achieve this?

I have tried now to establish the reality of the two-stress phrase and to mention some of its characteristics and the differences between it and the half-line of verse proper. I have attempted by reading to show that some understanding of the system enables us to see better how a sermon of Wulfstan was intended to be delivered and what he was doing as he composed. Allow me now to discuss briefly the way he handled Ælfric's rhythmical prose.

It is one of the curiosities of literature, this relationship between Ælfric and Wulfstan, and the finicky technical transformation that Wulfstan makes of the writing of the other. It would be interesting to know whether he was aware of the carefully constructed form he was destroying when he did this, or what Ælfric in turn thought of these episcopal transmogrifications. There are several notable passages where the process can be examined in detail. I think in particular of Wulfstan's rewriting of Napier viii which is printed as Napier vii,[20] of his version of *De falsis deis* (Napier xviii), and his doctoring of Ælfric's second *Pastoral Letter*. He has tampered less severely with this last than with the others, and it is in them that the thorough-going reviser can best be followed at work.

Here is a curious situation in a troubled age; one man produces a special kind of rhythmical writing with a distinct and recognizable texture, then another, heavily burdened with the cares and duties of an enormously responsible position, takes the trouble to dissect all this and reconstruct it according to the rules governing his own rhythmical practice. I do not wish to suggest, of course, that he was merely preoccupied with the metrical transformation. He is almost always concerned primarily with expanding the text, with adding his own material, though he is also careful from time to time to change words or phrases which happen to be alien to his own usage. But whenever he makes expansions or alterations it is in such a way that the prose emerges reshaped into his own rhythmical mode, and many of the minor changes he makes seem to be purely on account of the rhythm.

I cannot easily describe Wulfstan's modifications in detail without putting written material before you, but something can be said. In the first place it may be noticed that whether Wulfstan understood Ælfric's system of joining pairs of half-lines by alliteration or not, he certainly did not regard this procedure as sacrosanct, and felt quite at liberty to interpolate one or more of his own two-stress phrases between any two of Ælfric's half-lines. A large amount of the expansion is made in this way. But there are other modifications. Sometimes a rather rambling Ælfric half-line is turned by the addition of two or three syllables into two two-stress phrases. Thus in Ælfric (Napier viii, p. 58)[20] we have the whole line

Ælc *w*isdom is of *G*ode   forðam þe *G*od sylf is *w*isdom

a half-line of 7 syllables followed by another of 8. By the addition of another 4 words to these 11, 4 words which between them contribute only an extra 6 syllables, Wulfstan turns this line into *four* two-stress phrases containing respectively 4, 6, 6, and 5 syllables (Napier vii, p. 52[20]):

Ælc riht wisdom
is cumen of Gode
forðam þe God sylf is
se soða wisdom.

Many of Ælfric's half-lines are left untouched, and are accepted by Wulfstan because they happen to have the same rhythmical eligibility as the two-stress phrase interpolations by which they are often flanked. What is most striking and important is that whatever the basic purpose of particular modifications, they almost always help to produce in the finished revision a flow of two-stress phrases which, while necessarily a little less sure and characteristic of Wulfstan than those of his own independent compositions, are nevertheless remarkably similar. Here, then, we have another confirmation of the rhythmical system which Wulfstan followed with such relentless thoroughness.

IV

It is time now to ask, what other purposes are served by a careful analysis of this system? I can think of four; three I shall mention, the fourth I should like to consider in more detail. First, I believe that it should be possible to learn something about the stress system of late Old English from this body of material hitherto untapped for such a purpose.[21] Secondly, it is easier on the basis of a knowledge of the precise point at which a passage breaks rhythmically to clear up a few textual problems, or at least to suggest the right line of approach. One example is sufficient, that of a famous crux in the *Sermo ad Anglos* involving the phrase *þe for heora þrytan lewe nellað beorgan.* The pointing shows that the rhythm breaks between *þrytan* and *lewe*, and that any interpretation which seeks to place *lewe* in intimate syntactic association with *þrytan* rather than with *beorgan* is almost certainly wrong.[22] Thirdly, it is perhaps worth noting that some attention to the rhythmical scheme should lead one to beware, in any investigation of Wulfstan's language, of accepting as normal prose usage something which may have been controlled by the shape of the phrase patterns he allowed himself. This means especially that a study of word-order might have to reckon with certain aberrations, and that the choice of words and even inflexions[23] may sometimes have been dictated by the system. This also applies, of course, to Ælfric's rhythmical writing.

I come now to the fourth matter, the problem of the Wulfstan canon, which, if there were time, would call for much fuller treatment. Two questions immediately arise after we have asked ourselves whether Wulfstan's rhythmical habits will enable us to sort out the canon. The first is, did Wulfstan always write like this? In other words, if you find a piece of prose that does not have the characteristics I have tried to describe, is it then certainly *not* by him? I find this question very hard to answer. I should say that there is no evidence that Wulfstan ever wrote anything that does not have in a considerable measure the rhythmical features which are most strikingly present in an exhortatory piece like the *Sermo ad Anglos*. His calmer expository prose, whether it be in the sermons or in the laws, is sometimes slightly less crisply rhythmed, but it is never by any means to be confused with the language of ordinary conversation. At the same time we must remember that what I have called ordinary prose was common enough in his time. Are we to conclude, then, that with Wulfstan the other, more mannered, way of writing became so ingrained a habit that he soon found himself unable to write anything less stylized? I think we can hardly conclude this, but must say only that whenever Wulfstan was writing anything official or to be delivered orally, anything, in other words, of the kind which his successors thought fit to preserve, he dropped naturally into this style. That he used it in the laws is not surprising; they would frequently be cited orally, and their memorability and impressiveness would be the greater if they were in a rhythmical shape.

Here one wonders a little about the situations in which Ælfric deemed it proper to assume the high style. He uses it not merely for sermons but also in private letters, and in private letters to men who were not so illiterate that they would need to have them read out to them. We must remember, however, the modernity of the distinction between reading to oneself and reading aloud, and that in this age a man read aloud or at least moved his lips even in reading to himself, so that there would always be a direct sensory appeal in any rhythm or alliterative adornment.[24] It cannot, therefore, be said that there were any situations in which to compose in a rhythmical style was entirely without reason, provided your reader knew what you were about, and could read with reasonable fluency. So it is possible that Wulfstan grew so much into it that it became his habitual mode of writing, just as blank verse came frequently to be the vehicle of John Kemble's conversation. At the same time I would note that the letter of Wulfstan to Cnut,[25] though by no means without marked rhythmical characteristics, has not the same firm touch we find in the sermons or in most of the other work we know to be his. If here he was trying to write ordinary prose, it shows that by this time he was unable to depart radically from the other style which he had cultivated for so long.

So much for the first of my two questions; a sermon or an official document not in his usual style is not likely to be by him. The second question is, was Wulfstan one of a school which used this fourth Old English style, or was he quite apart? If he can be shown to be quite apart, then we are in a strong position, for anything which shows his peculiar features of rhythm must certainly be by him. Here, unfortunately, the situation becomes complicated. I have already suggested that the basis of this whole system of his is something essentially in tune with the make-up of the English language. If many generations of poets could absorb the more complex but linguistically related system of Old English verse, should we not expect the other style, heard in the lawcourts and from the pulpit, to spread widely once it had taken shape? I think we should, but first we ought to ask whether it first took shape in Wulfstan's hands or whether it is earlier. We know at least that many features of his style are found before his time; the fondness for phrases with two alliterating or rhyming elements of which the law texts furnish early examples is only part of a tradition in which there are other resemblances to his style. Nor are these things confined to English, and Professor Bethurum has shown that some of them have a venerable ancestry.[26] But what about the regularly recurring two-stress phrase? What is its history, how old is it? Was there a rhythmical tradition, say in the law texts or in homiletic literature, which was not that of the classical verse,[27] but which supplied a model which Wulfstan followed quite closely?

As to the laws, it must be noted that the early codes are by no means so highly rhythmed as the later ones. Of the surviving law texts which are likely to have been composed before his time, there is none which can be pointed to as a model which would satisfactorily account for Wulfstan's style.[28] It is possible, of course, that the early laws have lost some of their rhythmical character in the course of transmission, but I think it highly unlikely. If we turn from the laws to the homilies we shall find things of rather greater interest and significance. These can be studied in greatest concentration in the homilies of the Vercelli Book. It is interesting to note how intimate is the association in manuscripts of material preserved by Vercelli and of texts written by Wulfstan. This is probably no accident, and it is almost certain that Wulfstan was brought up in familiarity with the traditions which Vercelli represents.

The earlier history of sermon writing in the vernacular is obscure, and we cannot be sure how old the rhythmical traditions such as we find in the Vercelli Book are. Nor can we speak of one single style or technique there, but at least it may be said that the traditions which it preserves are earlier than Wulfstan and that among them are stylistic habits which have a remarkable similarity to his own. A passage from Napier xxx (p. 145^{15} ff.) will illustrate this; we have here a piece of text which is also found on folio 114^{b} of the Vercelli Book and which is mainly composed of a succession of two-stress phrases.[29] And despite significant differences in detail between the patterns of these phrases and those of Wulfstan, it is clear that a tradition represented by a passage of this kind could well have furnished the rhythmical inspiration for Wulfstan's own writing, and of course for that of others. Where this tradition came from I am unwilling to guess, but the material extant would indicate that it is only in the late Old English period that the two-stress phrase comes to be used in a variety of ways outside its very technical employment in the role of half-line in the classical verse. I would suggest that the very diversity of the different techniques which we find in the debased verse of some of the *Chronicle* poems, in the *Lives of Saints*, in the Vercelli homilies, and in Wulfstan himself is in itself a sign that the habit as a whole was not very old. It is not the diversity of decay, but, in Ælfric and Wulfstan at least, a systematic attempt to produce something stylized which led to different results in different writers because the traditions behind were not solid and established.

I have said that up to Wulfstan's time no one employed quite the same rhythmical system as he did, but that something closely akin was already in common use in homiletic writings. From the point of view of the canon of his works the problem of the antecedents to his style is less serious than its history from his own time onwards. At this juncture we run into those cloudy figures, the Wulfstan imitators, who are believed by some to have produced material which is indistinguishable from the work of the master. I think there can be no doubt that the traditions which the Vercelli homilies most clearly represent were passed on right to Middle English times, and the real problem is whether Wulfstan's (as I believe) individual modifications of these had sufficient cogency and appeal to lead other writers to adopt them and write exactly as he did. Though I should regard Wulfstan as the one man of his generation likely to have produced a definite school, its members would scarcely have as their main ambition a desire to pass off their work as his. And even if they had, it is probable that in such a situation, where they would be following what was not an age-old tradition, their own personal characteristics would appear in what they wrote, in rhythmical details as well as in matters of syntax and vocabulary.[30] Therefore, if a text seems in all these particulars to be characteristic of Wulfstan, it is extremely unlikely that anyone but he wrote it, or, indeed, could have written it.

There are some eleventh-century texts which are remarkably similar to his in rhythmical texture. Among these I should include the text printed by Liebermann under the title *Antworten auf Klage um Land* and also *Rectitudines Singularum Personarum* together with its companion piece *Gerefa*.[31] Nevertheless, I believe that a strict analysis of their two-stress phrases shows that they deviate significantly from those of Wulfstan; such an analysis is therefore quite valuable except, of course, when we have to deal with very short texts. Whenever problems of authorship arise, it need hardly be said that what the nature of the rhythms suggests must always be considered along with all other available evidence, and not by itself. At the same time I have often found it strikingly illuminating to begin by using it by itself, and it is no bad exercise to attempt to formulate conclusions on this basis alone, checking them afterwards with a fuller array of different information.

I had hoped here to say something precise about certain disputed texts and the evidence supplied about them by a detailed analysis of their rhythms.[32] But the facts must be presented in detail or not at all, so that I have to crave forgiveness if this lecture has turned out to be nothing more than a prolegomenon.

Some nine hundred years ago, in a text I have just mentioned, an Anglo-Saxon described in rhythmical periods the duties of a good reeve. I will end with his last words:

> Ic gecende be ðam ðe ic cuðe; se ðe bet cunne, gecyðe his mare.

'I have explained the matter as well as I knew how to; let him who is better informed explain it more fully.'

NOTES

1. See Dorothy Bethurum, 'Stylistic Features of the Old English Laws', *M.L.R.* xxvii, where many references are given; Dorothy Whitelock, *Sermo Lupi ad Anglos*, and references in section iii of her bibliography; 'Wulfstan and the so-called Laws of Edward and Guthrum', *E.H.R.* lvi; 'Wulfstan and the Laws of Cnut', *E.H.R.* lxiii. For some problems of vocabulary see R. J. Menner, 'Anglian and Saxon Elements in Wulfstan's Vocabulary', *M.L.N.* lxiii, and references.

2. The second of these is printed by E. V. K. Dobbie, *The Anglo Saxon Minor Poems*, p. 24 f. On pp. xxxii–xliii he discusses the various pieces of verse found in the *Chronicle*. To this type belongs the three-line poem inscribed on the shield of Eadwen. The text is found in F. Kluge, 'Zur Geschichte des Reimes', *P.B.B.* 9, pp. 422 ff., and a facsimile at the end of vol. i of Hickes, *Thesaurus*.

3. Attempts to prove that a different kind of popular verse coexisted with the 'classical' even in early Old English are not convincing. See J. W. Rankin, 'Rhythm and Rime before the Norman Conquest', *P.M.L.A.* xxxvi (1921), pp. 401–28.

4. See especially Dorothy Bethurum, 'The Form of Ælfric's Lives of Saints', *Studies in Philology*, xxix, p. 519, and W. W. Skeat, *Ælfric's Lives of Saints*, ii, pp. l–liii.

5. For the literature of this arid terminological controversy and related things, see the references in G. H. Gerould, 'Abbot Ælfric's Rhythmic Prose', *Modern Philology*, xxii. I may add that I do not agree with Gerould that Ælfric's rhythms in this kind of writing are explained by rhythmical features in Latin texts which he was using or with which he was familiar.

6. The poem of 959 is on the accession of Eadgar and is found in MSS. D, E, and in part, *sub anno* 958, in F; that of 975 is on the death of Eadgar, and is found in MS. D. On Wulfstan's authorship of these, see K. Jost, 'Wulfstan und die Angelsächsische Chronik', *Anglia*, 47, pp. 105 ff. Under the year 975 MSS. A, B, and C have a different poem, in classical verse, on the death of Eadgar, and D and E have a poem in debased verse which I have already discussed.

7. e.g. A. S. Napier, *Wulfstan: Sammlung der ihm zugeschriebenen Homilien*, 146^{31}–147^{6} *and se hæfde . . . þam byligeon* (xxx); 200^{10-14} (xlii). The problem of assessing passages like these is complicated by the fact that in some

cases they may be nothing more than paraphrases of real poems. An example of such a thing is found in Napier, 145[33] ff. (= Vercelli 114[b]) where we have a prose dilution of lines 3 ff. of *An Exhortation to Christian Living*. As it stands, this dilution looks like an example of irregular verse, 'debased' indeed, but preserving many of the metrical features of the original. See L. Whitbread, 'Two notes on Minor Old English Poems', *Studia Neophilologica*, xx, no. iii, pp. 192 ff. But there are examples of a less fortuitous debased verse of the kind I discuss, albeit markedly different from Ælfric, such as the piece in Napier pp. 186–7 beginning

> (in þam dæge us byð æteowed)
> seo ge*o*penung heofena   and *e*ngla þrym
> and hel*w*ihta hryre   and eorðan for*w*yrd
> *t*reowleasra gewinn   and *t*ungla gefeall. . . .

This is also found in a metrically less perfect form in the second and the twenty-first homilies in the Vercelli Book, from which it is printed (with variations from Napier) by Max Förster, 'Der Vercelli-Codex cxvii', in *Festschrift für Lorenz Morsbach*, pp. 90–2.

8. The Ely Charter. The interest of this document was first brought to my attention by the treatment of it in E. Sievers, *Metrische Studien*, iv, pp. 208, 575. The Latin and Old English texts are found in Stowe Charters No. 31 (British Museum), and are printed in W. de G. Birch, *Cartularium saxonicum*, Nos. 1266, 1267. There is a reproduction of the manuscript in *Ordnance Survey Facsimiles*, Part iii, no. xxxii. The Old English text is edited by A. J. Robertson, *Anglo-Saxon Charters*, pp. 98–102. Mr. N. R. Ker informs me that the Latin and the Old English texts are almost certainly in the same hand, which appears to be of the second half of the eleventh century. According to my analysis of its rhythmical characteristics it shows a surprising similarity to Ælfric's work in this kind; the same is true of the use of alliteration and indeed of all stylistic features. If the Old English version of the charter was really written in or soon after 970, this similarity is very odd, for there is nothing else like it till we come to Ælfric's own writing. Nevertheless, it is obvious that its rhythmical features cannot be used as evidence that Ælfric wrote it, for if the text is as early as 970, it could he held to prove that Ælfric was merely continuing an older tradition; on the other hand, if it is late, then it might be argued that it was the work of a successor or imitator. I turn therefore to some other points. It has already been mentioned (p. 114) that Ælfric was at pains on at least three occasions to write in praise of Eadgar. Now the author of the English version of the charter not only does the same, but he does it in phrases often identical with or similar to those used in one or other of the three acknowledged Ælfric texts, while other passages in the charter can be paralleled elsewhere in his work. It is therefore either by Ælfric or a very curious and ingenious pastiche by someone else, and since the style, diction, rhythm, and vocabulary is everywhere characteristic of Ælfric, I am led to the first of these two conclusions.

I give below some of the parallels. Some (e.g. *Eadgar cining*) may well be fortuitous, but I have considered it inadvisable to ignore these, especially such of them as occur in the very Ælfric texts which offer other, more striking, parallels. The line references to the charter are according to Miss

Robertson's numbering, and the following abbreviations are used; Hom.: B. Thorpe, *The Homilies of the Anglo Saxon Church*; Sk.: W. W. Skeat, *Ælfric's Lives of Saints*; Ep.: 'Epilogue to the Heptateuch', ed. S. J. Crawford, *E.E.T.S.* 160, pp. 414–17.

P. 98. 6, 7. *ðe . . . gewissað . . . gewylt*. Cf. the juxtaposition of these verbs in Hom. i. 78[15], *se Heretoga seðe gewylt and gewissað. . . .*

7. *ealra cininga*. Cf. Ep. 83–4, *ealra cininga swiðost.*

8. *Eadgar cining*. Cf. Sk. xxi. 445.

ofer Engla þeode. Cf. Ep. 82–4, and especially 84, *ofer Engla ðeode.*

9. *7 he hæfð nu gewyld*. Cf. Ep. 84, *7 him God gewilde.*

Scottas 7 Cumbras. Cf. Sk. xxi. 451, *Cumera and Scotta.*

10–11. *7 eall þ ðis igland . . . þ ic nu on sibbe gesitte mine cynestol*. Cf. Hom. ii. 306[1], *and he mid sige gesæt siððan his cynestol*; Sk. xiii. 148, *þaða þis igland wæs wunigende on sibbe*; xxi. 447, *and his cynerice wæs wunigende on sibbe* (a clear enough example at any rate of Ælfric's readiness to use his own material more than once).

12. *hu ic his lof arære*. Cf. Ep. 82–3, *Eadgar . . . arærde Godes lof. . . .*

13. *þurh ure asolcennysse*. Cf. Hom. i. 602[8], *ure asolcennysse.*

14–15. Cf. for general sense Sk. xxi. 446.

P. 100. 2–3. *þæs halgan mædenes þe ðær gehal lið oð þis*. Cf. Sk. xx. 106, *þæs halgan mædenes*, and 111–12, *seðe hire lic heold hal on ðære byrgene git oð þisne dæg.*

3. *on eall hwittre ðryh of marmstane geworht*. Cf. Sk. xx. 79–81, *ane mære þruh . . . gewohrt of marmstane eall hwites bleos*, and 83, *eac of hwitum marmstane.*

5. *7 hu heo Gode ðeowode on godre drohtnunge*. Cf. Sk. xx. 32–3, *þæt heo Criste moste þeowian on mynsterlicre drohtnunge.*

7 be hyre geendunge. Cf. Sk. xx. 71, *æfter hire geendunge.*

6. *swa swa Beda awrat þeodæ lareow on his larbocum*. Cf. Sk. xx. 118, *swa swa se lareow Beda on ðære bec sæde þe he gesette be ðysum*; xx. 24, *se halga Beda þe þas boc gesette.*

The date at which this text was composed is a matter of great interest. One naturally thinks of the possibility of Æthelwold having commissioned Ælfric to do it. But Æthelwold died in 984, and though there is no doubt that Ælfric could have been writing by then, there is certainly no evidence for his having used the rhythmical style till much later. The parallels would on the whole suggest that in this document he was drawing from the other three texts. A date around 1006, when he was engaged on the Latin *Life* of Æthelwold, is perhaps the most likely. I am not qualified to discuss the authorship of the Latin text, but I cannot agree with the view of Sievers (op. cit., p. 208 n.) who appears to have thought that both Latin and Old English were by the same author, and that the Old English version was the original. He does not consider the possibility of one or both being considerably later than 970. The authenticity of the Latin version has often been questioned, e.g. by Birch, Stevenson, and Plummer.

9. I have not attempted to make an exhaustive collection of writings which seem to me to be in the Ælfric manner, but two might be mentioned here. The first is Napier xxxi which opens thus:

We willað nu secgan sume bysne to þisum;
An munuccild wunode mid manegum gebroðrum
on Mauricius mynstre þæs halgan martyres,
þæt is on Muntgiu swa men farað to Rome.

Ða hæfde þæt munuccild   swiðe mærlice stemne
and his modor gecom   to þam mynstre for oft
and gehyrde gelome   hyre leofan sunu
hu myrge he sang   mid þam munecum symle
and hyre wæs myrge   on hyre mode þurh þæt.

It is found only in MS. E where another hand has given it the title 'Be ane munuccilde'. There can be no doubt that this is not by Wulfstan: aside from the rhythmical features, we may note that the verbs *hopian* and *befrinan* (Napier 152[20, 23]) are not recorded in Wulfstan's works. The whole piece seems to me to be characteristic of Ælfric in rhythm, style, and vocabulary.

The second text is the paraphrase of two passages from the Book of Daniel, and is preserved in MS. Vespasian D xiv. It is printed in full though not with complete accuracy by Rubie D. Warner in 'Early English Homilies from the Twelfth Century Manuscript Vesp. D xiv', *E.E.T.S., O.S.*, 152 (1917), p. 38 ff. The text is briefly discussed by Max Förster in *Englische Studien*, 54, p. 49 f. and the first part is printed in his *Altenglisches Lesebuch für Anfänger* (5th ed. 1949), p. 35. It begins:

On þære ilcan burh   Babilonie
(þe we embe specað)
wæs on Daries dagen   se wytege Daniel
Godes heh ðeign   haliges lifes man.

(*þe we embe specað* is clearly extra-metrical, and Förster suggests that it is 'jedenfalls als Zusatz des Kopisten zu streichen, anknüpfend an die vorhergehende Erzählung von Nebukadnezar'.) Like the first, this text seems to me to be remarkably similar to the known writings of Ælfric; it may be significant that it is preserved in a manuscript full of writings known to be by him. But nothing final can be said about the authorship of these two pieces and others like them until more is known about the rhythmical structure of eleventh- and twelfth-century writings as a whole.

10. The first passage is Napier 5[7–16]; the position of the two main stresses in lines 9 and 16 is somewhat doubtful (cf. introduction to note 19). The second passage read is printed in note 14. It is hardly necessary to add that the full rhythmical power of his prose is more clearly in evidence in this second passage.

11. *Anglia*, 7, Anzeiger, p. 200.

12. I do not propose here to discuss the various phonetic characteristics which would distinguish two such manners of enunciation, or which for that matter would have to be considered in any full analysis of the pronunciation of a two-stress phrase. There are problems not merely of rhythm (i.e. the length of time and exact degree of stress accorded to the different elements, among which we must reckon with *silences*), but also of intonation. It is perhaps worth calling attention to the fact that when one says that a phrase (either Old or Modern English) has two main stresses which are found in such and such positions, this is not really a description of the rhythmical character of the phrase. The relationship between stress, duration, and intonation is very intimate and I do not feel that stress can be said to be more important than the other two. Any statement, therefore, about the number and position of main stresses should not be accepted

as more than a rough directive from which (at least in contemporary English) we can make certain deductions about the nature of the other features.

13. It is well known that the most diverse kinds of speech material tend to shape themselves into a two-stress pattern. E.g. *Píccadilly Círcus* as readily as *Píccadílly*, *Wáterloo Brídge* as well as *Wáterlóo*, *hám and egg sándwich* beside *hám and égg*. For a demonstration of the dominant position of the two-stress phrase in all periods of English see Marjorie Daunt, 'Old English Verse and English Speech Rhythm', *Transactions of the Philological Society*, 1946, p. 56.

14. I print below the text of Miss Whitelock's edition, lines 55–68 with the pointing added from all five manuscripts, B, C, E, H, and I. The material from B and C (CCCC 419 and 201) comes from transcripts kindly lent to me by Miss Whitelock; that from I (British Museum Cotton Nero A i) was noted for me by Dr. B. J. Timmer. For convenience of printing I have not indicated the different kinds of punctuation marks used. A capital letter therefore merely indicates that the MS. for which it stands has some mark of punctuation at the point where the letter is printed:

Ne dohte hit nu lange EI
inne ne ute BCEHI
ac wæs here H 7 hunger BCEHI
bryne BH 7 blodgyte CEHI
on gewelhwylcan ende BCEI
oft 7 gelome BCEHI
7 us stalu BH 7 cwalu BCEHI
stric BH 7 steorfa BCHI
orfcwealm BCH 7 uncoþu BCEHI
hol BH 7 hete BCEH
7 rypera reaflac CEI
derede swyþe þearle BCEHI
7 (us) ungylda B
swyðe gedrehtan BCEHI
7 us unwedera E foroft BCI
weoldon unwæstma BCEHI
forþam on þysan I earde wæs C
swa hit þincan mæg BCEI
nu fela geara
unrihta fela BCHI
7 tealte getrywða E
æghwær mid mannum BCEHI
ne bearh nu foroft E
gesib gesibban BCEI
þe ma þe fremdan BCEHI
ne fæder his bearne BCHI
ne hwilum bearn
his agenum fæder BCEHI
ne broþer oþrum BCEHI
ne ure ænig
his lif (ne) fadode BEI
swa swa he scolde BCEHI

ne gehadode regollice BCHI
ne læwede lahlice BCEHI
ac worhtan lust us to lage I
ealles to gelome EI
7 naþor ne heoldan
ne lare ne lage
Godes ne manna I
swa swa we scoldan EI

Lines 35–40 are not in MSS. B, C, and H. Lines 3, 4, 7–10 are punctuated in the middle in some of the MSS.; this is a convention often adopted when two words of similar or opposite meaning are used together in a phrase. It is not a rhythmical pointing at all and is inherited from earlier Latin scribal tradition (see E. A. Lowe, *The Beneventan Script*, p. 233, and specimen no. 2 on p. 229). In the *Sermo ad Anglos* it is used most frequently by B, less so by H, with great rarity by C and I, and never by E. Concerning pointing at the ends of lines, we may note that lines 15 and 17 present the only conflicts. In 15 the agreement of BCI against E suggests strongly that E is wrong though plausible. In 17, I's pointing after *þysan* is patently an error. In the thirty-four lines found in all MSS., only three have no punctuation at all, a proportion which roughly applies to the *Sermo* as a whole.

15. See especially K. Luick, *Anglia* 23, Beiblatt p. 226, and references in his *Historische Grammatik der englischen Sprache*, paragraphs 55 and 60. For the pointing in the Cædmon MS. see J. Lawrence, *Chapters on Alliterative Verse*. It is important that editors of Old and Middle English texts should record the punctuation. If it is not actually printed, as it is by Skeat in the *Lives of Saints*, or by Joseph Hall in his *Selections from Early Middle English*, it ought at least to be noted in an appendix as it is by Fehr in his edition of Ælfric's *Pastoral Letters*.

16. I take this opportunity of suggesting that a careful analysis of the punctuation of the texts in Lambarde's *Archaionomia* might settle the question of whether he had access to sources no longer extant. For the clear demonstration by Mr. Kenneth Sisam (*M.L.R.* xviii, p. 98; cf. ibid., 253–69, *Beiblatt z. Anglia* 1924, p. 214, 1925, p. 345) of palpable sixteenth-century insertions in a few notable passages does not prove that *all* Lambarde's deviations from known manuscripts are of this kind. The punctuation of these texts is so much in conformity with Old English practice that it is not easy to believe that Lambarde himself produced it by the light of nature. So if it could be shown that his punctuation of any text is not taken over direct from any of the known manuscripts containing this text (either from one or in a composite fashion from more than one) then we should have strong evidence that Liebermann was right in supposing another source. The only text I have examined from this point of view is EGu (for the details of the punctuation in the two surviving MSS. B and H, I am indebted to Mr. John Bromwich and to Mr. A. J. Aitken). I know of no way of assessing such a complicated set of facts as these two MSS. offer, but briefly the position is as follows.

It is generally believed that Lambarde did not know of H when he compiled the *Archaionomia* (Liebermann, *Gesetze*, I, xxviii, col. 2) nor can I find any textual evidence to suggest that he did. If, however, he was relying solely on B, the deviations in punctuation are astonishingly numerous, though his own pointing contrives to be so 'good' that it deviates from that of H in only about one-fifth as many cases as it deviates from B. It so happens that the punctuation of H is better than that of B in the sense that (with numerous omissions typical of almost all manuscripts) it more faithfully divides two-stress phrases. It is therefore probably nearer to the original text than B is, at least in this respect. In the absence of any other textual evidence to the contrary, it is not easy to believe that Lambarde was using H. Yet I find it hard to believe that on his own he could have revised the pointing of the B version of EGu to produce a punctuation with so comparatively few deviations from that of H, and it seems to me more reasonable to suppose that he had access to another manuscript which had preserved a 'good' punctuation and which therefore frequently agreed with H. It may be noted that later when Lambarde produced a text of *Geþincþo* from H (*Perambulation of Kent*, published 1576), though his readings of the text itself remain as unreliable as elsewhere (he deviates from the manuscript in over a score of details) yet he does not radically alter the punctuation. He retains almost all that H has, and simply adds more of his own at certain fairly obvious points. It is clear that all the available material needs full investigation.

17. There has been a widespread tendency to ignore or to be insufficiently aware of the clear distinction between the rhythmical characteristics of Wulfstan and of Ælfric. See the pertinent remarks of Professor Bethurum, 'The Connection of the Katherine Group with Old English Prose', *J.E.G.Ph.*, xxiv. 561, footnote 26.

18. The doctrine is often repeated that D and E half-lines disappear in Middle English because of the loss of the old poetic compounds. One may note (*a*) that not all D lines involve compounds at all—*swutol sang scopes*, *flod blode weol* (*Beowulf*, 90, 1422), &c., nor even all E—*twelf wintra tid* (*Beowulf*, 147); (*b*) that the compounds which in O.E. form all or part of a D or E line are not always 'poetic' words such as are found only rarely after Old English times. The disappearance of types D and E must be connected rather with a change in the rhythmical basis of the language whereby the weight of syllables with subsidiary stress, e.g. in trisyllabic words, is no longer so distinctive that it can properly play its former functional role.

19. It is convenient to show in tabular form some facts about Wulfstan's rhythmical two-stress phrases. There is no method of analysis which is both simple and exhaustive (cf. note 12) and I have chosen to present the simplest possible description. It consists of marking the two syllables with main stress as / and the rest as ×; the symbol × here represents therefore not 'minimal stress', but 'any degree of stress short of main stress', e.g. *orfcwealm and uncoðu* / × × / × ×; *to gedwolgoda weorðunge* × × / × × / × ×. The analysis which follows is of the *Sermo ad Anglos*. It is necessarily somewhat tentative and I have ignored some phrases, not so much because they have any abnormality of pattern, but because it is not always easy to decide where the two main stresses fall, e.g. *and ut of þysan earde*, × / × × × / × or × × × / × / ×? I have also ignored the *Schwellvers* (Miss Whitelock's edition, lines 137–43, *þurh morðdæda . . . mistlice forligru*, and 167–72, *her syndan mannslagan . . . ryperas 7 reaferas*) on which see 5(*c*) on p. 138.

Patterns (ignoring anacrusis)	*Number of syllables before first main stress* 0	1	2	3	4	*Totals*	
/ × × × × / × × ×						0	15
/ × × × / × × ×		3	1			4	
/ × × / × × ×		1	3			4	
/ × / × × ×		1	2	1		4	
/ / × × ×		2		1		3	
/ × × × × / × ×	1	2	1			4	89
/ × × × / × ×	3	13	1	1		18	
/ × × / × ×	17	17	6	1		41	
/ × / × ×	4	11	4	2		21	
/ / × ×		1	3	1		5	
/ × × × × / ×	1	2				3	471
/ × × × / ×	45	56	13			114	
/ × × / ×	90	96	33	6		225	
/ × / ×	15	34	36	10		95	
/ / ×		2	30	1	1	34	
/ × × × × /						0	23
/ × × × /			1	2		3	
/ × × /	1	2	3			6	
/ × /		6	6	1	1	14	
/ /						0	
						598	

The enclosed figures are of those patterns used ten times or more.

The patterns recorded ten times or more from my material are only fifteen in number, and these account for about 86 per cent. of the text. They are:

Pattern	Count
× / × × / ×	96
/ × × / ×	90
× / × × × / ×	56
/ × × × / ×	45
× × / × / ×	36
× / × / ×	34
× × / × × / ×	33
× × / / ×	30
× / × × / × ×	17
/ × × / × ×	17
/ × / ×	15
× × / × × × / ×	13
× / × × × / × ×	13
× / × / × ×	11
× × × / × / ×	10
	516

If we disregard anacrusis, we can group these into seven basic types:

1.	/ × × / ×	219
2.	/ × × × / ×	114
3.	/ × / ×	95
4.	/ × × / × ×	34
5.	× / / ×	30
6.	/ × × × / × ×	13
7.	/ × / × ×	11
		516

The following comments may be made:

1. Varieties of the 'A' type including cases with anacrusis of one or two syllables, i.e. (× ×)/ ×(× ×)/ ×, account for about 70 per cent. of all phrases.

2. Anacrusis rarely (about 4 per cent. of cases) exceeds two syllables. The two examples in which it exceeds three, *swa þæt hy ne scamað na*, and *and þy us is þearf micel* (*Sermo*, 161, 198) are, in terms of the prosody of the O.E. classical verse, respectively B and C types where the preliminary unstressed material is not strictly speaking anacrusis at all. The amount of anacrusis in Wulfstan's phrases depends partly on the 'weight' of the rest of the phrase, and tends to be in inverse ratio thereto. This means that phrases which without anacrusis would have seven syllables rarely have more than one opening unstressed syllable, and those which would have six rarely have more than two. Trisyllabic anacrusis, which as I have said is not common anyhow, is mainly confined to phrases which would otherwise have three, four, or five syllables. This functional compensatory use of anacrusis is in accordance with the traditions of the classical verse where the conception of total weight of half-line is always important.

3. 'B' types of phrase, i.e. those ending with a syllable bearing main stress, are remarkably rare. This is in striking contrast not only with the classical verse (see p. 122) but also with Ælfric, in whom it is found in nearly 20 per cent. of half-lines. This is one of the most significant of Wulfstan's deviations from other rhythmical genres.

4. The pattern / × × (×)/ is so rare as to be suspicious. This makes the addition in MS. C after *yfelian swyþe* in line 7 of the *Sermo* somewhat suspect. The addition begins:

þis wæs on Æþelredes cyninges
dagum gediht.
feower geara fæce
ær he forðferde.

The phrase *dagum gediht* is the only clear example in the *Sermo* of a pattern beginning and ending with a main stress, and the pattern of the preceding phrase × × × / × × × / × × is not found again. Though the rest of the addition is metrically sound, it seems to me that the irregularity of the two opening phrases is rather against Wulfstan being their author. On the other hand the addition in C at line 48 is rhythmically above reproach.

5. The only cases where the *Sermo* does not divide regularly into groups with the above characteristics are these:

(*a*) Apostrophes and interjectory remarks. The *Sermo* has the following examples; *Leofan men*, 4; *La hwæt*, 48; *And la*, 102, 130 (different in C); *Eala*, 176; *Ac la*, 180 (C and H have *Ac nu*). It would be wrong to regard these as ordinary unstressed material preliminary to the phrase following them, for in each case this is rhythmically regular without them, though it may be noted that none of them has a punctuation mark after it except *Leofan men*, and this only in B. *Leofan men* and *La hwæt* (written *lá hwǽt* in H) have both two main stresses but are deficient in number of syllables, the minimum of which for a Wulfstan phrase is four.

(*b*) *Inquits* are often extrametrical; there are no examples in the *Sermo*, but one occurs in the first passage from Napier vi cited in note 27 below.

(*c*) Expanded rhythmical phrases. I have already mentioned two passages in the *Sermo* where the phrase-unit is markedly above normal dimensions and weight, and stands more or less in the same relation to the normal phrase as expanded half-lines of the classical verse do to normal half-lines. These expanded phrases are not common, they almost always occur in bunches and they are only used to achieve some specially powerful effect.

(*d*) It is possible that very occasionally, especially at the end of a period, three-stress phrases were used, e.g. *bét þonne we ær þýsan dýdan*, 17; *dó máre gif he mǽge*, 72; *Gód úre hélþe*, 210. But I am not sure that it is necessary to assume this at any point.

6. It may be noted that a particular pattern tends to be followed by itself more frequently than would be the case in a succession of patterns which formed a purely random series, e.g. lines 89–92 where (ignoring anacrusis) the pattern / × × / × occurs seven times in a row:

fylþe adreogað
an æfter anum
7 ælc æfter oðrum
hundum geliccast
þe for fylþe ne scrifað
and syððan wið weorðe
syllað of lande.

Lines 96–7 provide five consecutive examples of / × × × / ×:

fremdum to gewealde
ut of ðisse þeode
7 eal þæt syndan micle
7 egeslice dæda
understande se þe wille.

In the second passage it is interesting to note that the second line, which is found only in E, fits the prevailing pattern: not only does this suggest that it is an addition by Wulfstan himself, but it shows how carefully additions were woven into the text. This tendency for patterns to repeat themselves is important in any consideration of the problem of interpolations. It will be found that these (even when there is no doubt of their genuineness) often break up two originally adjacent phrases of the same rhythmical pattern, e.g. line 48 (/ × × × / × ×), 66–8 (/ × × / × ×).

7. It should be emphasized that the rhythmical structure of the *Sermo* does not differ radically from that of other Wulfstan texts. For purposes of comparison I list below the figures for a number of texts; the *Sermo*, Napier x, Napier xiii, EGu, and (for contrast) Ælfric's *Life of St. Oswald*. The numbers in brackets indicate the total number of phrases assessed in each text; in the lists the figures have all been raised by multiplication to the same scale as those for the *Sermo*.

Patterns (ignoring anacrusis)	*Sermo* (598)		*Napier x* (512)		*Napier xiii* (357)		*EGu* (172)		*St. Oswald* (500)	
/××××/×××	0		0		0		0		0	
/×××/×××	4		1		5		0		8	
/××/×××	4	15	5	16	10	23	3	10	4	23
/×/×××	4		9		3		7		7	
//×××	3		1		5		0		4	
/××××/××	4		0		4		0		5	
/×××/××	18		28		25		35		20	
/××/××	41	89	46	110	41	96	48	137	46	113
/×/××	21		29		18		37		36	
//××	5		7		8		17		6	
/××××/×	3		5		5		24		26	
/×××/×	114		120		104		91		66	
/××/×	225	471	226	451	190	452	203	437	138	345
/×/×	95		74		120		91		101	
//×	34		26		33		28		14	
/××××/	0		1		0		0		6	
/×××/	3		2		2		0		30	
/××/	6	23	7	21	3	27	0	14	51	117
/×/	14		11		22		14		30	
//	0		0		0		0		0	
	598		598		598		598		598	

20. The nature of Wulfstan's alterations to Napier viii is the subject of a dissertation by G. O. Zimmerman, *Die beiden Fassungen des dem Abt Ælfric zugeschriebenen angel-sächsischen Traktats Über die siebenfältige Gabe des Heiligen Geistes*, Leipzig, 1888. He discusses in detail the changes in vocabulary, the introduction of favourite Wulfstan phrases, &c. He is well aware that some kind of metrical transformation has taken place: 'Die Vierheber dieses Stückes (i.e. Napier vii) tragen nicht mehr das Ælfric'sche Gepräge. Sie scheinen mir nicht mehr als Langzeilen berechnet gewesen zu sein. Die verknüpfende Alliteration fehlt meist, und die Sätze resp. Gedanken endigen nicht mehr wie bei Ælfric am Ende eines Doppelverses nur, sondern nach jedem beliebigen Vierheber.' This is interesting as far as it goes, but the author offers no analysis of the exact ways in which the transformation is brought about. The term 'Vierheber' and its use here is of course due to the Einenkel school.

I print below a few lines from Napier vii, pp. 52^{20} ff. (= viii, pp. 58^{20} ff.) in a way intended to show the nature of the transformation. Normal type represents Ælfric's text, and each of his whole lines begins a new line on the printed page. Bold type represents Wulfstan's additions; when a word or a phrase of Ælfric has been omitted by Wulfstan, I print it in brackets. In this way the text as Ælfric wrote it is represented by everything not in bold type: as Wulfstan left it, by everything not in brackets.

A vertical bar represents the break between each of Ælfric's original half-lines, a full stop the rhythmical divisions as intended by Wulfstan:

Ælc **riht** wisdom. is **cumen** of Gode. | forðam þe God sylf is. **se soða** wisdom. |

and ælc man bið. **gesælig and** eadig. | þe hæfð þæne wisdom. | **þe of Godes agenre gyfe cymð.**

(gif he) **and ðurh þæt** his agen lif. | gelogað mid wisdome. |

Se wisdom is. (halig) | **swa we ær cwædon.** þæs halgan gastes gifu. |

and (se) deofol (forgifð) | **sæwð.** þærtogeanes. (dysig) | **unwisdom and swicdom. and gedeð swa þurh þæt.**

þæt (he) **unsælig man.** wisdomes ne (gyme) | **gymeð.** ne wislice. **his lif ne** (libbe) | **fadað.**

and gyt **eac gedeð.** þæt forcuðre is. | þæt he (telle) **talað þeh hwilum.** hine **sylfne. wærne and** wisne. |

and bið **eac for oft.** swa gehiwod | **licetere**. swylce he wis sy. | **byþ þeah smeagende. oftor ymbe swicdom. þonne ymbe wisdom.**

It will be noticed that in the process of expansion 16 half-lines of Ælfric have grown into 32 Wulfstan phrases, and that this has been brought about by the use of only 72 extra syllables (88 added and 16 removed) beside the 106 of the original.

A knowledge of the nature of these changes is valuable in any consideration of original Wulfstan texts which have themselves undergone revision, because it sometimes helps to show whether such revision is Wulfstan's own work or that of someone else. When the alterations are such that the original two-stress formation is unspoilt or even improved, the probability is that they are his own. The point has some relevance to a problem recently discussed by Mr. N. R. Ker, 'Hemming's Cartulary', in *Studies in Mediæval History presented to Frederick Maurice Powicke*, pp. 70–2. Mr. Ker mentions eight early-eleventh-century manuscripts in which a hand occurs —'not so much a professional as a scholar's hand'—which makes alterations and additions to texts some of which are by Wulfstan. He calls attention to the fact that such tamperings as are in English are 'Wulfstanian in character and language'. Mr. Ker has kindly shown me the relevant passages, and my own impression is that the added material, where it is copious enough to be assessed, shows the same careful attention to rhythmical considerations as that in the revisions of Ælfric. Whether the hand is Wulfstan's own it is not my business to decide. But I believe the revisions to be his, and since these are made by this hand in so many different manuscripts, it is more likely to be his own than that of anyone else. If it is, I should like to call attention to the interest of the fact that the considerable revisions on folios 115–16 of Cotton Tiberius A xiii (see footnote to Napier 4^{4}–5^{1}) include additional punctuation.

A good example of a Wulfstan text which has been tampered with by someone else is Napier lii. The version in *Polity* cap. xix is addressed to priests in the plural; the version in Napier uses the singular, with the result that metrically impeccable phrases of *Polity* are ruined in the transformation. Thus *sacerdas sculan* becomes *sacerd scel* (Napier 275^{15}); *ægðer hi sculon* becomes *æiþer he sceal* (ibid. line 17); *healdan sceolan* becomes *healdan sceal* (line 20). If Wulfstan himself had made this change he would have filled out these now defective phrases with extra words.

21. For this a full investigation of the very copious material would be necessary. The method would be similar to, though not perhaps as straightforward as, that which Sievers, using the evidence of the classical verse, expounds in PBB. 10.

22. The passage (lines 163–5 of Miss Whitelock's edition) reads thus:

hy scamað þæt hy betan EI
heora misdæda BCEI
swa swa bec tæcan BCEHI
gelice þam dwæsan BCH
þe for heora prytan BI
lewe nellað beorgan C(?), EI
ær hy na ne magan CEI
þeh hy eal willan BCEHI

It so happens that B begins a new side with the word *lewe* and it might be claimed that its mark of punctuation after *prytan* loses a little weight as a result. But I confirms it, and no manuscript has a mark after *lewe*. So it seems proper to take *þe for heora prytan* separately, with the meaning 'who on account of their pride'. The phrase occurs again in this sense in *Grið* (cap. 21, Liebermann, *Gesetze*, i. 472), a good deal of which, including this passage, seems to bear the mark of Wulfstan's hand. Compare also Napier 178[19]: *se ðe for his prydan Gode nele hyran ... witod he sceal misfaran*. It follows that the word *lewe* is intimately connected not with *prytan* but with (*nellað*) *beorgan*.

The passage is clearly related to that in another Wulfstan text, EGu 10 (Liebermann, *Gesetze*, i. 132–4), where we have (MS. H):

Gif limlæweo lama
þe forworht wære
weorþe forlæten
7 he æfter þam
ðreo niht alibbe
siððan man mot hylpan
be bisceopes leafe
se ðe wylle beorgan
sare 7 saule.

(On *limlæw* see Liebermann, iii. 91.) In the *Sermo*, MS. C actually has *sare nellað beorgan*, which I should regard as an intelligent substitution of a common word for a rare one of similar meaning. In EGu the phrase must mean 'who wishes to cure (*or* tend to) the injury (of the cripple)'. In the *Sermo* the basic sense of injury or infirmity seems to have taken on a more abstract colour, like that of the compound *synleaw* used two lines later, with a meaning 'moral infirmity'. I would therefore translate 'like the fools who though they really would like to, are prevented by their pride from curing their spiritual infirmities before it is too late'.

23. This has been discussed already by Professor Norman Davis in a review of J. Hedberg, *The Syncope of the Old English Present Endings*, in *R.E.S.*, xxv, pp. 160–1, where he suggests that in the phrase *æftan heaweð* (*Sermo* line 70) a syncopated form of the verb would be rhythmically ineligible. Cf. the remarks of R. J. Menner in a review of the same work, *J.E.G.Ph.*, xlvii, pp. 417–18.

24. See H. J. Chaytor, *From Script to Print*, pp. 13 ff. and references.

25. J. M. Kemble, *Codex Diplomaticus Aevi Saxonici*, vi. 177 (No. MCCCXIV).

26. In 'Stylistic Features' (see note 1) she cites many examples and discusses similar things in other Germanic languages. There is much illustrative material, curiously interpreted, in E. Sievers, *Metrische Studien*, iv.

27. I think it is inconceivable that Wulfstan should not have had some familiarity with the classical verse; but whatever the basis of his own style may have been, it is evident that he regarded such verse as no proper or practicable medium for what he had to say, even in his most impassioned and 'poetic' moments, despite the fact that it was not unusual to embody genuine 'poems' in homilies, cf. note 7.

On page 123 I have raised the question of whether Wulfstan knew what Ælfric's metrical intentions were. If he knew the classical verse, one would suppose that he would have seen what Ælfric was about, and there is one curious text which, if it is by Wulfstan, would show quite clearly that he himself tried something of the same kind. This is Napier vi, a most remarkable document. It contains almost nothing in vocabulary which can be shown to be alien to his own usage, nor so far as I am aware has its authenticity been doubted. It is remarkable not only because over large stretches 'half-lines' are joined in pairs by alliteration and even occasionally by rhyme, but because it has a strophic 'chorus' (used ten times, Napier $45^{12, 19}$, $46^{2, 10, 22}$, $47^{2, 9, 16, 22}$, 48^{3}) which goes thus:

Gyt I*s*aias furðor *s*æde
ealswa hit *aeode* on forsyngodre *þeode.*

A short passage (Napier 49^{18} ff.) will illustrate the style:

eala *l*eofan *c*ild (cwæð ure drihten) ge*c*yrrað ic *l*ære
and *w*endað hider to me *w*eorðaþ on rihtwege
and beseoð to *eo*wrum drihtne *a*csjað georne
hu betst sy to *f*arenne and *f*arað æfter þam wege;
þonne wyrðe *g*e geborgene *g*yt
gif *g*e *w*illað þæt *g*e ne for*w*eorðað.

In this same piece there are passages where the system is spoiled as it is in Napier vii. I print below an example from Napier 49^{28} ff., using the same conventions as in note 20:

Gehyrað **he cwæð**. Godes word | **nu ða**. and **doð swa ic lære**. godjað georne. |
(then come five whole lines without disturbance followed by)
ne hæðenscipes gymað. | **on ænige wisan**. eow sylfum to hearme. |
þonne weorðe ic mid eow. | **cwæð ure drihten**. æfre æt ðearfe. |

The additions here and elsewhere in the text which thus break up the structure of the original are clearly by Wulfstan. But he has only interfered with small sections of the text and I think it likely that the original version was also by him, an experiment which he did not follow up. In any case it is emphatically not an original Ælfric text worked over by him, as vii is.

There are one or two other passages in Napier which have a similar 'whole line' basis, e.g. the Lord's Prayer in xxvi, 125^{7-14}, but it is hard to say whether they are by Wulfstan or not. Cf. also Napier 121^{6-13} (the opening of Wanley's no. 45) of which there is a prose paraphrase in Napier 150^{23} ff. and in part at 144^{32} (cf. Vercelli 113^{b}). But I am inclined to doubt whether this is by Wulfstan. The favourite passage 143^{9-15} (cf. 67^{13-16}, 112^{6-7}, *Grið* 30 and the opening of *Polity* xxv) seems to be a slight revision by him of something of the same kind.

28. In the Kentish code of Hloþhære and Eadric there are numerous traces of the rhythmical pattern which becomes so regular in Wulfstan. The same is true of the code of Ine and, to a lesser extent, of that of Alfred. There are similar features in II Eadwerd and in the laws of Eadgar, and it may be noted that Wulfstan, without violating his own rules, is frequently able to incorporate passages from Eadgar into his own legal works without any alteration. But the *constant* occurrence of the pattern is a characteristic which is absent from the laws written before Wulfstan's time. Of laws belonging to the Anglian area we know little more than that there were some; there is evidence that Offa's code was known to Alfred. But I do not think it likely that they belonged to a different stylistic tradition which paid more attention to rhythmical matters, though it is just possible that these lost laws contributed something to Wulfstan's way of writing. For the laws of Edward and Guthrum see note 1.

29. Napier xxx is such a curiously complicated pastiche that it may be worth saying something about its components. The parts by Wulfstan can, I think, be picked out on rhythmical grounds with a fair degree of accuracy; the rest is by no means homogeneous. The beginning to 144^{28} seems to me to be Wulfstan's, though as I have suggested (note 27) 143^{9-15} is perhaps no more than a revision of somebody else's work. The passage 144^{29} to 145^{9} is of a quite different character, and is found in Vercelli f. 113^{b}; it is not quite ordinary prose, but such rhythmical features as it possesses are not very striking, and the two-stress phrase is not regularly in evidence. It is unlikely that Wulfstan incorporated it here—the pastiche is the work of a later man—and since 143^{9-15} itself seems to interrupt the flow of the text before and after it, it is probable that this too was not placed where it is by Wulfstan.

At 145^{9} begins something which with the slight revision of one line reveals itself clearly as a fragment of a genuine Old English poem:

we syndon *d*eadlice men   and to *d*uste sceolan
on *w*orulde *w*urðan   *w*urmum to æte
and of *eo*rðan *e*ft   *ea*lle arisan
(MS. eorðan we sceolan eft)
on *d*omes *d*æge   and *d*rihtene sylfum
æt*y*wan *ea*ll   þæt we ær dydon.

At this point the verse breaks down and a few lines later, 145^{15}, we continue with the passage from Vercelli 114^{b} which is rhythmed in something akin to Wulfstan's own manner, though it happens to include in 145^{33} ff. a paraphrase of part of the beginning of *An Exhortation to Christian Living* (see note 7). Then from 146^{8} on we have a collection of material from the ninth Vercelli homily and other sources. Not till about 150^{12} (or a little earlier?) do we come to material with a Wulfstan ring to it, and everything from there to the end is, I think, probably by him. Yet most of the text from 145^{15} to 150^{12} is mainly in two-stress phrases not unlike his own, and if Wulfstan knew Vercelli or the tradition it represents, he would have had such models constantly before him.

30. B. Fehr's contention (*Die Hirtenbriefe Ælfrics*, paragraph 170) that Wulfstan is easy to imitate is very properly challenged by Karl Jost (in a review of Fehr, *Englische Studien* 52, 105 ff.): 'Nach seiner (i.e. Fehr's) meinung ist Wulfstans stil "sehr leicht nachzuahmen"; es bedarf bloss einer reichlichen verwendung von formeln wie: *for ure þearfe, agen, georne, understande se þe cunne*, etc., um beispielsweise einen Ælfrictext in den Wulfstanstil zu übertragen. Persönlich stelle ich mir diese übertragung etwas schwieriger vor; ich vermag nämlich nicht zu glauben, Wulfstans stil sei nichts anderes als Ælfricstil plus häufiges *for ure þearfe, agen*, etc.'

31. Liebermann, *Gesetze*, i. 400, 444, 453.

32. I will make here only a few comments based on rhythmical evidence.

(*a*) Napier i: 3^{19} to the end (including what is in E) is very characteristic of Wulfstan. The rest is hardly his.

(*b*) Napier xvi: all except the very end is in a shakier rhythm than normal. The passage 98^{8}–101^{13} is unlikely to be his, and the homily up to that point, if put together by him, probably consists mainly of material he has revised only slightly.

(*c*) Napier xviii: this is certainly Wulfstan's work; it stands in the same relation to Ælfric's original as Napier vii does to viii (see note 20). For the Ælfric text see J. M. Kemble, *Salomon and Saturnus*, pp. 120 ff., and F. Kluge, *Angelsächsisches Lesebuch* (2nd ed.), p. 76.

(*d*) Napier xxiii: this is probably all his. MS. K has some passages, not found elsewhere, which also seem to be by Wulfstan. The material elsewhere preserved by K alone (e.g. in xxiv and xxvi) usually has an authentic ring.

(*e*) Napier xl: the rhythmical evidence would suggest that Wulfstan contributed the parts from the beginning to 182^{8} and from 188^{11} to the end.

(*f*) Napier xli: stylistically this resembles vi (see note 27) and I see no reason for doubting that Wulfstan wrote it.

(*g*) Napier xlii: the part from 202^{4} to the end is probably by Wulfstan.

(*h*) An analysis of the rhythmical patterns of the prose of *Polity* puts Wulfstan's authorship of it beyond reasonable doubt, and similar analysis confirms Miss Whitelock's views (see note 1) about the part Wulfstan played in the composition of the laws of Cnut. It also corroborates her opinion that he wrote EGu, and Jost's that he wrote the two *Chronicle* poems of 959 and 975 (see note 6).

Additional note. In the original version of this paper, in note 8 the word *sige* was inadvertently omitted between *mid* and *gesæt* (p. 131 line 13); attention to this was called by Professor John Pope in 'Ælfric and the Old English version of the Ely privilege', *England before the Norman Conquest . . . presented to Dorothy Whitelock*, ed. Peter Clemoes and Kathleen Hughes (Cambridge, 1971), p. 107. Some stylistic matters bearing on the establishment of the Wulfstan canon (cf. note 32 above) were more fully discussed by the author in his review of Karl Jost, *Wulfstanstudien* (Schweizer Anglistische Arbeiten, 23, Bern 1950) in *English Studies* 32 (1951), 163–8.

ANGLO-SAXON ROYAL GENEALOGIES

By KENNETH SISAM

Fellow of the Academy

AMONG the Germanic peoples, the Anglo-Saxons alone have handed down a number of royal genealogies, recorded as early as the eighth and ninth centuries. For a period when evidence is scanty they offer materials to historians and ethnologists, as well as to investigators of mythology and legend: at the very beginning of *Beowulf*, the student is faced with a genealogical problem. So it is not surprising that they have been examined by a succession of scholars eminent in Germanic studies:[1] Jakob Grimm, Kemble, Müllenhoff, Plummer, W. H. Stevenson, Olrik, Chadwick, R. W. Chambers. The inclusion of several Anglo-Saxon genealogies in the *Historia Brittonum* of Nennius has attracted the attention of another distinguished group:[2] Zimmer, Mommsen, Duchesne, Thurneysen, F. Lot. There are besides a number of special studies,[3] and many incidental references by workers in related subjects.

Yet anybody who wishes to form a general idea of the nature and value of these genealogies will not find the way easy. If the incidental references to them are assembled, they leave an

[1] J. Grimm *Deutsche Mythologie*, 1835, Appendix. J. M. Kemble *Über die Stammtafel der Westsachsen*, 1836; and Postscript to the Preface of his second edition of *Beowulf* ii (1837), pp. 1 ff. K. Müllenhoff *Beovulf*, 1889. C. Plummer *Two of the Saxon Chronicles Parallel*, 1892, esp. ii, pp. 1 ff. W. H. Stevenson *Asser's Life of King Alfred*, 1904, esp. pp. 152 ff. A. Olrik *Danmarks Heltedigtning*, 1903–10, with the revised and modified translation by L. M. Hollander *The Heroic Legends of Denmark*, New York 1919, esp. ch. viii. H. M. Chadwick *The Origin of the English Nation*, 1907. R. W. Chambers *Beowulf, an Introduction*, 2nd edn. 1932, esp. pp. 195 ff.

[2] H. Zimmer *Nennius Vindicatus*, 1893. Th. Mommsen *Historia Brittonum* in *Mon. Germ. Hist. Auct. Ant.* xiii (1894). L. Duchesne *Revue Celtique* xv (1894), pp. 174 ff. R. Thurneysen, esp. his review of Zimmer in *Zeitschrift für deutsche Philologie* xxviii (1895), pp. 80 ff. F. Lot *Nennius et l'Historia Brittonum*, 1934.

[3] e.g. R. Henning 'Sceaf und die westsächsische Stammtafel', *Zeitschrift für deutsches Altertum* xli (1897), pp. 156 ff. G. H. Wheeler 'The Genealogy of the Early West Saxon Kings', *English Historical Review* xxxvi (1921), pp. 161 ff. Erna Hackenberg *Die Stammtafeln der angelsächsischen Königreiche*, Berlin 1918, (factual and valuable). A Brandl 'Die Urstammtafel der Westsachsen und das *Beowulf-Epos*', *Archiv für das Studium der Neueren Sprachen*, &c., cxxxvii (1918), pp. 6 ff.

impression of incoherence which the longer studies do not altogether remove; and the documents themselves are baffling. Bare lists of names are intractable material, because they afford few sure holds from which criticism can work. It happens too that some of the genealogies appear in literary texts whose composition and authority is the subject of controversy: the *Anglo-Saxon Chronicle*, the *Historia Brittonum*, Asser's *Life of Alfred*. One soon becomes involved in a tangle of possibilities, where the temptation to be over-ingenious is always present, with the doubt whether time is well spent on these old names of kings or shadows.

Still I have persisted in a fresh attempt, working from the documents and using the critical literature as a subsequent check. When dealing with composite sources like the *Anglo-Saxon Chronicle*, I have tried not to base arguments on disputed theories of their origin and date; for it seemed best to segregate the genealogies, see what light they throw on the development of the literary texts into which they have been absorbed, and submit to correction by the results of other independent lines of investigation.

I

The Early Documents

(i) Bede, who finished his *History* in 731, gives the genealogy of Hengest and Horsa (*Hist. Eccl.* i. 15); of Hengest's descendants, the kings of Kent: *Aedilberct–Irminric–Octa–Oeric* or *Oisc–Hengist* (ii. 5); and Eorpwald's descent through Redwald and Tytil from Wuffa, the king of the East Angles who gave his name to the Wuffings (ii. 15). As alliteration is a feature of many Anglo-Saxon genealogies, and is sometimes used to test their authenticity, it is worth noting that the last has no alliteration. The second has vowel alliteration up to Hengist, and shows a use of alternative names *Oisc*: *Oeric* likely to confuse later records. The first also isolates the names of Hengist and Horsa in the alliteration: 'Hengist et Horsa . . . erant filii Uictgilsi, cuius pater Uitta, cuius pater Uecta, cuius pater Uoden, de cuius stirpe multarum provinciarum regium genus originem duxit.'

(ii) The Vespasian Group. An early collection of chronological materials, including lists of popes and English bishops, and royal genealogies, is found in three pre-Conquest manuscripts:

Vespasian B VI, CCCC 183, and Tiberius B V. The twelfth-century copy in *Textus Roffensis* is closely related to the Tiberius text.

Vespasian B VI, ff. 104–9 is a Mercian fragment, probably from Lichfield,[1] where it remained throughout Anglo-Saxon times. From the episcopal lists it can be dated fairly closely to the year 812. It contains tabular genealogies of the kings of Northumbria (Deira and Bernicia), Mercia, Lindsey, Kent, and East Anglia, in that order, all going back to Woden and Frealaf, and the Lindsey list still farther back to Geat. These have been printed in Sweet's *Oldest English Texts* pp. 167 ff. under the heading 'Genealogies (Northumbrian?)', which has led to the mistaken belief that it is a Northumbrian document. It is a Mercian compilation, reflecting Mercian political interests, and only the Mercian kings are brought up to date with Cenwulf (796–821), who was reigning when the manuscript was written. The royal lists begin and end: 'Haec sunt genelogiae per partes Brittaniae regum regnantium per diuersa loca.'

CCCC 183 contains similar lists, and regnal tables for Northumbria and Mercia, together with Bede's Life of St. Cuthbert in prose and verse. The lists of bishops for Canterbury (but not Rochester), and for Winchester, Sherborne, Wells, and Crediton, are brought up to around 937, so that it is fairly certainly a South-Western manuscript written about that date. Script and small initials are reminiscent of MS. Junius 27, a psalter with Winchester connexions, but the contemporary bishops of Winchester are inaccurately recorded. At the beginning is the picture of a king offering a book to a saint, which Plummer first connected with the statement in Simeon of Durham[2] that Athelstan gave the Life of Cuthbert in verse and prose to the shrine of St. Cuthbert, then at Chester le-Street. This attribution is confirmed by additions relating to the cult of the saint, a short inventory of church vessels in early eleventh-century Northumbrian, and the record of a gift by Walchear bishop of Durham (1071–80). Apparently the manuscript was prepared for the occasion. After the royal genealogies contained in Vespasian B VI, it gives

[1] K. Sisam *Cynewulf* (Brit. Acad. 1933), p. 6. For a description of the MS. see *Catalogue of Ancient MSS. in the British Museum, Part II Latin*, 1884, pp. 79 ff.; and A. Wilmart *Revue Bénédictine*, 1934, pp. 47 ff.

[2] Rolls Series i, p. 211; see Plummer *Baedae Opera Historica* i, p. cxlvii n.; and for more detail, J. A. Robinson *The Times of St. Dunstan*, pp. 51 ff. M. R. James gives a full description in his *Catalogue of the MSS. of Corpus Christi College, Cambridge*, i, pp. 426 ff. where the genealogies are printed.

the pedigree of Ine of Wessex, which it is convenient to divide into two parts: (i) Ine–Cenred–Ceolwald–Cuþwulf–Cuþwine–Celin–Cynric–Creoda–Cerdic; and (ii) (Cerdic)–Aluca–Giwis–Brand–Bældæg–Woden–Frealaf.

Tiberius B v is, at least in this part, a Christ Church, Canterbury, compilation of the time of Archbishop Sigeric (990–4),[1] whose Itinerary from Rome immediately follows the genealogies. It contains lists similar to those in CCCC 183, but adds before the genealogies a regnal table, without genealogical indications, of West Saxon kings from Cerdic to Æthelred; after the genealogies and the pedigree of Ine, it has a list of West Saxon kings beginning 'Eadweard and Eadmund and Æðelred æðelingas syndon Eadgares suna cyninges' and ending with the long West Saxon pedigree going back to Adam which will be discussed later.[2]

The relation of these three manuscripts is clear: Tiberius B v is not copied from CCCC 183,[3] and both derive from a copy (CT) very closely related to Vespasian B vi, but differing from it in some details like the bad spelling *Ceonreowing* (Vesp. *Cynreowing*) in Cenwulf's pedigree; the displacement of Æthelbald's line among the Mercian genealogies (which in CCCC 183 seems to be only a matter of columnar arrangement); and the inclusion of Ine's pedigree. The genealogies contain no clear evidence that this lost copy was independent of Vespasian B vi.[4]

[1] On Sigeric's dates see K. Sisam *Review of English Studies* vii (1931), pp. 15 f.

[2] These lists are printed by T. Wright *Reliquiæ Antiquæ* ii (1843), pp. 169 ff. On the list beginning 'Eadweard etc.', which is found also in *Textus Roffensis* ed. Hearne, 1720, pp. 61 f., see W. H. Stevenson's *Asser*, p. 158 and note. It goes with Chronicles B, C, D against the Parker MS., Asser, and Æthelweard. The statement that Ine 'getimbrade þæt beorhte mynster æt Glæstingabyrig' suggests that it was prepared or retouched at Glastonbury. This would fit well with its appearance in MS. Tiberius B v, if that MS. was put together at Christ Church soon after Dunstan's death: it contains a list of the abbots of Glastonbury entered in the margin of f. 23*b* as a supplement to the episcopal and genealogical tables. The series of West Saxon kings in this document from Edgar's reign includes Creoda as the son of Cerdic (see below, p. 196). It was often copied in Scandinavian texts, e.g. in the Prologue to the *Prose Edda*; and from a sentence in it: 'se Scef wæs Noes sunu and he wæs innan þære Earce geboren', they produced the name *Sescef*, as Sievers noted (Paul and Braune's *Beiträge* xvi (1892), pp. 361 ff.). Evidently they knew no tradition of Sceaf. The Scandinavian copies agree with Tiberius B v against *Textus Roffensis* in omitting Tætwa and Hwala among Woden's ancestors.

[3] It has not the confusion in the Bernician branches noted below, p. 183.

[4] In the East Anglian list, Sweet prints the strange form *T(y)twianing* (as if written with *wyn*), where CT has *Tytman*, which is probably right (Florence of Worcester *Tytmon*, miswritten *Titinon* in the late MSS. of Nennius). This

That Ine's pedigree was not originally part of the collection is indicated by its place at the end of the pedigrees in CCCC 183 and Tiberius B v; and by its absence from the earliest manuscript Vespasian B vi, where the colophon marks the completeness of the text. This manuscript, written about 812, contains evidence that the royal genealogies were retouched in the last decade of the eighth century. At that time there were good reasons for neglecting the kings of Wessex in a Mercian compilation. Since Ine's day Wessex had been ruled by many kings whose pedigrees were obscure to the West Saxons themselves, if we may judge from the Chronicle. The latest of these, Beorhtric, had married Offa's daughter Eadburg, and with Offa's help had driven Ecgberht, the heir of Ine's family, into exile. Until Ecgberht had established himself after his accession in 802, and perhaps until his heirs were established, a Mercian genealogist might well disregard the hereditary claims of the West Saxon kings. But as Ecgberht's influence increased, the lack of a West Saxon genealogy would be felt even in Mercia. At a guess, I should name his time (802–39) as the likeliest for the addition of his ancestor Ine's pedigree to the collection.

The episcopal lists in CCCC 183 supply evidence of the time at which the Mercian compilation came South. Whereas the lists for Canterbury, Winchester, and the South-Western sees are brought up to about 937, those for Lichfield and other Midland bishoprics represent the position about 840: so presumably a parent manuscript of CCCC 183 and Tiberius B v (I shall sometimes use CT for any parent of these two) came South after 840 and may influence Southern documents after that date. That it was influential is suggested by the association of CCCC 183 with King Athelstan, and of Tiberius B v with Glastonbury and Canterbury Cathedral.

The absence from CCCC 183, copied at the height of West Saxon power, of any pedigrees for West Saxon kings later than Ine, is a sign that in this part it reproduces an early source. One could wish for sure evidence that Ine's pedigree, which has the characteristic Woden–Frealaf ending of the Mercian compilation, was incorporated in it before it reached Wessex; and there is some confirmation in the forms *Creoda* and *Celin*. *Creoda* (CT)

would be decisive against derivation of CT from Vespasian B vi, but the MS. is rubbed here, and I am not satisfied that Sweet's reading is correct. The bishops' lists in CCCC 183 contain some evidence, e.g. the older form *Oiðil-wald* (Vespasian *Oeðil-*), that they are not derived from Vespasian B vi in the direct line.

should be *Crĭda* in standard West Saxon: all manuscripts of the Chronicle have *Crida* (*Cryda* Otho B xi according to Nowell and Wheloc) in the annal for 593, which possibly records the death of the Mercian king of the same name. *Celin* (CT), as Bede explains (*Hist. Eccl.* ii. 5) and recorded examples confirm, is the Anglian form of West Saxon *Ceawlin.*[1]

(iii) The Historia Brittonum[2] is a bewildering compilation of old and new materials which was assembled and worked over by Nennius in the first half of the ninth century. One reviser (whether Nennius or Samuel) omitted the genealogical section: 'Set cum inutiles magistro meo, id est Beulano presbytero, uisae sunt genealogiae Saxonum et aliarum genealogiae gentium, nolui eas scribere' (ch. 63). The version which preserves them survives in late eleventh- and early twelfth-century manuscripts and contains lists for Bernicia, Kent down to Ecgberht (673), East Anglia, Mercia down to Ecgfrith (whose reign began and ended in 796), and Deira,[3] in that order; but not for Lindsey or Wessex.

These genealogies are related to the corresponding lists in Vespasian B vi, and the following points of comparison deserve notice:

(*a*) The Vespasian lists begin with the latest king in the trunk pedigree, and work backwards: e.g.

Eduine Aelling
Aelle Yffing, &c.;

and when the succession passes to a branch line, they start from the latest king and work backwards to the trunk pedigree, e.g.

Ecgfrið Offing
Offa Ðincfriðing, &c.[4]

[1] On the forms and etymology, which are difficult, see O. S. Anderson *Old English Material in the Leningrad MS. of Bede's Ecclesiastical History*, Lund 1941, p. 92.

[2] Ed. Mommsen in *Mon. Germ. Hist.* (1894); F. Lot *Nennius et l'Historia Brittonum*, 1934.

[3] Followed by some confused branch lists that should be attached to the main Bernician line.

[4] Given the method, and the information whether from written or oral sources, the presentation found in the Vespasian B vi group is inevitable. When the trunk pedigree ceases to provide the king in the direct line, it naturally ends. When a branch ceases to provide the king, it also ends. R. W. Chambers *Beowulf, an Introduction*, p. 196, relies on the argument that a written pedigree must have been drawn up during the reign of the latest king

In the *Historia Brittonum*, where the extant manuscripts do not use the tabular form, the trunk lists begin with the remotest ancestor (in this case Woden): e.g. 'UUoden genuit Beldeg, genuit Beornec, &c.' But the Mercian branches follow the English order, indicating that it was original, at least in the Mercian list: e.g. 'Ecgfrid filius Offa, filius Duminfert [*sic*], &c.' The more natural form of Vespasian B vi makes it easy to add names at the remote end of a pedigree, the more artificial order usual in the *Historia* is convenient for adding recent names.

(*b*) The extant manuscripts of the genealogies in the *Historia* show confusion of the Deiran with the Bernician line in the immediate descendants of Woden. This points to an earlier copy or source in which these lists stood side by side, as they do in Vespasian B vi. So the order in the *Historia* is not old, and may, like the omission of some names found in Vespasian B vi, be due to errors in transmission.

(*c*) The lists in the *Historia* start from Woden, not from Frealaf; they do not include the Mercian king Cenwulf who succeeded Ecgfrith in 796; and at least one name *Soemil* (Vesp. *Soemel*) keeps an older spelling. Their source, then, seems to have been a form slightly earlier than that of Vespasian B vi.[1] They also contain two names which are not in the Vespasian group of manuscripts, but are in Florence of Worcester's lists: *Gueagon* (Fl. *Waga*) as the son of *Guedolgeat* (*Wađolgeot*) in the Mercian pedigree, and *Sguerthing* instead of *Uestorualcna* in the Deiran.[2]

in a recorded line, but it has force only if a descendant of that king succeeded him. Of the latest kings in the four Northumbrian and four Mercian lines or branches included in Vespasian B vi, none was in fact succeeded by his son; so that a modern historian, using this form of pedigree, would take the same latest names for his starting-points.

[1] In *Duminfert* [*sic*] the second element *-fert* for *-ferđ* shows that Nennius was not copying direct from Vespasian B vi which has *đincfriđ*. That CCCC 183 has *đingferþ* here is not necessarily significant; but there is some special relation between the contents of that MS. and the *Historia Brittonum*. Unlike Vespasian B vi it contains the Northumbrian regnal table which Nennius uses at chs. 63 f. It also begins a collection of computus material, &c. (some of which is found in Vespasian B vi) with the note that the Saxons were called in by Wyrtgeorn cccxlviiii years after Christ's Passion, during the consulship of Gratianus and Equitius. This appears in the *Historia* ch. 31, and has been the despair of editors: see F. Lot in his edition p. 172 n.; and Chadwick's objections to the general opinion that CCCC 183 borrows from the *Historia*, reported by M. R. James in his *Catalogue of the MSS. of Corpus Christi College, Cambridge*, i, p. 439 n.

[2] *Waga* may be a short form of *Wađolgeot*. *Swerting* is an epic name (*Beowulf* 1203), but in the *Historia* there is one clear example of the patronymic in *-ing* treated as if it were a primary name: *Eadlbald* filius *Alguing* for

Zimmer's contention[1] that English genealogies were already part of the *Historia Brittonum* at the end of the seventh century, and were later retouched, has not escaped challenge. Contact with a Mercian source not older than 796 is proved by the inclusion of Ecgfrith's line; the availability of such a Mercian source for all the lists is established by Vespasian B VI; and none of the many traces of an English original in the name-forms of the *Historia* requires a date earlier than 796. But the best ground for a decision is the selection of royal houses: Northumbria, Mercia, Lindsey, Kent, East Anglia in Vespasian B VI are what we might expect in Mercia under Offa;[2] and, except for Lindsey, the *Historia* gives the same pedigrees. A century earlier there were more kings to choose from; the outlook was different; and it would be hard to neglect Wulfhere's recent power in Mercia, or Ine's predominance in the South. I conclude that the genealogical tables were incorporated into the *Historia Brittonum* at the end of the eighth or in the first half of the ninth century, which is the period of Nennius's activity.

There remains the genealogy of Horsa and Hengest, through Woden to Geata, in a narrative part (ch. 31) of the *Historia Brittonum* which is generally thought to be old and which is fortunately preserved in the earliest manuscript. To this I shall return (p. 167 below).

(iv) THE WEST SAXON REGNAL TABLE. Bede refers to official reckonings of the reigns of English kings.[3] The earliest extant regnal list is that for Northumbria which appears at the end of the Moore MS. (*c.* 737) of his History,[4] and lists for Northumbria and Mercia are included in CT. Where the succession was regular from father to son, these lists correspond with the royal pedigree; and there was a risk of confusion, for a compiler of

Aeðelbald Alwing of Vespasian B VI. Florence makes *Swaerta* the grandfather of Westorualcna, but he sometimes built up what he could collect from his sources into orderly lists; see Plummer in his edition of the Chronicle ii, p. 2.

[1] *Nennius Vindicatus* 1893. Mommsen, in his edition p. 117, agrees that the genealogies were first assembled in the seventh century; but see F. Lot in his edition pp. 91 ff.

[2] For the historical background, see Stenton *Anglo-Saxon England*, ch. vii.

[3] Cunctis regum tempora computantibus (*Hist. Eccl.* iii. 1; cf. iii. 9). The Laws of Wihtred of Kent are dated in the fifth year of his reign, i.e. 695; cf. W. Levison *England and the Continent in the Eighth Century*, 1946, pp. 84 f., 270 ff.

[4] See P. H. Blair in *Chadwick Memorial Studies*, 1950, pp. 245 ff.

pedigrees, when dealing with remote times, might assume that successive kings were father and son, and so produce a false series.

The West Saxon regnal table includes two genealogies, Cerdic to Woden and Æthelwulf to Cerdic, which I shall call R^A and R^B. There are several copies,[1] but for present purposes three are enough: a Fragment in BM. MS. Addit. 23211 written in Alfred's reign;[2] the copy which prefaces the Parker Chronicle, written in or soon after 892; and another in Cambridge University Library MS. Kk. 3. 18[3] of the second half of the eleventh century. No one of these derives from another.

The Fragment begins with the years of Ecgberht's reign, continues with the accession of Æthelwulf, traces his pedigree to Cerdic (R^B), and then notes the reigns of his sons up to the accession of Alfred. R^B runs: Æðelwulf–Ecgberht–Ealhmund–Eaba–Eoppa–Ingild–Coenred–Ceolwald–Cuðuulf–Ceaulin–Cynnric–Criodo–Ceardic. As it contains the form *Eaba* for *Eafa*, it is usually said to be based on a record written as early as 750;[4] but medial and final *b* for *f* occurs in common words as late as 832 in Kentish charters,[5] so that it is not evidence of a written record before the ninth century. Between *Cynnric* and *Ceardic* the

[1] Stemmata in A. S. Napier *Modern Language Notes* xii (1897), pp. 110 f.; and E. Hackenberg *Die Stammtafeln*, &c., p. 8. N. R. Ker *Medieval Libraries of Great Britain*, 1941, p. 112 n. notes that Napier's MS. BM. Addit. 34652 f. 2 originally belonged to MS. Otho B XI. Professor Bruce Dickins in *The Genealogical Preface to the Anglo-Saxon Chronicle*, Cambridge 1952, prints the texts of the Parker MS., Tiberius A III (a leaf from Tiberius A VI with continuation to Edward the Martyr's reign), CCCC 383 (incomplete), and some excerpts entered in CCCC 138 by Robert Record in the sixteenth century. These last appear to be from MS. Kk. 3. 18.

[2] Printed by Sweet *O.E.T.* p. 179. This Fragment is one of two small leaves that have been used in a binding. It is headed by two lines of Roman numerals from i to xxviiii, written later than the text which begins: 'rice 7 heold xxxvii wint̄ 7 vii monað; ond ða feng æ[ðelwulf], &c.'; the bracketed letters were cut away when the leaf was used for binding. The lower half of the page is occupied by the East Saxon genealogies also printed by Sweet, p. 179, and they completed this part of the text: the verso begins *Versus de Lun̄* and ends with the heading *Versus de diebus*, so that more computus material in Latin followed. The other leaf, from the same MS., contains on both sides a fragment of the *Old English Martyrology*, ed. G. Herzfeld, E.E.T.S., 1900, with well-marked Mercian forms.

[3] In J. Schipper's *König Alfreds Übersetzung von Bedas Kirchengeschichte*, 1899, pp. 702 f.; and in T. Miller's edition (E.E.T.S.) i, pp. 486 f.

[4] Since Napier *M.L.N.* xii, pp. 110 f.

[5] Sweet *O.E.T.*, charters 38–40. *Liaba* for *Leofa* occurs in Alfred's charter of 873, Sweet's no. 32, and *ob* for *of* occurs in the Hatton MS. of *Pastoral Care*

fragment has *Criodo*,[1] and forms like this, as Sweet noted, indicate influence of or copying from a non-West Saxon dialect.

MS. Kk. 3. 18, a careful copy of Bede's History in the Old English version, has a complete form of the document, with Cerdic's pedigree (R^A) near the beginning: Cerdic–Elesa–⟨Esla⟩[2] – Gewis – Wig – Freawine – Freoðogar – Brond – Bældæg – Woden. Next it gives the length of reign for Cerdic and his successors: 'his son Cynric', Ceawlin, Ceol, Ceolwulf, &c. It does not say (as the Parker copy does) that Æthelheard and Beorhtric were descended from Cerdic, and the omission may possibly be deliberate, for Æthelheard's right was obscure,[3] and Beorhtric was the rival of Ecgberht. In tracing Æthelwulf's pedigree (R^B) to Cerdic, it adds the information, related to the Chronicle annal for 718, that Ine, Cuthburg, and Cwenburg, besides Ingild, were children of Cenred. It has the old spelling *Eaba*, and the error *Celming*, *Celm* where we should expect *Ceaulining*, *Ceaulin*. Creoda appears as Cerdic's son in this pedigree.

The Parker Chronicle MS., copied in or soon after 892, is given third place as a reminder that its greater age does not make it a better witness than MS. Kk. 3. 18. The copy of the regnal table it contains has the same names, not omitting *Esla*, in the pedigree of Cerdic (R^A). In the list of reigns it omits Ceawlin carelessly, and says both of Æthelheard and Beorhtric that their kin goes back to Cerdic. In the pedigree of Æthelwulf (R^B) it agrees with Kk. 3. 18 against the Fragment in the interpolation of Ine, Cuthburg, and Cwenburg, and in the error *Celming*, *Celm*; but it differs from Kk. 3. 18 and the Fragment in adopting the later spelling *Eafa*, and in the omission of Creoda. The omission is intentional, for the Parker MS. drops Creoda again in the Chronicle pedigree of Æthelwulf at 855, where other manuscripts of the Chronicle preserve it. In both places the purpose was to get rid of a name inconsistent with the Chronicle narrative, which makes Cynric the son of Cerdic.[4]

304/9 in the last decade of the ninth century. For Mercia, see the Worcester charter of Offa 791–6, Sweet's no. 15.

[1] The spelling *io* for the diphthong in *Criodo* was giving place to later *eo* in Alfred's time; see Sievers, *Zum angelsächsischen Vocalismus*, 1900, pp. 39 f.

[2] The omission is probably due to a scribal error, but it is repeated in some other copies, e.g. the early twelfth-century fragment at the end of MS. CCCC 383.

[3] The Chronicle gives no indication of Æthelheard's claim; see below, pp. 194 f.

[4] See below, p. 157 and pp. 195 f.

Clearly the Parker and Cambridge University Library manuscripts derive from a copy (PCa.) made in Alfred's reign, which differed from the Fragment in having the added names Ine, Cuthburg, and Cwenburg, and the error *Celming*, *Celm*. So it ought not to be assumed that the part missing from the Fragment was identical with PCa. in the pedigree of Cerdic (R^A). Both the Fragment and PCa. derive from an earlier manuscript, still of Alfred's reign, which read in the pedigree of Æthelwulf (R^B): Ingild – Coenred – Ceolwald – Cuðuulf – Cuðuine – Celin – Cynric–Criodo–Ceardic. But this, with Ingild instead of his brother Ine, is the pedigree of Ine to Cerdic in CT (above, p. 148). CT alone preserved the Anglian forms *Celin(in)g*, *Celin*[1] which account for the error *Celming*, *Celm* in the Parker MS., in Kk. 3. 18, and in most later copies of R^B. CT and this part of the Regnal Table represent a single document. And the indications are that the CT pedigree was incorporated into the Regnal Table, not extracted from it. The inclusion of long pedigrees in a regnal table is exceptional; and incorporation of a series of names from another source would explain its discrepancies from the list of reigns which precedes it. Besides, it is unlikely that an excerptor, working in the later ninth century with the Regnal Table before him, would choose just this piece of Æthelwulf's pedigree, adding only the name of Frealaf.

(v) *Asser's Life* of King Alfred was completed in 893, and survived until the Cotton fire of 1731 in a single manuscript, written about the year 1000.[2] In his classic edition W. H. Stevenson shows that Asser used a copy of the *Anglo-Saxon Chronicle* which differed in some details from the extant manuscripts, and in some appears to have been nearer the original. In the first chapter Asser gives an elaborate genealogy of the West Saxon kings from Alfred to Adam. To this I shall return,[2] noting here that it includes Creoda between Cerdic and Cynric, although in the next chapter Cynric is described as the son of Cerdic in accordance with the Chronicle narrative.

[1] I assume that *Celin* was rightly understood as *Ceaulin* in R^B in the Fragment, though the scribe was troubled by it, for he wrote *ceaulniing* (the first *i* altered from *n*?); but that it was not recognized by the scribe of the copy from which the Parker, Cambridge, and several other extant MSS. derive.

[2] On the date of the lost MS. see Stevenson's edition pp. xxxii ff. especially § 23 and footnotes; and K. Sisam in *Review of English Studies* vii (1931), p. 8 n. Nothing in the pedigree of Æthelwulf suggests that the work is later than Alfred's time.

(vi) *The Anglo-Saxon Chronicle*. For the text of the genealogies which appear in the annals of the Chronicle issued about 892, we have the evidence of the Parker MS. copied in or soon after that year at Winchester; of Otho B XI (*c.* 1025), a copy of the Parker MS. which Wheloc printed in 1643 before it was badly damaged by fire;[1] of the Abingdon version represented by Tiberius A VI (*c.* 1000) and Tiberius B I (*c.* 1050); and of the Northern version in the Worcester MS. Tiberius B IV (*c.* 1050).

The Northumbrian pedigrees given are: 547 Ida to Woden and Geat; 670 Oswiu to Ida-Eoppa; 685 Ecgfrith to Ida-Eoppa; 731 Ceolwulf to Ida-Eoppa; 738 Eadbryht to Leodwald who is in the previous lists. Under 560 the independent Deiran line of Ælle is traced to Woden. The Mercian pedigrees are: 626 Penda to Woden; 716 Æthelbald to Pybba, Penda's father; 755 Offa to Woden through Pybba. The Kentish line from Wihtred to Æthelberht is given under 694. These non-West Saxon pedigrees are based on the same materials as those of Vespasian B VI, and most differences seem to be due to carelessness in the Chronicle. So in Penda's pedigree (626), *Watholgeot* is missing and *Angeltheow* is substituted for *Angengeot*; in Ælle's (560), *Soemel* is omitted and the archetype seems to have had *Westerfalcna*, perhaps through misreading of the runic *wyn* as *f*; in Ceolwulf's (731), *Cuthwine* is preceded by the short form *Cutha*, as if that were the name of Cuthwine's son. Except that most of the lists stop at Woden, there is no decisive evidence of a relation with the *Historia Brittonum* against Vespasian B VI.

The West Saxon pedigrees, none of which occurs in Vespasian B VI, are: 552 Cynric–Cerdic to Woden; 597 Ceolwulf through Cynric–Cerdic to Woden; 611 Cynegils to Cynric; 674 Æscwine to Cynric–Cerdic; 676 Centwine to Ceolwulf; 685 Ceadwalla to Cynric–Cerdic; 688 Ine to Cynric–Cerdic. On Ine's abdication in 728[2] the pedigree of Oswald Ætheling is given. From that date up to and including 836 there is either no reference to the king's pedigree, or he is said to be of the kin of Cerdic. Then, under 855, Æthelwulf's lineage is traced back to Adam, and with this culmination of the genealogist's art, the Chronicle series ends.

[1] This is useful where the pedigrees in the Parker MS. have been erased. A distorted leaf of the MS. survives for Æthelwulf's pedigree of 855. Laurence Nowell's transcript of this MS. is now available in BM. Addit. 43703.

[2] I give the dates of annals from Plummer's print of the Parker MS. throughout without inquiring whether there are reasons, as here, for thinking them to be inaccurate.

II

The Genealogy of Æthelwulf

Having now surveyed the documents up to the end of the ninth century, I shall examine the genealogy of Æthelwulf, entered in the Chronicle under the year 855, in six sections: (1) up to Ingild; (2) Ingild (or his brother Ine) to Cerdic; (3) Cerdic to Woden; (4) Woden to Geat; (5) beyond Geat; (6) Biblical names. The names are usually cited from the Parker MS.

(1) *To Ingild*: Æþelwulf–Ecgbryht–Ealhmund–Eafa–Eoppa–Ingild. The Regnal Table (R^B) and Asser agree with the Chronicle. Of the names between Ecgberht and Ingild nothing is known, except a credible late tradition, recorded by a late-eleventh-century hand in the Canterbury Chronicle Domitian A VIII (= F) at 784, that this Ealhmund was king of Kent.

(2) *Ingild to Cerdic*: Ingild–Cenred–Ceolwald–Cuþa–Cuþwine – Ceawlin – Cynric (– Creoda) – Cerdic. Creoda is in the Abingdon (B, C) and Northern (D) versions; and his omission from the Parker MS. is due to a late-ninth-century editor who aimed at bringing the genealogy into line with the Chronicle narrative.[1] Asser, who preserves the older form *Coenred* for *Cenred* of the Parker MS., agrees in this part with the archetype of the Chronicle which was circulated about 892. Both agree with R^B in the Regnal Table, except that they have the short form *Cuþa* for *Cuþwulf*. And we have seen (p. 155 above) that in this series of names R^B agrees exactly with CT, and probably derives from it. The consensus is important because the other relevant West Saxon pedigrees in the archetype of the Chronicle of 892, viz. those at 597, 674, 685, 688, are inconsistent with one another, and Æthelwulf's pedigree from Ingild to Cerdic could not be deduced from them.[2] So this part of the 'official' royal pedigree of Alfred's time derives from an independent tradition, of which

[1] See above p. 296 for the omission of Creoda from R^B of the Regnal Table in the Parker MS.; cf. pp. 195 f. below.

[2] Plummer *Two Saxon Chronicles* ii, p. 2: 'It is lost labour to try and reconcile these inconsistencies.' G. H. Wheeler *English Historical Review* xxxvi uses these annals to construct a pedigree (p. 167) of the West Saxon kings after Cerdic, but is obliged to make several doubtful assumptions. E. Hackenberg *Die Stammtafeln*, &c., gets a very different table (p. 3) from the same materials. The evidence is insufficient to establish the true relationships of the kings who claimed to be descendants of Cerdic.

CT seems to give the earliest form. That tradition is not obviously wrong; and its first clear appearance in Æthelwulf's pedigree at 855 in the Chronicle of 892 fits, though it does not establish, the suggestion that the pedigree of Ine to Cerdic was in CT when it came south after 840 (above p. 149).

(3) *Cerdic to Woden*: Cerdic–Elesa–Esla–Giwis–Wig–Freawine–Friþogar–Brond–Bældæg–Woden. Here the pedigrees under 552 and 597 agree with 855. R. W. Chambers, who gives the latest survey of the genealogies, brings out the alliterative structure by printing:

> (Cynric Cerdicing), Cerdic Elesing,
> Elesa Esling, Esla Giwising,
> Giwis Wiging, Wig Freawining,
> Freawine Friðogaring, Friðogar Bronding,
> Brond Bældæging, Bældæg Wodening.[1]

He comments: 'These lines are probably very old. . . . Note, that not only do the names alliterate, but the alliteration is perfect. Every line attains double alliteration in the first half, with one alliterating word only in the second half. The lines must go back to times when lists of royal ancestors, both real and imaginary, had to be arranged in correct verse; times when such things were recorded by memory rather than by writing. They are pre-literary, and were doubtless chanted by retainers of the West-Saxon kings in heathen days.'

Yet this perfection raises doubts. As late as 1066 verses like

> Cyning cystum god clæne and milde
> Eadward se æðela eðel bewerede

were composed with triple alliteration, and there is no good evidence that uniform triple alliteration was ancient practice. Again, no other Anglo-Saxon genealogy shows the arrangement by regularly changing alliterative pairs; and it was certainly not the custom of Wessex in historical times. From Cerdic to the end of the seventh century, most West Saxon kings' names alliterate on *C*. For some reason Cenred did not become king, though he survived to advise Ine on his code of laws;[2] and, for some reason

[1] *Beowulf, An Introduction* (1932), p. 316.

[2] See the preface to *Ine's Laws*, ed. Liebermann i, p. 88. It is likely enough, in view of the family history, that Cenred had entered the religious life; cf. Liebermann *Gesetze* iii, p. 67; but the choice of names for his sons still needs explanation. Possibly there was danger in being an ostensible clairnant to the throne.

he broke away from the *C* alliteration in naming his sons Ine and Ingild, while retaining it for his daughters Cuthburg and Cwenburg. As a consequence, West Saxon and English kings' names have vowel alliteration from the year 802, when Cenred's descendant Ecgberht recovered the throne, till the line ended with Edgar the Atheling after the Norman Conquest. Given continuous hereditary succession, it was not hard to maintain this tradition; Æthelwulf named his sons Æthelbald, Æthelbryht, Æthelred, and Ælfred, and they succeeded in turn. But by what foresight could it be arranged, in the troubled days of migration and conquest, that the names of successive kings would make such perfect verse? We should have to suppose that some ancestor—Brand for instance—noticed that his name made a verse with those of his father Bældæg and his grandfather Woden; and, to provide the opportunity for a second verse, avoided a name beginning with *B* for that one of his sons who was to be ancestor of the West Saxon kings. Then that son, Frithogar, had to prepare the first half of a verse for himself by giving his son a name like *Freawine*, with initial *F*, and so on. Even if we discard the theory that kings were elected it is unlikely that early history was planned in this way. But the alternative is that the perfect verse pedigree is wholly or partly fictitious.

Here are three extracts from recorded genealogies:

UUoden	Woden	Woden
Belde⟨g⟩	Bældæg	Bældæg
Brond	Brand	Brand
Geuuis	Giwis	Benoc
Elesa	Aluca	Aloc
Cerdic	Cerdic	Angenwit [*sic*]

The first is the text of Asser, confirmed by the transcripts, before Stevenson's standard edition, following Wise (1722), conflated it with the 855 pedigree of Æthelwulf. The second is from the pedigree of Ine in CT (CCCC 183 agreeing with Tiberius B v) which has cropped up so often already as a probable source. With this support the manuscript text of Asser must stand. Evidently he had before him a version of the 855 pedigree, which in this part corresponded name by name with the pedigree from Ine to Woden in CT; which lacked the extraordinary alliterative regularity of the Chronicle list from Cerdic to Woden; and which is prima facie an earlier form of that list. Then either he transcribed a pedigree which was the basis of the Chronicle list, or he used a copy of the Chronicle which contained the 855 entry in an earlier form. Since the 855 annal is known to us only from the version circulated in 892, there is no evidence that it existed in exactly the same form before that date.[1]

Any way through the surface of a major historical source deserves to be explored; so at this point I shall digress, using conjecture to avoid an impasse.

The third column above is an extract from the pedigree of the Northumbrian king Ida as given in the Chronicle under 547. Its correspondence with the others is the more remarkable because *Aloc* represents *Alusa* of the Vespasian group, and *Aluson* of the *Historia Brittonum*.[2] Historians and ethnologists have been puzzled to find the West Saxon genealogy joining with the Bernician in Brand–Bældæg–Woden,[3] where Seaxnet, the god of the Saxons, or at least a separate line from Woden might have been expected. Besides, according to the Chronicle, Ida may have been born before Cerdic died; yet in CT Brand is Cerdic's third and Ida's seventh ancestor. The explanation is, I believe, that Cerdic's pedigree was copied from this part of Ida's, and that *Giwis* was substituted afterwards to give it a West Saxon colouring. The substitution exactly at this point might be made because the association of Bernic with Bernicia was obvious. Bernic, who appears only in the pedigree of Ida, is generally

[1] Unfortunately the early Fragment of the Regnal Table does not contain Cerdic's pedigree (R^A). The slightly later complete texts have the longer alliterative form; but as they all derive from a version which shows retouching of R^B (p. 155 above), the possibility cannot be excluded that the shorter form originally stood in R^A, as in CT and Asser.

[2] The corresponding part of Ida's pedigree in the Vespasian group varies from the Chronicle, but the name-elements are the same: Woden–Beldæg–Be(o)rnic–Wegbrand–Ingibrand–Alusa–Angengeot. The *Historia Brittonum* has Woden–Beldeg–Beornec–Gechbrond (for *Guechbrond*, but *Brond* appears in the corrupted Deiran pedigree)–Aluson–Inguec [*sic*]. *Alusa* is otherwise unknown; so is *Elesa*, unless it has the same etymology as *Elsa* in *Widsith* 117 (see R. W. Chambers's note in his edition, p. 220). *Aluca* (Chronicle *Aloc*) is formed like *Baduca*, and occurs in the Durham *Liber Vitae*: see R. Müller *Untersuchungen über die Namen des nordhumbrischen Liber Vitae*, 1901, pp. 72 ff. and 140 f. It may have been substituted for *Alusa* in Cerdic's pedigree in CT as the more familiar form, and there is a possibility of confusing *s* and *c* in some early majuscule hands.

[3] Müllenhoff *Beovulf*, pp. 65 f. notes the similarity of names in the two pedigrees. Chadwick *Origin of the English Nation*, pp. 60 f. considers and rejects the possibility that names in Ida's pedigree may be borrowed from Cerdic's, but overlooks the converse possibility, although the Northumbrian pedigree is on record nearly a century before the West Saxon. E. Hackenberg *Die Stammtafeln*, &c., p. 115 suggests borrowing by the West Saxon pedigree.

regarded as an eponymous king derived from the name of the Bernicians,[1] and Giwis, who appears only in the pedigree of Cerdic, seems to be derived in the same way from *Gewisse*, a name for the West Saxons which was already antiquated in Bede's time[2] and which only the Welsh preserved.[3]

It is more likely that the Northumbrian names were adopted by some mistake than that they were deliberately taken by a pedigree-maker. In the extant manuscripts of the *Historia Brittonum* the Deiran pedigree begins Woden–Beldeyg–Brond–Siggar instead of Woden–Wegdæg–Siggar in the Vespasian group and the Chronicle (560); and in Tiberius B v, eight kings from the Bernician Regnal Table appear as predecessors of Offa in the Mercian table which stands beside it. But the condition for such erroneous transfers is that the lists affected should be adjacent (above p. 151); there is reason to think that West Saxon royal pedigrees were not included at all in early collections like Vespasian B vi; and it is unlikely that the Bernician and West Saxon lists would be side by side in any early systematic collection. Again, my conjecture requires a transfer from a version of Ida's pedigree for which the Chronicle itself is the witness.[4]

[1] See, e.g., J. E. Lloyd *A History of Wales* i (1911), p. 163.

[2] *Hist. Eccl.* iii, p. 7. Had Bede known of a leader Gewis from whom the people took their name, he would hardly have missed this opportunity of saying so. Cf. Plummer's note to Bede ii, pp. 88 f.; Chadwick *Origin of the English Nation*, p. 33 and p. 156 n.; Stevenson on Asser, pp. 161 f.

In the Chronicle *gi-*, which is an earlier form of the prefix *ge-*, occurs only in *Giwis*. Except for this name, the prefix is regularly *ge-* in early West Saxon, early Kentish, and Mercian (there are examples of *gi-* in the oldest glossaries which are composite). In Northumbrian *gi-* is common early and late; but the almost contemporary MSS. of Bede's *History* have already *Geuisse*. *Gi(wis)* occurs in Welsh records, and probably preserves the form the English prefix had when the name was borrowed. So *Giwis* in CT and the archetype of the Chronicle of 892 (855 Parker MS. *Giwising, Giwis*; 597 Parker MS. *Gewising, Giwis*; 552 MS. B *Giwising, Giwis*) is best explained by ultimate borrowing from a Welsh written source and mechanical copying of the unfamiliar name thereafter. Here and elsewhere (see below, p. 196 and n. 3 and p. 199) we have to do with the transcription of an old name, not with the recording of a living tradition. The lack of such a tradition is confirmed by the fanciful development of this antiquarian people-name. Besides a name for Cerdic's ancestor, *Giwisse* provided a name for the land of the English in *Textus Roffensis*, and for an emperor's daughter in Geoffrey of Monmouth: see Stevenson loc. cit.

[3] Asser's version of the pedigree has: *Geuuis, a quo Britones totam illam gentem Geguuis nominant*. On the use in Anglo-Saxon charters see Stevenson's note; and G. M. Young *Last Essays*, 1950, p. 128.

[4] The identical list in Simeon of Durham ii, p. 366, is presumably derived from the Chronicle.

To meet these conditions I propose a solution which is necessarily speculative. Ida ruled in the time of Cynric, who is always associated with Cerdic, as his son, in the Chronicle narrative. And it is common ground that before the Chronicle there were older collections of short annals.[1] Suppose two successive entries:

> Her Ida feng to rice on Norðhymbrum.
> Her Cynric Cerdicing[2] gefeaht wið Brettas æt Searobyrig.

If later the pedigree of Ida were added to the first entry in the margin, it might spill over so that the latter part of it lay alongside the second entry. By this accident, Cerdic might appear as *Alusing* (or the like), and be assigned the Woden end of Ida's pedigree in a later copy. Two entries very near to these do in fact come together in the finished Chronicle, at 547 and 552, the first ending with a pedigree of Ida, the second with a pedigree of Cerdic. And as Cerdic and Cynric are mentioned in six previous annals, there is no obvious reason why their pedigree should be entered just here unless it is connected with or suggested by Ida's. But if the appearance of these two pedigrees together is significant, the assumed manuscript collection of annals would not only be the source of Cerdic's genealogy: it would have a place somewhere in the pedigree of the Chronicle narrative, and represent the stage in which the longer royal pedigrees from the Mercian compilation, known to us from Vespasian B vi and CT, appeared as accretions to short annals. I must in any case assume that the alliterative pedigree of Cerdic which stands in the developed Chronicle at 552, instead of the short pedigree supposed to originate there, has been carried through by a ninth-century editor, so that 552, 597, and 855 should agree: in a point so important disagreement would be intolerable. There is yet another implication: that the pedigree of Ida beyond *Angenwit*, which stands at 547, is a replacement of the part transferred to

[1] e.g. Stenton *Anglo-Saxon England*, pp. 20 ff. and 682; Chadwick *Origin of the English Nation*, pp. 26 ff.; Plummer in his edition of the Chronicle ii, p. cxii n.

[2] The Kentish kings descended from Hengest's son Oisc were called *Oiscingas* (Bede ii. 5); the East Anglian kings descended from Wuffa were called *Wuffingas* (Bede ii. 15). Felix in his life of Guthlac, written before 749, mentions Penwald, a Mercian of royal lineage descended from Icil, and the much later Old English version says the family were called *Iclingas* (ed. P. Gonser, Heidelberg, 1909, p. 104). So to describe Cynric as *Cerdicing* leaves unprejudiced the question whether he was Cerdic's son or his grandson through Creoda, and may possibly explain how the conflicting traditions arose.

Cerdic,[1] and is not necessarily identical with it: the original entry may have had *Bernic* for *Benoc*, and *Alusa* (possibly *Ealusa* or a form nearer *Elesa*) not *Aloc*.

The reader who is invited to consider the probability of such a chain of hypotheses may well ask when and where Ida's pedigree is supposed to have been inserted in the annals and misdivided. But there is not enough evidence. The mistake might be made soon after or long after the insertion. If the indications noted at p. 149 above are accepted, this mistake had been recorded in Mercia by about 840; if they are found insufficient, there is no evidence of it until Alfred's time, when it seems to be deep-seated. As the place and time most likely for the insertion of Ida's pedigree, and its confusion with Cerdic's, I have in mind Wessex in Ecgberht's reign (802–39).

However this detailed conjecture may be judged, if the framework of Cerdic's pedigree is somehow borrowed from Ida's, his real pedigree was almost certainly unknown. But that conclusion hardly strengthens the argument that Cerdic himself is a fiction. This Saxon invader with a Celtic name, who is described as *ealdorman* 'leader' by the Chronicle itself (495), may well have been *dux ex virtute*, not *rex ex nobilitate*, and so have had no remembered pedigree.

If no more is granted than the priority of the shorter form of Cerdic's pedigree, on the evidence of Asser and CT, then the suspiciously regular alliterative form is a fiction elaborated from it, probably in the ninth century, and is not a very ancient mnemonic in verse.

But we need not suppose that it was specially composed for the Chronicle circulated in 892: more probably, the compiler or editor knew it as an existing alternative, and preferred it because it gave more names and was more elegant in literary form. The motives for such an elaboration were comparatively innocent: flattery of the ruling house, emulation of the long lines that joined other English kings to Woden, or the desire to find a place for distinguished names that were remembered in no other pedigree or Liber Vitae. Materials were always at hand, because a true series of royal fathers and sons would contain only some of the great hereditary kings,[2] and would exclude most of the tribal gods and heroes, as well as unattached names from the

[1] See below, p. 170.

[2] For example, Ine was not in the direct line from Ecgberht to Cerdic; and Penda's son Wulfhere was not in the main Mercian line. Nor is there any place in the Anglo-Saxon pedigrees for famous ancestors on the female side.

common stock of legend. Old names are the stuff from which fictitious pedigrees are made, and must not be regarded as evidence of genuineness.

The conditions favourable to the production and establishment of the elaborate versified form are easy to define. The added names should be remote and timeless, so that their order is at the convenience of the versifier; they should not conflict with other well-known pedigrees; and the framework into which they are fitted must not be firmly fixed in tradition, so that doubts are raised by dislocation of its familiar order. The last condition is satisfied if Cerdic's pedigree had come into existence fairly recently through a mistake.

It will help the examination of the added names to distinguish them by brackets from the framework: Cerdic–Elesa–(Esla)–Giwis–(Wig–Freawine–Frithogar)–Brand–Bældæg–Woden. *Esla* is otherwise unknown in English, and is curiously like *Elesa*—too like if *Elesa* is etymologically the same name as *Elsa* in *Widsith* 117. *Frithogar* is not unusual, though no great chief or hero of that name is recorded. But Freawine and Wig, father and son, belong to heroic legend.

The chief Mercian genealogy in the Vespasian group gives the descending series: Woden–Waðolgeot–Uihtlæg–Uermund–Offa–Angengeot–Eamer–Icil, &c. Danish tradition, recorded first in the late twelfth- or early thirteenth-century Latin of Sven Aageson and Saxo Grammaticus, preserves a story of King Wermundus, son of Wiglet (= Wihtlæg) and father of Uffo (= Offa). With them are associated an ally or sub-king, Frowinus (= Freawine), his son Wigo, and his daughter whom Offa married.[1] There are strong reasons why their story should be well known among the Mercians. The great King Offa (†796) seems to have taken special pride in the ancestor to whom he owed his name, and perhaps had in mind an accomplishment of the older Offa when he fixed his boundaries by building Offa's Dyke.[2] The story of the first Offa is referred to in *Widsith* 35–44;[3] and in *Beowulf* 1944–62, where Wermund also probably appears

[1] For details see Chadwick *Origin of the English Nation*, ch. vi. Whether the Danish tradition is independent of the English is disputed; but in any case, it probably differs considerably from the story told in England three or four centuries earlier.

[2] See Sir Cyril Fox *The Boundary Line of Cymru* (Brit. Acad. 1940), pp. 20 f.

[3] Ed. R. W. Chambers, 1912, Introd. pp. 84 ff. It should not be assumed that this passage in *Widsith* was composed in the seventh century. Few texts offer such opportunities for accretion or show more signs that the opportunities were taken.

(miswritten *Garmund*), with Eomer (miswritten *Geomor*) who is described as his grandson. Its persistence in the Midlands and its association with the Mercian Offa are proved by the *Vitae Duorum Offarum* written at St. Albans in the late twelfth or early thirteenth century.[1]

English literary sources do not mention Wig or Freawine, and they could not be expected to appear in incidental references like those in *Beowulf* and *Widsith*. But it can hardly be doubted that they had a prominent part in the full story as it was told at the Mercian court, and I regard Cerdic's pedigree as evidence for it. A West Saxon embellisher of pedigrees would not dare to claim Wermund and Offa of Angel while Offa of Mercia and his pedigree were freshly remembered. But Freawine and Wig, the illustrious associates of Wermund and Offa, were claimed by no other dynasty; and during the period of Mercian predominance that ended with Beorhtric in 802, the analogy of existing relations may have established them in legend as Saxon rulers in the Continental home-land.

In the arrangement given below, it will be seen that, by the mere accident that has been supposed, the first and last lines set the unusual pattern of Cerdic's longer pedigree. If Wig and Freawine are added after Giwis, another verse is produced to the pattern, and alliteration fixes the place of insertion:

Cynric Cerdicing,   Cerdic Elesing,
Elesa X-ing,   X Giwising,
Giwis Wiging,   Wig Freawining,
Freawine Y-ing,   Y Bronding,
Brond Bældæging   Bældæg Wodening.

It would be straining coincidence to suppose that *Esla* arose by the accident of dittography; but to perfect the artificial verse form would call for no more technical ingenuity than the replacement of X by any name beginning with a vowel, and of Y by any name beginning with F.

(4) *Woden to Geat* (Parker MS.): Woden Friþowalding, Friþuwald Frealafing,[2] Frealaf Friþuwulfing, Friþuwulf Finning, Fin Godwulfing, Godwulf Geating. Of these Friþuwald, Frealaf, Friþuwulf, Godwulf are known only from genealogies. Finn is a Frisian king of heroic legend, Geat a god.

[1] Chambers *Beowulf, an Introduction*, pp. 217–43 prints the relevant parts.

[2] MS. *Freawining*.

Few will dissent from the general opinion[1] that the ancestors of Woden were a fanciful development of Christian times. There is no evidence of an ancient tradition about them among the Germanic peoples of the Continent and Scandinavia. Bede gives no hint of pedigrees going beyond Woden. The lists in the *Historia Brittonum* begin with him. Cerdic's pedigree (R^A) in the West Saxon Regnal Table, important because it is a text of Alfred's time earlier even in this part than the Parker MS., ends with Woden; and so do the Chronicle pedigrees, except Æthelwulf's under 855 and Ida's under 547.[2]

The genesis of a fiction is often easier to explain than that of an historical event. The need for an extension beyond Woden would first arise when a royal pedigree up to Woden had become settled in tradition or in authoritative records. Until then, there was still room for more names of old kings, heroes, and gods among his descendants. Thereafter, anybody who wished to express national pride or literary ingenuity by embroidering the genealogy had the choice of either adding names behind Woden, or producing a conflicting tradition which would raise doubts. And whoever first added names behind Woden in a king's pedigree had a good chance of general acceptance; for he gave new information where before there was nothing, and though Woden might have three sons or seven, he could have only one father, father's father, &c.

I take the documents according to the order in which their texts may be reckoned to have become fixed:

(i) *Vespasian B VI*: Frealaf, who appears as the father of Woden in all the genealogies of this manuscript, may be a hero or divinity who was remembered by the Mercians. His name seems to be a very recent addition, and only the pedigree of the kings of Lindsey goes beyond him: Frealaf Frioðulfing, Frioðulf Finning, Finn Goduulfing, Godulf Geoting.[3] All that we know of the

[1] See, e.g., R. W. Chambers *Beowulf, an Introduction*, pp. 320 ff.

[2] See below, pp. 169 f.

[3] In Vespasian B VI **gaut* appears regularly as *Geot-*, *-geot*. Of nine examples four are in the Northumbrian and five in the Mercian lists; so these forms, common in southern Northumbria (Bülbring *Altenglisches Elementarbuch*, § 108) were current in the central Mercian dialect of Lichfield. The South-Western MS. CCCC 183 (*c.* 937) has *Geating* (once), *-geot* five times, and the bad spelling *-giot* thrice; Tiberius B V (*c.* 1000) has *Eating* (once, perhaps by confusion with *Eata*) and *-geot* eight times. The *Historia Brittonum* derives from a source with *ea* spellings, which perhaps came from south Mercia. Although *gaut* was a very productive element in Germanic personal names (see Förstemann *Altdeutsches Namenbuch* s.v.), it seems to have become rarer in late

kings of Lindsey depends on this list, and on Stenton's convincing identification of *Aldfrið*, the latest name in it, with *Ealdfrid rex* who attests Offa's confirmation of a Sussex charter between 786 and 796.[1] His attendance on Offa gives a reason for including the obscure kings of this small and isolated kingdom in a Mercian compilation recorded soon after Offa's reign. And if the Lindsey pedigree was added to an older collection in Aldfrith's day, that would explain why the names from Friothulf to Geat are not carried through to the rest of the pedigrees in Vespasian B VI. It would explain, too, why the Lindsey pedigree is not in the tables of the *Historia Brittonum*, which derive from an earlier state of the collection.[2]

(ii) *Historia Brittonum*: So far, the indications favour a date round about the end of the eighth century for the extension to Geat. But what of the pedigree of Horsa and Hengest in the narrative of the *Historia Brittonum*, ch. 31, where the Chartres MS., whatever its value for the whole text, is the earliest witness?[3] It reads: '. . . Uuoden, filii Frelab, filii Freudulf, filii Fran [*for* Finn], filii Folcpald [*for* Folcwald], filii G⟨e⟩uta [*for* Geata], qui *fuit*, ut aiunt, filius dei, non deus exercituum, set unus ex idolis que ipsi colebant.'[4] Here Folcwald, the father of Finn in heroic poetry (*Widsith* 27, *Beowulf* 1089), replaces *Godwulf*, who appears in all other versions of the Woden-Geat series.[5] Most

Anglo-Saxon times, and to have troubled copyists. In the Chronicle *Angengeot* becomes *Angenwit* (through *-iut*?) in the pedigree of Ida (547) and *Angelþeow* in the pedigree of Penda (626, 755).

[1] 'Lindsey and its Kings' in *Essays in History* presented to R. L. Poole, 1927, pp. 136 ff.

[2] Above, p. 151.

[3] It has usually been assigned to the late ninth or early tenth century; but C. Samaran (quoted by F. Lot *Nennius et l'Historia Brittonum* i, p. 31), after an expert examination, inclines to the second half of the tenth century.

[4] On *Frelab* for *Frealaf* see p. 153, n. 5. *Freudulf* has the diphthong *eu* (for older *iu*, Vesp. B VI *Frioðulf*) which no other MS. of the *Historia* preserves. *Geuta*, corrected from *Guta*, is probably due to misreading the open or *u*-shaped form of *a*, which occurs both in Insular and Continental scripts. The other MSS. have *Geata*, except *Ieta* in Bibl. Nat. lat. 11108 which derives from an English recension of the late tenth or early eleventh century. The error *Fran* for *Finn* seems to be reflected in the Irish translation, said to be of the late eleventh century, which has *Finn–Frenn–Folcuald*.

[5] In the English genealogical tables Finn appears as the son of Godwulf. In the *Historia Brittonum*, *Widsith*, and *Beowulf* he is the son of Folcwald(a). The discrepancy does not require the assumption of two Finns, or two names for the Frisian hero's father. This is a fictitious, not a real pedigree. The unknown Godwulf alliterates with and is probably associated with Geat, who has a key position. Then if an unrelated hero Finn is to be included, a false

critics of the *Historia* before F. Lot seem to agree that this part of the narrative is old—perhaps as early as the seventh century.[1] But in a work which was certainly revised as late as the first quarter of the ninth century, there can be no assurance that this genealogy as a whole, or any detail in it, belongs to the old narrative. The concurrence of the Chartres and later manuscripts proves at most that it was part of the text issued by Nennius in the first half of the ninth century. But that is about the time at which special attention was given to the English genealogies. And certainly one man dealt with this passage and with the collection of genealogies at chs. 57 ff.; for there the other royal houses are derived from Woden, but the Kentish kings are not traced beyond Hengest because his pedigree is given at ch. 31.

Two fortunate chances help us in this case. First Bede, who was particularly well informed about Kentish history and tradition, gives the pedigree of Hengest and Horsa with no extension beyond Woden. Secondly, misspellings in the manuscripts of the *Historia Brittonum* prove that *Folcwald* derives from an original in which *w* was represented by the runic letter *wyn*.[2] It has been assumed that this use of *wyn* in English writing is very old, because it occurs in the charter of Oethilred, dated 692–3.[3] But there are other reasons for thinking that this is not a contemporary charter, but a copy made perhaps a century later.[4] I have noticed no example of *wyn* in English manuscripts that can be assigned to the first half of the eighth century with confidence.[5] It appears

linking is inevitable. If the composer of the fiction thought of the difficulty, he could justify himself by the argument that Folcwald had no better claim to be Geata's son or Godwulf's than had Finn.

[1] See R. Thurneysen *Zeitschrift für deutsche Philologie* xxviii, pp. 100 f.

[2] See Mommsen in his edition, Introd., p. 142. It follows that the compiler was using an English written source.

[3] So W. Keller *Angelsächsische Palaeographie*, 1906, p. 12. There is a facsimile in *Ancient Charters in the British Museum*, 1873, pl. ii.

[4] K. Sisam *Cynewulf and his Poetry*, p. 25; and *Studies in the History of OE. Literature*, 1953, p. 92 n.

[5] I do not accept as strictly contemporary Æthelbald's charter of 742 in Sweet *Oldest English Texts*, p. 432; facsimile in Ordnance Survey *Facsimiles of Anglo-Saxon MSS.*, vol. i, 1878. There is no example of *wyn* in St. Willibrord's Calendar of the early eighth century, or in the many names in Bede (Moore MS. *c.* 737, and Leningrad MS. *c.* 746). Its absence from the monumental script of the Durham *Liber Vitae* (early ninth century) is less significant for ordinary usage. It is fairly common in the Corpus Glossary, which Sweet (*O.E.T.*, p. 5) dated in the first half of the eighth century, but which is now assigned to the late eighth or early ninth centuries (E. A. Lowe *Codices Latini Antiquiores* ii, no. 122). In the Epinal Glossary *wyn* is scarce and sometimes crudely adapted to Latin script, but the date of the MS. is disputed. Sweet in

increasingly, though irregularly, in the latter part of the eighth century; but there is no instance, for example, in the original Sussex charter of Oslac dated 780, and its later confirmation by Offa;[1] *u*, *uu* are commoner in the early ninth-century Mercian Vespasian B vi; and as late as the beginning of the tenth century they are sometimes preferred.[2] The question requires more study, but unless earlier examples of *wyn* can be established, this indication suggests that *Folcwald* came into the text of the *Historia* not earlier than the second half of the eighth century; *Freudulf* is not a very old form; and the whole line from Woden to Geat may have been added by Nennius at the beginning of the ninth century. Evidence that Finn in this genealogy was so early understood to be the Frisian king is welcome.[3]

(iii) *Chronicle*: It is convenient to take the Chronicle before Asser.

Ida's pedigree at 547 runs in the Abingdon version (both manuscripts): Woden–Freoþelaf–Friþulf–Finn–Godulf–Geat. If *Freoþelaf*[4] is an error for *Frealaf*, this agrees with the Lindsey pedigree of Vespasian B vi; and with the *Historia Brittonum* except in its reading *Folcwald* for *Godwulf*. The pedigree has been erased from the Parker MS., the other independent witness to the text; but the fire-damaged manuscript Otho B xi, which was a close copy of the Parker MS., omits Frealaf (or Freoþelaf),

the facsimile edition (E.E.T.S. 1883), p. xi argued for the early eighth century against Maunde Thompson's opinion that it was early ninth. The question is primarily one for Latin palaeography, and the latest and best authority, Lowe in *Codices Latini Antiquiores* vi (1953), description of pl. 760, prefers the first half of the eighth century; but in the practice of the Epinal MS. the chance of *wyn* being used for any one instance of *w* is small.

[1] Published in facsimile by W. de G. Birch, 1892.

[2] e.g. in the original charter of Wærferth dated 904 in *Facsimiles of Ancient Charters in the British Museum*, vol. iii. In Caroline minuscule *uu* was retained for the spelling of English names, e.g. in the MS. of Æthelweard's Chronicle composed after 975.

[3] The balance of probability is against *Folcwald* being the earlier reading in the genealogies and *Godwulf* a later substitution. For, apart from the isolation of the *Historia* among the witnesses, it is unlikely that a reading *Finn Folcwalding*, supported by epic tradition, would be replaced by *Finn Godwulfing*. Presumably Nennius had access to an English form of the Kentish pedigree which had been influenced by the legend of Finn. F. Lot's view, op. cit., pp. 93 f. and 171 n., that Nennius simply transferred these names from the Lindsey pedigree in Vespasian B vi by a mistake, fails to account for *Folcwald*.

[4] This name occurs nowhere else in English genealogies but is prominent in Danish royal pedigrees. It should be regarded as a scribal error, due to *Freoþewulfing* which follows immediately.

giving Woden–Friþowulf–Finn–Godwulf–Geat.[1] There are two possibilities: the one that *Frealaf*, which is represented in all other versions of this series, was omitted by scribal error from Otho B xi (and presumably the Parker MS.); the other, more remote, that an older tradition omitted *Frealaf*; for it is conceivable that, in the Lindsey pedigree, his name is an intrusion from the other lists in Vespasian B vi. It remains to note that the extension from Woden to Geat at 547,[2] which is unique in the Chronicle before the great pedigree of 855, fits in with my conjecture that Cerdic's short pedigree was taken from Ida's. The conjecture implies that the remoter part of Ida's pedigree, as it now stands in the Chronicle, is a late replacement of the part from Alusa to Woden which was erroneously transferred to Cerdic.

In Æthelwulf's pedigree under 855 the Parker MS. gives: Woden – Friþuwald – Frealaf[3] – Friþuwulf – Finn – Godwulf – Geat. Here Friþuwald, who cannot be identified with any probability, has been added to the usual series. But the Abingdon (B, C) and Northern (D) Chronicles, and the list in Tiberius B v,[4] have neither the new name Friþuwald, nor Friþuwulf, both of which are in Asser and Æthelweard. This raises a question of some importance for the textual criticism of the Chronicle: which of the two lists offered by the extant manuscripts was in the archetype of the Chronicle of 892?

A curious point of form also deserves notice, now that all the variants of the series from Woden to Geat have been assembled. Although alliteration controls the variations, none of the recorded versions continues the alliterative scheme discussed at pp. 158 ff. above. In the first and last lines the lists[5] will run, e.g.

Woden Frealafing   Frealaf Finning
Finn Godwulfing,   Godwulf Geating

[1] Nowell's transcript and Wheloc's print show that in Otho B xi Ælle's pedigree at 560 ended: *Woden Friþowulfing*. The scribe, probably following the Parker MS. in which Ælle's pedigree has been erased, began to carry through the extension beyond Woden. In the Abingdon version (B, C) there are no names beyond Woden at 560.

[2] Æthelweard, whose version of the Chronicle differed from the extant texts in some points, says under this year that Ida's family derived from Woden, with no mention of Geat.

[3] MS. *Friþuwald Freawining*, *Frealaf Friþuwulfing*, where the scribe has caught up *Freawining* from the descendants of Woden. MS. Otho B xi repeated the error.

[4] See above, p. 148 n. 2.

[5] Except the *Historia Brittonum*, where Finn son of Folcwald regularizes the last line.

with single alliteration in the first half and double in the second. This reverses alliterative practice; and if this part of the pedigree was ever cast into alliterative verse, *Godwulf Geating* must be a first half-line, with something about Geat in the second half.[1]

(iv) *Asser*, in this part of the pedigree, agrees with the Parker list against manuscripts B, C, D of the Chronicle: 'UUoden, qui fuit Frithowald, qui fuit Frealaf, qui fuit Frithuwulf, qui fuit Finn, ⟨qui fuit⟩ Godwulf, qui fuit Geata, *quem Getam iamdudum pagani pro deo venerabantur*.' (Then he quotes ineptly some lines from Sedulius which refer to the slave Geta in Terentian comedy.)[2] Asser finished his work in 893, but does not use the Chronicle after 887; in the historical part of Æthelwulf's pedigree the manuscript (*c.* 1000) preserved one form *Coenred* which is older than *Cenred* of the Parker and other Chronicles though it was probably in their archetype; in Cerdic's pedigree as far as Woden, he has the earlier short form, where all the Chronicle manuscripts have the verse form developed from it (above, pp. 159 ff.). So in this place Asser's agreement with the Parker list (and Æthelweard also agrees) should settle the reading of the archetype of the Chronicle of 892, against the consensus of the Abingdon (B, C) and Northern (D) versions, which are thus shown to have some special relation here.

Asser's *Geata* for *Geat* has been explained by W. H. Stevenson[3] as due to influence of the Latin name *Geta*. Few scholars have been more familiar with the *Historia Brittonum*, but by some chance he overlooked *Geata*[4] in that text (above, p. 167 n. 4), which

[1] See below, p. 172.

[2] See Stevenson's note in his edition, pp. 162 f.

[3] In his edition, pp. 160 f.: rather, the form *Geata* suggested the false connexion with *Geta*. Asser's use of the *Historia* elsewhere is noticed at p. 186.

[4] *Geata* admits of a special explanation. In an Old English genealogy, the remotest name appears as a patronymic, e.g. *Geating*, not as an independent name; and *Geating* might be formed from *Geat* or *Geata*. Without a tradition to guide him, the compiler of the *Historia* might decide for *Geata*. The same consideration applies to *Sceaf*, an end-name in the West Saxon genealogy, which has been connected by Olrik with *Sceafa*, the name of the Langobard king in *Widsith* 32. Whether or not that identification is accepted, the difference between *Sceafa* and *Sceaf* is no objection; for the latter form is first recorded (as *Scef*) in Æthelweard, who wrote after 975, and may have derived it from *Sce(a)fing*. Similarly from an epic phrase like *Finn Folcwalding* (*Widsith* 27), either *Folcwald* or *Folcwalda* can be deduced. The first appears in the *Historia Brittonum* and is normal: there are many names in *-wald*, including *Folcuald*, in Bede and the Durham *Liber Vitae*, but no example of *-walda*. Here *Beowulf* 1089 *Folcwaldan sunu* is exceptional, and the weak form may be

is an obvious source for Asser's note that *Geata* was worshipped as a god. *Geat* is probably the name of a god (perhaps the tribal god of the Geats) whose cult was absorbed by Woden, for the equivalent *Gautr* is found in Norse as a name of Odin among the gods.[1] And as this section of the *Historia* derives from English tradition, it adds something to the possibility that there was a verse form of the genealogy in which *Godwulf Geating* was followed by a half-line containing the word *god*.

(5) *Beyond Geat.* We have seen that the tradition of the genealogy from Woden to Geat is compact, though in detail it was not fixed when Asser's *Life* and the Chronicle were written about 892. The names are held to the F and G alliteration, and no early witness to the text adds or omits or varies more than one name. Evidently the series was soon closed against considerable additions, and then anybody who wished to find a place in the royal genealogy for dimly remembered kings, heroes, or gods must add them behind Geat.

The extension beyond Geat cannot be traced behind the pedigree of Æthelwulf as it appeared in Asser and in the Chronicle circulated about 892; and the following later documents are necessary for the examination of this part.[2]

(α) Æthelweard's Chronicle, written in Latin in the last quarter of the tenth century, and preserved in one manuscript[3] of which only fragments survive since the Cotton fire of 1731. It is mainly a translation from the *Anglo-Saxon Chronicle*,[4] and the pedigree of Æthelwulf is given under the year 857.

(β) William of Malmesbury's *Gesta Regum*, written in its first form about 1125. He gives the pedigree of Æthelwulf at the regular place (855), referring to *Anglorum chronica*.[5]

(γ) *Beowulf*, the poem preserved in MS. Vitellius A xv (*c.* 1000),

a late development rather than the survival of an old formation. On the history of *-wald*, *-walda* see Förstemann *Altdeutsches Namenbuch* s.v.

[1] *Grímnis-mál* in *Corpus Poeticum Boreale* i, p. 76; cf. p. 357.

[2] I disregard late transfers to the royal pedigrees of other English kingdoms; and also the pedigrees recorded in Scandinavia, which are literary derivatives from the recension of Edgar's time mentioned above, p. 148 n. 2.

[3] Enough fragments of MS. Otho A x remain to show that it was written early in the eleventh century in a smooth round English form of Caroline minuscule. The text in H. Petrie's *Monumenta Historica Britannica*, 1848, follows Savile's print of 1596.

[4] See Stenton in *Essays in Medieval History presented to T. F. Tout*, 1925, pp. 19 ff. for Æthelweard's sources.

[5] Ed. W. Stubbs (Rolls Series), 1887, i, pp. 120 f.

and generally of much earlier composition; how much earlier in the relevant lines (3–57) is hard to say, because the passage is in parts confused and suspect.

The following table makes comparison easier:

Chronicle B, C	*Asser*	*Æthelweard*	*Beowulf*	*William of Malmesbury*
Sceaf(ing)[1]	Seth	Scef[3]	Scef(ing)	Strephius
Bedwig	Beduuig			Bedwegius
Hwala	Huala			Gwala
Haðra	Hathra			Hadra
Itermon	Itermod			Stermonius
Heremod	Heremod			Heremodius
				Sceaf[5]
Scyldwa	Sceldwea	Scyld	Scyld[4]	Sceldius
Beaw	Beauu	Beo	Beowulf (Dane)	Beowius
Tætwa	Caetuua	Tetuua	Healfdene	Tetius
Geat(a)	Geata[2]	Geat	Hrothgar, &c.	Getius

[1] CHRONICLE—Bedwig Sceafing id est filius Noe se wæs geboren on þære Earce Noes; so that it has been questioned whether Bedwig was the person supposed to have been born in the Ark.

[2] ASSER—quem Getam iamdudum pagani pro deo uenerabantur.

[3] ÆTHELWEARD—Ipse Scef cum uno dromone aduectus est in insula oceani quæ dicitur Scani, armis circundatus, eratque ualde recens puer, et ab incolis illius terræ ignotus; attamen ab eis suscipitur, et ut familiarem diligenti animo eum custodierunt, et post in regem eligunt; de cuius prosapia ordinem trahit Athulf rex.

[4] BEOWULF—'Scyld Scefing . . . after he was first found helpless' grew up to conquer the neighbouring peoples (3 ff.) . . . For his funeral ship 'they provided him with no less rich treasures than did those who in the beginning sent him out, a child alone, across the sea' (43 ff. *Maþmas* 'treasures' includes rich arms).

[5] WILLIAM OF MALMESBURY—Iste, ut ferunt, in quandam insulam Germaniæ Scandzam, de qua Iordanes historiographus Gothorum loquitur, appulsus, navi sine remige, puerulus, posito ad caput frumenti manipulo, dormiens, ideoque Sceaf nuncupatus, ab hominibus regionis illius pro miraculo exceptus, et sedulo nutritus: adulta ætate regnavit in oppido quod tunc Slaswic, nunc vero Haithebi appellatur. Est autem regio illa Anglia Vetus dicta, unde Angli venerunt in Britanniam, inter Saxones et Gothos constituta.

(i) *The Chronicle* list is taken from the Abingdon version (B, C) in the spelling of B (*c.* 1000). The Northern version (D) practically agrees, but has several careless spellings, particularly *Beowung Beowi* for *Bedwi(g)ing Bedwi(g)*.[1] The Parker MS. agrees up

[1] E. Björkman's suggestion, *Beiblatt zur Anglia* xxx (1919), pp. 23 f., that the Northern version of the Chronicle (D, *c.* 1050) preserves the original reading in *Beowung*, *Beowi*, does not deserve the favourable consideration it has had.

to Itermon, but goes on: *Hraþraing* [*sic*] *se wæs geboren in þære Earce*, so that the scribe has dropped several names that were certainly in the archetype.[1] This is proof, if proof were needed, that even at Winchester a scribe contemporary with Alfred could not be trusted to treat the royal genealogy with respectful care; and nobody bothered to correct him: MS. Otho B XI has the same mistakes. Of the names, *Tætwa*, *Itermon*, *Haþra*, *Bedwig* are otherwise unknown; and *Hwala* occurs only once elsewhere in Old English, in *Widsith* 14, where he appears as the best of rulers, alongside Alexander. *Heremod* is a not uncommon name in England, and a famous Heremod appears in *Beowulf* 901, 1709, and in the older Edda, *Hyndloljóþ* 7. Note that *Sceldwea* is separated from *Sceaf(a)* by the five names Heremod, Itermon, Haþra, Hwala, Bedwig.

(ii) *Asser* here adds nothing to the Chronicle, but confirms it. *Caetuua* and *Itermod* (influenced by *Heremod*?) seem to be scribal errors; and it is unlikely that Asser himself is responsible for a second Seth, son of Noah. Iafeth was usually regarded as the ancestor of the European peoples,[2] and the possibility that the last four letters of his name have something to do with the error *Seth* cannot be excluded; but a careless scribe may have substituted *Seth* for *Sceaf*.[3]

For (i) the likeness of *d* and *o* in some Anglo-Saxon scripts would equally account for *Beow*- as a misreading of *Bedw*-. (ii) *Beowung*, *Beowi* are impossible English forms from *Beow*, but *Bedwiing*, *Bedwi* are late forms from *Bedwig*. (iii) *Beowi*, in an Old English text going back to Alfred's time, cannot be explained from Latin *Beowius*; and there is no other evidence for that form before William of Malmesbury (who ends all the names in this part of the genealogy either in -*ius* or -*a*), or for the existence of a Latin source here. (iv) On the contrary, D here is closely related to the more careful MSS. B, C, which have *Bedwiging*, *Bedwig*. (v) They are confirmed by *Bedwig* in Asser, who has been shown to be a good authority for this genealogy; and all post-Conquest chroniclers, like Florence of Worcester, have forms of *Bedwig*. (vi) No explanation has been given either for the duplication of *Beow*, or for the order *Beow-Sceaf* which results. So the suggestion fails in every test.

[1] The spelling of this early MS. is: Geat Tætwaing, Tætwa Beawing, Beaw Sceldwaing, Sceldwea Heremoding, Heremod Itermoning, Itermon Hraþraing. Note that the strange form *Sceldwea* is established for the archetype by the agreement of this MS. with B (*Sceldweaing*) and Asser; and the artificial formations *Tætwaing*, *Sceldwaing*, are paralleled by *Cuþaing* for *Cuþing* in the Parker MS. of this genealogy, and at the years 597, 685, and 731. There is no need to ascribe these forms to a Latin source.

[2] See *Historia Brittonum*, ch. 17 and Mommsen's references to sources.

[3] The identification was made by Florence of Worcester (†1118) or an early reader of his chronicle. The good twelfth-century MS. CCC. Oxford 157, p. 47 reads *Seth saxonice Sceaf*. Florence there gives a table starting from

(iii) *Æthelweard* was descended from King Æthelred, Æthelwulf's son and Alfred's elder brother, and was the first noble of his time. His Preface is evidence enough that he took a special interest in the family tree, so that he is a good witness. In the pedigree of Æthelwulf, which appears at its usual place (857), he agrees with the Parker MS., against manuscripts B, C, D, and Asser, in omitting Creoda;[1] with the Chronicle manuscripts, but against Asser, he has the longer alliterative pedigree from Cerdic to Woden; and, agreeing with Asser and the Parker MS. against B, C, D, he has the fullest form of the series from Woden to Geat.[2] It is significant that he breaks away from all these texts by omitting the five names Heremod, Itermon, Hathra, Hwala, Bedwig; and so brings together Scyld and Scef to agree with *Scyld Scefing* in *Beowulf.*[3] But he is not dependent on *Beowulf.* He has *Beo*, with Asser and the Chronicle, as the son of Scyld, not the erroneous *Beowulf*[4] of the poem; Scyld's grandson is Tetuua, not Healfdene; Scef, not Scyld, is the unknown child who drifts ashore in a ship laden with precious weapons. In *Beowulf* Scyld's sea-funeral catches the poet's imagination, and his arrival as a helpless child is mentioned incidentally; but Æthelweard tells of Scef's miraculous arrival, with no mention of a funeral ship. His text points to a pedigree of Æthelwulf, possibly contained in the copy of the Chronicle used by Æthelweard but more likely to be preserved in a family tradition, from which the five names from Heremod to Bedwig were absent.[5] The natural

Adam, in which Seth appears as a fourth son of Noah; his descendants are copied from Asser; and collation with the Chronicle showed the equivalence of Seth and Sceaf. At the beginning of another good twelfth-century MS. of his work, CCCC. 92, *Sceaf* stands beside the sons of Noah; but the last four letters are by a later hand on an erasure, so that the MS. originally read *Seth*: see below, p. 177 n. 4.

[1] See above, p. 157. He also omits *Cutha* = *Cuthwulf* before *Cuthwine*, which is a natural slip, since *Cutha* is a short form for both the compound names.

[2] Above, p. 170.

[3] There is no chance of accidental omission, because he numbers Cerdic's ancestors, e.g. *nonus UUothen, nonus decimus Scef.* The agreement of Æthelweard and *Beowulf* in the spellings *Scyld, Scef* is not significant, for both MSS. are of the same age and these are the normal late West Saxon forms.

[4] Miswritten for *Beo(w)*, because some scribe confused the name with that of Beowulf the son of Ecgtheow, who is the hero of the poem. See Appendix B.

[5] Stenton in *Essays presented to T. F. Tout*, 1925, p. 23 n. suggests that Æthelweard's form of the pedigree is due to the lost version of the Chronicle which he used. But a different view does not conflict with his main argument. This is the special case of Æthelweard's own pedigree; there was a conflict of tradition; and he might decide against the authority of the Chronicle he was using. Up to Scyld this Chronicle seems to have had that most developed

explanation is that these five names represent a late accretion to the non-Biblical names in Æthelwulf's pedigree, which those who connected Scyld and Sceaf could not accept.

The four names that Æthelweard has in common with the Chronicle and Asser are all unusual among Old English personal names, and are remarkable because two, *Sceld-* and *Beaw*,[1] have non-West Saxon stem-vowels in the early witnesses; two, *Sceldwea* and *Tætwa*,[2] show suffixes that have not been satisfactorily explained; and three, *Sceaf*, *Sceld*, *Beow*, correspond with common words meaning 'sheaf', 'shield', and 'barley', which has suggested a mythological interpretation. These names are further discussed in Appendix B.

The five names omitted by Æthelweard—Heremod, Itermon, Haþra, Hwala, Bedwig—seem to be a heterogeneous group; for it is improbable that any ancient tradition made Heremod father of Scyld, or Itermon (if the name is authentic) father of Heremod,[3] or Hwala father of Haþra, or Sceaf father of Bedwig. But in *Beowulf* it is implied that Heremod had been king of the Scyldings (Danes) before Scyld. Somebody for whom this tradition was strong, and who felt that Sceaf must be the remotest of all the Germanic names, would be tempted to find a place for the legendary figure of Heremod by breaking the combination *Scyld Sceafing*. That would open the way for the interpolation of other unrelated names, especially those with H-alliteration.

(iv) *William of Malmesbury*: Here *Sceaf* and the note on him are obviously interpolated, for *Sceaf* alone among the names is not latinized, and the corruption *Strephius* (of which Stubbs reports a variant *Screfius* from the second recension) stands where we should expect *Scefius*, as the remotest non-Biblical name. If this interpolation is removed, there remains a pedigree

form of the pedigree which appears in the Parker MS., and for the part beyond Scyld it is unlikely that the names in Asser and all extant copies of the Chronicle were unknown to Æthelweard and his correspondents.

[1] The Chronicle MSS. C and D have *Beaw* with B and Asser; Æthelweard has the correct nominative *Beo*. *Beowa* occurs in *Beowan hammes hecgan* in the Wiltshire charter of 931 which also names *grendles mere*, but the identification of this name with *Beaw*, *Beo* involves more than one doubtful assumption.

[2] *Tætwa* might be the short form of a compound like *Tætwulf*, but that explanation will hardly serve for *Sceldwea*; if a compound *Sceldwulf* (ON. *Skeldulfr*) were assumed, the equivalence with *Scyld* would fail. See below, pp. 199 f.

[3] Some scholars take *Ecgwela* in *Beowulf* 1710 to be Heremod's father. The three *Ecg-* names in the poem, *Ecgtheow* father of Beowulf, *Ecglaf* father of Unferth, and *Ecgwela*, all seem to be inventions for the purposes of the Beowulf stories.

which agrees generally with the Chronicle, though not exactly with any one manuscript.[1]

The disputed question is whether William's note on Sceaf has independent authority. He was widely read, romantically inclined, and had a tendency to blend and vary sources, which is one of his claims to be an historian rather than a chronicler. As Stubbs says:

> Our author, even when following most closely the material details which he found in the books that he was using, does so for the most part in his own language. . . . His own mastery of Latin . . . tempted him continually to paraphrase, or modify in other ways, the language of his authority, and that to such a degree as occasionally to suggest that he had still more recondite materials before him.[2]

Now Æthelweard's Chronicle is one of the authorities that William mentions in his preface to the *Gesta Regum*, and it is the probable source for the addition of Sceaf at this point in the Chronicle genealogy. To infer that a distant ancestor of the English kings ruled in Anglia Vetus was natural, and the precise names *Slaswic* and *Haithebi* are derived from another place in Æthelweard's Chronicle,[3] which is good evidence that William had it before him. Again, the meaning of the common noun *sceaf* was familiar to any Englishman of the early twelfth century: the proper name is glossed *garba* in some late chroniclers.[4]

[1] Thus it has the remotest names *Hwala*, *Bedwig*, *Scef* which the scribe of the Parker MS. omitted. In the Woden-Geat series it has *Fridewaldus* with the Parker MS. and Asser, but omits *Frithuwulf* with Chronicles B, C, D. In the historical part, against B, C, D, and Asser, it omits *Creoda* with the Parker MS. and in accordance with William's own narrative; but *Chinricus Creodingii*, *Creodingius Cherdicii* is interlined in the first version (Stubbs's note ad loc.).

[2] *Gesta Regum* ii, Preface, p. xvi.

[3] Ed. Petrie, p. 502: 'Porro Anglia Vetus sita est inter Saxones et Giotos, habens oppidum capitale quod sermone Saxonico *Slesuuic* nuncupatur, secundum vero Danos *Haithaby*.'

[4] In CCCC 92, a good twelfth-century MS. of Florence of Worcester, a thirteenth-century reader has altered *Seth* to *Schef* (see above, p. 174 n. 3), added *i. garba* above it, and provided a footnote which develops the legend: 'On the testimony of old chronographers, a ship without oars (*sine remige*) drove ashore *in Saxonia*. The people of the country, coming to see what it contained, found a little boy, crying with no one to comfort him (*quendam puerulum vagientem, omni penitus solatio destitutum humano*). A sheaf had been placed under his head. The Saxons brought him up, and called him *Schef*, *i. garba, a manipulo videlicet capite suo supposito*. This Schef, reared among the Saxons, begot Beadwy.' It is William of Malmesbury re-vamped. Matthew Paris in his *Chronica Majora* (*c.* 1250), ed. Luard, Rolls Series, i, p. 444, is content to copy William of Malmesbury, adding after *manipulo* 'quem patria lingua *seaf* dicimus, Gallica vero *garbam*'.

So a writer of William's intelligence and classical training[1] might, as Olrik and others have suggested, give an etymological turn to the story by transmuting Æthelweard's phrases *ualde recens puer, armis circundatus* into *puerulus, posito sub caput frumenti manipulo, dormiens*. The alternative view requires more than the assumption that an ancient tradition explaining Sceaf's name survived into the twelfth century. If William gave his mind to the difference at all, why should he prefer this tradition to the clear and good authority of Æthelweard when it would have been easy to combine the two? And why did Æthelweard, who was dealing with his own pedigree, who went out of his way to give a tradition about Sceaf, and knew the common meaning of *sceaf*, make no reference to the explanatory story of a sheaf of corn if it were current in his time? On these considerations it is unsafe to treat William of Malmesbury as an authority for this genealogy independent of the Chronicle and Æthelweard.

(6) *Biblical Names*: The Biblical names show the artificial character of this lengthened pedigree and the crudeness of the connexions that passed muster. Otherwise they need not detain us. William of Malmesbury has noted their source in Luke iii. 36–38, and the dependence need not be direct. There are earlier instances of pedigrees being traced back to Adam through this series of names, e.g. Nennius chs. 17 and 18;[2] and the ultimate source, Genesis v, is a commonplace of Biblical and universal chronologies. Æthelweard does not mention the Biblical names, but it cannot be deduced from his silence that they were absent from his copy of the *Anglo-Saxon Chronicle*. He may have preferred family tradition to a written Chronicle for the part beyond Geat. Besides, he was a great patron of the revival of religion and learning that marked the second half of the tenth century, and scholarly friends like Ælfric would not encourage belief in the fabulous birth in the Ark of an ancestor Sceaf.[3]

[1] He was one of the best classical scholars of his times (see M. R. James *Two Ancient English Scholars*, 1931) and in this passage *sine remige* seems to be a reminiscence of a famous line in Virgil *Aeneid* iv. 588.

[2] Later Irish pedigrees are traced to Adam, usually through Mil of Spain. The late Scandinavian genealogies also go back to Adam through Saturn, Jupiter, Priam, &c. See too Plummer's notes to the Chronicle ii, pp. 81 f.

[3] The best authorities agree in identifying Æthelweard the chronicler with Ælfric's patron Alderman Æthelweard. But there are difficulties. (i) That an Anglo-Saxon layman should write a long work in Latin is extraordinary. (ii) The Latin style of Æthelweard's Chronicle is so artificial as to be sometimes unintelligible, but the Latin of Æthelwold and Ælfric is plain and

To sum up. Analysis of the pedigree of Æthelwulf has shown it to be a late and artificial composition, developed by well-marked stages in such a way that, as a rule, the remotest names represent the latest accretions. Thus:

1. Æthelwulf–Ecgberht–Ealhmund–Eafa–Eoppa–Ingild;
2. (Ine) – Cenred – Ceolwald – Cuthwulf – Cuthwine – Ceawlin–Cynric–Creoda–Cerdic;
3*a*. (Cerdic)–Elesa–Giwis–Brond–Bældæg–Woden;
3*b*. (Cerdic) – Elesa – Esla – Giwis – Wig – Freawine – Frithogar – Brond–Bældæg–Woden;
4. (Woden) – Frithuwald – Frealaf – Frithuwulf – Finn – Godwulf–Geat (with variations);
5*a*. (Geat)–Tætwa–Beaw–Sceldwea–Sceaf;
5*b*. (Geat) – Tætwa – Beaw – Sceldwea – Heremod – Itermon – Hathra–Hwala–Bedwig–Sceaf;
6. (Sceaf)–Noe–Lamech &c.–Adam.

The alternative 3*b* may have been added later than 4, and 5*b* later than 6.

It may be asked: where in this pedigree does fact end and fiction begin? There is no certain answer. From Ecgberht to Ingild, Ine's brother, it may reasonably be trusted in the

practical. This might be explained if Æthelweard wrote his Chronicle before he came under the influence of the reforming school. Yet according to Ælfric (English Preface to his *Grammar*) even among the English clergy Latin was at a very low ebb before the Benedictine Reform. The later Æthelweard's work is dated (see E. E. Barker in *Bulletin of the Institute of Historical Research* xxiv (1951), esp. p. 56) the shorter is the period in which he could have been uninfluenced by the new school. (iii) Ælfric's patron pressed him to translate the first part of Genesis, explaining that another man had translated the rest for him; yet the Vulgate Genesis would be simple to anybody who could write or read Æthelweard's Chronicle. (iv) So far from suggesting that his patron could read Latin for himself and was vain of his Latinity, Ælfric, who was a tactful man, implies the contrary. The English Preface to his *Lives of Saints* is addressed to Æthelweard and Æthelmær, whereas the Latin Preface refers to them in the third person; and the English Preface runs: 'thou, beloved, above all, and Æthelmær have asked me for such writings and received them from my hands, *to strengthen your faith with narratives which hitherto you had not in your own language*'. (v) Æthelweard's Chronicle shows verbal misunderstandings of the *Anglo-Saxon Chronicle* annals, e.g. for 658, 710, 755, which are hardly possible for a literate Englishman.

If the identification of the two Æthelweards holds good, the explanation of these difficulties may be that a Celtic-trained secretary was employed to turn Æthelweard's material into Latin, so that it could be sent abroad to his distant kinswoman Matilda, daughter of Otto the Great, who is addressed at the beginning of each of the four books. That an eminent layman should employ a Latin secretary for this purpose seems natural enough.

absence both of conflicting and corroborative evidence. From Ingild to Cerdic it is defensible, but there is conflicting evidence in the Chronicle on the immediate successors of Cerdic, and it is unlikely that the facts of the early period can be represented by orderly lines of hereditary succession. Beyond Cerdic all is fiction or error, and if the names themselves are old, they were not attached to the ancestry of the West Saxon kings by old tradition.

III

General Survey

The general development of Anglo-Saxon genealogies has been touched on so often in the analysis of Æthelwulf's pedigree that it will be convenient to continue with that subject, leaving the minor genealogies in the Chronicle to be dealt with in Appendix A.

Tacitus's account of Germanic custom: 'reges ex nobilitate, duces ex virtute sumunt',[1] seems to be a fair generalization, if the meaning of 'king' is not pressed too closely. It implies that, in times when there was only oral tradition, the ancestry of noble families was remembered. But since strict rules of hereditary succession were not the sole basis of choice, it does not imply the memorizing of very long pedigrees. To go beyond great-grandfathers, which is the normal limit of chronology in oral tradition, would seldom be necessary.

In the remains of heroic poetry, where the habits of the period before writing are most likely to be reflected, there is no evidence for long pedigrees. In *Beowulf* the ancestry of King Hrothgar is short and mainly fictitious: Healfdene–Beowulf Scylding–Scyld Scefing. We are told that King Hygelac was the son of King Hrethel, and was related, perhaps as nephew or grandson, to Swerting. The father of a hero is usually named: Sigemund is the son of Wæls (*Beow.* 897); Waldhere in the fragments of that story is the son of Ælfhere. When Beowulf son of Ecgtheow arrives unexpectedly at Heorot, Hrothgar at once recalls his father and mother;[2] and though there were special reasons in

[1] *Germania*, ch. vii.

[2] We are told also that Beowulf was of the kin of the Wægmundings (2814). Note that the names of Beowulf, Sigemund, and Waldhere, like Hengest's (above, p. 146), do not alliterate with the names given to their fathers. Others alliterate, e.g. Widia son of Weland in *Waldere*, Hagan son of Hagathien in the Latin *Waltharius*, Sigurd or Siegfried son of Sigemund in *Volsunga Saga* and *Nibelungenlied*; but nothing suggests that the latter combinations are the more primitive.

this case, great men of the Heroic period took pride in their memory for relationships. '*Chud ist mir al irmindeot*'—'I know everybody', says Hildebrand in *Hildebrandslied* 13 when he asks Hadubrand to name his father and kin. He means everybody of note, and a man is seldom mentioned in *Beowulf* without the name of his father or some distinguished kinsman. Still, the purpose seems to be the practical one of identifying him or establishing his own worth. Reflected glory from very remote ancestors is nowhere claimed. There is no evidence in Germanic or early Anglo-Saxon times that genealogies were recited on formal visits or at funerals; or used to fix the order of remote events.

Written pedigrees of Germanic kings first appear among the tribes that moved south-east into close contact with the Roman Empire. In the *Lex Burgundionum* which is assigned to the early sixth century, four ancestors or predecessors of King Gundobad are named,[1] and three of them, Gifica, Gislhere, and Guthhere, are mentioned in English heroic poetry, though the references in *Widsith* 19, 65 ff., 123 do not suggest a close relationship between them. In the seventh-century *Origo Gentis Langobardorum* the pedigree of King Rotharius is given to ten generations.[2] Free from the possibility of tampering between the original and the extant manuscripts is the Gothic pedigree of seventeen generations which Jordanes[3] copied from Cassiodorus, who wrote about the year 530: it ends with demigods (*ansis*, ON. *ǽsir*, OE. *ēsa* gen. pl.), so that invention was already at work to lengthen the lines. None of these East-Germanic royal pedigrees goes back to Woden.

Bede was the first to record some English royal pedigrees,[4] and in the parts before written records they are short. He notes that many kings or sub-kings traced their descent from Woden, but the one example he preserves has no claims to credibility: only three names come between Hengest, who flourished in the middle of the fifth century, and Woden, a spirit who was worshipped as a great god in the first century A.D.

There is evidence for the existence, some two generations after Bede's *History* (731), of a systematic collection of royal genealogies, witnessed by the 'Vespasian group' of manuscripts, by Nennius and the Chronicle.[5] For these lists we are fortunate in having the early MS. Vespasian B VI, which can be localized in

[1] *Mon. Germ. Hist. Leges* I (1892). ii. 1, p. 43.
[2] Op. cit. *SS. Rerum Langobardicarum* (1878), p. 6.
[3] Op. cit. *Auct. Ant.* v i (1882), p. 76 and footnote.
[4] Above, p. 146.
[5] Above, pp. 146–56.

Mercia (Lichfield) and dated close to the year 812. Whereas Nennius and the Chronicle end the pedigrees with Woden, Vespasian B VI shows that by 812 they had been taken a step farther back to Frealaf, of whom nothing is known. By this date too, the kings of Lindsey had been traced still farther back to Geat;[1] and though Nennius has not the Lindsey pedigree, in another context he carries Hengest's line beyond Woden to Geat. Evidently this last development is later than Bede.

The genealogies of the Vespasian collection cannot be analysed by the methods used for the more elaborate pedigree of Æthelwulf. All the copies seem to belong to a single tradition, and most of the lists present an impenetrable front. Fortunately there are enough of them to give opportunities for comparison; and some light can be thrown on their transmission, credibility, and historical setting.

For the transmission it is instructive to compare Bede's text of the early part of the Kentish pedigree, which is free from any suspicion of later corruption, with the lists in Vespasian B VI and in Nennius:

Bede i. 15 and ii. 5	*Vespasian B VI*	*Historia Brittonum*
Uoden	Uoden	UUoden
Uecta	Uegdaeg	Guectha
Uitta	Uihtgils	Guigta
Uictgils	Uitta	Guictgils
Hengist	Hengest	Hengest
Oeric *or* Oisc	Ocga	Ossa
Octa	Oese	Octha
Irminric	Iurmenric	Eormoric

The alternative *Oeric* might be expected to disappear, but it is surprising that *Oisc*, from which *Oiscingas* the family name of early kings of Kent derived, and which should have later forms *Oesc*, *Esc*, appears in the Vespasian group as *Oese*, by common scribal confusion of *c* and *e*; in Nennius as *Ossa*, with the doubling of intervocalic *s* which is a feature of Insular spelling; and

[1] Above, p. 166. In a letter written before 725 (*Mon. Germ. Hist. Epist.* iii (1892), pp. 271 f.), Bishop Daniel of Winchester advises Boniface how to confute the heathens from their own *falsorum deorum genealogia*. This implies no more than the practice of making the gods a family of fathers and sons, sisters and brothers, which is usual when they are given human attributes. It is not evidence for a long pedigree of the gods in heathen Germany of the early eighth century.

as *Æsc* in the Chronicle narrative.[1] Then again *Uegdæg* in the Vespasian group is not philologically equivalent to Bede's *Uecta*, Nennius's *Guechta*, and appears to be a late assimilation to *Uegdæg*, the son of Woden from whom the Deiran kings traced their descent: it is against the practice of these genealogies that the kings of Kent and Deira should be content to share a fictitious link with Woden.

The *Historia Brittonum* has neither the misreading *Ocga* for *Octa*, which may be due to the likeness of *t* and *g* in many Insular hands, nor the two inversions *Uihtgils : Uitta* and *Ocga: Oese* which distinguish the Vespasian group from Bede.[2] The one case where Bede provides a check may be exceptional; yet in a list of eight early names, it is disquieting to find that the Vespasian group, our chief authority for the genealogies, has two misreadings *Oese* and *Ocga*, one substituted form *Uegdaeg*, and two inversions of the order.

We have seen (above, p. 174) how carelessly the pedigree of the West Saxon royal family was copied at Winchester about the end of the ninth century; and clearly not all the genealogies copied at Lichfield a century earlier had been preserved with ritual precision by oral or by written tradition. Examples of the scribal corruption they suffered in comparatively late manuscripts have been noted incidentally; and to establish that transmission was careless throughout Anglo-Saxon times it will be enough to add a curious instance from MS. CCCC 183, which King Athelstan presented to St. Cuthbert's shrine. In it a Bernician branch runs:

Leodwald	Eadhelming
Ecgwald	Ocgting
Eadhelm	Iding
Ocg	Eating

because the scribe copied the column of patronymics separately,

[1] *Oesa* Vesp.: *Ossa* Nennius: *Esa* Chronicle appears in the pedigree of Ida of Bernicia. On *Æsc* see below, p. 196. For suggested etymologies of *Oisc* and *Oeric*, none of them convincing, see H. Ström *Old English Personal Names in Bede's History*, Lund 1939, pp. 73 f. The Ravenna Geographer, writing in the seventh century, gives the name of the leader of the Saxon invaders as MS. *Ansehis*, which editors correct to *Anschis* (v. 31). Chadwick *Origin of the English Nation*, p. 47 equates *Anschis* with *Oisc*, and notes that a slight variation would make MS. *Ansehis* correspond to *Oese*. Müllenhoff *Beovulf*, p. 61 n. suggests, with more probability, that *Anschis* comes through a Greek source which had ἄγχις = *Hangis(t)* = Hengist.

[2] Whether Nennius used Bede is disputed. Here he or his immediate source may have corrected the Vespasian text by reference to Bede; but he may have used it in an earlier, less corrupted form: see above, p. 151. In the

omitting *Ecgwalding* which should stand opposite *Leodwald*, and so gives grandfathers, not fathers, in the second column for this and the following branch.

Turning from the transmission to the substance of the genealogies, we are at once faced with a doubt. All the kingdoms for which genealogies are preserved—Deira, Bernicia, Mercia, East Anglia, Lindsey, Kent, Wessex, Essex—have lines going back to Woden (or Seaxnet). Were they all established by *reges ex nobilitate* whose remoter ancestors were kept in memory? In that case, the genealogies provide remarkable evidence of order, continuity, and respect for hereditary right in the period of migration and conquest. Or were some of the founders of kingdoms *duces ex virtute*, war-leaders and adventurers who won power in confused and violent times, and later acquired the pedigrees which no king need lack? There is information, legendary of course, about only two of the reputed first conquerors of kingdoms in England. Hengest of Kent, who is presumably the same as Hengest in the Finn legend,[1] was certainly a war-leader: the one story describes him as an adventurer or exile, the other makes him King Hnæf's principal retainer. His pedigree is a crude fiction that might have been produced at any time before it appears in Bede. Cerdic, the founder of the West Saxon kingdom, is called *ealdorman* in the Chronicle, which is precisely *dux*, not *rex*; and his pedigree seems to be the result of an error.[2] It may well be that some of the other founders of English kingdoms were not kings by heredity, and that the earlier parts of their pedigrees are fictions of the seventh and eighth centuries.

Doubt is confirmed by a curious feature of all these genealogies. They are represented by trunk lines to which branch lines are joined when necessary.[3] Four of the pedigrees, viz. the Deiran, Bernician, Mercian, and Kentish, are in all manuscripts of the Vespasian group, in the *Historia Brittonum*, and (except part of the Kentish) in the Chronicle, so that they belong to the nucleus of the collection. The trunk pedigrees for these kingdoms end with

narrative of the *Historia Brittonum*, ch. 38 *Octha* is given as the name of Hengest's son; and Æthelweard at the year 596 makes *Ochta* and *Ese* names of the same son.

[1] Finn in the genealogies, if he is the same as Finn Folcwalding of Finnsburh (above, p. 167 n. 5), is Woden's grandfather, while Hengest is Woden's great-great-grandson. But to argue from this that two different Finns are intended is to treat the prehistoric parts of the genealogies as true records or consistent fictions.

[2] Above, pp. 160 ff.

[3] Above, pp. 150 f.

kings who reigned at dates varying from the first half of the seventh to the second half of the eighth century, and to the name of the latest king in each trunk line I add a rough date for the end of his reign. Then from Edwin (632) to Woden, inclusive, there are 14 names in the Deiran line; from Ecgfrith (685) there are 15 names in the Bernician;[1] from Æthelred (704) 14 names in the Mercian; and from Æthelberht (762) 14 names in the Kentish. The East Anglian line may belong to the original group, since it is in the *Historia Brittonum* and the Chronicle has no occasion to use it: from Ælfwald (749) there are 14 names. The Lindsey pedigree, which seems to be a later addition to the Vespasian collection, is exceptional. Apparently it had become settled with only 11 names from Aldfrith (790) to Woden; and, as if to make up for the deficiency, it alone is carried back to Geat, making 16 names in all as compared with 15 in most other pedigrees that include Frealaf as Woden's father.

The regularity of numbers extends to the two Saxon pedigrees that supplement the Vespasian collection. From Ine (726) of Wessex to Woden there are 14 names in the CT list; and the East Saxon line in BM. Addit. 23211 tallies with 14 names from Offa (709) to Seaxnet.[2] The law of averages can produce remarkable uniformity; but here, in the extreme case, the Lindsey pedigree professes to cover a period of some 9 generations more than the Deiran; yet in only 2 out of the 8 lines is the total one more than the norm. The conclusion that there was a recognized standard length for these trunk pedigrees can hardly be avoided.

The agreement can be tested at earlier stages. Starting from three contemporaries, Æthelberht I of Kent, Ælle of Deira, and Æthelric of Bernicia, there are 9 names to Woden in the Kentish line, 13 in the Deiran, 12 in the Bernician. Starting from the first kings (not necessarily contemporary) who founded dynasties in England,[3] there are 6 names from Cerdic of Wessex to Woden in CT, 7 from Oisc of Kent, 8 from Icil of Mercia, 9 from Wuffa of East Anglia, 11 from Ida of Bernicia. So the regularity of numbers is not early. It was attained in the late eighth century; and the influence that could level out variations up to that time must have operated then.

[1] The *Historia Brittonum* and the Chronicle, which derive from a text that did not go beyond Woden to Frealaf, have both 14 names here; but they are not good evidence for that number in their archetype because they disagree in important details; see p. 302 n. 2. They show that the text of the Bernician pedigree was unstable.

[2] See above, p. 153 n. 2.

[3] See above, p. 162 n. 2.

The explanation I suggest is that the original of this collection was a late-eighth-century compilation in a tabular form which is best preserved in the earliest manuscript, Vespasian B VI, though it is there disturbed by undoubted additions in the Mercian branches.[1] The chance agreement in length of two or three important lines, such as the Kentish and the Mercian, would establish a normal length for the columns. Because any irregularity is unpleasingly conspicuous where the columns stand side by side, and perhaps because there seemed to be a certain fitness in having the same number of generations in each trunk line, others of the original collection were made to conform, more probably by choice of alternatives or expansion than by omission. Trunk pedigrees incorporated later, or recorded elsewhere in imitation of the standard collection, would be made to match them. Thus a rigid form was imposed on materials still comparatively fluid.

So although recent writers who have weighed the evidence for the Anglo-Saxon conquest have treated them with respect,[2] the Anglo-Saxon genealogies are not primitive documents. Counting their generations will not lead us back safely to Continental chiefs or kings of the fourth or fifth centuries. For it is exactly their remoter parts, the details of which had no practical importance, that would be fluid enough in the late eighth century to be moulded into standard form by a compiler of tables. I suspect particularly the long Northumbrian pedigrees of Ida and Yffi. They agree so closely together in the number of generations to Woden, and differ so much from the short pedigree of Hengest, that one would expect a master of chronology like Bede to notice them, if they existed in his time and were believed to be authentic. The possibility of Celtic influence on these long prehistoric lists cannot be excluded, for both the Irish and the Welsh

[1] The royal pedigrees of the Vespasian collection can be displayed on one page of moderate size (they occupy the lower three-quarters of the large page of Vespasian B VI); and two pedigrees of about fourteen lines each make a convenient column. How the branches for Northumbria and Mercia were arranged in the original is hard to guess; but at least the latest Mercian branch in Vespasian B VI must be reckoned an accretion. Even so the scribe has managed to end each of his three columns with *Frealaf* in a line across the foot of the page: the Lindsey addition Frioðulf–Finn–Godulf–Geat projects below from the middle column. The arrangement in CCCC 183 and Tiberius B V is further disturbed by the insertion of regnal tables among the genealogies.

[2] Thus J. N. L. Myres *Roman Britain and the English Settlements*, 1936, p. 403 n. approves 'the increasing tendency of scholars to treat the genealogies as archaic and primitive documents'.

seem to have kept pedigrees in early Christian times,[1] they were more fanciful than the Anglo-Saxons, and more inclined to pride themselves on very distant ancestors.

The early names of the Mercian genealogy are the best authenticated: Penda (†655) – Pypba – Crioda – Cynewald – Cnebba – Icil–Eamer–Angengeot–Offa–Uermund–Uihtlaeg–Watholgeot–Woden. Bede (ii. 20) says that Penda was of the Mercian royal stock. Felix, writing before 749, makes St. Guthlac the descendant of Icil through a line of famous kings. *Beowulf* 1960 mentions Eomer (MS. *Geomor*) as if he were a son of the Continental Offa. Offa–Wermund–Wihtlæg have the same relation as Uffo–Wermundus–Viglet in late Danish tradition, which may or may not be independent.[2] Still, the possibility cannot be excluded that legendary heroes of the tribe were absorbed into the royal line; and there are some discrepancies in the tradition. *Waga*[3] in Florence of Worcester and Nennius is an important variation, unless it is a by-form of *Watholgeot*. In *Beowulf* 1957 ff., granted that MS. *Garmund* represents Wermund, Eomer appears to be son of Offa and grandson of Wermund, not, as in the Vespasian collection, grandson of Offa and son of Angengeot (Nennius *Ongen*, Chronicle *Angelþeow*). As historical records, all the genealogies in their early parts fail because fact, fiction, and error cannot be distinguished.

Their historical development is firmer ground. It is no chance that the Vespasian collection can be traced to Mercia in the last decades of the eighth century, for then Mercian power was at its height under King Offa (757–96). To the Pope and to Charlemagne he represented England as no previous king could have done, and so became a force to be reckoned with in European diplomacy. There were still many lesser English kings, whom he controlled by conquest or by marriage alliances; and it was his policy to sustain them in their hereditary kingdoms, so long as they fell in with his purposes. Charlemagne's example may have guided his ambitions, but what is known of their relations shows

[1] I am obliged to Dr. D. A. Binchy for information about early Irish genealogies, and for a reference to T. F. O'Rahilly's *Early Irish History and Mythology*, Dublin 1946. Mr. O'Rahilly thinks that an exaggerated age and authority have been attributed to the Irish documents, see esp. pp. 266 ff. and pp. 408 ff. The difficulty with them and with the Welsh genealogies is that they are recorded in late manuscripts, and the present investigation shows how dangerous it is to assume that late copies of such material accurately reproduce sources that were in existence many centuries earlier.

[2] Above, p. 164.

[3] Above, p. 151 n. 2.

that he set his royal dignity as high as Charlemagne's. No contemporary king could surpass him in the ancestors that tradition gave him among the kings of Angel. And there was besides a strong reason why he should wish to glorify hereditary kingship —his devotion to his only son, and his determination to spare no means that would secure him in the succession.[1] Nine years before his own death he had Ecgfrith crowned; and for the first time in England, as far as records show, the religious rite of anointing was used to make the ceremony more solemn and binding.[2]

These conditions favoured the assembly of the Vespasian pedigrees of ruling kings, together with lists of popes and English bishops which recall Offa's policy of playing a leading part in Church affairs; and the collection was influential in following centuries because of the usefulness of the information it contained, and the advantage in dissemination that a Mercian compilation had when Mercia's authority was widest spread. The direct record of Offa's reign is slight; and the best hope of learning more about his character and policy lies in the possibility that documents like this may be traced back to it.

Offa's hopes were disappointed. Within a few months of his own death, Ecgfrith died; the great kingdom passed to a collateral line, and another generation saw the breakdown of Mercian supremacy. Within a year of Ecgfrith's death Alcuin laments that 'hardly one remains of the old stock of kings, and the more obscure their origin, the more they lack valour'.[3] Though he had reasons for gloom in the state of Northumbria, his words are a reminder that the Church, which had the means of recording royal genealogies, favoured hereditary succession. Its interest as well as its teaching were on the side of legitimate birth, continuity, and civil peace.

With the fall of most of the hereditary kings, emulation and interest in royal genealogies was bound to decline. When Ecgberht died in 839 only the old Wessex line was strong and secure. The record of literary activity in his day is scanty. About the time of his death the expanded form of the Vespasian collection

[1] 'Nam, sicut scis optime, quam multum sanguinis effudit pater eius ut filio regnum confirmaret'; Alcuin in *Mon. Germ. Epist. Karol. Aevi* ii, p. 179; cf. p. 182 foot. See also his letter to Ecgfrith op. cit., p. 105: 'Ecce quam nobilissimus natus es parentibus, quam magna enutritus cura.'

[2] See Stenton *Anglo-Saxon England*, p. 217.

[3] Op. cit., p. 192. See also the following letter (p. 193) in the same sense; cf. Stenton in *Essays on History presented to R. L. Poole*, p. 142.

which I have called CT came South,[1] where copies were made up to the twelfth century. But not till the reign of his grandson Alfred is there written evidence of pride in the history of the West Saxons. Alfred noted some information about the royal family in his lost *Handbook*; his interest may have encouraged the preservation of minor West Saxon pedigrees in the Chronicle of 892; and his prestige is reflected in the pedigree of his father Æthelwulf which surpasses all the rest in its fantastic development.

After a succession of strong kings, Edgar's reign marks a new high point in the political and cultural history of the West Saxon kingdom; and in his time the Regnal Table was brought up to date in the version beginning: 'Eadweard and Eadmund and Æðelred æðelingas syndon Eadgares suna cyninges.'[2] That is the end of the development. The decline of Ecgberht's house followed swiftly. Great enthusiasm for hereditary English kings is not to be expected in the reigns of Edward the Martyr, Æthelred 'the Unready', Cnut the Dane and his sons, or Edward the Confessor. The Conquest was still more unfavourable to interest in Anglo-Saxon royal genealogies. They are dropped from the post-Conquest Chronicles E and F; and at Christ Church, Canterbury, the writer of F erased many of them from the Parker Chronicle to make room for other matter. But under Henry I the new antiquarian school of native chroniclers—Florence of Worcester, Simeon of Durham, William of Malmesbury—collected and recorded all they could find about the Anglo-Saxon kings; and Florence or a continuator revised the Vespasian lists of kings and bishops. Later chroniclers did little more than add to the corruption of forgotten names. For the pedigrees of English kings the fantastic pedigree of Æthelwulf served as a model throughout the Middle Ages; and Kemble[3] quotes from rolls at Cambridge and Paris a curious fifteenth-century collection of the royal genealogies of various countries. There Henry VI is traced back to Adam through Gothus–Cinrincius (Cynric)–Boerinus (Beowius)–Sceldius–Sceph and other old names derived from William of Malmesbury.

[1] Above, p. 149.

[2] Above, p. 148 n. 2.

[3] Postscript to the preface of *Beowulf* ii (1837), p. vii. The names are quoted from the Trinity College, Cambridge, roll O. 5.54.

APPENDIX A

Genealogies and the Structure of the *Anglo-Saxon Chronicle*

Some questions affecting the compilation of the Chronicle are assembled here because the genealogies supply clues.

(i) Was There a Chronicle Ending at 855? Many critics agree with Plummer[1] that an earlier form of the Chronicle ended at 855, and they rely on the great pedigree of Æthelwulf entered under that year, regarding it as a final flourish. Its evidence is at best indecisive. Politically Æthelwulf's last years were clouded, so that a contemporary would scarcely choose his death (858 entered at 855) as the occasion for such a flourish. Since he was father of four succeeding kings, his pedigree might be added to honour or flatter any of them, and particularly Alfred after he had re-established the prestige of his kingdom: Æthelwulf's pedigree gave Alfred's, as well as Ecgberht's.

But did this long pedigree exist before Alfred's reign? It is first witnessed by the Chronicle of 892, and (with a significant variation) by Asser,[2] who wrote about the same time. The West Saxon Regnal Table, compiled or revised after Alfred's accession in 871, does not carry the line beyond Woden, the old end-point for most of the royal genealogies; and that is not easy to explain if the longer form had already won sufficient status to be adopted in a chronicle up to 855.

It might still be maintained that a chronicle up to 855 was produced very early in Alfred's reign. But the pedigree of Æthelwulf is joined to its annal in the same way as are the pedigrees in eighth-century annals, e.g. Offa's at 755. In the context it reads more likc additional material, artlessly tacked on, than the studied close of a work ending at 855.

(ii) The Regnal Table and the Chronicle. Plummer insists that the West Saxon Regnal Table[3] was drawn up to be the Preface of a chronicle composed in Alfred's reign.[4] W. H. Stevenson says the Table was probably older than Alfred's time.[5] The question raised by this

[1] Edition ii, p. cxiii n. For discussion see R. H. Hodgkin *A History of the Anglo-Saxons*, 1935, ii, p. 707.

[2] Above, p. 159.

[3] See pp. 152 ff. above.

[4] Edition ii, pp. lxxxix ff. and cvi; *Life and Times of Alfred the Great*, 1902, p. 146.

[5] *Asser*, p. 153 and note. The reasons given are not compelling. Even if the forms *Celin* and *Eaba* (above, p. 153 n. 5) were out of date in Alfred's time, a compiler might take them over from an older source. So it is with *Creoda* (below, pp. 195 f.). The references to Alfred's lost *Handbook* in Florence of Worcester and William of Malmesbury show that it contained genealogical information about the West Saxon royal family, but hardly point to this particular regnal table.

difference of opinion between two masters of the subject is interesting for the history of the Chronicle of 892.

One expects a preface that covers matter dealt with in the text to be based on the text or on the same sources; but the Regnal Table disagrees with the Chronicle annals in many points and is clearly based on other sources.[1] In his examination of these discrepancies Plummer distinguished 'the writer of the genealogical Preface' from 'the compilers of the Chronicle',[2] without explaining further. But the discrepancies are easier to account for if the Regnal Table was an older independent document of some official standing, which the compiler of the Chronicle adopted without critical scrutiny. Its divergences might then escape notice, as they could scarcely do if it was composed as part of the plan of the Chronicle.

There is a better reason for thinking that the Table was originally an independent document. The Fragment from Alfred's time shows the earliest state of the text: it has correctly *Ceaulin*, not *Celm*, and it omits the details of Cenred's family which are related to the Chronicle annal for 718.[3] It accompanied a martyrology, and is followed not by a chronicle but by computus matter—genealogies of the East Saxon kings and Latin verses on calendarial subjects. This is the natural context of a regnal table. Its association with the Chronicle of 892 seems to be secondary; and an independent origin might explain why only a minority of the later copies and extensions are found in manuscripts containing the Chronicle.

That the 'genealogical Preface' was in the archetype of the Chronicle of 892 follows naturally from Plummer's view. If that view is rejected the question becomes an open one. Certainly it has the function of a preface in the Parker MS. The same text appears on the leaf in BM. MS. Addit. 34652 which originally belonged to MS. Otho B XI;[4]

[1] Even in spelling it was not assimilated to the text of the Chronicle. *Ceardic*, which appears at different places in the Fragment, in MS. Kk. 3. 18, and in the Parker MS., was evidently the spelling of the Table. The text of the Chronicle (Parker, B, C, D, E) has regularly *Cer-*. *Ceard-* twice in the late MS. F from Canterbury is not significant.

[2] Edition ii, p. 1.

[3] See above, p. 154.

[4] Above, p. 153 n. 1. Plummer (ii, pp. xcix f.) satisfied himself that the Chronicle in Otho B XI was a close derivative of the Parker MS.; and had he known the origin of the leaf printed by Napier he would not have treated its text of the Regnal Table, which repeats glaring errors of the Parker MS., as an earlier stage from which corruption in the Parker Table can be explained (ii, pp. 2 f.). The Parker Table omits Ceawlin's reign altogether. After Cynric's reign the Otho B XI leaf has: 'þa he gefor þa feng Ceol[win] to þam rice 7 heol seofan gear. þa he gefor þa feng Ceol to þam rice 7 heold syx gear. þa he gefor þa feng Ceolwulf, &c.' Napier noted that [win] is added by an early modern hand. It has no authority, and the duplication of *Ceol* must be explained as an error made in copying from the defective Parker text.

but as the Chronicle in this manuscript is a derivative of the Parker text (A), it adds nothing to the evidence.

The only other manuscript of the Chronicle with which the Regnal Table is associated is Tiberius A VI (B), which has the annals up to 977, and once contained a regnal table (now in MS. Tiberius A III)[1] continued up to the accession of Edward the Martyr in 975. If this leaf immediately preceded the Chronicle it should be decisive for the archetype, since B is independent of A both in the annals and in the Table: it keeps Creoda whose name has been excluded from the Parker MS.[2] But the original position of the leaf is uncertain. Its modest opening line does not suggest the beginning of a major work. Joscelin's transcript in Bodleian MS. Laud Misc. 661 puts the Table at the end of the Chronicle. MS. C of the Chronicle, which up to 977 is closely related to B, and which continues the annals beyond that date, does not contain the Table. These facts would be conveniently explained if the Table followed the Chronicle in Tiberius A VI. If so, the Parker MS. is the only evidence that the Table served as preface to the archetype of 892. Still, prefaces that are not closely bound to their texts are likely to be dropped in late copies; and the interpolation of Cuthburg and Cwenburg is best explained by association with the Chronicle.

(iii) THE POSITION OF PEDIGREES IN THE CHRONICLE. Pedigrees usually come at the ends of annals. This might be due to the compiler's plan; but longer additions to an existing framework would naturally have the end-position. Then it is worth noting the places where something follows a pedigree, viz. 676, 685, 716, 731. In every case the following matter comes from Bede's *Epitome* (*Eccl. Hist.* v. 24). This is consistent with Earle's opinion, advanced on general grounds, that the almost complete incorporation of Bede's *Epitome* was late;[3] and as the pedigrees at 685, 716, 731 are from the Vespasian group, that source appears to have been incorporated before the Epitome. In the annal for 626, where matter from the Epitome precedes Penda's pedigree from the Vespasian source, the beginning of the Penda entry seems to be defective. The usual formal statement of his accession is lacking, and it may have fallen out as a result of the insertion of a sentence from the Epitome at this point. We seem here to catch a glimpse of a draft of the Chronicle in which the patchwork of compilation was visible.

Other copies show that the sentence containing Ceawlin was differently worded: 'þa he forðferde þa feng Ceawlin to, his sunu, and heold, &c.'

[1] For the authorities, see Plummer ii, p. xc n. There is a facsimile in Thorpe *The Anglo-Saxon Chronicle* (Rolls Series) i (1861), pl. vii. Robert Cotton himself may have removed the regnal tables from his MSS. Tiberius A VI and Otho B XI when he was compiling the genealogy of James I, which he carried back to Alfred. [See now N. R. Ker, *Catalogue*, p. 249].

[2] See p. 154 above.

[3] *Two Saxon Chronicles Parallel*, 1865, pp. viii f. Plummer agrees in his edition ii, p. cxiii.

(iv) THE CHRONICLE AND THE OE. BEDE. The Old English version of Bede's *History* omits the Epitome. Plummer notes that, even where it depends on the History, the Chronicle of 892 does not agree in expression with the *OE. Bede*, as it often does with the *OE. Orosius*. He infers, unconvincingly, that Bede had not yet been translated in 892,[1] and explains that the Epitome was omitted from the *OE. Bede* because it was already available in the Chronicle.[2]

There is another indication. The pedigrees of the early kings of Kent—Hengest to Woden and Æthelberht to Hengest—are exceptionally omitted from the Chronicle of 892. The likeliest reason is that they were available in two of the most important chapters of Bede for Anglo-Saxon history,[3] one giving the Continental origins of the English invaders,[4] the other recording both the arrival of Augustine and the names of the Bretwaldas or overlords of all England. So here, as in the treatment of the Epitome, there is evidence that the two works were regarded as complementary. If the *OE. Bede* was not earlier than the Chronicle of 892, it must have been a related project carried out at the

[1] Edition ii, p. cviii; cf. the fuller discussion in his *Life and Times of Alfred the Great*, pp. 156 ff. Without touching on the large questions of Alfred's part in the compilation of the Chronicle and in the translation of Bede, it is difficult to examine this argument. Underlying it is the assumption that these two works and the *OE. Orosius*, all from the last decade of the ninth century, have the same literary and linguistic background. But on that assumption one would expect likenesses of expression between the Chronicle and the *OE. Bede*, whichever was the earlier. Their absence points to a different literary and linguistic background for the *OE. Bede*. See also p. 196 n. 3 below.

There is another underlying assumption—that Alfred himself translated or rather adapted Orosius. The view now prevalent, which I accept provisionally, is that he encouraged, or planned, or perhaps contributed information to the Chronicle of 892, but did not himself compile it. How then is the likeness with *Orosius* to be explained? One possibility is that the compiler (or a compiler) of the Chronicle of 892 and the adapter of Orosius were the same person, whom the king commissioned to do both works. It would argue some vanity and administrative weakness in King Alfred if, having conceived a great plan of education through the vernacular, he made the provision of the books 'most necessary for all men to know' depend too much on his own health and his leisure for translating.

The attribution of the *OE. Orosius* to Alfred rests on William of Malmesbury *Gesta Regum* (Rolls Series) i, p. 132. The *OE. Bede* is attributed to him by William of Malmesbury ibid.; by a Latin couplet in MS. Cambr. Univ. Lib. Kk. 3. 18; and by Ælfric *Catholic Homilies* ed. Thorpe ii, p. 118.

[2] Edition ii, p. cviii, note 6.

[3] See above, p. 146. The short pedigree of the East Anglian king Eorpwald, also in Bede, might have been given under 632, but its omission is not significant.

[4] Additions from this chapter are made in Chronicle E (which takes over Hengest's pedigree), and by a hand of *c.* 1100 in the Parker MS. The passage on the Bretwaldas is elaborated in all copies of the Chronicle.

same time. The almost negligible use of the text of Bede (as distinct from the Epitome) in the Chronicle of 892[1] is further evidence of a plan of work to avoid overlapping. So there is reason to think that the Epitome was first incorporated in the Chronicle about 892.

(v) THE SHORTER WEST SAXON PEDIGREES. The non-West Saxon genealogies of the Vespasian group were drawn on up to Offa's accession, entered at 755, by which date their usefulness was exhausted. But the shorter West Saxon pedigrees in the list at p. 156 above end with 728. Under that year, at the accession of Æthelheard whose parentage is not given, the pedigree of Oswald 'the Atheling', against whom he fought, is taken back to Ceawlin. The Anglo-Saxons were often content to state bare facts where we expect them to be coloured or explained. So this pedigree, with the mention of Oswald's death in 730, seems to be the only record of a serious contest for the throne, derived from a source which supported the unsuccessful Oswald as having the hereditary right.

Of King Æscwine also nothing is known, except that the Chronicle gives his pedigree on his accession in 674, and notes that he fought against Wulfhere of Mercia in 675 and died in 676. But the pedigree is there because he belonged to a collateral line which had not produced a king for several generations. So it is with his successors: Centwine who became king in 676, Ceadwalla who 'began to fight for the kingship' in 685, and Ine whose reign began in 688. If Ceolwulf (597) and Cynegils (611) are brought in for completeness, it appears that the Chronicle gives the pedigree of each early West Saxon king on his accession, if his hereditary claim could be stated in pedigree form and he was not thought to be the son of the preceding king.

These short Wessex genealogies, found only in the Chronicle, are an integral part of its plan, and should be distinguished from the longer ones which are by comparison excrescences: the honorific genealogies of Æthelwulf (855) given at his death, and of Cerdic (552) given long after his death and the accession of Cynric; the antiquarian genealogies of Ida of Bernicia (547), Ælle of Deira (560), Penda of Mercia (626).[2]

Beyond the routine statement that their 'kin goes back to Cerdic', neither the Chronicle annals nor the Regnal Table gives pedigrees for the kings who ruled Wessex from 728, when Oswald the Atheling failed to secure the throne, till 802 when Ecgberht re-established an hereditary succession. There is no sign that any of the kings without pedigrees—Æthelheard, Cuthred, Sigebryht, Cynewulf, Beorhtric—was the natural heir to his predecessor; the alliteration of names is broken, and the

[1] Plummer ii, p. lxi n.

[2] The pedigrees of Wihtred of Kent (694) and Offa of Mercia (755) might belong to either group. Both follow a struggle for the throne; but they give additional information about great neighbouring kings, and derive from the same source as the longer pedigrees.

violence of the times is epitomized in the famous annal at 755, which brings together the deposition and murder of Sigebryht, and the deaths of his brother Cyneheard and King Cynewulf (786) in a surprise bid for revenge and power. In such times it would be useless and might be dangerous to record royal pedigrees.

So the cessation of short pedigrees after 728 is not good evidence of a change in the authorship of the Chronicle annals soon after that year:[1] rather, it indicates a change in the conditions of kingship.

Nor is there much weight in the argument that pedigrees like those of Æscwine and Oswald the Atheling must derive from a contemporary written source because these princes were forgotten or negligible in the ninth century.[2] Kings and strong claimants to the throne are not quickly forgotten. One may still find villagers who, without a written record, can trace back their descent through a century and a half to an undistinguished great-grandfather. In Anglo-Saxon times when the conception of kindred was vital, the descendants of kings might reach back still farther in memory: thus Alfred's mother Osburh was reputed to come from Jutish stock, of the kin of Stuf and Wihtgar,[3] the sixth-century rulers of the Isle of Wight. In the ninth century, when hereditary succession was firmly re-established, a careful investigator of family traditions could have recovered the pedigrees of Oswald and Æscwine, and devised short pedigrees for much earlier kings of Wessex at least as credible as those in the Chronicle. But such an investigator, working when the quarrels of the eighth century were no longer active, would surely have had the curiosity to recover the pedigrees of some of the kings who ruled between 728 and 802. That none of them is recorded is an indication that pedigrees like those of Æscwine and Oswald the Atheling came from an eighth-century written source; and there is a presumption that the same source contained a pedigree of Ine.

(vi) Creoda.—In the early part of the Chronicle there is little sign of the patient investigation by a co-ordinating mind that distinguishes Bede's *History*. No doubt some attempt was made, in Alfred's time and earlier, to collect obvious sources of information; but they were slight and scrappy, and chance plays a great part in the record. One such chance sets the problem of Creoda, who has been mentioned incidentally above, pp. 154, 157. Creoda is unknown to the Chronicle narrative. That narrative seems to be based on a tradition in alliterative form which named a succession of fathers and sons in pairs as the builders of the pre-Christian West Saxon kingdom—Cerdic and Cynric, Cynric and Ceawlin, Ceawlin and Cutha. Because later West Saxon kings claimed descent from them, Cerdic and Cynric probably enjoyed a pre-eminence

[1] Chadwick *Origin of the English Nation*, p. 27.

[2] Wheeler *E.H.R.* xxxvi, pp. 161 f.

[3] Asser, ch. 2. For the preservation of such a tradition a detailed pedigree is not necessary.

in eighth- and ninth-century tradition greater than that they had in earlier times. But from the later ninth century onwards a rival account, which makes Creoda Cerdic's son and Cynric's father, has troubled chroniclers and historians; and this problem of conflicting traditions can now be clarified:

First, Creoda occurs only in one context, the pedigree of Ine (or his brother Ingild) to Cerdic, which is the same in CT and the West Saxon Regnal Table (R^B), and (except that they have the short form *Cutha* for *Cuthwulf*) in Asser and the archetype of the Chronicle circulated in 892. All represent one document which ran, as we have seen:[1] 'Ine Coenreding, Coenred Ceolualding, Ceoluald Cuðuulfing, Cuðuulf Cuðuining, Cuðuine Celining, Celin Cynricing, Cynric Crioding, Criodo Ceardicing'; and had it not turned up in West Saxon court circles in the second half of the ninth century, no hint of a West Saxon Creoda would have reached us.

Secondly, historians must decide whether there was a Creoda son of Cerdic, not by the evidence of alliteration, which suits both alternatives;[2] nor by proof that his name stood in the archetype of the Chronicle at the year 855, because the Chronicle has both traditions; but simply on the value they attach to this lost document as against the Chronicle narrative. Its authority should not be prejudiced by the pedigree of Cerdic (R^A) to Woden which, in shorter or longer form, is associated with it.

Thirdly, there is no ninth-century or later evidence for a living tradition of Creoda in Wessex, as distinct from this slender thread of written tradition. The West Saxon form of the name is *Crĭda* (*Crȳda*); yet in the three copies of the Chronicle which contain it (B, C, D), in CT, in R^B of the Regnal Table, in Asser, and as late as the correcting hand of William of Malmesbury's *Gesta Regum* and Matthew Paris, the West Saxon form never appears—always the non-West Saxon *Creoda*. There are other examples where an obsolete form of a forgotten name is retained as a kind of fossil. *Bieda* is the early West Saxon form of Anglian *Beda*, and *Bieda* the son of Port keeps the spelling with *ie* at the year 501 in all late Chronicle manuscripts (B, C, E, F) and in William of Malmesbury, where a living tradition would give *Byda* or *Bida*. Again, Bede's *Oisc* son of Hengest should be represented in ninth-century West Saxon or Kentish by *Oesc*, later *Ēsc*; yet *Æsc* (24 instances), presumably with a short vowel, appears in all manuscripts of the Chronicle, whatever their date and place of origin, through a misreading of the unfamiliar *oesc* in a written source and mechanical copying thereafter.[3]

[1] Above, pp. 155, 157.

[2] I cannot follow this part of W. H. Stevenson's argument in his *Asser*, pp. 158 f.

[3] Æthelweard ii, ch. 2 has *Ese* (from *Oese*), and William of Malmesbury *Gesta Regum* i, ch. 8 has *Eisc*, a misreading of Bede's *Oisc*; but both have *Æsc* from the Chronicle in their narrative. *Oisc* in the Annals of St. Neot's is better explained by direct reference to Bede than by an old copy of the

APPENDIX B

The Danish Royal Pedigree in *Beowulf*

The royal pedigree near the beginning of *Beowulf* is treated separately, because it professes to give the descent of a Danish, not an Anglo-Saxon, king. It has been discussed by critics of the poem with a wealth of suggested explanations; and there is room for differences of opinion. I propose to run over the scanty evidence afresh, without being drawn too far away from genealogies; and to start from what seems relatively firm ground: that in its remoter parts the pedigree of Æthelwulf in the Chronicle is a fiction of the late ninth century.[1]

In the following table, which should read with the notes on p. 173 above, Æ is taken from Æthelweard's West Saxon genealogy; B is the Danish genealogy from *Beowulf*; D the Danish genealogy according to the tradition of Denmark recorded by Sven Aageson *c.* 1190.

Æ	B	D
Scef	Scef	——
Scyld	Scyld	Scyld
Beo	Beowulf	Frotho
Tetuua, &c.	Healfdene, &c.	Healfdene, &c.

With Tetuua in Æ and Healfdene in B and D the lists separate and take on a national character; but the likeness of the English documents Æ and B in the first three names cannot be mere coincidence, and since both lists are fictitious, it is to be explained by borrowing or conflation.

That *Beowulf* here has the greater authority of a record from the seventh or eighth century should not be taken for granted. Whether the text recorded *circa* 1000 was all put into verse by one author, or is the product of two or more who worked at different times, is a matter of opinion: there is no old tradition or fair presumption which gives a preference to one view unless the other can be established. But those who have regarded *Beowulf* as to some extent composite are agreed that the Introduction contains comparatively late work; and they include such accomplished critics as Müllenhoff, Ten Brink, Bradley, who noted that it stands outside the numbering of sections, and Schücking, who

Chronicle used by the annalist, as Stevenson suggests, *Asser*, p. 105. *Æsc* for *Oesc*, *Esc* seems to be characteristic of the Chronicle tradition. The Vespasian group has *Oese*, *Oesing* by scribal confusion of *c* and *e* (cf. Nennius *Ossa*). In the rendering of *Hist. Eccl.* ii. 5 the MSS. of the *OE. Bede* have *Oesc* (so B; *Oese* C, O, and Ca), *Oescing*, *Oesces*, except Tanner 10 which has *Æsc*, &c., perhaps by influence of the Chronicle. It is noteworthy that the archetype of the *OE. Bede* had *Oesc*, and the archetype of the Chronicle had *Æsc*, although any one person applying his mind to both texts could not fail to see that they represent the same king; cf. p. 193 n. 1 above.

[1] See above, pp. 179 f.

assembled differences of syntactical usage.[1] This has a bearing on two famous difficulties in the genealogy it presents.

First, it twice names as Scyld's son a Beowulf, not mentioned elsewhere, who is brought into no relation with the hero of the poem. 'Beowulf' is a rare name: outside the poem it occurs once in English pre-Conquest documents, once (*Bjólfr*) in Icelandic; and it is not in the tradition of Denmark. So the odds are long against a legendary Danish Beowulf appearing at the commencement of a poem about Beowulf the Geat.[2] And if two legendary Beowulfs happened to come into the same narrative, one would expect some reference to the strange coincidence—that Hrothgar, for instance, when he greets the visiting hero, would mention that his own grandfather bore the same name. The other English documents—Asser, the Chronicle of 892, Æthelweard—support the sequence Sceaf–Scyld–Beo. If the English poem is brought into line by reading *Beo* for *Beowulf* in lines 18 and 53, the difficulty is removed; no further consequential change is needed for metrical or other reasons; and a possible explanation of the confusion is provided. A reader or copyist, beginning the adventures of Beowulf the Geat, might hastily assume that *Beo* in the Introduction stood for the name of the hero. Such a superficial error could be made at any stage up to the surviving copy, and if it was made late, no adjustment in the rest of the narrative need be expected. The proposal to read *Beo* is old and well known. Few conjectures have so strong a claim to be received into the text. Its acceptance leaves unprejudiced two interrelated questions which lie outside the present scope: whether Beo and Beowulf the Geat are ultimately connected, and whether Frotho's dragon-fight is the same as that described in *Beowulf*.[3]

The second difficulty is in the expression *Scyld Scefing* which normally means 'Scyld, son of Sceaf'. Scyld in the Danish genealogy is reasonably accounted for as an eponymous king whose name has been deduced from *Scyldingas*, i.e. 'people of (or with) the shield', so that he ought not to have a known father. Again, the story of Scyld referred to in *Beowulf*—that he arrived as an unknown child, alone in a boat laden with treasures—is of a type used elsewhere to account for a hero whose origin is unknown. Æthelweard tells the story of Sceaf, and the two accounts cannot be reconciled. It has been suggested that *Scyld Scefing* in *Beowulf* means

[1] H. Bradley in *Encyc. Brit.* (1910) s.v. *Beowulf*; see his *Collected Papers*, 1928, p. 207; L. Schücking *Beowulfs Rückkehr*, Halle 1905, pp. 53, 72.

[2] R. C. Boer *Beowulf*, Halle 1912, pp. 110 ff. argues that the Danish king Beowulf was originally the hero of the dragon-fight in *Beowulf*, and that this part of the Introduction was once attached to the dragon-fight. But the objection to two Beowulfs holds, and is not weakened by Boer's elaborate construction at pp. 142 ff. of the same book. It is not as if *Beowulf* meant etymologically anything like 'monster-killer'.

[3] E. Sievers *Berichten der Kgl. Sächs. Gesellschaft der Wissenschaften* (1895), pp. 181 ff. noted that Frotho, who occupies the place of Beo(wulf) in the genealogy from Denmark, was the hero of a dragon-fight.

'Scyld of the Sheaf'. The purpose of this unusual interpretation is to make *Beowulf* consistent, but the objections outweigh that advantage. (i) Æthelweard, the reviser of the Regnal Table in Edgar's reign,[1] and fairly certainly Asser and the Chronicle of 892, take *Sceafing* to mean 'son of Sceaf'. If the rare meaning 'of the sheaf' were possible, they might be wrong, though such an error would imply that they did not know a story of Scyld and the sheaf. (ii) Names of tribes like *Scyldingas*, *Helmingas* 'people of the shield', 'helm', are not really parallel to *Scyld Scefing* in the sense 'Scyld who on a particular occasion was associated with a sheaf'. (iii) There is no hint of the sheaf story in any pre-Conquest authority. It may well be an etymological fancy of William of Malmesbury,[2] and he tells the story of Sceaf, not of Scyld. Then, on a balance of probabilities, *Scyld Scefing* in *Beowulf* means 'Scyld, son of Sceaf'; and Sceaf and Beo, unknown in Scandinavian tradition, have been adopted from English sources into the Danish genealogy given in the English poem. On this view the story of Scyld's mysterious arrival, which is not in the tradition of Denmark, is likely to be borrowed from the English legend of Sceaf. It must be borrowed from somewhere if, as the leading authorities agree, the Danish ruler Scyld has been deduced from the people-name *Scyldingas*.

There is good evidence for an eponymous Danish Scyld. Was there also another Scyld, whose existence in native English tradition provided a false link between the English and Danish genealogies? The occurrence of Sceaf–Scyld(Sceldwea)–Beaw in the fantastic part of Æthelwulf's pedigree is not clear evidence. By 892–3, when these names first appear, the Danes had been raiding in England for a century and had made extensive settlements in the rich and populous eastern counties. Not much is known about them before the late tenth century, but as intermediaries between English and Scandinavians, as an audience for the oral literature of both peoples, and as possible preservers of heathen legends that had lost their hold in the long-christianized South, the inhabitants of the Danelaw cannot be neglected. It is noteworthy that Æthelweard, whose province is generally agreed to be the English South-West, gives the Scandinavian form *Uuithar* for Woden's son in the genealogy of Hengest, not Bede's *Uecta*, or *Uegdæg* of the Vespasian group.

A related question should be taken first: Does *Sceldwea* (for that is the archetypal form proved by the agreement of Asser, the Parker MS., and *Sceldweaing* in Chronicle B) represent the same name as *Scyld*? Æthelweard, a good authority on this point, thought that it did, and I prefer to follow him. With no satisfactory explanation of the ending *-wea*[3] a

[1] See above, p. 148 n. 2. [2] See above, pp. 177 f.

[3] If the tradition of Scyld was borrowed from or revived by the Danish invaders and settlers, it is just possible that *w* in *Sceldwea* may reflect the old ending of the nominative in the *u*- stem, which seems to have survived as late as the ninth century in Norse usage. But in these rigmaroles a jingling

doubt must remain; but those who take *Sceldwea* and *Scyld* to be distinct names whose likeness caused confusion between the English and Danish genealogies, cannot fairly use the following Abingdon story as evidence for a native English Scyld. It is not reasonable to postulate an English Sceldwea, an English Scyld and a Danish Scyld, all different, in order to explain the recorded genealogies.

The Abingdon story was first adduced by Kemble, and has been accepted as witness to an ancient tradition by such good authorities as Chadwick and Olrik.[1] It appears in the thirteenth-century chronicle of Abingdon,[2] and may be summarized:

> In the reign of King Edmund (939–46) a dispute arose between Oxford claimants and the monks of Abingdon about a meadow called Beri,[3] lying between the Thames and Gifteleia (Iffley). After prayer and fasting, the monks were divinely inspired with a plan for settling the rightful ownership. Rising at dawn on an appointed day, they took a round shield, placed upon it a sheaf of corn, and above that a wax candle of suitable size. They lighted the candle, floated the shield with its freight in the Thames near their church, and a few of them followed it in a boat. It moved from side to side of the river, pointing out the monastery's lands as with a finger. When it came to Beri, which is an island in winter and often in summer, the candle left mid-stream and passed right round the island-meadow, thus proving it to be the property of the monks of Abingdon.

The credibility of this story is easily shaken. It is recorded late in a chronicle which is full of inventions. It is not in the twelfth-century Abingdon chronicle Claudius C IX.[4] It comes from a monastery noted for falsifications, and its motive is the establishment of Abingdon's claim to disputed land by a kind of judgement of God given at a time beyond the reach of memory. Edmund's reign may have been chosen because Abingdon had so little authentic history until Edmund's successor Eadred, by his grant to Bishop Æthelwold, transformed it from a small, neglected monastery into one of the most influential in England.[5] That the experiment described was ever made is impossible, except by

tendency may corrupt the endings: cf. *Aloc*, *Benoc* in the Chronicle pedigree of Ida, or *Sceldius–Beowius–Tetius–Getius* in William of Malmesbury.

[1] H. M. Chadwick *Origin of the English Nation*, pp. 278 ff.; A. Olrik *The Heroic Legends of Denmark* transl. L. M. Hollander, New York 1919, ch. viii.

[2] Ed. J. Stevenson, Rolls Series, 1858, i, p. 89.

[3] *Berig* occurs again at p. 126 of the same volume in the Anglo-Saxon boundaries of 20 hides said to have been given to Abingdon by King Ine. See Birch *Cartularium Saxonicum* Nos. 906 and 971. Mr. G. B. Grundy identified Berig as 'the great eyot which extends from the Gut to the railway bridge over the Thames at Kennington'; and Mrs. Gelling, who is preparing the Berkshire material for the English Place-Name Society, regards this identification as reasonable.

[4] See F. M. Stenton *The Early History of the Abbey of Abingdon*, 1913, pp. 2 ff. for the relations of the texts.

[5] Stenton op. cit. esp. pp. 7 ff.

a miracle (which is no doubt intended); for the shield and its freight moved along the Thames against the main stream, which runs from Oxford to Abingdon. Still, it may be argued that the association of a shield and a sheaf is beyond the inventive power of the Abingdon monks, that it was suggested by some ancient ritual, and so points to an old connexion between the shadowy Sceaf and Scyld. I doubt whether we can set such limits to invention in the most fertile age of romance. So far from suggesting an old ritual, the chronicler claims that it was a divinely inspired plan for a very exceptional occasion; and it cannot be assumed that disputes about eyots were frequent enough to preserve the memory of an ancient rite for settling them. The germ of the story is the observation that in a backwater of a slow river, like the Thames near Oxford and Abingdon, the current sometimes runs in a direction opposite to that of the river that feeds it. Under favourable conditions an object floating down the river might pass round an eyot bounded by the main stream and a backwater.

Then again, the candle, lighted in the daytime and in the open air, is as prominent as the sheaf, more prominent than the shield. It has all the appearance of a Christian symbol of divine guidance and illumination, and is easier to explain as the fancy of a monkish chronicler than as a survival from primitive ritual practice. By the same symbolism, a sheaf, which is light and conspicuous, could represent the produce of the disputed land. The 'raft' should be something dignified and free from the suspicion of contrivance. A shield might suggest defence of the right; but apart from that, could anything more suitable be imagined than the round shield, buoyant, saucer-shaped, floating without bias towards any direction, and convenient for displaying the candle and sheaf to the onlookers? It may be granted that there is not much evidence for the practical use of the round shield after the Conquest, but even if no specimens were preserved in old stores of arms, the round shield could be seen in carvings, tapestries, and the illustrations of books. Anybody who has dealt with the falsifications of charters will not underestimate the antiquarian interests of the Abingdon monks, or their ingenuity in supporting claims to land. Only by giving it the benefit of every doubt can this late story be converted into evidence that the early Anglo-Saxons knew of two closely associated personages or spirits, an English Sceaf and an English Scyld.

Another consideration bears on the identity of Scyld. The only indication that Heremod was connected with the English is in the fantastic pedigree of Æthelwulf, a Saxon not an Anglian king, and in the part of it which his descendant Æthelweard omits. As evidence it is worthless. But in *Beowulf* 901 ff., 1709 ff. it is implied that Heremod ruled the Danes before Scyld, and late Scandinavian tradition also suggests that he was a ruler of the Danes.[1] If then a Danish Heremod is

[1] See the brief summary by A. Heusler in J. Hoops *Reallexikon der Germanischen Altertumskunde* (1915) s.v. *Heremod.*

borrowed into Æthelwulf's pedigree in the Chronicle, Scyld (Sceldwea) who appears as his son in the same pedigree was probably understood to be the Danish Scyld, ruler of the Scyldings.

To suppose that there was only one legendary ruler called Scyld has the advantage of simplicity, for the name is rare. Curiously enough, when a rare legendary name appears in Anglo-Saxon in more than one context, some critics of standing assume that there were two namesakes: two Beowulfs, two Germanic Finns, two Hengests. A strange coincidence is always possible, though one of this kind would be so confusing in legend that we should hardly expect it to survive. But a monotonous repetition of the same coincidence is improbable. The old rule against multiplying entities beyond what is necessary favours one Scyld, and perhaps should tilt the balance in favour of one Sceaf(a), the same that *Widsith* makes the legendary ruler of the Lombards.[1]

It should be plain that this discussion of the pedigree in *Beowulf* has led to little more than an expression of opinion, or rather of a number of interrelated opinions. From the nature of the evidence, one cannot make each step secure: nor, after several choices between alternative possibilities, is there the satisfaction of showing that the result fits neatly into another group of established facts. It is, and is likely to remain, a problem with too many unknowns.

Still it may be worth while to complete the interpretation by suggesting a way in which Sceaf, Scyld, Beo might appear in that order in three Anglo-Saxon documents. In the earliest recorded, the pedigree of Æthelwulf from the Chronicle of 892, the stem-vowels of *Sceld-*, *Beaw* are non-West Saxon (*Sceaf* is general Old English). So it may be inferred that, at that time, the names did not belong to West Saxon tradition, but were imported into Æthelwulf's pedigree from a non-West Saxon source; and, on the analogy of forms like *Creoda*,[2] from a written, not from an oral source. Again, all three names are distinguished by having simple meanings 'sheaf', 'shield', 'barley', which suggests myth and remoteness in time. And they have yet another feature in common. *Sceaf* is connected with *Scani* by Æthelweard; the names alliterate; and if Sceafa of the Lombards in *Widsith* is the same, the Lombards had a strong tradition that they came from *Scadanau*.[3] Scyld, if he is the eponym of the Scyldings (Danes), had the same kingdom, *Scedenig* in *Beowulf* 1686, and his name also alliterates. According to *Beowulf* 19, Scyld's son Beo[wulf] ruled *Scedelandum in*. All the place-names[4] stand for the southern part of Scandinavia, which later gave its name to the whole peninsula.

[1] See above, p. 171 n. 4.

[2] Above, p. 196.

[3] Cf. *Origo Gentis Langobardorum* in *Mon. Germ. Hist. Rerum Langobardicarum*, &c. (1878), p. 2; Paul the Deacon's *Historia Langobardorum*, same volume, i, ch. 1.

[4] For the etymological relations of this group of names, see E. Björkman *Studien über die Eigennamen im* Beowulf, Halle 1920, pp. 99 f.

There is plenty of early evidence for genealogical speculation and systematization. Tacitus's notice (*Germania*, ch. ii) of the god Tuisto, with a son Mannus and three grandsons from whom the German tribes derived, was developed by the sixth century to account for the derivation of the peoples of Europe from Alanus, a descendant of Japhet.[1] We have seen how gods and heroes were arranged in neat lines of descent in the remoter parts of Anglo-Saxon royal genealogies. *Widsith* is evidence of a learned and antiquarian interest in collecting and arranging the rulers and tribes of Germanic legend. Then it seems likely enough that the question would be asked: Who was the first ruler in *Scedenig*, the traditional homeland of so many Germanic tribes? Was it Sceaf, or Scyld as the Danes claim, or Beo who, according to others, belongs to the earliest times? And somebody whose knowledge of legend was reckoned authoritative, might have settled on the order Sceaf, Scyld, Beo, assuming a natural succession of grandfather, father, and son.

For the man who introduced these names into Æthelwulf's pedigree this would be a scrap of antiquarian learning, to be copied exactly. By Æthelweard's time—the last quarter of the tenth century—it had become traditional in the royal genealogy of Wessex. In the Introduction to *Beowulf*, which may or may not be derived independently, the story of Sceaf's arrival from the sea was transferred to Scyld, the founder of Hrothgar's kingdom, and Beo was confused by a scribe or reader with Beowulf the Geat, the hero of the poem. These developments would be possible if the order Sceaf, Scyld, Beo was established as late as the ninth century, when the Danes had overrun much of non-West Saxon England; though an earlier date is not excluded if any evidence requires it.

POSTSCRIPT

How much did the Anglo-Saxons know about their early history in England, and about persons associated in legend with still earlier Germanic times? When a name appears incidentally in a sixth-century annal of the *Anglo-Saxon Chronicle* or in *Beowulf*, did it unlock a store of well-ordered information in the mind of an intelligent Anglo-Saxon? Or did it often convey no more than the vague impression of remote times that adds to the enjoyment of old stories? Evidence bearing on such questions is hard to find. Modern scholars, whether expressly or by implication, seem to prefer the first and more congenial opinion. Yet scattered through this examination of the Anglo-Saxon genealogies there is a considerable amount of evidence in the other direction. As examples: we should expect agreement on the names of Hengest's

[1] A further development is in Nennius *Historia Brittonum*, ch. xvii.

son and grandson because the kings of Kent claimed descent from them and Bede records them; yet of the five witnesses (up to and including Æthelweard) who might be reckoned intelligent, no two agree both in the names and their order (pp. 182 f. and 196 f.). The variant forms of Æthelwulf's pedigree (pp. 159 ff.) could not have arisen or survived if consistent legends about the heroes or gods in its remoter parts had been well known in the ninth century. Sometimes the stereotyped spelling of names tells against a living tradition (p. 196). And there are instances of surprising carelessness (pp. 174 and 183).

This evidence covers a long period. It begins in the early eighth century, and in the ninth century, when comparisons become possible, the number of variants or errors is already large. It might be objected that all the genealogies have come down to us through clerical channels which were indifferent or hostile to secular legend. But Æthelweard was a layman; the compiler of the Chronicle of 892 should have been more than usually well versed in tradition; on the most sceptical view of King Alfred's share in that Chronicle he is likely to have read it attentively; and a well-informed audience might be expected to restrain fanciful or erroneous variations. In any case, if *Beowulf*, as is now commonly supposed, was a written composition, or was recorded in writing in the eighth century, it too must have come down to us through similar channels until the extant copy was made as late as Æthelweard's time.

To put the issue more clearly: there is good evidence that old stories were told throughout Anglo-Saxon times, and that some stories about persons of the Heroic Age outlived the Norman Conquest. But there is little if any evidence to show whether the same stories were always attached to the same names, or whether, if all the stories could be assembled, an historian or a mythographer would be likely to find them consistent. So it is reasonable to give full weight to the evidence from the genealogies, and in any work of interpretation, to allow room for inconsistency, vagueness, and error in Anglo-Saxon tradition.

SIR ISRAEL GOLLANCZ MEMORIAL LECTURE

PLACE-NAMES AND THE ANGLO-SAXON SETTLEMENT

By A. H. SMITH

Read 29 February 1956

ENGLISH place-names have assumed considerable importance as one of the sources of information on the origin and growth of the English nation, on the development of the language, and on the steadily increasing exploitation of the natural resources of the country-side by settlement and land-utilization. The authority that place-names seem to have acquired would justify a restatement of the restrictions we should be prepared to accept for this sort of evidence and a brief re-examination, from a linguistic viewpoint, of the relevance of some types of place-name, and particularly those formed in one way or another with the suffix *-ing*, to the problems of the Anglo-Saxon settlement.

In the last thirty years the English Place-Name Society has assembled and analysed material in such measure that only the most patient of readers will discover its riches. As the survey has advanced, a surer insight into the linguistic processes of name-giving adds increasing reliability to the interpretation of that material. The fact that it now requires two large volumes to report and illustrate the word-stock embodied in English place-names[1] is a sign of the abundance of the linguistic material, and the introduction to each county survey an indication of its special contribution to historical and dialect studies. As one who has had the time and the facilities to scrutinize the work of the survey, I should pay tribute to the learning, the enthusiasm, and the diligence of the founders of this great national project, the late Sir Allen Mawer and Sir Frank Stenton, as well as to Professor Eilert Ekwall and Professor Bruce Dickins.[2] The British Academy, a generous foster-parent of some thirty years' standing, should find satisfaction in

[1] *English Place-Name Elements* (English Place-Name Society, vols. xxv, xxvi, Cambridge, 1956).

[2] Any study of English place-names must now to a great extent be based on the publications of the English Place-Name Society and on the materials which the society and scholars working for the survey are bringing together for future publications. Professor Ekwall's own independent contributions have a singular importance in the development of methods and in linguistic interpretation.

the results of the Society's youthful vigour in the past, and I am very sincerely grateful, not only for the honour of delivering the Sir Israel Gollancz Memorial Lecture, but also for the occasion it provides for me to express to the Academy itself the gratitude of all place-name scholars for its continued interest and help in this field of inquiry.

We must be cognizant of certain obvious limitations in place-name evidence. Adequate and decisive medieval material is frequently not yet available for many names in *-ing* and *-ingham*, and these we cannot at present place in their proper category or their proper time-range. The survey itself is far from complete and many areas like Kent or the west midlands remain to be examined.[1] These are critical regions for the history of the English settlement and for the characteristics of our earliest dialects and their geographical distribution. Although we think we can recognize as typically south-eastern such words as OE *harað* 'a wood' (in Hardres K)[2] and *spic* 'brushwood' (in Speach Sr, Poles Pitch Sx), or such forms as *nīge* for *nīwe* 'new' (in Nyetimber Sx, Nizell's Heath K) or the unmutated *hāð* for *hǣð* 'heathland' (in Hoath Sx, Hoathly K), evidence of primitive distinctions in the oldest language of Kent and its relation to the linguistic background of the Netherlands and the Cimbric peninsula, and indeed to the neighbouring counties of Surrey and Sussex, is not yet available; nor has the final pattern yet emerged of the regional distribution of important dialect features like Mercian *wælla* for Anglian *wella* 'a spring' (as in Colwall He).[3]

[1] J. K. Wallenberg's *Kentish Place-Names* (Uppsala, 1931), a study of the place-names in the Old English Kentish charters, and *The Place-Names of Kent* (Uppsala, 1934) contain a great deal of useful early material, but both these works are marred by somewhat unfortunate etymological experiments, by their lack of analyses, and by their failure to perceive or indicate the significance of the material in either the history or the linguistic background of Kent. In the west midlands work is now in progress on the surveys of Gloucestershire, Herefordshire, Staffordshire, and Cheshire, and *The Place-Names of Derbyshire* is in the press.

[2] The abbreviations for sources and counties are those commonly used in place-name studies. In these notes EPNS denotes the publications of the English Place-Name Society; Ekwall, *Dictionary* denotes E. Ekwall, *The Oxford Dictionary of English Place-Names* (Oxford, 1947), and *Elements* A. H. Smith, *English Place-Name Elements* (EPNS xxv, xxvi, Cambridge, 1956): these all provide the necessary bibliographical information, full discussions, and further examples of the place-name elements mentioned in this lecture. Early spellings of place-names are not usually cited but can be found in the relevant county volumes.

[3] This Old English dialect feature is discussed by E. Ekwall, *Contributions to the Study of Old English Dialects* (Lund, 1917), 40–65. Regional features of

Apart from a few counties like Lancashire, Derbyshire, or Worcestershire, where material is adequate, we have as yet only an impression of the essential Mercian character of the language in a region stretching in the western half of the country from the Ribble and the Wharfe in the north to the Vale of Gloucester in the south. The deficiency is one which time and industry will alone correct.

Secondly, the independent value of place-name evidence is readily lowered by the assumptions that have to be made when, as is so often the case in the older names, linguistic information for their interpretation is not available. The interpretation of old *-ing* names is an obvious example, but the difficulty can be well illustrated by a couple of fairly common names, Windsor and Ludgershall, for on the meaning of these names place-name scholars have long exercised those arts of linguistic ingenuity in which they seem to be singularly gifted.[1] In the past it has been thought that the function of a genitive singular form in the first element of a compound place-name was restricted essentially to the idea of personal possession, and for that reason Windsor and Ludgershall have been derived from personal names, Windsor from an OE *Windel* (combined with *ōra* 'a bank, a slope') and Ludgershall from an Old English personal name *Lūtegār* (combined with *halh* 'a nook of land'). Neither personal name is

this kind are often obscured by the spelling habits of individual scribes or scriptoria and most often by the West Saxon orthography of much of our Old English literary and charter material. They become evident again, however, in the new orthography of Middle English. In late Middle English the local pattern is again disturbed by the spread of east midland spelling habits.

[1] The names in question are Windsor Brk, Co, Winsor D, Ha, Broadwindsor Do, all usually with Middle English spellings such as *Windlesore* (discussed in *Place-Names of Devon* (EPNS viii), 262–3, and Ekwall, *Dictionary*, s.n.), and Ludgershall Bk, W, Luggershall Gl, Lurgashall Sx, a lost *Lotegoreshale* Ess, and the OE *æt Lutegaresheale* (ASWills), which is identical with one or another of the modern names mentioned. The latter names are discussed in *Place-Names of Buckinghamshire* (EPNS ii), 104–6, *Place-Names of Sussex* (ibid. vi), 111, and *Place-Names of Wiltshire* (ibid. xvi), 367–8 (all proposing a personal name *Lūtegār*); A. Mawer, *Problems of Place-Name Study* (Cambridge, 1929), 87 (taking the names as compounds of OE *hlyte* 'lot' and an unrecorded OE *gærs-halh*, 'grassland on a *halh* allotted by lot') and J. K. Wallenberg, *Kentish Place-Names* (Uppsala, 1931), 333–4 (with an etymology similar to Mawer's but from a variant **hlut*, or alternatively from another root related to OE *holt* 'wood'); and Ekwall, *Dictionary*, s.n. (from OE *lȳt* 'little' and *gærs-halh*). The reasons for rejecting some of these proposals are summarized in *Elements*, ii. 28–29, which agrees with E. Tengstrand's important discussion and suggestion of OE **lūte-gār* 'spear-trap' in *A Contribution to the Study of Genitival Composition in Old English Place-Names* (Uppsala, 1940), 222 ff.

recorded in Old English, but *Windel* at least does conform to an established type of personal name formed with the suffix *-el* and has a parallel in Old High German *Windul*; this suggested personal name is also thought to occur in Windlesham Sr. The other personal name *Lūtegār*, supposed to enter also into *Lutegaresberi* (the old name for Montacute So) and to be the source of a fourteenth-century Somerset surname John *Lotegar*, could only be explained on phonological grounds as a continental German name, for no native personal name-theme *Lūte-* is known in Old English. The series of coincidences of the unrecorded *Windel* always being the owner of an *ōra* or slope, of the suspicious *Lūtegār* being the possessor only of 'nooks of land' and a single *beorg* or hill, and of a supposedly continental German name *Lutegar* appearing in English place-names scattered over a wide area in Essex, Sussex, Buckinghamshire, Gloucestershire, Wiltshire, and Somerset, one of them recorded in a late Old English will, is at least suspicious. Appellatives rather than personal names would remove these difficulties of coincidence as of phonology. In Windsor we do not have a personal name in the genitive, but apparently a word *windels*, formed from the root *wind* with the well-established noun-suffix *-els*[1] and the source of the somewhat obscure Modern English word *windlass*; although this too is an assumption, it provides a reasonable descriptive compound for Windsor, 'slope or bank with a windlass' (for pulling up boats and the like). With Ludgershall we must recollect that in Old English the genitive had attributive functions besides possession, and enough evidence is now available to show that these functions extended to the simple syntactical relationships that can be expressed in place-names: appellatives used as first elements in the genitive are common enough in Scandinavian place-names, and can be established in English usage. Tengstrand's suggestion, therefore, of an OE *lūtegār* 'spear-trap' at least has the merit of being a possible compound of the known root of OE *lūtian* 'to hide, to skulk' with *gār* 'a spear', of denoting a trapping device well known amongst the hunters of Scandinavia, and of explaining its frequent composition with *halh* 'a nook of land', which is the kind of place where such traps would be located; the Somerset surname *Lotegar* may equally well be a Middle English local name of similar origin.

However complicated might be the circumstances attending

[1] This ancient noun-forming suffix is common enough in Old English words like *græfels* 'quarry' (from *grafan* 'to dig'), *byrgels* 'burial-place', and many other place-name themes (cf. *Elements* i. 150).

the creation of a place-name, the name itself will be a simple factual statement, and its frame of reference can only be completed from other sources. Some names, for example, which are compounds of an animal name with the word *hēafod* 'head', cannot on topographical grounds describe either 'a headland' or 'the source of a river, the top end of a valley', which are common meanings of *hēafod* in place-names, but Professor Dickins has shown that place-names like Farcet Hu from OE *fearr* 'a bull'[1] recall a feature of Germanic heathen religion, by which only the head of a sacrificed animal was offered to the god. The relevant *head*-names themselves do no more than establish the practice for England, and are unique evidence there, but for the scanty details of the custom we have to turn elsewhere, to Adam of Bremen's account of the great Swedish festivals at Uppsala and like sources. In the same way, names like Follifoot YW (which means 'fight of the foals') or Rosewain Cu ('horse-fight') establish the bare fact of horse-fighting in Viking England, but for any details of this sport (in which two horses are driven on to fight each other by men armed with goads) we have to turn to the pictorial stones of Sweden and Gotland and to the Icelandic Sagas.[2] Besides such simple records, or the valuable evidence about the physical state of the English landscape, rudimentary ideas about the structure of early society are implicit in the meaning of *-ing* or the use of personal names and personal designations and in the semantic development of common terms like *hām* 'homestead, manor', *tūn* 'enclosure, farmstead, manor, estate', *þrop* 'outlying farmstead', *stōw* 'place of assembly, place with religious associations', but the little that has so far been gleaned must be interpreted through a knowledge of the material culture provided by the archaeologist and through the memories of ancient times preserved in historical documents, in folk-lore, and in heroic literature.

Thirdly, it is essential to recall that we do not get a comprehensive picture of English nomenclature before the great fiscal

[1] *Place-Names of Surrey* (EPNS xi), 403–6.

[2] Follifoot YW and a lost name *Follithwaite* YW, which Ekwall, *Dictionary*, s.n., rightly interprets as from an OE *fola-gefeoht* 'foal-fight', and Rosewain Cu, which is to be derived from ON *hross* 'horse' and OE *gewinn* 'fight'; *Place-Names of Cumberland* (EPNS xxi), 334, derives this name from ON *hross* and ON *vin* 'meadow', but this is improbable because the medial *-i-* in ME spellings like *Rossiwin* does not represent an Old Norse genitive plural *-a*, and because ON *vin* was not used to form place-names as late as the Viking Age (cf. V. Jansson, *Nordiska Vin-namn*, Uppsala, 1951). On the significance of these names compare A. H. Smith in *Arv*, ii. 104–8.

land-survey of Domesday Book and that some six centuries had elapsed since the first coming of the English to Britain. The great events through which we must penetrate to reach the days of the early settlement are the evolution of the kingdom, which mutilated and removed the oldest tribal boundaries; the conversion of the English to Christianity in the early seventh century, which provides one of the most illuminating pieces of chronological evidence in place-names; the Viking invasions and occupation; and the Norman Conquest. In this long period, there were important changes in economic and legal institutions, and there were many far-reaching linguistic developments; ancient words and archaic place-name structures disappear and are replaced by others more appropriate to new functions in name-giving demanded by a developing countryside, and much of our Old English place-name material—none older than the late seventh century and of very uneven geographical distribution—is in the standard orthography of West Saxon and often an inaccurate reflection of the spoken language of other regions where this orthographic system had become current. These affairs draw a heavy curtain over the scene of English life in the first two scantily documented centuries. Even if we accept Bede's simple traditional account of the tribal settlement and the implications about the continental home, we do not commit ourselves to the acceptance of either the ethnic or the linguistic purity of the Anglo-Saxons or indeed of the tribal components of Angles, Saxons, and Jutes, for the account is by no means complete. The great tribe of the *Hwicce* in Worcestershire and Gloucestershire has no place in that tradition and its origin is obscure. In Kent there may have been Frisian settlers, if we accept that interpretation of the material culture of south-eastern England, but neither place-names nor language can yet confirm it.[1] But there is evidence of shifting and merging population amongst the Anglo-Saxon tribes. In Wessex we have isolated settlements of East Saxons at Exton Ha, of Kentish men in Canterton Ha, and of Angles in Englefield Brk; in Anglian territory we have settlements of Saxons at Saxon C and elsewhere, and amongst the Mercians similar small colonies of Kentish men at Conderton Wo and Angles at Engleton St.[2] Similar inferences may be drawn from

[1] The only direct place-name evidence so far available is for isolated Frisian settlements in the Danelaw, and some names like Friesthorpe and Firsby L or Frisby Lei certainly belong to the Viking Age. Others like Frieston L, Friston Sf, or Fryston YW may do so.

[2] A convenient survey of these racial and tribal names is made by E. Ekwall in *Namn och Bygd*, xli.

other groups of names like Spalding L and Spaldingmoor YE, both of which may be connected with the *Spalda* of the seventh century Tribal Hidage (BCS 97); Whiston Nth, Wichnor St, and Wychwood O all seem to refer in one way or another to the tribe of the *Hwicce*[1] and places as far apart as Uxbridge or Uxendon Mx and Whitsun Brook Wo are named from the *Wihsa*,[2] another midland folk also mentioned in the Tribal Hidage. Although racial or tribal place-names of this kind cannot designate more than isolated groups living in alien surroundings, the implications for the history of culture are as important as they are obvious.

It is with such limitations in mind that we should view those types of place-names that are thought to bear on the history of the Anglo-Saxon settlement; it is the independent linguistic aspect that needs emphasis. In particular we should examine the meaning and chronology of names in *-ing*, especially when related to other common terminals like *hām* 'a homestead, a village', *tūn* 'an enclosure, a farmstead, an estate', or *þrop*, *wīc*, and *stoc* 'dependent farmstead', as well as topographical terms like *burna* 'a stream' or *lēah* 'a woodland glade', for names in *-ing* and *-ingham* have been much used as evidence of the range of the earliest English settlement. Most scholars have accepted Ekwall's classical work as the standard guide, and any survey of the problem must inevitably start from his illuminating illustrations of the origin of certain types of *-ing* names, as well as from Karlström's parallel investigation of *ing-* compounds. Considerable new light on the origin of these types of names has come from Ståhle's penetrating examination of Swedish and other material; the gradual accretion of new English material allows us to place our own *-ing* names in their proper categories with greater certainty.[3]

The suffix *-ing* has a long and complicated history and it is necessary to distinguish its several functions and forms in place-names, for these were not all in use at the same time and not all belong to the earliest part of the Anglo-Saxon period. This old Germanic suffix seems to have the primary meaning of 'that which pertains or belongs to something or someone', and, as far

[1] *Place-Names of Worcestershire* (EPNS iv), xv.

[2] *Place-Names of Worcestershire* (ibid.), xix; *Place-Names of Middlesex* (ibid. xviii), xiv. 49, 54.

[3] E. Ekwall, *English Place-Names in -ing* (Lund, 1923); S. Karlström, *Old English Compound Place-Names in -ing* (Uppsala, 1927); C. I. Ståhle, *Studier över de svenska ortnamnen på -inge* (Lund, 1946).

as sense goes, even if not form, it has affinities with the common Old English adjectival suffix *-ig* (modern *-y*). All its later meanings arise from this idea of general pertinence, sometimes with a personal, sometimes with an impersonal concrete application. Besides the noun-forming suffix *-ing*, *-ung* in common nouns like *cyning* 'a king', *cēping* 'a market', or *falding* 'an enclosure', which are relevant only because they are to be found in a good many place-names and so can be confused formally with true *-ing* names, the chief name-forming suffixes to be distinguished are:

1. Final *-ing* (singular), as in Deeping L 'the deep place', Clavering Ess 'the clover place'.
2. Final *-ingas* (nominative plural), as in Hastings Sx 'the people of *Hǣst*', Avening Gl 'the dwellers on a river *Avon*'.
3. Medial *-inga-* (genitive plural of *-ingas*) in compound place-names like Goodmanham YE (Bede's *Godmunddingaham*) 'homestead of the *Gōdmundingas* or people of *Gōdmund*', Hertingfordbury Hrt (ME *Hertfordingeberi*) 'the fortification of the men of Hertford'.
4. Medial *-ing-*, as in Teddington Wo (OE *Teottingtun*) '*tūn* or farmstead associated with Teotta', Sinnington YN (DB *Siuenintun*) '*tūn* associated with the river Seven'.

The orthographic distinction between singular and plural forms persists generally until the thirteenth century, and as a rule early Middle English spellings (*-ing* singular, *-in*(*g*)- connective, *-inges* nominative plural, *-inge-* genitive plural), when they are available, leave us in no doubt about the morphological structure of these different categories of names.

The singular place-name-forming suffix *-ing* (the Deeping type) is not common in Old English—there are fewer than fifty examples—but there is ample evidence for it in names like Balking Brk (OE *Baðalacing* BCS 1121 'the place of Baðulac') or Guiting Gl (OE *Gytinc* BCS 1299 'the gushing stream' from OE *gyte*), and its paradigm (as, for example, *on Gytincges æwylm* (BCS 1299) 'to the source of the Guiting') proves that it is singular in number. It is also found in Old English literary sources; besides *Riffeng* for *Riphaei montes* in the Orosius, there is a significant phrase in *Wonders of the East* which reads: *in þære stowe þe is haten Gorgoneus, þæt is wælkyrging* 'in the place that is called *Gorgoneus*, that is *Wælkyrging*'; in the context the latter can only mean 'place of the *wælcyrge* or sorceress'.[1] The formation is therefore

[1] *King Alfred's Orosius*, ed. H. Sweet (EETS 79), 8 (OE *of Riffeng þæm beorgum*, Lat. *Riphaei montes*; cf. also *þa beorgas Riffen* (ibid. 16). The reference to *wælkyrging*, cited by Ekwall, *English Place-Names in -ing*, 21, is

clearly one that could be used long after the settlement, and is one that is no doubt to be found in many more *-ing* names than has been allowed for. In Scandinavia it is a very common formation, and Swedish parallels make a distinction between nature-names like *Sanding* 'the sandy place' (which are *a*-stem declensions) and settlement-names like *Steninge* 'the settlement of the Stenings' (which are *-ja*-stem nouns formed from old plural folk-names, in this example 'the dwellers at a place called *Sten*'); although there is no such clear grammatical distinction in English, palatalized forms like Wantage Brk or Garlinge K are best explained as *ja*-stem settlement-names, whilst semantically names like Balking Brk and others which contain personal names are just as likely to be new settlement-names formed from old folk-names: in some of these the palatalized ending *-incg* has been frequently adjusted analogically to the very common Old English *a*-stem type *-ing*. In the same way Garlinge K and Swathling Ha may be derivatives denoting settlements from such old place-names as *Grēne-lēah* 'green glade' or *Swæð-lēah* 'glade with a track'; but others like Clavering Ess ('the clover place'), Nursling Ha ('the nut-shell place'), or Guiting Gl would seem to be old nature-names. It is, of course, difficult to distinguish place-names of this kind from common nouns in *-ing* like *cēping* 'a market' or *rydding* 'a clearing', as well as other compound place-names like Dickering YE ('dike-ring') or Eakring Nt ('circle of oaks'). Though some may be old, we cannot safely regard *-ing* names of this type as evidence of early settlement.

The plural *-ingas* names are originally folk-names, falling into two clearly marked groups: one includes names like Hastings or Reading formed from personal names (*Hǣst* or *Rēada*), and the other includes names like Twyning or Avening Gl formed from old local names, in one case an old elliptical place-name '(place) between the rivers (Avon and Severn)' and in the other a lost river-name *Avon*. This second group may also contain some formed directly from appellatives, as Spalding L (from OE *spalde* 'a ditch'), Meering Nt (from OE *mere* 'a pool') or Sompting Sx (from OE *sumpt* 'a swamp'), but even in these there may also have been an intermediate stage in which the appellative had already become a local name before the folk-name was created. Spalding may in fact take its name from a branch of the *Spalda*, the

Narratiunculae Anglice Conscriptae, ed. O. Cockayne (London, 1861), 35; cf. also *Wonders of the East* (EETS 161), 55. Bosworth, misunderstanding the function of *-ing*, translates the word as 'one that belongs to the race of the *wælcyrgan*' (*Anglo-Saxon Dictionary*, ed. T. N. Toller, s.v. *wæl-cyrgan*).

Mercian folk mentioned in the Tribal Hidage, and Meering may mean 'the people dwelling at a place called *Mere*' rather than 'the *mere*- or pool-dwellers'; they would properly fall in the second class. The significance of making this distinction is that the first group of *-ingas* names formed from personal names is ancient, whereas the second group formed from older place-names could have been created at any time in the Old English period.

The older *-ingas* names from personal names belong to a type shared at least from classical times by all the Germanic peoples. The use of *-ingas* here ranges from such simple family or dynastic designations as the Kentish *Oiscingi* 'the dynasty founded by *Oisc*' or the Norse *Knýtlingar* 'the dynasty of *Knút*' to others more general like the *Scyldingas* of *Beowulf* which denoted not only the dynasty of *Scyld* but also the whole Danish people, and to others more specific like the *Gunbadingi* 'those who obeyed the *Lex Burgundionum* of King *Gundobad*'.[1] In Old English the formation is limited to certain place-names, to the earlier heroic poetry, and to the oldest historical traditions; the East Anglian kings, according to Bede (ii. 15), were called the *Uuffingas* from the sixth-century king *Uuffa*, grandfather of Redwald. But an occasional allusion like that of Felix to the *Guthlacingas*, from whom St. Guthlac was said to have been named, brings a faulty memory of its use down to the eighth century.[2] The generalized meaning of these folk-names in *-ingas* is 'an association of people dependent in some way or another upon the leader whose name forms the first theme'. The dynastic use is a particularization of this, just as the patronymic use of *-ing* in the singular in personal names like *Wulf Wonreding* (also *sunu Wonredes*) in *Beowulf* or *Ecgbryht Ealhmunding* 'Ecgbryht son of Ealhmund' is a highly specialized use of the singular form of this particular suffix found only in West Germanic (Old English, Frisian, and medieval Swiss-German)[3] but not in Scandinavian; it is almost unnecessary to add that names like Hastings or Reading do not mean 'the sons of *Hǣst*' or 'the sons of *Rēada*', for some of these folks like the Hastings were such large groups that blood relationship with a single leader is out of the question. These names first denoted communities of people (the leader, his family, and his

[1] Cf. F. Kluge, *Nominale Stammbildungslehre* (Halle, 1926), § 26*c*.

[2] Cf. F. M. Stenton in *Introduction to the Survey of English Place-Names* (EPNS i, part 1), 168; the reference is to the *Prose Life of St. Guthlac* (Anglistische Forschungen, xxvii), 106.

[3] Cf. C. I. Ståhle, *Studier över de svenska ortnamnen på -inge* (Lund, 1946), 81 ff.

dependants and followers) and then seem to have denoted the districts occupied by these folks before they became stabilized as the names of some place within the district: the name *Berecingas*, from which Barking Ess is derived, was described as the *prouincia In Berecingum* by Bede, and it was only later restricted to the principal settlement in the province. Something like this is implied in groups of names like Hastings, Hastingford Sx, Hastingleigh K, all named from the *Hæstingas*. Lack of evidence for creation of folk-names from personal names in later times leads us to believe that such folk-names belong to the age of migration and early settlement.

The *-ingas* folk-names in the second group are derived from old local names and denote 'the dwellers in the place named'. Again it is a type which has its counterpart in Scandinavia and elsewhere: Swedish *skåning* describes 'a man from *Skåne*', Icelandic *Norðhymbringar* 'the men of Northumbria'. In Old English it is well attested in the boundaries of contiguous estates in phrases like *Bromleaginga mearce* (BCS 506) 'the boundary of the men of Bromley K'. That it was a living form in the ninth, tenth, and eleventh centuries is proved by such expressions as *Berclingas*, which described the members of the religious community at Berkeley Gl, *Eoforwicingas* 'the men of York', or *Fifburgingas* 'the men of the Five (Danish) Boroughs',[1] for these are not permanent stabilized folk-names but living colloquialisms. Although the occurrence of this type of *-ingas* name in other Germanic languages suggests the possibility of its early use in England, it clearly continued active throughout the Old English period, and names like Avening Gl 'the folk living near a river *Avon*' or Twyning Gl, which in Old English was simply an elliptical prepositional name *Bitwinæum* '(land) between the rivers (Severn and Avon)' and does not appear with an *-ing* suffix till Domesday Book, are not necessarily old.[2]

A similar distinction in chronology is to be made when these folk-names in *-ingas* are combined (in the genitive plural *-inga*) with other elements. The older type formed from personal names is well represented in compounds with *hām* 'a homestead' as in Wokingham Sr named from the *Wocingas*, whose name also

[1] *Berclingas* 804 BCS 313; *Eoforwicingas* ASC 918BCD; *Fifburgingas* ASC 1013CE: the last name cannot of course be older than the early tenth century when the Five Boroughs of the Danelaw were first recognized.

[2] It is possible that the type was used even later, for Barf Hill near Aike (*Place-Names of the East Riding* (EPNS xiv), 161) was known in the twelfth century by the alternative names *Berghe juxta Ake* and *Akinga-*, *Akeneberghe*, that is, 'hill of the inhabitants of Aike'.

survives in Woking Brk, or Goodmanham YE (from *Gōdmundingas* 'the people of Gōdmund'), as well as with other elements like *burna* 'a stream' in Pangbourne Brk (from 'the folk of *Pǣga*'), *feld* 'open country' in Redlingfield Sf (from 'the folk of *Rǣdla*'), or *lēah* 'forest glade' in Hastingley K named from the *Hǣstingas*. Such names are old. There are also examples of toponymic formations like Stockbury K (formerly *Stochingeberge* 'the fort of the men of Stoke'), the lost *Esthallingebrouk* Sx 'the brook of the men of the nearby East Hale', or even Westmorland (OE *Westmoringaland*)[1] 'the district of the men living west of the moors'. Similar folk-names seem to have been formed from old British place-names: Archenfield He[2] is 'the *feld* or district of the *Ercingas*', whose name is ultimately to be connected with that of the old Roman station of *Ariconium*, and Glastonbury So[3] 'the *burh* of the *Glæstingas*', whose name appears to be connected with the British root *glasto-* 'blue-green' probably used as a river-name and to be a parallel formulation to Avening. In this group of compound *-ing-* names we also find some elliptical forms in which only the first element of an old place-name is used to create the folk-name: Buckingway C is 'the road of the men of Boxworth' (where the *worth* is lost), Wetheringsett Sf 'the dwelling of the men of Wetherden'. This kind of ellipsis of the second element of the place-name which forms the folk-name is not unique, for it occurs often enough with other words like *hǣme* or *sǣte* which also denote 'dwellers'; OE *Dræghǣme*[4] denotes 'the dwellers in Drayton Nth', Somerset 'the folk belonging to Somerton So'. This may be a disturbing feature in the interpretation of *-ing* names since it is not always certain that the folk-name in *-ingas* is created directly from a personal name, in which case it would be old, or from an elliptical form of an older place-name, in which case it need not be old. Happing Hundred Nf, for example, may be 'the folk of a man called *Hæpp*' (who also gave his name to Happisburgh Nf), but it could formally be 'the folk belonging to Happisburgh'. Such cases are fortunately rare, but it does mean that folk-names in *-ingas* need to be examined critically and in their local setting when we think in terms of their antiquity.

[1] *Westmoringaland* ASC 966E.

[2] *Ircingafeld* ASC 918A.

[3] OE *Glestingaburg* 732–55 Holder, *on Glæstingabyrig c.* 1000 Saints, from an older *Glastonia* (cf. Ekwall, *Dictionary*, s.n.).

[4] *Dræghæma gemære* KCD 736; cf. Drayton (*Place-Names of Northamptonshire* (EPNS x), 20).

The medial connective *-ing-* is well exemplified in a name like Teddington Wo (OE *Teottingtun*),[1] which consists of a personal name *Teotta* linked by *-ing-* to *tūn* 'a farmstead'. In such a context *-ing-* is of obscure origin and meaning. Some scholars have explained it as a variant of the genitive plural of the old folk-name in *-ingas*, either as a stress variant in oblique cases, an original nominative *Teottinga-tūn* 'farmstead of Teotta's folk' having become *Teottingtūne* in the dative or quasi-locative, or as a simple reduction of that folk-name in a polysyllabic place-name.[2] There is no support for these views in the extant Old English material, which is plentiful, and we must therefore regard the independent existence of a connective *-ing-* as beyond dispute, for it is found in other West Germanic place-names, Old Saxon as well as Old High German.[3] In order to emphasize that *-ingtun* is not a variant of *-ingatūn*, Mawer and others have noted some Old English place-names where the reference is to an individual and not to a group of people (as it would be if the *-ing-* were a reduced form of an old folk-name in *-inga-*). In certain place-names the medial *-ing-* alternates with a normal genitive singular inflexion: the charter which refers to Wilmington K calls the place *Wieghelmestun* 'Wighelm's farmstead' and is later endorsed *Wigelmignctun*,[4] whilst Tiddington Wa appears as *æt Tidinctune* and *Tidantun* 'Tida's farmstead' in almost contemporary documents.[5] Secondly, in a name like OE *biscoping dene*[6] from the word *biscop* 'bishop', *-ing-* is unlikely to be patronymic or collective in function. And thirdly, certain place-names with this connective *-ing-* have been identified with known individuals, Kemerton Gl with *Cyneburg*, the late-seventh-century Abbess of Gloucester, or *Badenoðingland* with the *Badenoð* to whom the estate was granted in 845.[7] Such examples are also

[1] BCS 286 (cf. *Place-Names of Worcestershire* (EPNS iv), 168). The personal name *Teotta*, not recorded in independent use, is a pet form for some name in *Þēod-*, and it is worth noting that a few hundred yards away from the hamlet and now in Gloucestershire there is still marking the site of the old hundred meeting-place the Tibble Stone (*Tedboldstane* DB), which is 'Theodbald's stone'.

[2] On these interpretations of *-ingtūn* cf. *Elements*, i. 292.

[3] Cf. C. I. Ståhle, op. cit. 83–99; A. Bach, *Deutsche Namenkunde* ii (*Die deutschen Ortsnamen* i).

[4] BCS 97. Birch's form *Pleghelmestun* in BCS 98 is a misreading of *Wieghelmestun*.

[5] BCS 1232; KCD 561.

[6] BCS 378.

[7] Kemerton Gl is *Cyneburgingctun* 840 BCS 430; *Badenoðingland* KCD 449. On these names compare S. Karlström, *Old English Compound Place-Names in -ing* (Uppsala, 1927), 75.

important in showing that the formation was a living one till at least the ninth century and it does not therefore necessarily belong to the period of early settlement. The function of the medial *-ing-* is certainly not possessive, for that would have been expressed by the genitive. The intention, as Mawer held, was to denote a looser relationship of the place to the person, and Teddington means 'farmstead associated with Teotta' and not 'Teotta's farmstead'. This function is in fact simply a variant of the common suffix *-ing* which expresses the notion of general pertinence, 'that which pertains to someone or something', a function also implied by its use in linking river-names to *tūn*, as in Sinnington YN[1] '*tūn* on the R. Seven'. Morphologically, medial connective *-ing-* could be a stem-formation and it need not be part of its function to express number, individual or collective; if we sought to convey the same notion in modern English we should have to say 'the Nicholson house' (in which there is a similar ambiguity of number) as distinct from 'Nicholson's house' (where the genitive is a signal of possession by an individual). It is possible that the so-called uninflected genitive in many north midland and northern place-names like Osbaldwick YN or Bishopton YW[2] performs a similar function of unparticularized association in a somewhat later period. The medial *-ing-* is usually found with *tūn*, and indeed in the midlands generally it is the normal method of linking a personal name to *tūn*. But it occurs with other elements like OE *cot* 'a cottage, a shed' (as in Didcot Brk), *mynster* 'a church' (as in Lyminster Sx), or *land* 'a plot of ground' (as in Snodland K). There was an overlap in time in the use of *hām* 'a homestead' and the connective *-ing-*, and some apparently archaic names like Manningham or Addingham YW, where there is too little or no evidence in early Middle English for a genitive plural *-inga-*, belong here; they need have no great age. With others of these *-ingham* names, however, we find ourselves, because of the absence of early and decisive material, in a position that can only be described as ambivalent.

This short survey of the different types of *-ing* names is enough to show that the different functions of *-ing* are by no means coeval and emphasizes the need for a careful examination of the morphology and etymology of individual names if they are to be allocated to their proper categories.

[1] *Siuenintun* DB; cf. *Place-Names of the North Riding* (EPNS v), 76.

[2] Osbaldwick, *Osboldeuuic* DB (*Place-Names of the North Riding* (EPNS v), 10); Bishopton, *Biscoptun c.* 1030 YCh 7.

In English place-names generally an absolute chronology in terms of date is rarely possible, and we are almost restricted to the time of the conversion to Christianity in the early seventh century, the Viking settlement, and the Norman Conquest as our only guides, but the presence or absence of certain elements in regions like the south-western part of the West Riding, which cannot have been settled before the fall of the British kingdom of Elmet in the early seventh century, or west Devon, which was not occupied before the early eighth century, may throw some light on the problem. There were changing fashions of usage and of composition which produce recognizable and predominating patterns of nomenclature at different periods, and for them we can establish at least a chronological order.

The methods deserve a more critical examination than is possible now, but some of the better known at least merit a passing mention. Textual evidence of usage has shown that the singular *-ing* type of place-name (the Deeping type) could be formed as late as the ninth century and folk-names (of the *Berclingas* type) formed from local names throughout the Old English period. The identification of known persons with particular place-names points to the use of *-ingtūn* at least in the eighth and ninth centuries, whilst later on places named from men who can be identified as owners or tenants illustrate the continued activity of certain terms like *tūn*, *burh*, or *bý* till the twelfth and thirteenth centuries: Blackmanstone K is named from *Blacheman*, tenant in the time of Edward the Confessor; Quinbury Hrt was granted by Queen Maud to her chamberlain in Stephen's reign; Baggaby YE was named from the local twelfth-century Bagot family.[1] Such identifications cannot be made for *-ingas*, *hām*, or *worð*.

Archaic themes, known from other languages but not surviving long enough in Old English to be recorded in literature, belong to the older of our place-names, but by themselves do not constitute strong evidence, for not only is the chance of survival involved, but also the chance of any word that may have survived finding a place in the records: even very common elements like *lēah* 'a glade' or *þrop* 'an outlying farm' are extremely rare in literary sources. Personal names like the *Hǣst* of Hastings or the *Gensa* of Gensing Sx are not only monothematic names of a type which becomes less common as the period advances[2] but

[1] Cf. J. Tait in *Introduction to the Survey of English Place-Names* (EPNS i, part 1), 116–18; O. von Feilitzen, *The Pre-Conquest Personal Names of Domesday Book* (Uppsala, 1937), 32–33.

[2] On the changing fashions in personal nomenclature in the OE period

are from stems otherwise unknown in England: *Hǣst* can be connected only with Gothic *háifsts* 'strife' and *Gensa* with OHG *Gan*. In the same way, for a word like *gē* 'a district', unknown in England except for certain south-eastern names (like Surrey, or Eastry, Wester, and Sturry in Kent), we have to turn to German *gau* or Frisian *gē* for proof of its existence amongst the Germanic peoples. Even the form of the first element in some of these names, *sūðer* 'south' in Surrey, *ēaster* 'east' in Eastry or *wester* 'west' in Wester, is archaic, surviving only in more ancient records like Bede, where the East Angles are called *Eastrangli*, and in older place-names like Westerham K. This decay of ancient vocabulary results in difficulties of interpretation of certain groups of place-names in *-ing* and *-ingham* (compared with those in *tūn* or *-ingtun*) which invest them with a high degree of antiquity.

Certain names, which recall the religious practices of the heathen English, include those denoting temples, the *alh* in Alkham K, the *hearg* in Harrow Mx or Harrowden Bd, Ess, Nth, the *wīg* in Wye K, Patchway Sx or Willey Sr (which was 'a grove' named from the nearby temple at *Cusanweoh*); some denote groves and hills devoted to the service of the gods, *Woden* in Woodnesborough K, *Thunor* in Thundersley Ess and Thundridge Hrt, or *Tīw* in Tuesley Sr; such place-names can safely be ascribed to a period older than the conversion of the English in the early seventh century. A like age must be given some of the head-names[1] and to others containing OE *bēl* 'funeral pyre' as Beald C (on a hill formerly called *Dedehil* 'death hill'), *bēl-stede* (recorded in *Beowulf* 3097 in the sense 'place of the funeral pyre') as in Belstead Ess, Sf, or OE *bēl-haga* 'funeral pyre enclosure', as in Belaugh Nf or Byley YE, all of which recall the heathen practice of cremation in the disposal of the dead. Unfortunately, apart from Alkham, such allusions are generally limited to topographical features, and throw little light on the age of words denoting habitation sites.[2] On the other hand, words with a Christian

compare M. Redin, *Studies in Uncompounded Personal Names in Old English* (Uppsala, 1919), 187 ff.

[1] Cf. 71 *supra*.

[2] Some place-names with heathen reference may of course have been created in Christian times out of a traditional folk-memory and a certain antiquarian interest. This is particularly true of names containing *byrgels*, *byrgen*, &c., describing heathen burial sites and of names like Wansdyke ('Woden's dike') or Grimsditch ('Grim's, that is, Woden's ditch') which denote ancient earthworks considered to be the work of Woden and, later, of the Devil.

association, such as *biscop* (in Bishopton YW, Bispham La), *munuc* (in Monkton D, Do, Du, &c.), *prēost* (in Preston, Prescott, &c.), or saints' names, all obviously no older in English usage than the later seventh century, are not infrequent with certain common elements like *tūn* or *stōw* or *wīc*, but are very rare with *hām*, and never known with *-ingas* or *-ingahām* names.

When English place-names are examined in the light of these and other chronological tests, we are left in no doubt about the great antiquity of folk-names formed from personal names, whether they are used alone or in combination with *hām* and other elements like *burna* or *lēah*. From its combination with archaic words like *wester* (in Westerham K) or heathen association (as in Alkham K) the word *hām* also belongs to the earlier phases of the settlement, but a few sporadic Christian references as in Bispham La ('bishop's manor') bring its use in place-names at least to the later seventh century; it is of doubtful occurrence in Devon, but makes sporadic appearances in the far northwest.[1] The suffix *tūn* may have been in regular use from the time of the earliest settlements, for it is commonly used for sixth-century Saxon settlements in Normandy, but there are far too few signs of age in the great majority of examples of this most productive of all Old English place-name terms. On the other hand, its use with Christian appellatives or personal names, the identification of individuals whose names are compounded with *-ingtūn* (in the eighth and ninth centuries) and with *tūn* much later, and its common combination with racial names like *Norðman* 'Norwegian' (in Normanton) or *Īri* 'Irishman' (Irton YN), which cannot be older than the tenth century, make it typical of the middle and even the last stages of the Anglo-Saxon period.

It is, therefore, upon a very restricted number of place-names that we can estimate the range of the Anglo-Saxon settlement in its first phase. Folk-names in *-ingas* which can safely be derived from personal names (the Hastings type) are common in east and north Kent and in the coastal districts of Sussex and eastern Hampshire. In the Thames valley they are less common, but they are frequent in Essex and East Anglia. There is a sprinkling of such names in the east midland counties and in the East and North Ridings of Yorkshire. Names in *-ingahām* (the Wokingham type) are much less frequent in the south-eastern counties, but occur in greater numbers in East Anglia, the north-east midlands and the East Riding, but elsewhere in the north they are

[1] Ekwall, *Dictionary*, xii–xiv, discusses the age of OE *hām* in place-names.

very rare: *-ingahām* in fact seems to be more characteristic of Anglian territory than of the south. Similarly OE *hām* is common in the south-eastern counties, in East Anglia, and in the more easterly parts of the northern counties: it is of course found in most other counties to the west, but its appearance in the south-west, the midlands, the west midlands, and the north-west is very sporadic. Names of heathen origin have a very uneven distribution. They are unknown in the north and the north midlands (apart from one or two names like Grimsdike YW),[1] in the west midlands (except for Staffordshire), the south-west, the middle Thames valley, and the Weald. Even in the remaining parts of the east and south-east the majority are in certain localities like the Canterbury district, the Wey valley in Surrey, in Essex, and scattered along the rest of the Thames valley.

A broad agreement of the distribution of such archaic place-names has been sought with that of heathen English burial grounds, but there are undoubtedly anomalies in the pattern. In Essex burial grounds do not give us the same picture of an intensive and widespread settlement as do that county's archaic place-names, but that may be due to the casual circumstances which so often attend the discovery of these archaeological sites. On the other hand, in the Trent valley along the Fosseway to the Warwickshire Avon, even almost to Tewkesbury, heathen burials far outnumber the archaic place-names. The discrepancy may be accounted for by our inability to distinguish other types of archaic place-names which might have had a greater frequency in these districts. It is in fact noteworthy that folk-names of the type found in the names of the *Hwicce* of the south-west midlands, the *Hrype* from whom Ripon YW was named, the *Hicce*, whose name survives in Hitchen Hrt, and others recorded in the Tribal Hidage, are better known in these midland counties than elsewhere. In other areas, where archaeological material is wanting, scattered *-ing* names are found, but these are not necessarily of an ancient pattern. In the West Riding, for example, names like Bowling and Cowling are either simple appellatives in *-ing* or place-names formed with the singular *-ing* suffix from *bolla* 'a depression' and *coll* 'a hill-top', and other names like Addingham or Manningham appear to be 'homesteads associated with *Adda* or *Mægen*' with the connective *-ing-* rather than to contain old folk-names. The same is true of the Cumberland names Addingham, Hensingham, and Whicham: signs of the old genitive plural, which we should expect if these are from old

[1] *Grymisdyk* 1257–85 YD ii; the name describes a defensive earthwork.

folk-names, rarely occur in the early spellings of these place-names. In Somerset, the only name with any sign of age is Locking and this is as likely to denote 'the men of Loxton' (a place to the south of Locking) and to be a folk-name of local origin; such a name need not be old.

The absence of archaic names in certain districts, such as Romney Marsh, the Weald of Kent and Sussex, or the Fenlands round the Wash, has an obvious explanation in the character of the local landscape; in others, like the Hertfordshire Chilterns, the south-western part of the West Riding, or the far west, their absence is to be sought in the longer survival of a British population. Yet even in Hertfordshire a heavily wooded terrain unsuitable for their occupation probably discouraged encroachment by the East Saxons or the Angles and permitted the continued existence of a British community; the few archaic names that county possesses, Braughing, Tewin, or Thundridge, belong to its north-eastern parts.[1] A study of the exact location of these ancient settlements which can be ascertained only from their names is as significant as their general distribution, for the siting of such settlements seems to have been largely determined by the physical characteristics of the country-side.

The history of later colonization and of exploitation of virgin land around each parent settlement is reflected in the types of name that belong to the later centuries. OE *tūn* for example, as I have already observed, lacks those signs of age that we note in OE *hām*; it is comparatively rare in the south-eastern counties but increases in frequency in the midlands and towards the west and in the north, but its increasing frequency in village-names in the midland counties and in the west generally[2] suggests that the high mark of its use in place-names comes soon after the initial Anglo-Saxon settlements and its use with certain tribal names[3] makes it a sign of secondary colonization. But the evidence for the naming of secondary sites is complicated and three special features are to be noted.

[1] Braughing (which is also the name of the only medieval Hertfordshire deanery that belonged to the Bishopric of London to the east) is a folk-name from a personal name *Brahha*. Thundridge contains the name of the heathen god *Thunor*. Tewin is thought to be from a personal name *Tīwa*, connected with the god's name *Tīw*, but a folk-name of local origin from an OE *tīwe*, a variant of *tīg* 'a meeting-place', is also possible, as the names of the heathen gods do not appear to be used of mortal men in either England or Scandinavia.

[2] On the distribution of *tūn* compare the section Distribution of Elements s.v. in the various county surveys.

[3] Cf. *supra*, 72.

In the oldest extant place-name material, such as that in Bede or the earliest charters, the only element which denotes a habitation site is *hām* 'a homestead', for *tūn* is primarily an enclosure and *burh* and *ceaster* in those days referred to old Roman or British sites. In Bede, for example, there are only 7 names involving old folk-names in *-ingas*, there are 3 with *hām*, 2 with *tūn*, and 1 with *wīc*, but 13 with *ceaster* or *burh*. On the other hand, there are 31 names of purely topographical origin—names compounded with OE *feld* 'open country', *ford* 'ford', *eu* 'island', *dun* 'hill', *burna* 'stream'—and, as in the oldest charters, these topographical names have by the seventh and eighth centuries come to denote centres of human habitation. This we learn partly from their description as *villa* or the like or from the context and partly from a simple rule of usage which both Bede and the charter compilers observed,[1] that the preposition *æt* was not used in place-name forms when they were the names of original habitations like *Godmunddingaham* or of natural features like *Hæthfeld* or *Briodun*, but the preposition *æt* (or its Latin equivalent *ad*) was prefixed to old nature-names which had by this time been transferred to habitation sites, as in Bede's *Ad Baruæ id est Ad Nemus* from *bearu* 'a grove' or in *æt Clife* 'at Cliff' for Bishop's Cleeve Gl.[2] There is good chronological evidence for the great age of some of these topographical terms, like *lēah*, *dūn*, or *burna*,[3] for they are combined with old folk-names (as in Pangbourne Brk, Sittingbourne K, or Repton Db) and heathen associations are not wanting. The fact that so many of these topographical names have become parish names and had already become the names of Domesday manors bears witness to the readiness with which such names were transferred to secondary settlements in the older period. The later addition of a word like *tūn* to old toponymics, as in Carhampton So ('the *tūn* at a place called *æt Carrum*', from *carr* 'a rock') or in Tiverton D ('*tūn* at a place called *æt Twifyrde*', that is, 'the double ford') and many other so-called

[1] Ekwall discusses this interesting distinction (*Dictionary*, xvii–xviii).

[2] BCS 246.

[3] Of these examples, *lēah* continued in active use till Middle English times, especially in the sense 'woodland clearing', and since it was then sometimes used in the plural it was confused (and in poetic usage remains confused) with *lǣs* 'a meadow'. OE *dūn* remained in use throughout the Old English period. OE *burna* was supplanted in common use by *brōc* 'a brook' and often in the Danelaw by ON *bekkr* 'a stream', the main area of its survival being Northumberland; *burna* is combined with the archaic element *hām* but not with *tūn* (except in the Northumberland name Brunton), whereas *brōc* is very frequently combined with *tūn*, but never certainly with *hām*.

triple compounds,[1] is a conscious adjustment made in the adoption of the name of a natural feature as that of a new settlement.

Another striking feature of our oldest nomenclature is the rarity of words denoting buildings. OE *bōðl* or *bold* 'a dwelling' has a restricted currency in the north and midlands, *hall* 'a hall' is extremely rare until after the Norman Conquest, *hūs* is for the most part confined to the Danelaw (except in modern names) and its use is probably largely of Scandinavian origin, whilst *ærn* 'a house', *cot* 'a cottage', and *wīc* 'a dwelling', common enough in late Old English, often denote buildings in which certain crafts or other activities were practised, as in Crockern D, Do, Potterne Do, W (where crocks and pots were made), Hordern La ('store-house'), Glascote Wa (from *glæs* 'glass') or Salcote Ess (from *salt*), Chiswick Mx (*cēse* 'cheese') or Saltwick Nb (*salt*). Many other words like *hulc*, *scræf*, or *scydd* meant no more than 'shed' or 'hovel', and all are lacking in signs of antiquity. Indeed, the frequent use of *new* with some of the commoner elements, *hūs* (as in Newsham La, YN 'at the new houses'), *bōðl* (as in Newbottle Bk, Du, Nt, or Newbold Ch, Db, Wo, &c.), or *timber* 'a timbered building' (as in Newtimber, Nyetimber Sx), indicates a certain modernity in names which describe the dwellings of men. It may well be that the impermanence of early Anglo-Saxon dwellings rendered the use of such terms superfluous in early place-names, and that it was the *tūn* 'the enclosure' or the *worð* 'the curtilage' that mattered most. A man's own dwelling, his *cot*, assumes importance only in the later days of secondary colonization.

The third characteristic type of secondary names is the so-called simplex place-name, which consists of a single theme without any defining adjunct, Cotes, Lee, Stow, Stoke, Wike, or Thorpe. Functionally such names when derived from the commoner elements denoted places of restricted local importance. Apart from *lēah*, which continued in living use until Middle English, such words do not seem to have been in active use in place-names in the oldest period, and the fact that comparatively few of them became parochial names and many have not survived also points to the minor character of the settlements they describe and to their general lateness in the chronological

[1] These two examples clearly show that the so-called triple compounds may well originate as normal two-theme place-names consisting of an old place-name to which another element has been added: Brafferton YN is to be interpreted as 'the farmstead at a place formerly called *Bradford*' rather than 'the broad ford farmstead'.

ordering of English place-names. At the same time the absence of any kind of administrative independence of such outlying farmsteads and colonies would partially explain the absence or rarity of some of these elements in the oldest sources, and it is possible that some like *stede* 'a place, a site', so common in the south-eastern counties and East Anglia, or *þrop* 'an outlying farmstead', found chiefly in the Thames valley from Essex to Gloucestershire, occasionally in Northumbria, but never in Kent, Sussex, southern Hampshire, or the far south-west, have an older currency than the extant material suggests.

The general picture that we get of the spread of English settlement, however, is a basic nucleus of ancient sites indicated by a limited number of place-names in *-ing*, of major movements towards the west where names in *tūn* preponderate and words like *cot* become more frequent, and of the steady clearing of ground and the growth of outlying farms around all these primary settlements, an expansion at first represented chiefly by the use of old topographical names and later by the increasing use of special terms like *þrop* or *stoc* or *wīc*, and last of all by words like *rydding* 'clearing' and the like.

We are now achieving a greater measure of certainty in the names and types of names that have a bearing on the problem of the early Anglo-Saxon settlement. Through the pursuit of small clues and the application of comparative methods only possible with the advance of the survey, we understand more surely the temporal evolution of style in name-giving that follows a changing language and a developing country-side, and we are discerning differing regional patterns that depend partly on these evolutionary changes (as with *-ing*) and partly upon local differences in dialect or landscape that are original (as with *þrop*). At the same time the comprehensive picture of place-names in relation to the settlement can only be completed with the detailed surveys of the eighteen remaining English counties, when the contextual study of adequate material will allow us to put each name into its proper type and time.

SIR ISRAEL GOLLANCZ MEMORIAL LECTURE

THE OLD ENGLISH BEDE

By DOROTHY WHITELOCK

Fellow of the Academy

Read 14 February 1962

THE homilist Ælfric in his homily on St. Gregory, in the second volume of his *Catholic Homilies*, issued in 992, refers to Bede's history as the *Historia Anglorum* 'which King Alfred translated from Latin into English'.[1] From that day until the appearance of Henry Sweet's *Anglo-Saxon Reader* in 1876 no one, to my knowledge, called this attribution in doubt. Sweet questioned Alfred's authorship because of the over-literalness of the translation.[2] A stronger attack appeared in 1890, when Thomas Miller published the first volume of his edition of the Old English Bede,[3] a work to which all subsequent scholars in this field are greatly indebted. In the introduction he claimed that much of the vocabulary was not West Saxon, but Mercian, and that the work 'shows some familiarity with Scotch localities and circumstances' as well as 'a tender regard for things of Scotland'. He held that such sympathies were likely in the churches of Mercia, an area originally converted by the Scots from Iona, and he tentatively suggested Lichfield as the place where the translation was made.[4] From this date the war has been on.

There have been writers who simply ignored Miller's views, but from the first linguists appreciated the force of Miller's linguistic argument. I do not intend to reopen the question of the Anglian nature of the work. A number of subsequent studies in Old English vocabulary have supported Miller's claim for non-West-Saxon origin and have shown that the affinities lie with works surviving from Mercia and Northumbria.[5] Some of the evidence seems to point specifically to Mercia.[6]

But among those who have accepted Miller's claim, there are current several explanations of the presence of Mercian features in a work attributed to Alfred. We can dismiss that view which airily accounts for them as the alterations of later scribes, for Miller was undoubtedly right in claiming that such features were present in the common original of all surviving manuscripts, each of which, in greater or less degree, sporadically replaced

Anglian words and forms by West Saxon equivalents. If the work had originally been written by a West Saxon, we should then have to suppose that his version was lost and that all our manuscripts come from an Anglian copy of it[7]. It would be odd if no later copyist, eager though they all were to remove non-West-Saxon features, could find a West Saxon text as his exemplar. The Otho manuscript was written at Winchester:[8] it is inconceivable that even there only an Anglian copy was available of a West Saxon work.

Similar difficulties lie in the way of Deutschbein's suggestion in 1901, that two independent translations of Bede were made, one by an anonymous Mercian, one by King Alfred, and that the extant version is the former, whereas Ælfric is referring to the latter.[9] Why should all the later West Saxon copyists have chosen to reproduce the Mercian work, rather than Alfred's version? A further objection to this view is the fact that Ælfric does not merely refer to a vernacular version which he attributes to King Alfred; he actually uses it, and his phraseology shows clearly that he had our extant version in front of him.[10] Surely, then, it is this which he assigns to King Alfred.

Alfred's Mercian helpers, Werferth, Plegmund, Athelstan, and Werwulf, have often been called in, to account for the dialect colouring of the Old English Bede. This explanation assumes that a translation of Bede formed part of Alfred's scheme for educating his people, and hence the work was later attributed to the king himself. His precise connexion with it can be variously conceived: he could have commissioned it from a single Mercian scholar, as he did Gregory's *Dialogues* from Bishop Werferth; he could have laid the task on a team of helpers. In either case, he might have done no more than commission the work; or he might have given general instructions on what to omit and what to retain; he might have exercised some supervision in the course of production, either reading parts of it, or revising the whole.

This does not exhaust the possibilities. In 1898 Schipper suggested that Alfred had a text of Bede's Latin which had been provided with an interlinear gloss,[11] and Professor Kuhn developed this view in 1941.[12] He held that a text with frequent double glosses supplies the reason for the translator's practice of rendering one Latin word by two English equivalents. This is not the only way of accounting for this feature,[13] but even if it were, it is difficult to assume that this postulated gloss fully explains Mercian vocabulary and Mercian sympathies in a work by Alfred. Leaving aside for the present the alleged Mercian sympathies, can one suppose that Alfred, by no means a slavish translator, would use words which were alien to his own speech, even for simple conceptions like 'go', 'ask', 'call', 'thing', 'cause', 'manner', or for conjunctions and adverbs like 'unless', 'yet', 'almost', merely because they were in a gloss to the text?[14] Whether or not the translator was working from a glossed manuscript, this would not explain the use of these non-West-Saxon words in a work by Alfred.

Another theory was advanced by Hecht in 1907, that the translation was made by a Mercian teacher at Alfred's palace school, with omission of parts unsuitable for his pupils' reading, i.e. learned material, documents, citations, epitaphs, religious discussions, &c. He suggests that an improved version was later made at the king's request; but he does not develop his theory.[15]

So we have a wide choice. Yet there is still another possibility, which has received little attention:[16] that King Alfred had nothing whatever to do with the Old English Bede. It was attributed to him almost a century after his time. One could find parallels for a wrong attribution of a work at this distance of time. Alfred left a reputation as the translator of Latin works. Ælfric's contemporary, the chronicler Æthelweard, says he translated *volumina numero ignoto*.[17] Can one dismiss the possibility that translations which owed nothing to him could have been assigned to him, and that the Old English Bede could have been one of these? Not, I think, without looking more closely at the evidence for this attribution. This is the more necessary, because, if we cannot safely connect the work with Alfred, we must re-examine the evidence for its date.

Ælfric, who believed the work to be by Alfred himself, had access to at least a part of it, the section on St. Gregory.[18] It is, of course, possible that he saw a manuscript which had some indication of authorship, such as a preface by Alfred; but, since no extant manuscript has any such indication, we have no right to assume this. Ælfric's attribution is supported by William of Malmesbury, who lists the *Bede* with the *Orosius*, the *Cura Pastoralis*, the *Boethius*, and the *Handbook*, calling them Alfred's principal works.[19] This shows that the belief in Alfred's authorship was not confined to Ælfric, but it does not prove the attribution correct. On the other hand, the Middle English poet Laȝamon would hardly have made the blunder of assigning the Old English version to Bede himself if he had been aware of its attribution to Alfred.[20]

Two other arguments sometimes brought forward in support of Alfred's authorship must be rejected. One can be disposed of easily; Mr. Neil Ker has shown that a couplet referring to Alfred as author in the late eleventh-century Cambridge manuscript is in a hand of the sixteenth century.[21] Thus it merely represents the opinion of an antiquary, probably based on William of Malmesbury.

To refute the second argument requires some technical discussion. This same Cambridge manuscript inserts between Bede's preface and the list of chapters a West Saxon regnal list, which ends with Alfred, and this has often been used as evidence for an original connexion with the king. But the only other manuscript which has the beginning intact, that at Corpus Christi College, Cambridge, known as B (from the old name of the college, Benet), of the early eleventh century, does not contain this regnal list. Moreover, it can be shown that it was also lacking from the Otho manuscript known as C;[22] for this manuscript was available to the seventeenth-century editor of the Old English Bede, Abraham Whelock, before it was largely destroyed in the fire of 1731. He took his text from the Cambridge manuscript, giving variants from B and C; but when he prints the regnal list, the variants from what he calls B cannot be from the B manuscript of the Old English Bede, which has not got the list. They are from another Corpus (Benet) manuscript, the Parker manuscript of the Anglo-Saxon Chronicle. His readings from what he calls C come from the Cottonian manuscript Tiberius A iii, f. 178, a single leaf which once belonged to the version of the Anglo-Saxon Chronicle in Tiberius A vi. They agree with this completely,[23] and include a wrong date, CCCCXCIII for CCCCXCIIII, which is an easy misreading by Whelock of the figure in Tiberius A iii, where one of the minims has been almost entirely obscured by a small tear.[24] Whelock would hardly have referred to this manuscript simply as C, the letter by which he normally refers to the Otho manuscript of the Old English Bede, if the latter had contained the regnal list; and he would surely have referred to its readings if it had.[25] A list missing from both the B and the C manuscripts of the Old English Bede is extremely unlikely to have formed part of the original work. There is no evidence that it was inserted earlier than the Cambridge manuscript. The fact that it ends with Alfred is no safe argument that it was added in his reign, for the scribe who inserted it would be likely to copy the version available to him, without troubling to bring it up to date. When in the early eleventh century the Parker manuscript of the Anglo-Saxon Chronicle was copied into Otho B xi, the scribe was content to let the regnal list (which survives as a detached leaf, Additional MS. 34652, f. 2) end with Alfred.[26] Thus the regnal list in the Cambridge manuscript of the Old English Bede is valueless as evidence for a connexion of this work with Alfred.

On general grounds, one can argue that Bede's *Ecclesiastical History* would be very likely to be included in Alfred's scheme for providing translations of works 'most necessary for all men to know',[27] unless he knew that an English version was already available. If we take his words in the prefatory letter to his *Cura Pastoralis* at their face value, we must assume that when he planned his course of action he was not aware of a translation of Bede; for he says: 'I wondered exceedingly at those good and wise men who formerly were throughout England and had fully studied all those books, that they would not turn *any part of them* into their own language.' Yet the possibility remains that, unknown to Alfred, a translation of Bede had been made by an Anglian scholar. I should like something firmer than an attribution of almost a century later and an argument from general probability before accepting Alfred's connexion with the translation of Bede as an established fact.

It has sometimes been suggested that the Old English Bede can be shown to have formed part of Alfred's scheme because it omits certain matters which are dealt with in the other works translated, and hence that the translation was planned in relation to these. Before we examine these suggestions, we ought first to consider the translator's general practice, rather than argue from this or that omission, judged in isolation. By a selection of evidence one can prove almost anything. It is high time that we looked at the Old English Bede, without prejudging any issues.

Bede's *Ecclesiastical History* is a very long work. The translation greatly shortens it. In this it differs from the translations of the *Dialogues* and the *Cura Pastoralis* of Gregory the Great, which are given almost complete, perhaps out of reverence for the 'Apostle of the English'. Much is omitted from the Old English translations of Orosius, Boethius, and the *Soliloquies* of St. Augustine. Bede's book has been cut with remarkable care. The translator is anxious not to leave loose ends: he omits cross references to passages which he has left out; on occasion, he supplies information when a passage is no longer clear because of a previous omission.[28] Without any of our modern aids, such as an indexed

Bede, he has left a coherent account in spite of much condensation. He was very familiar with the text, for he can avoid repetition by omitting material which recurs later on in the book. There are discernible principles in his selection, consistently carried out. These things, even taken alone, suggest that a single mind was responsible for the form of the work. It does not read like team-work.[29] They suggest also that, though certain errors in detail in all manuscripts show that the version from which they descend was not the author's autograph,[30] it had not moved far from his intentions on larger matters.

One principle of selection was to omit most of the letters, documents, epitaphs, and poems quoted by Bede. True to this principle, the translator omitted the long document of Gregory's *Responsa* to Augustine's queries from its proper place in book i, and took pains to smooth over the gap by altering the words which follow. Later, however, he added the *Responsa* after the end of book iii. I shall consider the reason for this later.

A second principle of selection is of greater interest. The translator's main concern is with the ecclesiastical history of the *English* nation. It is significant that when Bede, near the end of his work, calls it *historia ecclesiastica Brittaniarum, et maxime gentis Anglorum*, the translator alters to 'the history of the church of the English nation in Britain',[31] a description which fits the work he has produced better than Bede's words do. His tendency to confine himself to English affairs explains not only the omission of much that concerns the internal affairs of the Celtic churches[32] and the dropping of the accounts of the foreign saints Germanus, Columba, Ninian, and Adamnan,[33] but also the omission of most of the Roman history in book i, of the account of the Pantheon,[34] of the parts of the chapter on Gregory[35] which do not relate to the English church, of the synod of Rome in book iv, ch. 18, of the details about the second synod which dealt with Wilfrid's suit in Rome,[36] and of the chapters from Adamnan's *De locis sanctis*.[37] Some minor references to foreign affairs are omitted also. Seen in this wider context, the omission of some references to the observance by the Celtic churches of a wrong date for Easter will not bear the weight that has often been placed on it. As the claim to 'a tender regard' towards Scottish susceptibilities mainly rests on the translator's treatment of the Easter controversy, it is necessary to look at this more closely.

If he had omitted all references to it, I should have suggested that he did so because it was an old and dead controversy, and I should have compared his lack of interest in Pelagianism and

Arianism. But he did not omit all the references; he made a significant selection. He retains the parts concerning the efforts of Augustine, Archbishop of Canterbury, to correct the errors of the British church,[38] and of Laurentius, Archbishop of Canterbury, to bring to the proper observance both the British and the Irish churches.[39] He retains also the accounts of how the Englishmen, Ecgberht, Aldhelm, and Ceolfrith, respectively converted from this error the Irish in Iona, the British in Wessex, and the Picts.[40] He omits the attempts of popes to win the Celtic churches to the truth, and those of the Irishman Adamnan;[41] the English church was not concerned in these efforts. More striking is his omission of all reference to the unorthodox practice of Aidan, the missionary to Northumbria,[42] and of the statement that the British bishops who helped to consecrate Chad observed the wrong Easter.[43] The long chapter on how the question was settled at the synod of Whitby goes out also, and consequently the following chapter on the departure of the defeated Colman,[44] and we can see how deliberate this omission was when we note that in the chapter on Wilfrid in book v even the few words of Bede mentioning his part at the synod of Whitby are expunged.[45] In fact, if we did not possess the Latin Bede, we should gather that the Irish missionaries brought their error into England only from the statements that Archbishop Theodore taught the English to celebrate the right Easter,[46] that Wilfrid on his return to Britain taught orthodox observances,[47] and that the Scots who preceded him in Ripon did not observe Easter rightly.[48] Though one cannot claim that the former unorthodoxy of part of the English church has been completely suppressed, it has certainly been robbed of any prominence. If this had been in order to avoid wounding the Scots, why then did the translator fail to expunge the accounts of the efforts of Laurentius and Ecgberht to reform them? My impression is that he was not deeply interested in this old controversy—he omits all Bede's demonstrations of where the error in calculation lay[49]—nor was he eager to call attention to any previous unorthodoxy in the English church; but he could not forbear to claim for the English church all possible credit for its share in reforming the Celtic churches.

If, then, the view that the translator betrays sympathy for the Irish church has no foundation, we can drop the idea that this sympathy showed him to be a Mercian. By itself, this never was a strong argument, for why should only Mercians feel gratitude to the Irish church, which also converted the Northumbrians and the East Saxons? Any argument for Mercian origin must stand or fall on linguistics alone, unless stronger evidence than this for Mercian sympathies is forthcoming. If the translator's selection shows special sympathies, they are those of an Englishman more interested in Englishmen than in foreigners, and this is unhelpful in localizing the work.

Miller makes a few minor points to support the thesis he based on the handling of the Easter question, but none is convincing.[50] The rendering of *transmontanis Pictis ad aquilonem* as 'in the moors which are to the north part of the kingdom of the Picts'[51] is claimed as evidence of close familiarity with Scotch localities; it reads more like the mistranslation of a man who did not understand the former divisions of Pictland. Little weight can be attached to the omission of Bede's remark that Iona belonged *ad ius quidem Brittanniae*,[52] in view of the translator's habit of shortening or omitting geographical descriptions. When Bede says Columba was called 'by some' Columcille, and the translator is specific, saying that 'the Scots afterwards called him Columcille',[53] this is surely only a natural inference. The claim that the reproach to the Scots implied in *fraudium*[54] was softened by the use of a milder word, *gestrodo*, suitable to the border foray, is false; it is not a milder word; it renders *rapinis* in the Vespasian Psalter. It is from the verb *strūdan* 'to plunder', and it is an excellent rendering of *fraudium* in the sense in which Bede is using it.

The translator did not trouble to soften the words: 'From that time no king of the Scots dared to come to battle against the English nation up to this present day.'[55] Nor was he interested enough in Scotland to retain the descriptions of the Firth of Clyde with its city of *Alcluith*[56] or of the Firth of Forth with its town of *Giudi*.[57] No safe conclusions regarding his locality can be drawn from his omission or inclusion of geographical data. He omits the accounts of the Antonine Wall, Heavenfield, Lindisfarne, Bangor, Reculver, and the Mevanian Isles,[58] and greatly shortens the description of Britain in Bede's first chapter. He retains short statements on Thanet, London, Lindsey, Sussex, Ely, and Abercorn, and most of the account of the Isle of Wight and its tides.[59]

Similarly, an examination of the forms of the place-names gives little result.[60] Many of Bede's forms are left unaltered, and these can be helpful only if we have reason to suppose that they were no longer the current forms and hence their retention may suggest that the place was unfamiliar to the translator. Sometimes he does replace Bede's forms with those current in his time. We can ignore the names of important places like York, Lincoln,

Chester, Winchester, the Thames, Severn, and Trent, where he uses the forms found in the Anglo-Saxon Chronicle and elsewhere; for no matter what his provenance, he would know of these places. His occasional use of *Lundenceaster* beside *Lundene* and *Lundenburh*, the forms normal in other records, can hardly be used, as Miller uses it, to show he was not a southerner. It is of greater interest that he is familiar with the current names of Bamburgh, Hexham, Whithorn, and Coldingham, which he could not have learnt from the Latin version;[61] but Bamburgh was a place of importance, Hexham and Whithorn were sees, whose names any ecclesiastic might be expected to know, and, though the history of the monastery of Coldingham after Bede's time is obscure, its name might be kept alive by its being the place at which St. Æthelthryth, a popular saint, first took the veil.[62] Knowledge of contemporary usage seems implied in his rendering of *uicum Cataractam*, *uico Cataractone*, as *Cetreht tune*, *Cetrehtan*, *Cetreht weorþige*.[63] On the other hand, he could not recognize Gateshead in *Ad Caprae Caput*, but puts *æt Rægeheafde*;[64] this is, however, a possible place-name, perhaps the origin of Read, Lancashire.[65] A man closely familiar with Northumbria might have altered the archaic form *Loidis* for Leeds,[66] and have used a more modern name than *Lugubalia* for Carlisle.[67] One cannot tell if his *in Donafelda* is anything more than a translation of Bede's *in Campodono*,[68] for the name does not survive. In the Midlands, *Teolfingaceastre* for Bede's *Tiouulfingacaestir*[69] looks like a genuine contraction of this lost name; but since the place is probably Littleborough on Trent, where the Roman road from Doncaster to Lincoln crosses the river, it may have been well known. When mentioning places in the south of England, he did not replace Bede's *Mean-* in *Meanware* by *Meon-*,[70] nor give the correct form for the important waterway, the Wantsome; he retained the misspelling of his C-type Latin text, writing *wantsama* instead of *wantsuma*.[71] It was left for the common exemplar of manuscripts C, O, and Ca to make the necessary correction.

The work has been shortened also by the leaving out of some explanatory comments, like that on the difference between a wall and a *vallum*,[72] or on the Latin and Greek names for a peninsula,[73] and almost all the interpretations of place-names; also some of Bede's rhetorical flourishes, for example that Oswald's fame spread 'rays of healing light' across the ocean,[74] or that from Theodore and Hadrian 'rivers of wholesome knowledge daily flowed to water the hearts of their hearers'.[75] The clause giving the year of the incarnation is often omitted. That this cannot be put down to scribal carelessness is indicated by a measure of selection of what dates to omit. In nine cases the year of the consecration or death of a bishop is omitted,[76] though the day and the length of the episcopate are usually retained. The year of the battle of *Degsastan* and of Hatfield[77] is omitted, and that of the baptism of Edwin and of Ceadwalla.[78] Accidental omission would not have spared all the dates of royal accessions; nor is it accident which replaces the clause by 'and after this'[79] or 'and two years later'.[80] For the purpose of observing an anniversary it is enough to know the day, and the clause by which incarnation dates are given is a lengthy one; yet an author who so often lessens his labours by omitting it cannot have regarded dates as of primary importance, a fact to be borne in mind when considering his omission of Bede's chronological summary.[81] The translator did not share Bede's passion for chronology: he omits the date calculated from the foundation of Rome[82] or from the coming of the English[83] as well as two of the four references to the indiction;[84] he frequently disregards Bede's cautious use of *ferme* or *circiter* in relation to dates.

Since it is possible to distinguish a high degree of care and consistency in the translator's procedure, it may be worth while to examine his handling of those places where Bede says or implies that persons are living or things surviving until the present day. Where it is obvious that Bede is speaking in his own person, as in the preface, or where it is definitely stated that the conditions of 731 are being described,[85] these things present no problem and the statements can be allowed to stand. Otherwise, when survival to the translator's day is impossible, he normally omits the statement, or alters the tense of the verbs. There is an exception when Bede's remark that James the deacon lived into 'our time' is retained,[86] and another when we are told that Daniel still holds the see of Winchester.[87] But a few lines later when Bede's statement that Forthhere 'is alive to this day' is kept in the translation, it is immediately followed by the words 'so said the writer'. In view of the normal practice of avoiding by some means the depicting of persons as still living, it seems fair to assume that in these two exceptional cases some such saving clause, like 'said Bede',[88] or 'said the author of this book',[89] has been omitted. When Bede says that Willibrord is alive, having held his episcopate for thirty-six years, the translator says he held it for thirty-six years and then died.[90] When Bede predicts that Acca will continue on his virtuous course until he receive his reward from God, the translator replaces the future tense by the past.[91]

In these cases, survival to the translator's day is impossible. In some other places, where he knew that conditions had since changed, he modernized. Thus, when Bede says the see of Selsey ceased 'until to-day', the translation reads 'for many years'.[92] Both references to the holding by the Jutes of the mainland opposite the Isle of Wight[93] are omitted, and so is the mention of a church of the Four Crowned Martyrs at Canterbury,[94] perhaps because it no longer existed. From the ninth statute of the synod of Hertford, concerning the need for more sees, the final clause 'but this was passed over for the present'[95] is dropped. More sees had since been created. Are these instances of modernization enough for us to assume that in general, where Bede's statements that conditions survive to the present day are left unchanged, this is because they are still true, or because the translator had no means of knowing that they were not, or because he was not sufficiently interested in the particular matter to go to the trouble of altering them? Or was he simply inconsistent, in which case such passages will not help to date or locate the work?

One can leave out of count claims that saints were being honoured, relics preserved, or miracles performed by relics and at places of martyrdom, at St. Albans or Lichfield or Ely or Lindisfarne,[96] or at foreign places such as Brie, Péronne, or near the Rhine.[97] He would be unlikely to question such claims.[98] He may have known that Edwin's gold chalice was still preserved at Canterbury,[99] or have had no reason to doubt it. He might be prepared to believe that places still bore the name of James the deacon[100] or of Tunna the priest,[101] whether he knew them or not; that the site of the heathen temple at Goodmanham was still being pointed out;[102] or that Aidan's oratory was still visible at Lindisfarne.[103] But did he omit Bede's statement that the church at Lincoln was roofless in his day[104] because he knew it was so no longer? Was it because he doubted its truth that he omits the mention of Horsa's monument as visible in Kent,[105] or was he uninterested in a monument to a heathen chieftain?

There are some places where Bede's statements are left unchanged when we know they were no longer true. He says that the bodies of all archbishops of Canterbury are buried in the monastery of St. Peter and St. Paul.[106] Though the evidence for a great conflict between this house (later called St. Augustine's) and Christ Church over burial rights in the mid-eighth century is post-Conquest and open to suspicion,[107] there seems no reason to doubt that Archbishop Cuthbert was buried in Christ Church in 760, and that after that date the only archbishop to be buried in the monastery of St. Peter and St. Paul was Jænberht, a former abbot of that house; and it would be unusual if a church had relinquished burial rights without resistance. One would have expected the translator, if consistent in his practice, to have altered the tense and have written 'in which the bodies of all bishops of Canterbury *were* placed'; especially would he have been inclined, one would have thought, to make this little adjustment if he were closely connected with Christ Church. Yet it may be that by the late ninth century the Christ Church claim had been so long and so securely established that even inmates of that church had ceased to be sensitive on the matter.

The translator retains Bede's tirades against the British Church for its clinging to the false date of Easter, though this had been relinquished as early as 768.[108] If he had retained only the remarks in book v, ch. 23, this would be understandable, for here it is explicit that it is the conditions holding in 731 which are being described. But in the preceding chapter he says that the Britons 'hold yet to their old customs and halt from the right paths'. However, he could not have omitted this accusation, false though it was by his time, without relinquishing the contrast which Bede is making to illustrate the divine justice, namely that the Irish, who helped to convert the English, received from them in return the gift of orthodoxy, whereas the British, who refused to take part in the conversion, remain in error.

One may also doubt whether it was still true that in the translator's time English monks were holding Mayo in Ireland,[109] though it is not possible to discover just when this community came to an end. There were English monks there certainly until about 800; Irish records long continue to call it 'Mayo of the Saxons', but the name could survive the presence of the English. In any case, the translator would be unlikely to have means of knowing what was happening there.

Of greater importance is his retention of the present tense when referring to the monasteries of Bardney, Lastingham, Whitby, and Hackness,[110] and to his acceptance of the information that remains of the monastic life established by Chad at Barrow in Lincolnshire are still visible,[111] that St. Cuthbert's relics are at Lindisfarne[112] and that East Anglia has two bishops until this day.[113] He nowhere gives a hint that any changes had been wrought in these areas by the Danish invasions and settlements.

If only we could be sure that he was reasonably consistent in his practice of bringing such references up to date, we might offer variant explanations of his failure to give such a hint: that he was writing before these settlements; that, though writing after them, he had no clear idea of what was happening beyond the Danish frontier; or that the Danish settlements were not so completely nor so immediately catastrophic in their effects on the church as we tend to assume.[114] Yet perhaps it is safest to suggest that he altered his source only when he could do so with little trouble, and where his interest was specially aroused. The clearest examples of modernization concern the south of England.

There is another alteration which should be considered. When he chooses, the translator can give a competent summary of a letter which he omits. He does so with regard to Pope Vitalian's letter on the provision of an archbishop of Canterbury after the death of Wigheard at Rome.[115] This makes one wonder whether the vagueness and inadequacy of the summary he gives of an important letter of St. Gregory is deliberate. From his words: 'he sent Bishop Augustine . . . a letter, in which he signified how he should consecrate other bishops and in what places he should establish them',[116] one would not easily recognize that famous letter which makes it clear that Gregory envisaged London, not Canterbury, as the eventual metropolitan see of the southern province, and that he did not intend the southern archbishop to take precedence over the Archbishop of York after Augustine's death. When one recalls that Cenwulf of Mercia, when taking steps to secure the abolition of the archbishopric of Lichfield founded in Offa's reign, tried to transfer the primacy to London,[117] relying no doubt on this very letter, it seems understandable that the translator might shrink from spreading more widely a knowledge of its dangerous contents. It is easy to see that a Canterbury writer might have a strong motive for its suppression, but on this matter the letter was equally inconvenient for the claims of Lichfield, or, indeed, of any see except London. It is true that in Alfred's reign some anxiety was being felt for the privileges of Canterbury. Pope John VIII wrote in 877 or 878 to Archbishop Æthelred:

> We indeed wish to preserve for you unimpaired and beyond doubt the privilege of your see, in the manner of the blessed Augustine, sent there by St. Gregory for the salvation of many and the conversion of the king, and we enact and command that it is to be observed for ever by all orders, whether ecclesiastical or lay, according to the (statute) of the same St. Gregory.[118]

He also says that he has written to King Alfred, who, he implies, has been threatening the rights of Canterbury. But he does not specify in what way, and it is unlikely that the threat concerned the primacy of Canterbury.[119] There would be many in the southern province besides the Canterbury clergy who would not wish to see the existing arrangement disturbed, or to spread Gregory's views on the equality of the northern archbishop, although this does not appear to have become an issue until much later. Although on general grounds it is tempting to suggest that it was Plegmund, Archbishop of Canterbury, who was eager that Bede's *Ecclesiastical History* should be one of the works translated, I doubt whether the vagueness of the reference to Gregory's letter, even if this were deliberate, affords strong support to such a view.[120]

The papal correspondence surviving from the ninth century supplies a reasonable explanation of the translator's change of mind with regard to the inclusion of Gregory's *Responsa*. There seems no logical reason for their removal from the proper place in book i to a position between books iii and iv. It would appear that the translator decided to include them after he had already started book iii. Now, between 872 and 874, Pope John VIII complained to Burgred of Mercia that 'many men of your kingdom presume to marry nuns and women dedicated to God, and women of their own kindred, disregarding the statute of St. Gregory, which of necessity was decreed for the newly-converted people'.[121] Writing to Archbishop Æthelred in 877 or 878, the same Pope says: 'Neither are you to permit anyone to marry within his own kindred, by the established decree of our holy predecessor Gregory, the teacher of your race.'[122] These passages show that in the second half of the ninth century Gregory's *Responsa* could not be dismissed as a dead letter, and this may account for the translator's second thoughts on their inclusion. The diction shows that it was he, and not a later writer, who added them, and he was using the same type of Latin text, a good version of what Plummer calls the C-type,[123] as for the rest of the work. It is therefore highly improbable that the omission of the *Responsa* from book i was occasioned by a lacuna in the Latin manuscript he was using.

So far we have found nothing in the translator's alterations that points to Alfred. The rendering of a passage in Bede's preface must next be considered. Bede wrote to King Ceolwulf: 'You desire that the said history should be made more familiar to yourself as well as to those over whom the Divine Authority has set you to rule, from your regard to the general welfare.' The Old English version has: 'I wrote this for your benefit and for your people; because God chose you as king, it behoves you to teach your people.'[124] On this change, Klaeber remarks: 'One can in fact hardly avoid the thought that this interpretation of the passage is inspired by King Alfred.'[125] Alfred certainly acted on this conception of a king's duties; but when one remembers the example of Charles the Great and the interest taken by Charles the Bald in the encouragement of learning, can one be certain that this view was uncommon at a time when Frankish influence was not negligible?

It is now time to examine the claims that the Old English Bede is proved to have been undertaken at Alfred's instigation by its omission of matter which was, or would be, in the other works translated, or, conversely, that these omitted matter which was, or would be, available in the translation of Bede. First, one must note that where there remains any overlap between the Old English Bede and any of the other works, the rendering is independent. The Anglo-Saxon Chronicle made no use of the Old English Bede, nor did the translator of Orosius in the material common to both works; Werferth did not use the parts where Bede is based on Gregory's *Dialogues*[126] and the translation of Gregory's *Responsa* was not consulted when a similar passage occurs in the *Cura Pastoralis*.[127] The translator of Bede shows no knowledge of the wording in these vernacular works. There is, therefore, no sign of direct influence; all one could hope to establish would be that the translation of Bede was planned in relation to one or more of these works.

Much of what Bede quotes from Orosius in book i is omitted from the Old English version. To assume that this was done because a translation of Orosius had been, or was to be made, is to ignore the similar omission of material drawn from Pliny, Prosper of Aquitaine, and Marcellinus Comes, as well as of the chapters from Constantius's *Life of Germanus*. The selection from Orosius in the two Old English works does not fit well a theory of a concerted plan, for both retain the parts about Severus and his wall, the accession of Marcus Antoninus, Diocletian's persecution, Constantius in Britain and the birth of his son Constantine, and Alaric's sack of Rome. Hence, though it may be strange that the translator of Bede should have omitted all or most of the account of Caesar's invasion of Britain,[128] it hardly seems an adequate explanation that in this one place he wished to avoid duplicating a section of the Old English Orosius. Even in the latter, the account is much curtailed. The omission from the Old English Bede of passages from Orosius is otherwise in line with the translator's lack of concern with foreign affairs. As for the omissions by the translator of *Orosius*, he has become very selective indeed by the time he reaches this, the seventh book of Orosius's long work; we need not assume that he left out some things because they were in Bede. There are noticeable differences between the translations. One is that while the Old English Bede retains the statement, based on Orosius, on the mildness of the climate of Ireland, the translator of Orosius replaces the words *sed caeli solique temperie magis utilis* by the remark that Ireland has much worse weather than Britain.[129] One should also contrast the lack of interest in geography betrayed by the translator of Bede with the remarkable reconstruction of the geography of north-east Europe supplied by the translator of Orosius, surely the most original and constructive addition to the translations of Alfred's reign. It is difficult to see the same mind behind these two works.

The omission by the Old English Bede of much of the chapter on St. Gregory has occasioned comment.[130] Almost everything that concerns England is kept, and also the date of his death and his epitaph.[131] The rest, including the account of his works, is omitted. But this can hardly be because it was felt redundant when translations of the *Dialogues* and the *Cura Pastoralis* had been provided, for this would be no good reason for omitting also his parentage, his career, his commentary on Job, his *Synodicus Libellus*, and his additions to the canon of the Mass. It is arguable that all this part seemed to the translator irrelevant in a history of the English church.

There remains the question of relationship with the Anglo-Saxon Chronicle, and this must be given careful consideration, partly because it concerns not only the connexion of the Old English Bede with Alfred, but also that of the Anglo-Saxon Chronicle, and partly because the view that a concerted plan lay behind these two works has the support of a great scholar with whom I normally find myself in complete agreement. Dr. Sisam writes: 'There is evidence that the two works were regarded as complementary.'[132] He argues that, while there is no sign of influence of the translation of Bede on the wording of the Chronicle, or vice versa, the omission from the Old English Bede of the chronological summary is to be explained by the presence of most of this in the Chronicle, whereas the tendency of the chronicler to confine himself to this summary suggests that he knew that the full work was, or would be, available in English. He sees further support for this view in the failure of the chronicler to supply a genealogy of the kings of Kent, a failure which he ascribes to an awareness that it was in two of the most important chapters in Bede.[133] One must take these points in order. It has been shown above that the translator of Bede is not greatly interested in chronology;[134] moreover, he tends to shorten his labours by getting rid of repetitions.[135] Almost all the entries in the chronological summary repeat what has been related in the body of the work; hence he may have thought it waste of labour to include it. That the chronicler, on the other hand, made great use of the summary requires no other explanation than that he took the shortest route to his goal. An annalist has to be interested in dates. Nevertheless, he did sometimes take matter from the rest of Bede's history, especially in order to add events of West Saxon history not mentioned in the summary. Thus he extracts the account of the expulsion of Cenwealth of Wessex by Penda of Mercia after he had divorced Penda's sister,[136] and also the information on the division of the West Saxon see.[137] He repeats Bede's list of kings who had held the *imperium*, in order to add the name of Ecgberht of Wessex.[138] It is hardly surprising that he passed over the discreditable incident of the sending of a West Saxon assassin to kill Edwin of Northumbria, with its sequel of Edwin's vengeance,[139] or the atrocities committed by Ceadwalla of Wessex in the Isle of Wight.[140] Otherwise, the only datable event of West Saxon history omitted by the chronicler is the victory over the apostate kings of Essex about 616, and to this Bede has only a brief passing reference.[141] The reason why the chronicler made comparatively little use of the text of Bede need not be because a translation was available; it could be because it contained little that was relevant to West Saxon history. For the rest, the chronological summary served him well enough.

There remains the argument drawn from the absence of the Kentish genealogy. Besides the genealogies of the West Saxon royal house, the chronicler supplies those of Bernicia (547, 670, 685), Deira (560), Ceolwulf of Northumbria (731), and the Mercian kings, Penda (626), Æthelbald (716), and Offa (755); but, though he traces the descent of Wihtred of Kent back to Æthelberht I (694), he nowhere takes it farther back. Yet it is unnecessary to assume that he meant his readers to get the Kentish genealogy from the translation of Bede. He obtained all the Northumbrian and Mercian genealogies from the collection which has come down to us in Vespasian B vi[142] and this has the Kentish genealogy. It would therefore have been easy for him to include it, whereas it would have been no light task for his readers to compile it for themselves from two chapters in Bede. But can we be sure that he would have thought it important? For three generations Kent had been ruled by the West Saxon royal house, which based its claim from at least one generation earlier. Why should the chronicler be at pains to demonstrate the descent from Woden of a previous dynasty of kings of Kent? He gives no genealogies for the kingdoms subject to Wessex in his day. It may be that none was known for Sussex, but that of the kings of Essex survives in a text of his time.[143] Yet he does not include it. It seems to me therefore that one cannot safely claim that the chronicler knew that a translation of Bede existed or was in preparation.

Hence my investigations have failed to find evidence that the translation of Bede was undertaken as part of Alfred's scheme. On the other hand, they have not proved that it was not so undertaken. If we had reason to suppose that there ever was a conference to decide what parts of the proposed works could be omitted, to avoid overlap, then the absence of any trace of concerted planning in relation to the Old English Bede might imply that it lay outside the scheme. But there are no grounds for postulating such a proceeding. So we reach a negative result.

The Old English Bede impresses me as the work of a man of an unusually orderly mind, which he applied carefully to the task before him. He knew his author well. He thought out some general principles of selection, and adhered to them with remarkable consistency. He was singularly exact in his rendering of Bede's terminology.[144] When one has said this, the fact remains that one cannot read his work without being conscious of the great decline of scholarship since the days of Bede. We are in a different intellectual climate. This impression does not depend solely on his inferior Latinity.[145] He lacks Bede's inquiring mind. Not only is there an increased insularity; his interests are narrower in other ways. He lacks Bede's interest in geography, chronology, and etymology. Moreover, he does not share his passion for precision and accuracy, and he is less careful than Bede was always to record the sources of the information. His handling of Bede's preface is careless, betraying a lack of understanding of the importance of evidence or of Bede's aims. In it he omits Nothhelm's researches into the papal archives at Rome, and he appears to number Chad and Cedd among Bede's informants, thus violating chronological possibility, though it is possible that this error arises from manuscript corruption.[146] He leaves out altogether the words with which Bede ends his preface:

And I humbly entreat the reader, if in these things . . . he find anything not delivered according to the truth, he will not impute this to me, who, as the true rule of history requires, have laboured sincerely to commit to writing such things as I could gather from common report, for the instruction of posterity.

This treatment of Bede's preface suggests that the decision to omit the documents quoted by Bede was not dictated solely by a desire to economize space, but also by a failure to appreciate the value of sources. He found room for all the miracle stories except one.[147] He probably regarded the work as in the first place one of religious edification. Bede's attitude to evidence has sometimes been described as modern; it lay outside the conception of the translator.

Just as he is inferior to Bede, so are those for whom he is writing inferior to the readers Bede had in mind. Hence the need to add explanatory comments, where Bede could count on being instantly understood. Biblical references are expanded with details of the incident referred to: a brief allusion to the lame man in Acts iii. 2–8 is much filled out from the source, to make the intended parallel clear,[148] and a rather subtle argument in Gregory's *Responsa* drawn from the story of John the Baptist's death is replaced by a direct narrative of the incident.[149] The translator adds that references to 'the law' are to the law of Moses,[150] that Genesis is the first book of Moses,[151] that it is St. Paul who is cited as 'the distinguished soldier of the heavenly army',[152] that the patriarch cited in book i, ch. 34 is Jacob,[153] that Caiphas was the chief of the priests,[154] that Constantinople is the chief city of the Greeks,[155] that balsam is 'the most precious spice and sweetest of those which were in the world',[156] and that *eclipsis solis* means 'the falling off of the sun so that it had no light and was terrible to look on'.[157] In short, the Old English Bede supports Alfred's complaints of the decline of scholarship, the justice of which was made clear by Sir Frank Stenton when commenting on the Latin of ninth-century charters.[158]

To deal with the style of the translation would require a whole lecture. Only a few points may be made here. The author was the product of a school of translating similar to that which trained Bishop Werferth. He shares with this author a fair amount of diction, including fixed renderings for a number of Latin words, and a fondness for rendering a single Latin word by two English synonyms. Whatever may be the origins of this practice, in these two writers it amounts to a mannerism. They both often translate over-literally, retaining Latinate constructions and using a word order unnatural to English, to an extent which suggests that they were influenced by the practice of interlinear glossing of a text. Yet the similarities between them can be over-emphasized. There are enough dissimilarities to show that Werferth was not the translator of Bede.[159]

Moreover, the Old English Bede is not consistently an over-literal rendering. Beside passages which are stiff and clumsy can be set others which are vigorous and idiomatic. One may cite the account of Gregory's meeting with the Anglian youths for sale in Rome (even the stylist Ælfric did not disdain to borrow from this),[160] or the rendering of the famous simile of the sparrow flying through the royal hall,[161] where *paruissimo spatio* is happily translated *an eagan bryhtm*, 'the twinkling of an eye', and the simple 'it rains and snows and storms outside' makes *furentibus . . . foris per omnia turbinibus hiemalium pluuiarum uel niuium* sound heavy. The two accounts of storms are made more vivid,[162] and there are instances of free and terse renderings of Latin phrases.[163]

The translator has a liking for words with a poetic ring:[164] some of his compounds are otherwise recorded only in poetry, e.g. *bædewæg* (*poculum*), *ellenwodness* (*zelum*), *eðelturf* (*patria*), *gylþgeorn* (*gloriae cupidissimus*), *wilsiþ* (*cupito itinere*), and *wilfægen* (*voti compos*). His use of the poetic *iumenn* 'men of old' puzzled the C scribe.[165] Some of his compounds are not recorded elsewhere: e.g. *heofonflod* (*inundantia*), *swiðstreme* (*meatu rapidissimo*), *arþegn* (*hospitium ministerio deseruiens*), *on bearnlufe* (*loco adoptiuo*), *se hwatesta fyrdesne* (*iuuenis bellicosus*).[166] Whether or not these are his own coinages, one can talk too much about the over-literalness of a writer capable of choosing such terse expressions.

The variation between literal and free translation runs through the work, and words characteristic of this work can occur in passages in either style. One cannot neatly divide the work between two authors of different habits.[167] It might be more difficult to outrule the possibility of a partial revision of a literal translation by a writer of better English. Yet it seems to me that the facts are not incompatible with a view of a single author, perhaps working in haste, unable to shed the habits of a school of interlinear glossing, who nevertheless was capable of vivid writing when his interest was stirred.

If, however, we wish to postulate a reviser, could that reviser be King Alfred? My own answer would be 'No'. There is too little agreement in diction with Alfred's works; and in these, even in the *Cura Pastoralis*,[168] which is a more faithful rendering than are the *Boethius* and the *Soliloquies*, greater liberties are sometimes taken with the text than in the Old English Bede. In these three works of Alfred, there is a tendency to expand the original, to elaborate—often unnecessarily—the similes and metaphors, and even to add such to make the meaning clearer.[169] These works show little sign of the power of the translator of Bede to reduce a Latin phrase to a single compound. In his prose works Alfred shows no fondness for poetic vocabulary, and neither these nor his verse translation of the *Metra* of Boethius suggest any outstanding ability in the formation of compounds.

To sum up: I see no evidence that Alfred took part in the actual translation of Bede. As regards the general plan, I would doubt whether he would have been willing to sacrifice so many types of interesting information in the interests of a rigid adherence to the main theme. That the translator and the king shared the view that it was the duty of a king to educate his people does not by itself seem to me enough to prove direct influence. That the work was undertaken at Alfred's instigation remains a probability. I have found no evidence against it, and it is the simplest way to explain the belief in 991 that the work was his. A detailed study of the list of chapter-headings, which I hope to publish elsewhere, may suggest, though it stops short of proof, that there was an early multiplication of manuscripts which lends itself to comparison with the circulation of the *Cura Pastoralis* and of the Anglo-Saxon Chronicle in the later years of Alfred's reign.

But if these things do not add up to certainty, how do we date the work? Fortunately, a final date is given by the quotation of three excerpts from it in Domitian ix, in a hand little, if at all, later than the end of Alfred's reign.[170] By the time we get the Otho manuscript, in the mid-tenth century, we are at least three removes from the original work. Unless we are convinced that it could not have been in existence when Alfred made his plans about 890 without being known to him, it is more difficult to establish the earliest limit of date. We are thrown back on linguistic evidence and are then faced with a shortage of comparative material from the Anglian areas. In any case, linguistic evidence cannot hope to date a work very closely.

I began these investigations in the hope that a detailed re-examination of the Old English Bede might allow of a definite statement on its connexion with Alfred's educational reforms. It has not done so. There is room for further study of this text, and others may find indications of date and authorship which I have missed. Meanwhile, such studies should not be restricted by too firm a faith in 'King Alfred's *Bede*'.

NOTES

I am indebted to Sir Frank Stenton for reading this paper and giving me valuable advice, and to Professor B. Dickins, Dr. K. Sisam, and Miss Celia Sisam for allowing me to consult them on various topics.

In the following notes, the Old English version of Bede is cited by page and line of Miller's edition (see n. 3 below). The Latin text is cited as H.E., by book and chapter, and if the chapter is long a page reference is added, which refers to the edition by Charles Plummer, *Venerabilis Baedae Opera Historica*, vol. i, Oxford, 1896.

1. *The Sermones Catholici or Homilies of Ælfric*, ed. B. Thorpe, London, 1846, ii, pp. 116 f.: *Manega halige bec cyðað his drohtnunge and his halige lif, and eac 'Historia Anglorum', ða ðe Ælfred cyning of Ledene on Englisc awende.*
2. H. Sweet, *An Anglo-Saxon Reader*, Oxford, 1876, p. 195: 'This passage alone is enough to prove that the translation is only nominally Alfred's.'
3. *The Old English Version of Bede's Ecclesiastical History of the English People*, ed. T. Miller, part i, 1, 1890, part i, 2, 1891, part ii, 1 and 2, 1898 (E.E.T.S. Original Series 95, 96, 110, 111), henceforward cited as Miller. The work had been edited twice before: i.e. by Abraham Whelock, in his *Historiæ Ecclesiasticæ Gentis Anglorum Libri V*, Cambridge, 1643 and 1644, and by John Smith in his *Historiae Ecclesiasticae Gentis Anglorum Libri Quinque*, Cambridge, 1722. Another edition was made by J. Schipper, *König Alfreds Übersetzung von Bedas Kirchengeschichte* (Bibliothek der angelsächsischen Prosa iv), Leipzig, 1899. Miller gives the text of MS. T (filling the lacunae from C, O, and Ca) with textual variants from all extant manuscripts; Schipper gives the text of O and B, with variants from the other manuscripts. Since then a transcript, made by Laurence Nowell, of the mainly destroyed MS. C has been discovered. It is BM. Addit. MS. 43703, on which see R. Flower, 'Laurence Nowell and the Discovery of England', reprinted in this edition, pp. 8, 25–7. I use my own collation of this transcript.
4. Miller, i, pp. lvii–lix.
5. See R. Jordan, *Eigentümlichkeiten des anglischen Wortschatzes* (Anglistische Forschungen 17), Heidelberg, 1906; F. Klaeber, 'Zur altenglischen Bedaübersetzung', *Anglia*, xxv (1902), pp. 257–315, xxvii (1904), pp. 243–82, 399–435; G. Scherer, *Zur Geographie und Chronologie des angelsächsischen Wortschatzes, im Anschluss an Bischof Wærferths Übersetzung der 'Dialoge' Gregors*, Berlin, 1928; H. Rauh, *Der Wortschatz der altenglischen Übersetzungen des*

Matthäeus-Evangeliums, Berlin, 1936; R. J. Menner, 'Vocabulary of the OE. Poems on Judgment Day', *Publications of the Modern Language Association*, lxii (1947), pp. 583–97; idem, 'The Anglian Vocabulary of the *Blickling Homilies*' in *Philologica: The Malone Anniversary Studies*, ed. T. A. Kirby and H. B. Woolf, Baltimore, 1949; J. J. Campbell, 'The Dialect Vocabulary of the OE. Bede', *Journal of English and Germanic Philology*, l (1951), pp. 349–72. Cf. also K. Sisam, *Studies in the History of Old English Literature*, Oxford, 1953, pp. 89, 129. For the Anglian character of the accidence see O. Eger, *Dialektisches in den Flexionsverhältnissen der angelsächsischen Bedaübersetzung*, Leipzig, 1910.

6. Certain words used in OE. Bede occur only in Mercian texts, but it must be remembered that there are no comparable Northumbrian texts until nearly a century later. The linguistic features of the archetype from which all extant manuscripts descend need more careful study, with due regard to the Nowell transcript and to the evidence of a connexion between MS. B and those of the other branch of manuscripts (see n. 22 *infra*). Yet it is clear that a Mercian *e* for *æ* has sometimes led later copyists into error, e.g. at Miller, 394. 28, where it must have been a form *lete* for *læte* 'late' which caused them to confuse it with the preterite of *lǣtan*, or at Miller 382. 6, where *beþinge* (T, B, for *bæþinge* = *fomentis*) leads to the error *beþenum* in C, O, and Ca. A sprinkling of examples of *ea* as back-mutation of *a* occurs in all manuscripts (lists are given by M. Deutschbein, 'Dialektisches in der ags. Übersetzung von Bedas Kirchengeschichte', *Beiträge zur Geschichte der deutschen Sprache und Literatur*, xxvi (1901), pp. 227 f., and by F. Klaeber, *Anglia*, xxv, pp. 264 f.). The Nowell transcript supplies further examples, and shows how this feature could lead copyists into error; one may assume that it was a form *deagum* for *dagum* which lies behind the error *deaglum*. The archetype included features which differentiate it from the Mercian of the Vespasian Psalter, e.g. *user*, *usse*, &c., where the Psalter has *ur*, and unsmoothed forms like *deagum*, *heago-*; *ðassum* for *ðissum* (a form recorded for northern texts) is shown to have occurred in the archetype by its presence in the Zupitza fragment (104. 12), in the original text of O (248. 3) and in T (422. 19). For other indications of a dialect not identical with that of the Psalter see Klaeber, *Anglia*, xxv, pp. 269 f., 297 f., 302, xxvii, pp. 262, 275, 401, 417, 427 f. It must also be borne in mind that the archetype was not the author's autograph (see n. 30 below).

7. As by Schipper in the introduction to his edition. Its improbability was shown already by Binz when he reviewed this work in *Englische Studien*, xxvii (1900), pp. 122–4. It was a common practice in the later Anglo-Saxon period to turn Mercian writings into literary West Saxon, but not vice versa.

8. See N. R. Ker, *Catalogue of Manuscripts containing Anglo-Saxon*, Oxford, 1957, p. 234.

9. Deutschbein, op. cit., p. 177.

10. This is clearly shown by the almost identical translation of *candidi corporis, ac uenusti uultus, capillorum quoque forma egregia*. OE. Bede reads: *wæron hwites lichoman 7 fægres ondwlitan men 7 æðellice gefeaxe*; Ælfric has *gefexode*, but otherwise only spelling differences. Compare also *mercatoribus: cypemen* OE. Bede, *cypmenn* Ælfric; *pueros uenales*: *cypecneohtas* OE. Bede, *cypecnihtas* Ælfric: *adludens ad nomen ait: plegode he mid his wordum to þæm noman 7 cwæð* OE. Bede, *gamenode mid his wordum to ðam naman 7 cwæð* Ælfric. Other

agreements include the omission by both of the words: *tantaque gratia frontispiccii mentem ab interna gratia uacuam gestat.* Ælfric uses the parts of this chapter which OE. Bede omits, but as far as this went he used it. Deutschbein recognized this fact, but strangely concluded that for the parts not in OE. Bede he used a lost version by King Alfred. But if he had two Old English versions, why did he mention only one? For the parts not in OE. Bede he presumably went to the Latin text.

11. J. Schipper, *Die Geschichte und der gegenwärtige Stand der Forschung über König Alfreds Übersetzung von Bedas Kirchengeschichte* (Sitzungsberichte der phil.-hist. Klasse der Kais. Akad. der Wissenschaften, cxxxviii, Abhandlung vii, Wien, 1898), p. 8.

12. S. M. Kuhn, 'Synonyms in the Old English Bede', *Journal of English and Germanic Philology*, xlvi (1947), pp. 168–76.

13. There are extant examples of this type of glossing, but it cannot alone account for the use of tautological pairs of words. Many examples of these pairs occur in other works, e.g. in the *Cura Pastoralis*, while in Werferth's translation of Gregory's *Dialogues*, as in OE. Bede, they are so frequent that they are best regarded as a stylistic feature. On this matter, see P. Fijn van Draat, 'The Authorship of the Old English Bede. A Study in Rhythm', *Anglia*, xxxix (1916), pp. 319–46.

14. The words *leoran* 'go', *(ge)frignan* 'ask', *(ge)cigan* 'call', *wise* 'thing', *intinga* 'cause', *gemet* 'manner', *nemne* 'unless', *gen*, *ge(o)nu* 'yet', *lytesne* 'almost' are alien to Alfred's usage, as are a great number of other words common in OE. Bede.

15. H. Hecht, *Bischofs Wærferth von Worcester Übersetzung der Dialoge Gregors des Grossen* (Bibliothek der angelsächsischen Prosa, v, Abt. 2), p. 23.

16. I would now modify my statement in *After Bede* (Jarrow Lecture 1960), p. 11, that 'there can be no doubt' that the translation of Bede was part of the king's scheme.

17. *Monumenta Historica Britannica*, p. 519A.

18. Ælfric makes use of Bede's history in several other places, but nowhere else does he mention or make use of the vernacular version. Resemblances in his account of Drihthelm's vision (*Catholic Homilies*, ii, pp. 348 ff.), i.e. *saeculi curis absolutus; all weoruldþing forleorte* OE. Bede, *forlet ealle woruldþing* Ælfric; *calefierent et siccarentur: gewermedon 7 adrugedon* OE. Bede, *wearmodon 7 adruwodon* Ælfric, are the obvious translations of the Latin. When Ælfric tells the story of Imma from H.E. iv. 22 in his *Catholic Homilies*, ii, pp. 356 ff., he mentions no English version, although in the same homily when he refers to Gregory's *Dialogues* he says this has been translated into English. I find no trace of his use of OE. Bede in this homily, nor in those on St. Alban (*Saints' Lives*, no. xix), St. Æthelthryth (ibid., no. xx) or St. Oswald (ibid., no. xxvi). It is perhaps useless to speculate on why he used OE. Bede only once. He may have had access to it only for a short time; he may, after using it once, have preferred to translate from the Latin himself; he may never have seen more than an extract from it. His words in the Gregory Homily: *seo foresæde boc nis eow eallum cuð, þeah ðe heo on Englisc awend sy*, may suggest that copies of OE. Bede were not easy to come by.

19. *De Gestis Regum Anglorum*, ed. W. Stubbs (Rolls Series, 1887), i, p. 132.

20. See Miller, i, pp. lviii f. He also calls attention to Giraldus Cambrensis, who, in his *Descriptio Kambriæ*, book i, ch. 6, speaks of *omnes libros Anglicos*

Bedæ, Rabani, regis Aeluredi. Giraldus may have attributed the OE. Bede to Bede himself, or he may merely have had a vague idea that works written by Bede in English had survived.

21. Ker, op. cit., p. 37.

22. There are five manuscripts of the OE. Bede, in addition to three short extracts in Domitian ix, f. 11 (cited as Zupitza):

T = Tanner 10 in the Bodleian Library, of the first half of the tenth century;
B = Corpus Christi College, Cambridge, MS. 41, of the first half of the eleventh century;
C = Cotton MS. Otho B xi+Otho B x, ff. 55, 58, 62 mainly of the mid tenth century, but with Bede's autobiographical note added some fifty years later;
O = Corpus Christi College, Oxford, MS. 279, part ii, of the beginning of the eleventh century;
Ca = Cambridge University Library, Kk. 3. 18 of the second half of the eleventh century.

(For descriptions of these manuscripts see Ker, op. cit., whose dating I have accepted.)
The current view of their relationship can be expressed as follows:

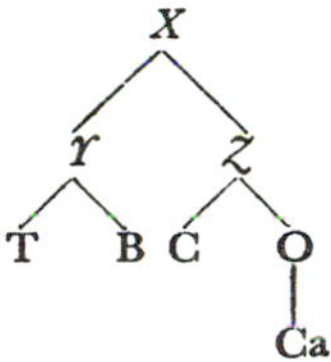

where *X* is the archetype, and *Y* and *Z* the postulated exemplars of the two branches. There were probably intervening stages. This scheme is true in outline, but it is far too simple. It fails to take into consideration signs of later contamination between the two branches. There are agreements in error between B and C, between B and O (and Ca), and between B and Ca where this differs from its exemplar O. But the arguments in this paper are not affected by this manuscript contamination.

23. A. S. Napier in 'Two Old English Fragments', *Modern Language Notes*, xii (1897), col. 106–14, mistakenly believes that Whelock was not referring to Tiberius A iii by the letter C, because where Ca allots a reign of *syxtyne winter* to Cuthred, Whelock gives *gear* as a C variant for *winter*, and Napier thought that the whole of the passage referring to Cuthred was missing from Tiberius A iii. This is not true. What is missing is the length of the *preceding* reign, and the mention of Cuthred's accession. The length of his reign is given as *7 heold xvi gear*. This explains Whelock's variant *gear*.

24. The figure was misread as 493 not only by Whelock, but by Nowell, who transcribed Tiberius A iii at the beginning of BM. Addit. MS. 43703, and by Napier in the article cited in the preceding note.

25. Nowell's transcript of C omits all the preliminary matter and begins with book i, 1.

26. In Tiberius A iii the list is continued to the reign of Edward the Martyr.

27. Yet one need not go all the way with J. W. Pearce, *Modern Language Notes*, vii, col. 105: 'Would it not have been passing strange if Alfred had

translated anything at all, and had neglected the history of his own country?'

28. An example of this occurs in n. 47 *infra*.

29. See, e.g., J. W. Pearce, 'Did King Alfred translate the *Historia Ecclesiastica?*', *Publications of the Modern Language Association*, viii (1893), Proceedings, pp. vi–xiii. The great measure of consistency in the rendering of Bede's terminology is an argument against multiple authorship. See n. 144 *infra*.

30. I append only a few examples of error common to all versions which cannot have originated from the translator himself: (i) Miller, 372. 11. All manuscripts read *beran* when either *feran* (sic Miller) or *leoran* (sic Klaeber) is required. Thus *ad eius uidendam gratiam simul transeamus ad caelos* has become *to heofenum beran his gife þær to geseonne*; (ii) 418. 9. *de milite factus . . . monachus* is rendered *wæs he ærest from cyninges þægn 7 þa wæs eft munuc geworden*. Here *from* no doubt originally translated *de*, but was mistaken as the adjective *from* 'strong, brave' and the sentence then altered to fit this; (iii) 332. 17. The rendering of *coronam . . . aeternam* as *þone ecan sige* probably conceals an original *þone ecan bige*. For other examples see Miller's notes to 72. 14, 80. 33, 118. 31, and those in Klaeber, op. cit. to 100. 4, 118. 31, 190. 27, 268. 29, 384. 8. Whatever may have been the original reading at 400. 21, both branches of manuscripts would hardly have had an almost identical corrupt reading (*on eall ðone* T, *on eal þane* C, &c.) if the archetype had been correct.

31. Miller, 480. 20: *by stære Ongelþiode cirican on Brytene*.

32. H.E. ii. 19, iii. 4.

33. Germanus in H.E. i. 17–21, Columba and Ninian in H.E. iii. 4, Adamnan in H.E. v. 15. Adamnan's correction of the Easter observance of the churches of Ireland is mentioned in the list of chapters, but the chapter is not in the text. I hope to demonstrate elsewhere that the list of chapters was made to agree with the state of the OE. text by someone other than the translator. This person retains the heading of the missing chapter v, 15 but joins it to the heading of ch. 18, a fact which suggests that he was misled by a reference in ch. 18 to the correction of Easter observance into the belief that this was what the heading of ch. 15 referred to, though, in fact, it is Aldhelm's conversion of the British church which is dealt with in ch. 18.

34. H.E. ii. 4 (p. 88).

35. H.E. ii. 1.

36. H.E. v. 19 (pp. 327 f.).

37. H.E. v. 16, 17.

38. H.E. ii. 2.

39. H.E. ii. 4.

40. Ecgberht in H.E. v. 22, Aldhelm in H.E. v. 18, Ceolfrith in H.E. v. 21. An earlier, shorter passage on Ecgberht's conversion of Iona in H.E. iii. 4 is omitted, probably to avoid repetition.

41. H.E. ii. 19, v. 15.

42. H.E. iii. 3, 17. The mention of Aidan's unorthodoxy is included in the version of H.E. iii. 17 contained in the group of MSS. C, O, and Ca, but this version was not that of the translator, and for the purposes of this paper it can be ignored. I agree with S. Potter, *On the Relation of the Old English Bede to Werferth's Gregory and to Alfred's Translations* (Mémoires de la Société

Royale des Sciences de Bohême. Classes des Lettres, 1930), pp. 30–33, and with J. J. Campbell, 'The OE. Bede: Book III, Chapters 16–20', *Modern Language Notes*, lxvii (1952), pp. 381–6, that, where in book iii from the second part of ch. 16 to the end of ch. 20 there are two versions of the translation, the one in manuscripts T and B is the work of the original translator.

43. H.E. iii. 28 (p. 195).
44. H.E. iii. 25, 26.
45. H.E. v. 19: *detecta et eliminata, ut et supra docuimus, Scottorum secta.*
46. H.E. iv. 2, Miller, 258. 8 f.
47. H.E. iii. 28, Miller, 246. 29 f. When in the words which follow immediately Bede only says that, as the Catholic observance increased, the Scots dwelling among the English either conformed or returned home, the translator finds it necessary, since he has omitted the previous account of their false Easter, to say: 'the Scots who dwelt among the English and were opposed to the catholic doctrine both in the observance of the right Easter and in many other things.'
48. H.E. v. 19 (p. 325), Miller, 456. 18–25.
49. It is only in the version in MSS. C, O, Ca (see n. 42 *supra*) that one of Bede's passages of explanation is retained.
50. Miller i, pp. lvii f.
51. H.E. v. 9 (p. 297), Miller, 410. 20 f.
52. H.E. iii. 3 (p. 132), Miller, 160. 2 ff.
53. H.E. v. 9 (p. 297), Miller, 410. 23 f. Cf. *An Old English Martyrology*, ed. G. Herzfeld, p. 92: *þone nemnað Sceottas Columchille.*
54. H.E. v. 23 (p. 351), Miller, 478. 33.
55. H.E. i. 33, Miller, 92. 24 f.
56. H.E. i. 1 (p. 13).
57. H.E. i. 12 (p. 25).
58. H.E. i. 5, iii. 2 (p. 129), iii. 3 (p. 132), ii. 2 (p. 84), v. 8 (p. 295), ii. 9 (p. 97).
59. H.E. i. 25, Miller, 56. 27 ff.; H.E. ii. 3, Miller, 104. 16 ff.; H.E. ii. 16, Miller, 142. 32 f.; H.E. iv. 13, Miller, 300. 30 ff.; H.E. iv. 19 (p. 246), Miller, 324. 6 f.; H.E. iv. 26 (p. 267), Miller, 358. 20 ff.
60. Many of the conclusions drawn by Miller in *Place Names in the English Bede* (Quellen und Forschungen zur Sprach- und Culturgeschichte, lxxviii, Strassburg, 1896), regarding the localization both of the archetype and of individual manuscripts are no longer valid, since more work has been done on comparative sources and on OE. dialects. For my purpose only forms which appear to be in the archetype need be considered.
61. Bede refers to Bamborough only as a royal town called after Queen Bebba; he uses only the adjective *Hagostaldensis* when speaking of Hexham, whereas the form in OE. Bede, *H(e)agost(e)aldes ea* has the support of the northern recension of the Anglo-Saxon Chronicle (s.a. 681 E, 766 D, E) which did not use the OE. Bede; *Candida Casa* would not have been given as *æt hwitan ærne* without knowledge of the current name, for *casa* is otherwise always translated *hus*; with *Coludisbyrig*, *Coludesburg*, for Bede's *Coludanae urbis*, *Coludi urbem*, one may compare *Coludesburh* in the northern recension of the Chronicle, s.a. 679 E, F, and in the CCCC MS. 196 of the *Old English Martyrology*, p. 102.
62. Hence its occurrence in the *Old English Martyrology*, a work whose composition may have been earlier than the translation of Bede.
63. H.E. ii. 14, 20, iii. 14, Miller, 140. 19, 150. 28, 194. 18.

64. H.E. iii. 21 (p. 170), Miller, 222. 13.
65. See E. Ekwall, *The Place-Names of Lancashire*, Manchester, 1922, p. 79. Werferth in Gregory's *Dialogues* translates *caput caprae* as *buccan heafod* (ed. Hecht, p. 232).
66. H.E. ii. 14, iii. 24, Miller, 140. 25, 238. 8.
67. H.E. iv. 29, Miller, 370. 27. It is called *Luel* in the *Anonymous Life of St. Cuthbert*, and Bede in his prose *Life of St. Cuthbert* says: *ad Lugubaliam ciuitatem quae a populis Anglorum corrupte Luel uocatur*. See B. Colgrave, *Two Lives of St. Cuthbert*, pp. 116, 122, 124, 242.
68. H.E. ii. 14, Miller, 140. 21.
69. H.E. ii. 16, Miller, 144. 14.
70. H.E. iv. 13, Miller, 302. 6.
71. H.E. i. 25 (p. 45, n. 1), Miller, 56. 29, where B's reading *wantsama* corresponds with Tiberius C ii *uuantsamu*. There is a lacuna in T.
72. H.E. i. 5.
73. H.E. iv. 13 (p. 232).
74. H.E. iii. 13 (p. 152).
75. H.E. iv. 2 (p. 204).
76. H.E. ii. 3, 7, 9, iii. 14, 27, v. 6, 8 (*bis*), 11.
77. H.E. i. 34, ii. 20.
78. H.E. ii. 14, v. 7.
79. H.E. ii. 3, Miller, 104. 12.
80. H.E. iv. 12, Miller, 298. 28.
81. See p. 17 *infra*.
82. H.E. i. 3.
83. H.E. ii. 14.
84. He omits those in H.E. ii. 4 (p. 88) and iv. 17 (p. 240). He retains the indiction in the acts of the synod of Hertford, H.E. iv. 5, Miller, 276. 15, and of the synod of Hatfield, H.E. iv. 17, Miller, 310. 17.
85. H.E. v. 23.
86. H.E. ii. 16 (p. 118), Miller, 144. 20.
87. H.E. v. 18, Miller, 446. 19.
88. Miller, 144. 9.
89. Cf. Miller, 216. 23, and also the rendering of *qui nunc usque superest* (H.E. iv. 31) as *cwæð, þæt he ða gena lifgende wære, þa he þis gewrit sette* (Miller, 378. 12 f.).
90. H.E. v. 11 (p. 303), Miller, 422. 16 ff.
91. H.E. v. 20 (p. 332), Miller, 466. 27 f.
92. H.E. v. 18 (p. 321), Miller, 448. 19 f. Note also that when in H.E. iv. 13 Bede says that Wilfrid's successors still hold Selsey, probably meaning that it was a family monastery, the translation says: *ðæt git to dæge his æfterfylgend bisceopas habbað 7 agon* (Miller, 304. 27 f.).
93. H.E. i. 15, iv. 16.
94. H.E. ii. 7.
95. H.E. iv. 5 (p. 216).
96. H.E. i. 7 (p. 21), Miller, 40. 27 ff.; H.E. iv. 3 (p. 212), Miller, 270. 31 ff.; H.E. iv. 19 (p. 246), Miller, 322. 35 f.; H.E. iv. 30, Miller, 378. 5 f.
97. H.E. iii. 8 (p. 144), Miller, 176. 20 f.; H.E. iii. 19 (p. 168), Miller, 218. 30 f.; H.E. v. 10 (p. 301), Miller, 418. 13 ff.
98. The translator replaces Bede's words *usque hodie* in H.E. iv. 6, which refer to the preservation of Eorcenwald's litter, by 'long afterwards' (Miller, 282. 3), probably because Bede said it was preserved by his disciples.

99. H.E. ii. 20 (p. 126), Miller, 150. 12 ff.
100. H.E. ii. 20, Miller, 150. 27 f.
101. H.E. iv. 22 (p. 250), Miller, 326. 26 f.
102. H.E. ii. 13 (p. 113), Miller, 138. 12 ff.
103. H.E. iii. 16, Miller, 202. 12 f.
104. H.E. ii. 16, Miller, 144. 4.
105. H.E. i. 15 (p. 31), Miller, 52. 11.
106. H.E. v. 8 (p. 294), Miller, 406. 24 f.: *in ðære alra ðara biscopa lichoman Contwara burge gesette seondon.*
107. Eadmer, the Christ Church historian, in his *Vita Bregwini* (*Anglia Sacra*, ii, p. 186), says that Archbishop Cuthbert had a church built in honour of John the Baptist to the east of the main church, partly in order that the archbishops should be buried in it, abrogating the ancient custom of burying them in the church of St. Peter and St. Paul. William of Malmesbury (*Gesta Pontificum*, ed. N. E. S. A. Hamilton, p. 15) tells a story that Cuthbert ordered his own illness to be kept quiet, so that when the monks of St. Peter and St. Paul came for his body, he had already been buried in his own church. More developed forms of this tale appear in later Canterbury writers, e.g. Gervase of Canterbury in his *Actus Pontificum* (*Opera*, ed. W. Stubbs, ii, p. 345), and William Thorne in his *Chronica de rebus gestis abbatum S. Augustini Cantuariæ* (ed. R. Twysden, *Scriptores Decem*, ii, col. 1772 f., translated by A. H. Davis, *William Thorne's Chronicle*, pp. 26–28). The quarrel on other matters between the two houses in Lanfranc's time (on which see D. Knowles, *The Monastic Order in England*, pp. 115 f.) would cause grievances to be revived or even invented, but as the tombs of the archbishops were identifiable, we can accept the claim that after Cuthbert, Jænberht was the only archbishop to be buried in the monastery of St. Peter and St. Paul.
108. *Annales Cambriæ: Pasca commutatur apud Brittones . . . emendante Elbodugo homine Dei.* J. E. Lloyd in *A History of Wales* (3rd edit. i, p. 203) regards as a later invention the claim of the Gwentian Brut that South Wales did not yield without a conflict; and even in this, the dispute is not referred to after 809.
109. H.E. iv. 4, Miller, 274. 15 ff.
110. Bardney in H.E. iii. 11 (p. 148), Miller, 182. 15; Lastingham in H.E. iii. 23 (p. 176), iv. 3 (p. 206), v. 19 (p. 326), Miller, 232. 13 f., 260. 26 f., 458. 11; Whitby in H.E. iv. 23 (pp. 252, 254), Miller, 330. 28, 334. 5, 342. 1; Hackness in H.E. iv. 23 (pp. 257 f.), Miller, 338. 33, 342. 1.
111. H.E. iv. 3 (p. 207); Miller, 262. 9 f.
112. Though the chapters on Cuthbert's translation and miracles do not actually say that the body is still at Lindisfarne, this is implied by the retention in H.E. v. 1 of the statement that his successor Oidelwald 'is buried in St. Peter's church in Lindisfarne beside the bodies of the aforementioned bishops' (Miller, 386. 22 f.).
113. H.E. iv. 5 (p. 217), Miller, 280. 19 f.
114. One should compare the evidence of the *Liber Eliensis* which shows that a monastery could survive the Danish invasions and attract the benefactions of early Danish converts. See D. Whitelock, 'The Conversion of the Eastern Danelaw', *Saga-Book of the Viking Society*, xii (1941), p. 169.
115. H.E. iii. 29, Miller, 248. 17–27.
116. H.E. i. 29, Miller, 90. 4 ff.

117. See F. M. Stenton, *Anglo-Saxon England* (2nd edit., Oxford, 1947), pp. 216, 223–7.

118. Best edition by E. Caspar, *Mon. Germ. Hist.: Epist. Karol. Aevi*, v, pp. 71 f.; translated by D. Whitelock, *English Historical Documents, c. 500–1042*, pp. 811 ff.

119. It is far more probable that Alfred had been demanding more help from the church for the defence of his kingdom than it thought in accordance with its privileges.

120. G. F. Browne, *King Alfred's Books*, p. 204, suggested that the omissions in H.E. i. 29–32 were because Alfred did not wish to make known to the unlearned how far short of Gregory's forecast the development of bishoprics had been; or, alternatively, that these passages were regarded as only of antiquarian interest.

121. D. Whitelock, op. cit., pp. 810 f.; Latin text in E. Caspar, op. cit., p. 293.

122. This is from the letter cited above; see n. 118.

123. For some of the peculiarities of the C-type text see Plummer, op. cit. i, pp. xciv f., and for his comments on the OE. version see pp. cxxviii f. Many examples could be added to his list of agreements with Tiberius C ii. A close connexion is suggested by the name *Berhtwini*, Miller, 308. 1, for Professor Mynors has informed me that the other C-type texts, Kassel Landesbibliothek Theol. Q 2 and Hatton 43, do not share the Tiberius C ii reading *Berchtuuini*, but have that of other early manuscripts, *Bernuuini*; moreover the erroneous *per x et nouem annos* (Plummer, i, p. 201, n. 10) which is the source of *anes wonðe twentig wintra*, Miller, 252. 9, occurs in Tiberius C ii, with *x et* on erasure, but not in other C-type MSS. Nevertheless, the manuscript used by the translator was free from many of the errors of Tiberius C ii. It had correctly *consonanter*, which is translated *geþwærelice*, Miller, 312. 2, when both Kassel and Hatton share the Tiberius error *constanter* (Plummer, i, p. 239, n. 9), and *quia liquido*, rendered *forþon hluttorlice*, Miller, 330. 24, when all these three manuscripts have the error *qui aliquando* (Plummer, i. p. 252, n. 1). With Kassel, it read *descendere*, rendered *astigan*, Miller, 270. 24, when Tiberius and Hatton have *descendentium* (Plummer, i, p. 211, n. 8); yet it agreed with Hatton in the correct reading *renitens*, rendered *wiðwinnende*, Miller, 368. 16, when Tiberius and Kassel have *paenitens* (Plummer, i, p. 272, n. 6). Hence it was a good text, but not superior in all respects to the common original of Tiberius C ii, Kassel and Hatton, and not siding consistently with any one of them. I am indebted to Professor Mynors for information on the Kassel and Hatton readings.

124. Miller, 2. 12 f.: *For þinre ðearfe 7 for þinre ðeode ic þis awrat; forþon ðe God to cyninge geceas, þe gedafenað þine þeode to læranne.*

125. *Anglia*, xxv, p. 264: 'Man kann sich in der that kaum des gedankens erwehren, daß diese fassung der stelle vom könig Ælfred inspiriert sei.'

126. See H. Hecht, *Bischofs Wærferth von Worcester Übersetzung der Dialoge Gregors des Grossen, Einleitung* (1907), pp. 16 ff., where the use in H.E. ii. 7 and iv. 22 of *Dialogues*, i. 6 and iv. 57 is pointed out. The extent of the borrowing, however, is too slight for either translator to be likely to notice it.

127. *King Alfred's West Saxon Version of Gregory's Pastoral Care*, ed. H. Sweet, p. 417, ll. 19–36, should be compared with H.E. i. 27 (p. 61), Miller, 86. 25–34. Here again, neither translator need have noticed the connexion.

128. Bede's chapter on Caesar, H.E. i. 2, is missing from MS. B; a brief mention of the invasion is in Ca, and in Nowell's transcript of C. Since T is defective at the beginning, it is impossible to tell whether this sentence was added to the C, O and Ca branch, or whether B omitted it. Plummer, *The Life and Times of Alfred the Great*, Oxford, 1902, p. 158, assumed the former alternative, and argued from the omission that Alfred had already translated Orosius.

129. Compare H.E. i. 1 (p. 12), Miller, 28. 30 ff., with *King Alfred's Orosius*, ed. H. Sweet, p. 24, ll. 17 ff. Other differences include the avoidance by the translator of Orosius of the erroneous translation of *creatus* as 'born' instead of 'created'; his tendency to use contemporary instead of Latin names of places; his form *Alrican* where OE. Bede retains *Alaricum*; and his addition of English inflexions to Latin nominatives. One small point of contact between the printed texts of OE. Bede and the *Orosius*, the form *Bellica* for *Belgica*, is not supported by the Nowell transcript of C, which has *Belgica*. It is only the late MSS. B and Ca which agree with the *Orosius*.

130. e.g. G. F. Browne, op. cit., p. 207, calls it 'curious', but considers that to explain it by the existence of translations of the *Dialogues* and the *Cura Pastoralis* would imply unfamiliarity with literary conditions of the time; P. G. Thomas, *English Literature before Chaucer*, London, 1924, p. 46, says it is 'still unexplained'; S. Potter, op. cit., pp. 11 f., suggests that the omission is from motives of literary economy, and that the passages where Bede's language is reminiscent of the Latin of Gregory's *Dialogues* were perhaps omitted because 'the translator saw no need to repeat what had already been given to the people in their birth tongue'.

131. This is the only verse passage of the original to be retained. The only omission relating to the English church is that of the passage on Gregory's joy at the conversion, and as in book i the translator has included the mention of letters and gifts sent by Gregory when he received the good news, he may have felt it redundant.

132. K. Sisam, 'Anglo-Saxon Royal Genealogies', reprinted in this edition, pp. 193–4.

133. H.E. i. 15 gives the line from Hengest back to Woden, ii. 5 that from Æthelberht I to Hengest.

134. See pp. 235–6 above.

135. e.g. he omits the first reference to the conversion of the monks of Iona to the true Easter in H.E. ii. 4, since it is described in H.E. v. 22; he omits the quotation from Gregory's *Responsa* at the end of H.E. iv. 27, presumably because it occurs earlier in the work.

136. H.E. iii. 7 (p. 140), ASC 658.

137. H.E. v. 18, ASC 709.

138. H.E. ii. 5, ASC 827.

139. H.E. ii. 9.

140. H.E. iv. 16.

141. H.E. ii. 5 (p. 92).

142. On this see K. Sisam, op. cit., pp. 147, 149, 166–7, 181–3, 186.

143. BM. Addit. MS. 23211, ed. H. Sweet, *The Oldest English Texts*, p. 179.

144. See H. R. Loyn, 'The Term *Ealdorman* in the Translations prepared at the Time of King Alfred', *English Historical Review*, lxviii (1953), pp. 513–25, and 'Gesiths and Thegns in Anglo-Saxon England from the Seventh to the Tenth Century' ibid. lxx (1955), pp. 534–7. One should note also the

consistent or almost consistent rendering of several Latin words, e.g., *celebrare* as *mærsian*, *congruus* as *gerisen*, *custodia* and *observatio* as *gehælde*, *eruditio* as *gelærednes*, *feruor* as *wylm*, *incuria* as *ungemen*, *industria* as *georn(ful)nes*. *ingenium* as *gleawnes*, *operatio* as *wyrcnes*, *profanare* as *aidlian*, *ratio* as *riht*, *regimen* as *gerece*, &c. This list, which could be much longer, excludes renderings which on the evidence of Werferth's and Alfred's writings appeared to represent a fixed practice.

145. Glaring errors, like Miller, 152. 23 *in municep þære byrig* for H.E. iii. 1 *in oppido municipio* (i.e. York), are not common. The word *tragicus* seems to have puzzled the translator, for in the same chapter he renders *tragica caede* as *on gelicnesse þæs traiscan wæles* (where in B *troianiscan* has been written above *traiscan*), and in H.E. iv. 16, where early manuscripts read *stragica caede*, but some later manuscripts *tragica caede*, we get *gelice þy troiscan* (sic T; *treiscan* B, *treoiescan* O and Nowell, *troiescan* Ca) *wæle* (Miller, 306. 20 f.). He occasionally chooses a wrong meaning of a word in its context, e.g. *persona* rendered *hade*, Miller, 78. 28, when it means 'person', and *habitabant* rendered *eardodon* when it means 'were situated', Miller, 120. 4. It is not always possible to distinguish between misunderstandings and deliberate alterations, but some examples of the former occur at Miller, 30. 4 ff., 74. 11 ff., 218. 15, 292. 19 f., 296. 26 f., 316. 4 f., 334. 7 f., 394. 23 ff., 468. 28.

146. The preface survives only in the late MSS. B and Ca of OE. Bede. Ca reads: *7 þurh Cedde þone arwurðan Myrcna bisceop 7 Ceaddan ymbe Myrcna þeode 7 Eastseaxena*; B reads: *7 ðurh Cedde þone arweorðan Myrcna bysceopes ymb Myrcna ðeode 7 Eastseaxena*. Since the Latin has *per ministerium Ceddi et Ceadda religiosorum Christi sacerdotum*, it is possible that the original began: *7 þurh þegnunge Ceddes þæs arweorðan Myrcna bisceopes 7 Ceaddan* and that an accidental omission of *þegnunge* led to the corruption of the whole passage. But it is also possible that the translator misunderstood the passage by failing to construe *per ministerium* with *ad fidem Christi . . . peruenerit*.

147. He omits the short second miracle in H.E. iv. 23 recording how the soul of St. Hilda was seen to ascend to heaven.

148. H.E. v. 2 (p. 284), Miller, 390. 6–11.

149. H.E. i. 27 (p. 51), Miller, 70. 21 ff.

150. H.E. i. 1 (p. 11), iv. 29 (p. 276), Miller, 26. 27, 374. 12.

151. H.E. iv. 24 (p. 261), Miller, 346. 7.

152. H.E. i. 27 (p. 61), Miller, 88. 16 f.

153. Miller, 92. 11.

154. H.E. v. 14, Miller, 442. 29 f.

155. H.E. i. 13, Miller, 48. 14.

156. H.E. iii. 8 (p. 144), Miller, 174. 30 ff.

157. H.E. iii. 27 (p. 191), Miller, 240. 20 f.

158. *The Latin Charters of the Anglo-Saxon Period*, Oxford, 1955, pp. 39–43.

159. On the relation of Werferth's *Dialogues* to the OE. Bede see Klaeber, *Anglia*, xxvii, p. 264; Hecht, op. cit., *Einleitung*, pp. 122–6; P. Fijn van Draat, op. cit., pp. 319–46; S. Potter, op. cit. Professor Potter overstates the case for agreement when he says that 'no word has a consistently different rendering' in the two works (p. 19). Yet he does not claim identity of authorship. One should note the following differences. Werferth mistranslates *gratia* in the sense 'for the sake of' (e.g. *Dialogues*, 170. 1 f. *mid geneosunge gife* = *visitationis gratia*, cf. 75. 35 f.); the translator of Bede renders it correctly, *for intingan*. Werferth is puzzled by the expression (*quidam*

nostri) prouectioris aetatis, and puts (*ure freond*) *manige* (43. 27; the reviser corrects to *ure yldran freond*); it and the variant *aetate prouectae* appear in OE. Bede as *gelyfdre ylde* (Miller, 174. 1, 342. 20). On the other hand, Werferth understands the phrase *beatae memoriae*, which OE. Bede mistranslates up to H.E. iv. 19, where he says 'from the blessed memory of Pope Agatho' instead of 'from Pope Agatho of blessed memory' (Miller, 314. 11). There are also consistent differences of rendering. Werferth translates *rusticus* as *ceorl*, *ceorlisc man* (and *verbo rustico* as *ceorliscum wordum*); OE. Bede as *folclic man* (*rustica loca* as *folcstowa*, *plebem rusticam*, as *ðæt ungelærede folc*); Werferth translates *barbarus* as *elreordig* 'of different speech' only once, when it refers to language, using otherwise *elþiodig*; OE. Bede always uses *elreordig*. *Per culpam incuriae* is *þurh gymeleasnesse* in Werferth, always *þurh ungemenne synne* in OE. Bede. The latter translates *aptus* as *geþungen* when it refers to persons, *gescrepe* (a word not in Werferth) with reference to things, whereas Werferth uses *gecoplic* (a word not in OE. Bede). *Mons* is *mor* in OE. Bede, *munt* in Werferth; *verax* is *arwyrðe* or *soðfæst* in OE. Bede, *soðsagol* in Werferth; and *devotus* is *wilsum* in OE. Bede, *estful* in Werferth. This list could be extended. Words common in OE. Bede but absent from Werferth include *instæpe* (*statim*, *confestim*, *extemplo*, *continuo*), *lytesne* (*pene*, *prope*), *swæsendu* (*prandium*, *epulae*, *dapes*, *caenum*, *esca*), *bensian* (*benedicere*), &c.; less common are *feoung* 'hatred', *gelis* as one rendering of *studium*, *risan* 'to seize', *hloþ* (*praeda*) and its derivative *hloþian*. Some of Werferth's words never occur in OE. Bede, e.g. *wenunga* 'perhaps', *wyrd* in the sense of 'deed', *ymbhoga* (*cura*, *negotium*), *teolone* or *teolung* (*studium*), *ymbhygdlic* (*sollicitus*), *arod*, *arodlice*, *arodness* (*promptus*, *constanter*, *instanter*, *constantia*). Though one may expect an author to vary his vocabulary to some extent at different periods of his life, the cumulative evidence that Werferth did not translate OE. Bede is strong.

160. See n. 10 *supra*.

161. H.E. ii. 13 (p. 112), Miller, 134. 24–136. 5.

162. H.E. iii. 15, v. 1, Miller, 200. 9–19, 384. 19–386. 14.

163. Note for example: *7 hine þider wel gescyrpte*, Miller, 454. 10 = *cunctis simul, quae necessitas poscebat itineris, largiter subministratis*; and the replacement of the long clause, *Quae ne facile a quopiam posset contemni, in transgressores dignas et competentes punitiones proposuit*, by two words, *bi witerædenne*, Miller, 172. 9.

164. Klaeber, op. cit., *Anglia*, xxv and xxvii, often calls attention to the use of words found mainly in poetry, e.g. *dogor*, *rodor*, *from* 'strong', *bestryðan* 'to heap up', *leod* 'man', *genge* 'effective', *uðgenge* 'fleeting', *til* 'good'. Some of these may have been current in the translator's dialect. In *Anglia*, xxvii, p. 256 he points out that *feorh(h)yrde* 'protector of life' occurs otherwise only in the poetic *Gloria*.

165. Klaeber, *Anglia*, xxvii, p. 433.

166. Ibid., p. 257: 'Die kühne komposition ist ganz im stil der Bedaübersetzung.'

167. The attempt of J. W. Pearce, 'Did King Alfred translate the *Historia Ecclesiastica*?', *Publications of the Modern Language Association*, viii (1893), Proceedings, pp. vi–xiii, to distinguish different authors does not convince me.

168. On Alfred's connexion with the translation of the *Cura Pastoralis* see S. Potter, op. cit., and also idem, 'The Old English "Pastoral Care"',

Transactions of the Philological Society, 1947, pp. 114–25. In the former work, p. 52, he claims that it stands apart in style of translation from the *Orosius*, *Boethius* and the *Soliloquies* of St. Augustine, yet on p. 55 he allows some share to Alfred. Alfred's own words, as Professor Potter realizes, are unambiguous: after mentioning help from Plegmund, Asser, Grimbald, and John (three of them foreigners) the king says, 'I translated it into English'. There are in my opinion a number of agreements in vocabulary and stylistic features between this work and the *Boethius* and the *Soliloquies* to prove that this was no empty boast.

169. As this feature has often been demonstrated from the *Boethius* and the *Soliloquies*, I confine my examples to the *Cura Pastoralis*. For the expansion of similes, compare *ut ad lectoris sui animum ordinatis allegationibus quasi quibusdam passibus gradiatur* with *ðætte ðeos spræc stigge on ðæt ingeðonc ðæs leorneres, suæ suæ on sume hlædre, stæpmælum near 7 near, oððæt hio fæstlice gestonde on ðæm solore ðæs modes ðe hi leornige* (ed. Sweet, p. 23); or note how Gregory's comparison of the mind with a ship going upstream, which *uno in loco nequaquam stare permittitur, quia ad ima relabitur, nisi ad summa conetur*, is spun out to *Ðæt scip wile hwilum stigan ongean ðone stream, ac hit ne mæg, buton ða rowend hit teon, ac hit sceal fleotan mid ðy streame; ne mæg hit no stille gestondan, buton hit ankor gehæbbe, oððe mon mid roðrum ongean tio; elles hit gelent mid ðy streame* (p. 445). Concrete illustrations are added, e.g. where Gregory speaks of the surface and depths of the mind, this is rendered the rind and the pith (p. 55); St. Paul, cultivating the vineyard of the church, is compared to the *ceorl* in his orchard (p. 293); and *praeconis officium* is defined as *friccan scire 7 foreryneles ða her iernað beforan kyningum, 7 bodigeað hira færelt 7 hiera willan hlydende* (*sic*) (p. 91). On pp. 121 f. the parable of the wicked servant (Matthew xxiv, 48 ff.) is expanded with four lines to point a contemporary moral. There are places in Bede which would have lent themselves to this type of expansion, but the opportunity is not taken. On the differences in rhythm between the translation of the *Cura Pastoralis* and that of the *Dialogues* and of Bede, see P. Fijn van Draat, op. cit., pp. 321 ff.

170. This single leaf, first published by J. Zupitza, 'Drei alte Excerpte aus Älfreds Beda', *Zeitschrift für deutsches Altertum*, xxx (1886), pp. 185 f., has on its recto the last two statutes of the synod of Hertford (Miller, 278. 28–280. 6), the beginning of H.E. i. 27, mentioning Augustine's consecration in Arles and his return to Britain (Miller, 62. 26–30), and the beginning of H.E. ii. 3, which describes his consecration of Mellitus to London and Justus to Rochester, altered to confine it to Mellitus (Miller, 104. 12–19). These excerpts may have been made at Canterbury, or London. Ker, op. cit., pp. 188 f., dates it 's.x in.'

SIR ISRAEL GOLLANCZ MEMORIAL LECTURE

THE COMPILATION OF THE ANGLO-SAXON CHRONICLE, 60 BC to AD 890: VOCABULARY AS EVIDENCE

By JANET BATELY

Read 10 May 1978

THAT lexical features can be used to determine the date, dialect, and authorship of Old English texts has long been recognized. It is, for instance, nearly ninety years since Thomas Miller first cited a number of features pointing not to a West Saxon (and Alfredian) origin for the Old English Bede but a Mercian one,[1] and appended a list of 'rare words from the version' with 'one or two recognised Anglian words' to 'give further comparisons'.[2] Sixteen years later Richard Jordan published the results of a much wider-ranging investigation of Old English dialect vocabulary, considerably enlarging Miller's list

I am indebted to Professor Dorothy Whitelock for reading this paper and giving me valuable advice, also to Dr R. Page for his helpful comments when I consulted the Parker Manuscript.

In the following notes references to the Chronicle are taken from *Two of the Saxon Chronicles Parallel*, ed. C. Plummer, Oxford, 1892–9, repr. with two notes by D. Whitelock, 1952, and in particular from Plummer's text of MS A. Readings from A that have been erased or altered by later hands are restored. Short titles of other texts and abbreviations (based on the lists in *ASE* iv, 1975) are as follows: Old English Bede (Bede), see *The Old English Version of Bede's Ecclesiastical History of the English People*, ed. T. Miller, EETS, os 95, 96, 110, 111, Oxford, 1890–8, repr. 1959, 1963; Alfred's Boethius (Bo), see *King Alfred's OE Version of Boethius' De Consolatione Philosophiae*, ed. W. J. Sedgefield, Oxford, 1899; Gregory's Dialogues (GD), see *Bischof Wærferths von Worcester Übersetzung der Dialoge Gregors des Grossen*, ed. H. Hecht, Leipzig and Hamburg, 1900, 1907, repr. Darmstadt, 1965; Laws (Law), see *Die Gesetze der Angelsachsen*, ed. F. Liebermann, Halle, 1903–16, repr. Aalen, 1960; Martyrology (Mart), see *An Old English Martyrology*, ed. G. Herzfeld, EETS 116, 1900, repr. Krause, New York, 1975; Orosius (Or), see *The Old English Orosius*, ed. J. Bately, EETS, ss 6, 1980; Pastoral Care (CP), see *King Alfred's West-Saxon Version of Gregory's Pastoral Care*, ed. H. Sweet, EETS 45, 50, 1871–2, repr. 1958; Paris Psalter (PPs), see *Liber Psalmorum: The West-Saxon Psalms*, ed. J. W. Bright and R. L. Ramsay, Boston, 1907; the Soliloquies (Solil), see *King Alfred's Version of St. Augustine's Soliloquies*, ed. T. A. Carnicelli, Cambridge, Mass., 1969.

[1] *Old English Bede*, i, pp. xxvi–lix. [2] Ibid. pp. xlix–li.

of words characteristic of texts of Anglian origin.[1] And since 1906 there have been further contributions to the subject,[2] though Jordan's findings have remained substantially unmodified. Less attention has been paid to lexical differences between early and late texts and the establishment of a standard; however, here too a significant contribution has been made in recent years, in particular by Kenneth and Celia Sisam and Helmut Gneuss.[3] As for vocabulary as evidence of authorship, this has increasingly been the subject of scholarly investigation, and it is on this aspect of lexical studies and its possible contribution to an understanding of the manner of compilation of the Anglo-Saxon Chronicle that I wish to concentrate in this paper.

In theory, a study of the vocabulary of an Old English prose text should provide us with information of at least three different kinds, matters of date and dialect apart. It should enable us to identify positive features of authorship, that is, to identify certain words and collocations as typical of the author of that text; it should enable us to identify negative features of authorship, that is, to draw up a list of words and collocations not typical of the author because rarely or never used by him; and it should enable us to determine whether the text is the work of one author or several. In practice, however, things are not so simple. Admittedly, similarities of usage between, for instance, the Institutes of Polity and homilies by Wulfstan enable us to identify the author of the former with the archbishop.[4] A number of other anonymous prose works can be attributed on similar grounds to Ælfric.[5] Differences of usage allow us to

[1] R. Jordan, *Eigentümlichkeiten des anglischen Wortschatzes* (Anglistische Forschungen 17), Heidelberg, 1906.

[2] See, e.g., R. J. Menner, 'Anglian and Saxon elements in Wulfstan's vocabulary', *MLN* lxiii (1948), pp. 1–9, and 'The Anglian vocabulary of the Blickling homilies', in *Philologica: The Malone Anniversary Studies*, ed. T. A. Kirby and H. B. Woolf, Baltimore, 1949, pp. 56–64; *The Life of St. Chad*, ed. R. Vleeskruyer, Amsterdam, 1953; also J. J. Campbell, 'The dialect vocabulary of the Old English Bede', *JEGPh* l (1951), pp. 349–72, and O. Funke, 'Altenglische Wortgeographie', *Anglistische Studien, Festschrift zum 70. Geburtstag von Professor Friedrich Wild* (Wiener Beiträge zur Englischen Philologie 66), Vienna, 1958, pp. 39–51.

[3] See, e.g., *The Salisbury Psalter*, ed. C. Sisam and K. Sisam (EETS 242), Oxford, 1959, repr. 1969, and H. Gneuss, 'The origin of Standard Old English and Æthelwold's school at Winchester', *ASE* i (1972), pp. 63–83.

[4] See *Die 'Institutes of Polity, Civil and Ecclesiastical'*, ed. K. Jost (Swiss Studies in English 47), Bern, 1959, esp. pp. 16–33.

[5] See *Homilies of Ælfric: a Supplementary Collection*, ed. J. C. Pope (EETS 259–60), Oxford, 1967–8, esp. pp. 94–105.

claim with some confidence that neither the author of the Old English Bede nor that of the Old English Orosius could have been the author of the Boethius, King Alfred,[1] while, as Professor Clemoes has recently shown, the distinctive pattern in which similarities and differences are combined in the Hexateuch points to multiple authorship of that work, with part of the translation attributable to Ælfric and part to another author, whom he would identify with Byrhtferth of Ramsay.[2] However, the three kinds of evidence cannot in fact be kept rigidly apart. In the majority of cases the presence of a certain word in a given text is of potential significance only if it can be shown to have been used at the expense of another word, or to be restricted to one of several possible contexts or groups of contexts.[3] So too with preferences, where one word is used much more frequently than another: these are significant only if other texts can be shown to have different preferences and it can be demonstrated that they are indeed the preferences of a single author, and not due to scribal interference or arising from multiple authorship, whether through collaboration, the incorporation of material by other hands, or subsequent rewriting or expansion.[4] And in considering the possibility of

[1] See D. Whitelock, 'The Old English Bede', reprinted in this edition, pp. 227–60; E. M. Liggins, 'The authorship of the Old English *Orosius*', *Anglia*, lxxxviii (1970), pp. 289–322; and J. M. Bately, 'King Alfred and the Old English translation of Orosius', idem, pp. 433–60.

[2] *The Old English Illustrated Hexateuch, British Museum Cotton Claudius, B. iv*, ed. C. R. Dodwell and P. Clemoes (*EEMF* 18), Copenhagen, 1974, esp. pp. 44–6 and 50–2.

[3] Thus Jost identifies as usages typical of Wulfstan *namian* not *hatan*, *genamod* and *genemnod beon* not *gehaten*, *geciged beon*; see K. Jost *Wulfstanstudien*, Bern, 1950, pp. 155 f. That Wulfstan also consistently uses the word *deofol* is in itself not significant—though, of course, his preference for the word on its own, without the demonstrative *se*, is a feature which helps to distinguish his writings from those of Ælfric, who uses both *deofol* and *se deofol* to refer to Satan: see *The Homilies of Wulfstan*, ed. D. Bethurum, Oxford, 1957, p. 47 n. 5.

[4] In the Old English Bede, for example, certain exceptional usages are found in a section of the work for which there are two separate versions, in the version which appears to be non-original; others occur in the list of chapter-headings, which may, in part at least, be the work of someone other than the translator of the text. Similarly, in the Old English Orosius, untypical forms which are confined to the reports of Ohthere and Wulfstan are probably not the author's own. See D. Whitelock, 'The list of chapter-headings in the Old English Bede', *Old English Studies in Honour of J. C. Pope*, ed. R. B. Burlin and E. B. Irving, Jnr., Toronto, 1974, pp. 263-84; Bately, *Anglia*, lxxxviii, p. 439 n. 31; and *The Old English Orosius*, Introduction, section V. 2. iv; and see below, pp. 278 n. 1, 291 n. 4, 294 n. 3.

multiple authorship we must bear in mind the fact that a single author's usage can be subject to considerable variation—as J. C. Pope says of Ælfric, 'he had such a rich vocabulary that each fresh homily is likely to contain something new'—while it is the 'core of familiar words that recur again and again' that is of the greatest significance in terms of authorship.[1] A prerequisite to any consideration of authorship is a corpus of sufficient length to provide such a core, with the desirable bonus of a number of manuscript copies to allow us to attempt to distinguish (as far as it is ever possible to do so) between the author's usage and that of subsequent scribes.

Ælfric provides us with both the sufficiently large corpus and the range of manuscript copies, some very close in date to the composition of their contents, one set with corrections actually in the author's own hand.[2] The earliest version of the Anglo-Saxon Chronicle that has come down to us (a version which appears to reflect an act of compilation and circulation of manuscripts round about the year 890 and which I shall refer to as the 890 Chronicle)[3] has also survived in a number of manuscripts, with one—MS A, the Parker MS—containing the whole section 60 BC–AD 891 in a single hand dated late ninth or early tenth century and, it has been suggested, possibly associated with the place of compilation.[4]

However, the seven manuscript copies are not seven independent witnesses to the original text. MS G is apparently a direct copy of MS A; B and C are for long stretches so close to

[1] *Homilies of Ælfric*, i, p. 99.

[2] See *Ælfric's First Series of Catholic Homilies, British Museum Royal 7 C. xii, fols. 4–218*, ed. N. Eliason and P. Clemoes (EEMF 13), Copenhagen, 1966, p. 28.

[3] See *English Historical Documents*, i, ed. D. Whitelock, London, 1955, rev. 1979, pp. 121–2, and, for a chronicle ending at 890, R. H. Hodgkin, 'The beginning of the year in the English chronicle', *EHR* xxxix (1924), pp. 507–8. A number of scholars include the annal for 891 in the 'first' chronicle, while some write of a Chronicle of 892: see, e.g., K. Sisam, 'Anglo-Saxon royal genealogies', reprinted in this edition, p. 190. However, the entry for 891 is absent from MS E (Oxford, Bodley MS Laud Misc. 636) and it is possible that this annal, like the annals from 892 onwards, was added after the 'original' compilation had been completed, its presence in MS D (British Library MS Cotton Tiberius B. iv) being the result of collation. See further below, pp. 268 n. 4, 279 n. 3, 283 n. 1.

[4] See M. B. Parkes, 'The palaeography of the Parker manuscript of the *Chronicle*, laws and Sedulius, and historiography at Winchester in the late ninth and tenth centuries', *ASE* v (1976), pp. 149–71. See further below, p. 292 and n. 5. MS A is Corpus Christi College, Cambridge, MS 173.

one another that Neil Ker has suggested that part of C is a direct copy of B; F is believed to be the work of a scribe who used the archetype of E as his base but also had before him MS A, which he proceeded to collate with his base, deleting entries and parts of entries in order to insert new material, while MSS D and E appear to have had a common archetype for their versions of the 890 Chronicle, a revision commonly known as the 'northern recension'.[1] Moreover, the evidence of Latin texts with material derived from the 890 Chronicle is that all the surviving manuscripts of the Old English version shared a common ancestor which was at least one remove from the original compilation.[2] As a result, the most we can hope to achieve by collating the manuscripts is a tentative reconstruction of the archetype and not necessarily the 'original' itself. At the same time, the limited subject-matter of the 890 Chronicle and the sparseness of entries for certain periods mean that the core of familar words is necessarily a small and selective one. None the less, there is sufficient material for us to reach certain conclusions about both the compilation and the authorship of the 890 Chronicle.

[1] For a valuable survey of the manuscripts and their relationships see Whitelock, *EHD* i, pp. 109–21. For MS G (British Library MS Otho B. xi) see Angelika Lutz, 'Zur Rekonstruktion der Version G der Angelsächsischen Chronik', *Anglia*, xcv (1977), pp. 1–19; for the relationship of MSS B and C (British Library MSS Cotton Tiberius A. vi and B. i) see N. R. Ker, *Catalogue of Manuscripts containing Anglo-Saxon*, Oxford, 1957, no. 191, 4, and *EHD* i, p. 112. Here Professor Whitelock argues most plausibly that the change in relationship between MSS B and C noted by Ker from annal 653 on must be connected with the dropping of annal numbers at this point by MS B: 'Up to 652 there is no reading which suggests that "C" had access to any other manuscript than "B". But after this date "C" is not solely dependent on "B"; in several places a comparison with other versions shows "C" to have better readings than "B". It can hardly be accidental that this change in the relationship comes at the exact point where "B" stops inserting the annal numbers. If the scribe of "C" were copying "B", he would now have to find some other authority for his dates; and he might then sometimes prefer the readings of this other authority. Nevertheless, he did not discard "B" at this point. "B" and "C" continue to share readings against those of other manuscripts, and, as Ker has noted, the relationship from about 945 to 977, when "B" ends, is again very close.' I would venture to add that on the evidence of the manuscript readings this other authority cannot have been MS A or indeed a manuscript of the 'northern recension'; however, it could have been an ancestor, or be derived from an ancestor, of B which had all the annal numbers and was free from some but not all of B's errors and variants, in which case there is no obligation to suppose that the scribe of C collated MS B and this second manuscript.

[2] See *EHD* i, esp. pp. 117–18.

Earlier scholars had no doubt as to who the person behind the compilation was. Plummer, for instance, writes:

To whom are we to attribute this earliest form of the national Chronicle? I have no hesitation in declaring that in my opinion the popular answer is in this case the right one: it is the work of Alfred the Great. I do not mean that the actual task of compiling the Chronicle from the earlier materials was necessarily performed by Alfred, though I can well fancy that he may have dictated some of the later annals which describe his own wars. But that the idea of a national Chronicle as opposed to merely local annals was his, that the idea was carried out under his direction and supervision, this I do most firmly believe.[1]

This view of Plummer's, that King Alfred was in some way involved in the compilation of the 890 Chronicle, has persisted until today: R. H. C. Davis, for instance, supports the idea of a national chronicle history composed in the king's court and accepts the suggestion that Alfred may have dictated some of the later annals.[2] However, the belief that the whole of the 890 Chronicle was, as Hodgkin puts it, 'substantially a product of Alfred's reign'[3] has never gained universal acceptance. Indeed, according to one school of thought, the Alfredian Chronicle is an extension of an older compilation, made probably during the reign of Alfred's father, Æthelwulf, and itself a highly composite document,[4] and E. E. Barker has recently put forward the theory that it was this pre-Alfredian version that was the basis of Ealdorman Æthelweard's Latin chronicle in the late tenth century: 'We believe that if his copy were available to us it would prove to be written in one hand down to the annal for 855 and to have subsequent material added at various times in different hands.'[5] Mr Barker also believes that some of the

[1] Plummer, *Two Saxon Chronicles*, ii, p. civ.

[2] R. H. C. Davis, 'Alfred the Great: Propaganda and Truth', *History*, lvi (1971), p. 177.

[3] R. H. Hodgkin, *History of the Anglo-Saxons*, Oxford, 1935, 3rd edn., 1952, ii, p. 624.

[4] See, e.g., F. Liebermann, review of Plummer, *Archiv für das Studium der neueren Sprachen*, civ (1900), pp. 188–99; also A. Brandl, *Geschichte der altenglischen Literatur*, in Paul's *Grundriss*, 2nd edn., Strasbourg, 1909, iii, pp. 1054 ff.; H. M. Chadwick, *The Origin of the English Nation*, Cambridge, 1907, repr. 1924, p. 25; and H. A. Rositzke, *The C-Text of the Old English Chronicle* (*Beiträge zur Englischen Philologie* 34), Bochum-Langendreer, 1940, pp. 7 ff.

[5] E. E. Barker, 'The Anglo-Saxon Chronicle used by Æthelweard', *Bulletin of the Institute of Historical Research,* xl (1967), p. 78. Mr Barker goes on to comment that the presumption that Æthelweard's copy of the Chronicle was a pre-Alfredian one 'may possibly account for certain small

material in the pre-855 section was added after 855 and in this he has the support of other proponents of the theory of a two-stage compilation, though these differ from him in matters of detail. For instance, although Mr Barker sees some of the entries based on Bede Epitome (the chronological summary at the end of Bede's Ecclesiastical History) as included in the Æthelwulf Chronicle and others as being a later addition,[1] Antonia Gransden assigns all the Bede Epitome material to the first compilation;[2] we may compare Plummer's belief that both Bedan and world history annals were inserted 'only . . . in the last stage of the compilation of the Chronicle (up to 892), in order to furnish an introduction to the whole'.[3] Before any attempt is made to discuss the involvement of King Alfred in the compilation of the 890 Chronicle, therefore, it is necessary

variations in the annals shortly after 855'. However, his claim that Æthelweard has nothing to correspond with the last words of annal 855 as recorded in MS A is incorrect, while the fact that Æthelweard also lacks the *7 se Æþelbryht ricsode v gear* of MS A 860 is surely without significance, the five-year reign being implicit in his references to an event which happened four years after Æthelbryht's accession and to the king's death one year after that. As for the mention of King Æthelbryht's burial place s.a. 866 not 860, this, as Mr Barker himself admits, occurs more naturally here and surely could be the result of editing of the Chronicle version by Æthelweard.

[1] Op. cit., p. 77. Also seen as added later is a series of 'Canterbury annals'. For a refutation of some of Barker's theories see J. Bately, 'Bede and the Anglo-Saxon Chronicle', *Saints, Scholars and Heroes*, ed. M. H. King and W. M. Stevens, 1979. For Bede Epitome see *Baedae Opera Historica*, ed. C. Plummer, Oxford, 1896, i, pp. 352–6.

[2] A. Gransden, *Historical Writing in England, c. 550–c. 1307*, London, 1974, p. 37. Dr Gransden, although maintaining that 'the Anglo-Saxon Chronicle was begun in King Alfred's reign' (p. 32), also assigns to the first stage of compilation lists and genealogies of kings, lists of bishops and the like, as well as a series of mid seventh to mid eighth-century West Saxon annals. The annals for the period 495 to the mid seventh century, however, which Barker takes to be part of an Æthelwulf chronicle and which Stenton and Harrison argue are the work of the author of a proto-chronicle composed 'at or shortly after the middle of the seventh century', she sees as a later addition: 'Clearly this section was compiled in Alfred's time, but it probably used oral traditions, partly in the form of epic poems', while the entries about Ceawlin, between 550 and 593, she believes are 'clearly derived from a separate saga about this king'. See further F. M. Stenton, 'The foundations of English history', *TRHS*, 4th ser. ix (1926), p. 166, also K. Harrison, *The Framework of Anglo-Saxon History to A.D. 900*, Cambridge, 1976, pp. 133 f.

[3] *Two Saxon Chronicles*, ii, p. cxiii. Plummer is here following E. Grubitz, *Kritische Untersuchung über die angelsächsischen Annalen bis zum Jahre 893*, Inaugural dissertation, Göttingen, 1868.

to examine linguistic evidence both for and against what may be called a unitary, as opposed to a two-stage, chronicle, and for and against the participation of more than one individual in different parts of the compilation. And it is necessary to consider the possibility of what may be called editorial interference.

What happens when an Anglo-Saxon chronicler extends an existing chronicle, and what happens when he reworks earlier material, can both be demonstrated from surviving Chronicle versions. In MSS D and E, for instance, we have the results of the intervention of the so-called northern recensionist (probably writing in York in the tenth century), who not only inserted a number of pieces of additional material of primarily northern interest into his copy of the 890 Chronicle, but also rewrote and enlarged existing entries which the 890 Chronicle had derived from Bede Epitome.[1] There is sufficient new material for us to obtain a reasonable idea of the recensionist's linguistic habits and to see that he made no real attempt to impose his preferences on the old material.[2] There are admittedly some alterations to the vocabulary in passages not rewritten or containing new material, but these are no different in type from, nor more numerous than the alterations made deliberately or accidentally by scribes of the Old English Bede or the Martyrology or the Pastoral Care.[3] And collators of manuscripts of the Chronicle can show similar lack of interest in lexical variation, as an examination of MS D reveals.[4]

[1] See Plummer, *Two Saxon Chronicles*, ii, pp. 1–40, *passim*.

[2] For the only apparently significant exception (in annal 571) see below, p. 277 n. 2. The normal usage of the author of the 'northern recension' appears to have been *forþferde*, with pp. *forþ(ge)faren* and a single instance of *for to Criste*, 616.

[3] In connection with certain characteristic features in MSS T and U of the *Pastoral Care*, Dorothy Horgan comments that these manuscripts seem to descend from a common archetype, whose scribe 'belonged, it would seem, to a centre . . . where conscientious transcription went side by side with an awareness of the changes which had taken place in syntax and vocabulary'. See D. M. Horgan, 'The relationship between the OE MSS of King Alfred's translation of Gregory's *Pastoral Care*', *Anglia*, xci (1973), p. 162.

[4] For the suggestion that certain entries in MS D are the result of collation see *EHD* i, pp. 113–14, and *The Peterborough Chronicle*, ed. D. Whitelock, EEMF 4, Copenhagen, 1954, pp. 28 f. Professor Whitelock suggests that the manuscript used in the collation was of the same type as C. For a different type of revision see GD, where MS H represents the result of a recollation of the original Old English translation with a manuscript of the Latin: see further D. Yerkes, *Studies in the Manuscripts of Gregory's Dialogues*, unpublished dissertation, Oxford, 1976.

At the same time, that chroniclers adding chronologically later material to an existing chronicle did not necessarily trouble, or think it desirable, to undertake a fundamental revision of the vocabulary of that existing chronicle, can readily be demonstrated by a comparison of the manuscripts of the Chronicle, and not just that part of the Chronicle up to 890 but subsequent sections also.[1] It would be unrealistic therefore to expect to be able to differentiate (except in the most exceptional circumstances) between a unitary and a compound 890 Chronicle, that is, between the work of a single compiler or group of compilers drawing on a variety of sources of which some at least were documents in the vernacular, and a multistage compilation with, for example, a chronicle compiled in the time of Æthelwulf being brought up to date by a later chronicler or chroniclers writing in or after 890. At the most, one can hope to identify groups of annals which differ significantly from one another and which could therefore have had different origins, and groups of annals which do not differ in this way and which could thus have been composed, or rewritten, or translated under similar circumstances and possibly by the same person.

Here the problem arises as to which differences between groups of annals can be considered significant and which cannot. There is undeniably an impressive number of variations of usage within the 890 Chronicle. However, Sir Frank Stenton warns against 'too much regard for minute differences of style and syntax',[2] and this warning cannot lightly be disregarded, especially in view of the very limited occurrence of many of the concepts in the Chronicle. If we take as one of our yardsticks the distribution of similar forms outside the Chronicle, we have indeed either to dismiss a large proportion of these variations

[1] Once again the type of alteration found does not differ in essentials from that normally found in manuscript copies.

[2] F. M. Stenton, 'The south-western element in the Old English Chronicle', *Essays in medieval history presented to T. F. Tout*, ed. A. G. Little and F. M. Powicke, Manchester, 1925, p. 15, repr. in *Preparatory to Anglo-Saxon England* (*PASE*), ed. D. Stenton, Oxford, 1970, p. 106. At the same time it must be remembered that in spite of variations in origin, 'stylistic continuity is (with exceptions such as the entry at 755) well maintained', and as the author of this comment, Cecily Clark, convincingly argues, the restricted vocabulary and phrasing, 'annal after annal using the same semi-formulaic language' must be interpreted in the light of 'the special stylistic principles' observed by the annalist. See C. Clark, 'The narrative mode of *The Anglo-Saxon Chronicle* before the Conquest, in *England before the Conquest*, ed. P. Clemoes and K. Hughes, Cambridge, 1971, pp. 215–35.

as non-significant because they are elsewhere found together in unitary texts, or to consider them only in a supporting role. For example, although the 890 Chronicle has a variety of expressions for 'become (or be made) bishop or archbishop', 'occupy the see', as AD 35 *gesæt biscepsetl*, 670 *feng to biscepdome*, 745 *onfeng biscepdome*, 741 *wæs to ærcebiscepe gehalgod*, 759 *wæs to ercebiscepe gehadod*, a similar and indeed wider range is found in the Old English Bede.[1] In the Bede, of course, variation in the Old English often reflects variation in the Latin original, and in the Chronicle too the wording of source material may have had an influential part to play. This is demonstrably the case in annals based on Bede Epitome, the *wæron gehadode* of 664 and *wæs gehalgod* of 731 corresponding to *ordinantur* and *consecratus* respectively in Bede.[2] At the same time, a number of variations which mark off one set of annals from another may be no more than the result of historical accident, due either to changing circumstances or to differences of emphasis in the source material. For example, though the annals for 866–76 are characterized by their use of the expression 'took up winter quarters there', *þær wintersetl namon*, the absence of this expression from earlier annals is in no way indicative of different authorship but merely reflects a change in strategy on the part of the Danes.[3] Similarly, comments such as that in 473, that the Britons fled from the English as from fire, *þa Walas flugon þa*

[1] See, e.g., Bede 54/25–6 *feng to biscophade*, 90/13 *biscopseðle onfeng*, 116/24 *feng to þam biscopseðle*, 170/7–8 *onfeng biscopscire*, 170/32 *to biscope gehalgode*, 164/15–16 *þa biscophade onfongen hæfde*, 478/2 *sæt biscopsetl*. Similarly such variants as the Chronicle's *geflieman* (871) and *aflieman* (836), *lædan* (827) and *gelædan* (871), *oferhergian* (796) and *forhergian* (686) are found together in a range of texts including Bede, Or, and the Alfredian canon.

[2] Similarly the choice of the verb *abrecan* in annal 409 *Gotan abræcon Romeburg* is determined by the use of the corresponding Latin verb *frangere* in Bede Epitome *Roma a Gothis fracta*, while the selection of *gesohte* (annal 46, altered to 47, MS A) for Bede Epitome *adiens* must be seen in the context of the normal rendering of *adire* by *gesecan* in texts such as the Old English Bede and Gregory's Dialogues. For the possibility of certain linguistic practices resulting from educational training see *The Old English Illustrated Hexateuch*, pp. 44–5 and H. Gneuss, *ASE* i, pp. 63–83; see also S. Potter, *On the Relation of the Old English Bede to Wærferth's Gregory and to Alfred's Translations*, Prague, 1930, pp. 17 ff. It should be noted, however, that in the Chronicle there is no attempt to match the variety of Bede Epitome, with *forþferde* rendering *obiit*, *defunctus est*, *migravit ad Dominum*, and *transiit*.

[3] Non-linguistic factors are also responsible for the limited occurrence of such concepts as 'island', 'booty', 'Britain'. Possibly to be included here are the collocations *faran up on*, *faran up onlong*, concentrated in the section 882–7. See below, p. 278 n. 3.

Englan swa fyr,[1] or 584, that Ceawlin took many towns and an enormous amount of booty and 'angry he returned thence to his own folk', *ierre he hwearf þonan to his agnum*, comments which stand out from the rest of the 890 Chronicle with its plain style and generally unemotional language, reflect a difference in subject-matter, the compiler possibly here drawing on an ultimately poetic, oral source.[2]

If we take as the starting-point of our investigation the annals dealing with events up to the death of Æthelwulf, that is, the section that some scholars see as forming a first-stage chronicle, we find that the majority of variations between annals and groups of annals are either paralleled elsewhere in unitary texts or are of a type that is not necessarily incompatible with the theory of a single compiler or translator. The 'world history' annals, AD 1–110, for instance, are distinguished from all the other annals by their use of *swealt* and *aswalt* 'died' (AD 3 and 45)[3] as well as the 'normal' *forþferde* (AD 63 and 101), and of *gefulluhtud* (AD 30) instead of the usual *gefulwad*, *gefullod*, 'baptized'; however, the verb *sweltan* and its compounds are found alongside *forþferan* in Wærferth's translation of Gregory's Dialogues, while the apparently rare *(ge)fulwihtian*[4] likewise occurs

[1] MS A originally *swa þer* (or *þær*) *fyr*; transcript of MS G *swa þær fyr wære*; see CP 90/19 and, for further instances of the construction *swa þer*, the note on CP 90/19 in I. Carlson, *The Pastoral Care edited from British Museum MS. Cotton Otho B. ii*, i, Stockholm Studies in English xxxiv, Stockholm, 1975, p. 150. In view of the reading of MS A here I find Carlson's suggestion of an original reading *swa oþer* in CP unconvincing.

[2] See H. Sweet, 'Some of the sources of the Anglo-Saxon Chronicle', *EStn* ii (1879), pp. 310–12. Sweet sees 'strikingly poetical diction' in some annals, notably 457 ('with superfluous and probably poetical amplification'), 491 ('with alliteration and poetical diction'), 501 (which 'looks like an attempt to eke out a few poetical epithets into an historical statement'), and Professor Whitelock (private communication) would add the annal 626 where 'the impossible round figures for Penda's age and length of reign are "30" and "50".' See also Harrison, p. 132 n. 10. The presence of allegedly poetic features in these entries (and I am not altogether convinced by Sweet's claims) does not rule out the possibility of an intermediary Latin version.

[3] In MS A the annal numbers 44, 45, and 46 have been altered to 45, 46, and 47.

[4] Bosworth and Toller, *Anglo-Saxon Dictionary*, cites only this instance and one from a fragment printed by O. Cockayne, *Leechdoms*, London, 1866, iii, p. 422, 'Of St. Mildrið, Tanet', where it occurs in the same sentence as the verb *gefullian*. However, see also *Angelsächsische Homilien und Heiligenleben*, ed. B. Assmann, Kassel, 1889, repr. with supplement by P. Clemoes, Darmstadt, 1964, ii. 21 and xvii. 29. For *fulluhtere* as a variant of *fullere* see GD 13/17 and Mart 102/24, beside 156/11.

alongside the more common *gefullian*. There is nothing in these annals that requires us to suppose that the man who translated the world history material[1] could not also have translated Bede Epitome or provided other pre-855 annals. So too with the section AD 449–584: though this is marked off from the rest of the Chronicle by its regular use of the formula 'the place called', as in the annal for 455, *þære stowe þe is gecueden Agæles þrep*, and 477 *þa stowe þe is nemned Cymenes ora*, this distinctive mannerism could already have been present in a Latin or vernacular source used by the compiler,[2] and its absence from surrounding annals does not of itself rule out the possibility of a single act of compilation for the whole section, 60 BC to the end of the seventh century. At the same time a certain unity is given to this section by the selection in its constituent parts of such potentially significant forms as *ealond* not *iglond*, 'island', *adrifan* not *adræfan*, 'drive out', normal *forþferde* for 'died', both *onfon rice* and *fon to rice* for 'succeed to the throne', *feohtan* and *gefeohtan* for 'fight', and *on* and *in* for 'in', 'into'.[3]

These lexical items occur also in the section that follows, in the annals for the eighth and early ninth centuries;[4] indeed, in the majority of entries up to and including the annals for the beginning of Egbert's reign, that is up to about 830, there is nothing that requires us to suppose a change of compiler, variations being either explicable in terms of differences in the

[1] For the possible Latin sources of the world history material see my article, 'World History in the *Anglo-Saxon Chronicle*: its sources and its separateness from the Old English Orosius', *ASE* viii, 177–94.

[2] In the Old English Bede, for instance, constructions of this type are normally (though not exclusively) used to render similar expressions in the Latin: see, e.g., 92/18 *on þære mæran stowe þe cweden is Degsastan*, Bede, HE I. xxxiv *in loco celeberrimo, qui dicitur Degsastan*; 140/16 *in þære stowe þe Mælmen hatte*, HE II. xiv *in loco qui vocatur Maelmin*. Instances in vernacular charters are paralleled in Latin ones. In the Old English Orosius, on the other hand, the 'is' or 'was called' formula is used freely without equivalent in the Latin source, apparently as a stylistic mannerism of the translator's. It is significant that in both the Bede and the Orosius as in other texts of the period the formula is found throughout the work, not concentrated in one small area as here in the Chronicle. The formula returns to the Chronicle in the 'continuation' 891–7; it is also a feature of the style of the northern recensionist. See further below, pp. 274 f., 279 n. 3, 282 n. 2, 291. Does the use of *Wihte ealond* (annals 530 and 534) beside the *Wiht* of 661 and 686 reflect a similarly worded Latin or vernacular source? See, e.g., Be, where *Wiht* (*þæt*) *ealand* regularly translates Latin *Uecta insula*?

[3] See further below, p. 282.

[4] For the verb *adræfan* (755) beside *adrifan* (823) see below, pp. 274 f.; *ealond* is confined to the BEp material in the annal for 716.

source material or paralleled in unitary texts. However, a handful of annals stand out from the rest. These are a group of early eighth-century annals and the entry for 755. The early eighth-century annals (stretching from at least 716 to 741)[1] are distinguished by their use of the collocation *lic resteþ* (716, 738) not *lic liþ* in referring to a man's burial place, *ferde* (721, 728, 737) in preference to *for* (confined here to an annal based on Bede Epitome), and *gewon* (741) beside the usual *feaht*, *gefeaht* (722, 725, 728, 743). Taken individually none of these items is of itself significantly distinctive; however, in combination[2] they must lead us to treat with caution the theory that the annals for the early eighth century, like those for preceding centuries, were originally composed in Latin,[3] and were subsequently translated by the compiler of this part of the Chronicle.[4]

[1] Annals 716 and 741 are merely the identifiable limits of this group, which could well extend beyond these annals in both directions. For the suggestion that the compiler may have had access to a series of annals for the end of the seventh and the first part of the eighth century see, e.g., F. M. Stenton, *Anglo-Saxon England*, Oxford, 1943, 3rd edn., 1971, p. 692.

[2] See also below, p. 279 n. 4. *Feran* is found also in certain ninth-century annals, but in a quite different combination. *Resteþ* could reflect the Latin verb *requiescere*; the normal *lic liþ* is found ten times elsewhere in the 890 Chronicle. For *gewon* see below, p. 290 n. 2.

[3] Items translated from Bede Epitome of course excepted. There is no evidence that the Bede Epitome entries, which stretch from 60 BC to AD 731, were not all translated by the same person, nor is there anything conclusive in the order of Bede Epitome and other material in individual annals to show the stage in the compilation at which they were added or to support Sisam's claim (*PBA* xxxix, p. 334 p. 192 above, agreeing with Earle and Plummer) that the incorporation of the Bede Epitome material was late. Quite often BEp material opens an annal (as, e.g., 710 and 725); where it does not, it is usually the nature of the material that determines the order of items (as, e.g., 675, where there are chronological considerations, or 685, where West Saxon material takes first place), though sometimes it may well have been the amount of space available to the compiler and its physical location that has done so. Moreover, in none of the four places 'where something follows a pedigree' (cited by Sisam as consistent with the theory of late incorporation) is the order of items arbitrary. Thus, in the annal for 676 we have the order West Saxon material + relevant pedigree + BEp material; in 685 we have West Saxon material incorporating the relevant pedigree + BEp material + relevant pedigree + further BEp material; in 716 the annal begins and ends with BEp material, the pedigrees being inserted at appropriate points in the course of the entry; in 731 we have Northumbrian material + relevant pedigree + BEp material, with the Northumbrian material possibly derived from or replacing an entry in Bede Epitome dated 729.

[4] An alternative possibility is that the compiler was here drawing on a vernacular source and that his linguistic usage at this point was influenced

Of the exceptional nature of the annal for 755, on the other hand, there can be no doubt. This is the annal incorporating the story of the heroic confrontation between the followers of Cynewulf and Cyneheard, an account (possibly from a saga or lay)[1] which, like a number of other items in the Chronicle, contains features that demonstrate clearly that it was added as an afterthought or additional comment to an existing entry, and so need not be the work of the author of that entry.[2] It is therefore not surprising that a study of vocabulary should reveal a number of differences of usage between this account and other

by the language of that source (see Plummer, ii, p. cxi, with arguments with which I disagree). However, if so, it does not necessarily follow that that text was composed in the eighth century: a translation of an original Latin document or documents could have been provided for him. For the suggestion that most if not all of the early material was originally composed in Latin see, e.g., Stenton, *Anglo-Saxon England*, p. 15. 'The foundation of the work was a set of West Saxon annals, possibly written in Latin, which came down to the middle of the eighth century', and ibid., p. 692; also Chadwick, p. 26. Chadwick follows W. H. Stevenson, 'The beginnings of Wessex', *EHR* xiv (1899), pp. 32–46, in drawing attention to certain apparent archaisms involving proper names, 'which make it probable that the annals were written in Latin'. However, modern scholarship would not agree with all Stevenson's interpretations of forms. It would be tempting to see the use of *rex* and *dux* in annals 792, 837, and 851 as an indication of Latin sources for these annals also were there not other possible explanations for this, as, for instance, the adoption by the compiler or scribe of Latin titles. See *Sweet's Anglo-Saxon Reader*, rev. D. Whitelock, Oxford, 1967, xxxiv, ll. 1 and 2.

[1] See, e.g., C. L. Wrenn, 'A saga of the Anglo-Saxons', *History*, xxv (1941), pp. 208–15.

[2] Indeed after the account of the feud the entry resumes as though the digression had never been made, 'in this same year . . .'. See further Wrenn, p. 213. Other annals with material of this type include the entries for 658 and 709; see also annals 787, 827, and 836. Of annal 827 Professor Whitelock observes (private communication quoting from her forthcoming book), 'One cannot help wondering why the chronicler has made so much of Egbert's conquest of Mercia when it was of such short duration. It may be that he saw a parallel between Egbert's position in 829 and that achieved by Alfred a few years before he was writing, when he was ruling the Mercians as overlord of Ealdorman Æthelred . . . The chronicler may have wished to stress that there was precedent for the rule of a West Saxon king over the Mercians.' And Professor Whitelock goes on to suggest that if this is indeed so, 'it would mean that the source the Chronicle is using for Egbert's reign might have quite a simple annal at 827 (for 829), stopping perhaps at *Miercna rice* (or at *besuþan Humbre wæs*) and not continuing until the last sentence about the submission of the Northumbrians'. Annal 827, it should be noted, contains one of the two instances of *geþwærnesse*, taken by Hodgkin to give unity to the section 823–78; the other occurs s.a. 860.

pre-855 annals, as, for instance, *adræfan* not *adrifan*, *haten* not *genemned*, *gecueden*, etc., while an important syntactical difference is the use no fewer than three times in the Cynewulf and Cyneheard material of the expanded form *wæron feohtende*, where other annals have only the simple form. For comparable features we have to look to the annals not of the eighth century or before, but of the ninth century, and more specifically to those annals that relate to the close of the reign of Egbert and to the times of Æthelwulf and his sons, 835 Chronicle dating onward.

As we have seen, supporters of the theory of a two-stage compilation take as the end of the first stage the annal for 855, and some go so far as to suggest that the material for the last twenty-five years or so of this section was quite probably provided by the compiler himself. In this view they are joined by J. B. Wynn, who comments that 'Down to about 830 the man responsible for the first recension, whether it ended at 855 or 891, was dependent for most of his information upon a number of older sources, especially Bede's *Historia*, and a series of seventh, eighth, and early ninth-century annals. After 830, or thereabouts, his work was more in the nature of an independent account, based on a first-hand knowledge of events'.[1] Other scholars, however, detect the hand of an Alfredian chronicler or chroniclers well before this date. Sir Frank Stenton, for example, contrasts annals 800–39 Chronicle dating, which deal with the reign of Egbert and the early part of Æthelwulf and which he takes to be all contemporary, with the subsequent entries from 840 to 865, which he points out are inconsecutive. Some of these annals, he says, must have been written down appreciably later than the events which they relate and are probably 'the work of the man who wrote the subsequent "Alfredian" section from 865 to 891'.[2] Hodgkin, on the other

[1] See J. B. Wynn, 'The beginning of the year in Bede and the Anglo-Saxon Chronicle', *MÆ* xxv (1956), p. 77. For the generally accepted view that for the second half of the eighth century and the first thirty years of the ninth century the compiler had virtually no West Saxon material at his disposal see, e.g., Chadwick, p. 26, also Stenton's comment, *Anglo-Saxon England*, p. 692, that it is doubtful whether, for the period 750–800, any written material lay before the compiler. As Professor Whitelock kindly informs me, it seems likely that the few records available to him were supplemented from Mercian sources.

[2] Stenton, *Anglo-Saxon England*, p. 692. See also A. J. Thorogood, 'The Anglo-Saxon Chronicle in the reign of Ecgberht', *EHR* xlviii (1933), pp. 353–63, and Chadwick, p. 25 n. 3, 'the paucity of entries between 840

hand, while agreeing with the theory of the involvement of an Alfredian chronicler in the Æthelwulfian annals, firmly rejects the theory that the earlier annals were contemporary, administering a stern rebuke to those not holding this view: 'If [they] had paid attention to the contrast in style and phraseology of the Chronicle before and after 823 [they] could scarcely have maintained that the annals for the reign of Egbert are a distinct entity and contemporary.' For Hodgkin the change comes *c.*823, and he claims that the entries 823–71 are all of a piece and must have been composed in Alfred's reign.[1]

In support of his claim, Hodgkin lists five distinctive features of 'style and phraseology' occurring between 823 and 878, which, he says, give this section a unity and in varying degrees link it with other Alfredian writings. These are *micel wæl geslægen* (823 etc., to 871), *micel wælsliht* (839 and 871), *gefægene wærun* (855 and 878), *geþuærnesse* (827 and 860), and *micle* (or *lytle*) *werede* (823, 871, 878). However, the unity that they give is, as he himself emphasizes, not necessarily the result of common authorship—most of the items being found in a range of texts by different authors—nor does their presence here of itself require us to suppose that all the entries were composed in Alfred's reign.[2] What is more, since the evidence that we have shows the Chronicle to follow the wording of its source material faithfully,[3] and there is no evidence of imaginative rewriting of the type found in the Orosius,[4] absence of Hodgkin's distinctive features from earlier annals does not necessarily imply a change of compiler. The majority of annals before 823 simply do not offer opportunities for the use of these or alternative forms and

and 865 is worth noticing'. Annals 822 (for 824) and 823 (for 825) still begin the year at Christmas, the first clear indication of the commencement of the year in the autumn (apparently the normal usage from that point to 890) comes in the entry for 851. See Professor Whitelock's note in Plummer, *Two Saxon Chronicles*, ii, pp. cxl–cxli, and *EHD* i, p. 125. For 'appreciably later' entries see below, p. 280 n. 4.

[1] Hodgkin, *History of the Anglo-Saxons*, ii, p. 627. See also pp. 745–6.

[2] For the occurrence of *micel wæl geslean* in later parts of the Chronicle see, e.g., 905D and 982C. Like the expressions *miclum* or *micle werede* it appears also in both the Old English Bede and Or; *gefægen beon* is found in the Alfredian canon, and *geþwærnes* in Be, Or, and CP.

[3] Additions and omissions apart, there are very few changes in translating material from Bede Epitome, the most important involving the substitution of active for passive constructions.

[4] See *The Old English Orosius*, Introduction, Section VIII, pp xciii-c, and commentary, *passim*.

constructions.[1] So, for instance, in the annal for 800 the Chronicle reports a great battle in which two ealdormen were slain and the people of Wiltshire had the victory: that the author of the annal does not use the words and phrases cited by Hodgkin and add that one side or the other came with a large force (or only a small one), or that there was much slaughter, or that the victors rejoiced, or that there was subsequently concord between the antagonists, need mean no more than that he had no access to information about such matters.

However, there are a number of less obvious but none the less significant lexical variations which do appear to indicate changes of authorship. To take first the annals for 866–90, relating to the reigns of Æthelred and Alfred, the evidence of vocabulary is that these fall into two groups centred on the 870s and 880s respectively. The most striking difference between these groups lies in their choice of words for the concept 'die'. In the annals of the 870s 'die' is consistently rendered by *gefaran*; in the annals of the 880s it is rendered no less consistently by *forþferan*.[2] The potential significance of this difference is demonstrated by the distribution of these two euphemistic expressions in other Old English texts of the ninth century. In these *forþferan* and *gefaran*, though common, normally never occur side by side in the same text, exceptions apparently being the result of the

[1] Indeed the only entry between 60 BC and AD 823 to refer to 'much slaughter of human beings' is 592, *Her micel wælfill wæs æt Woddesbeorge*, which we may compare with 839 *Her wæs micel wælsliht on Lundenne* and 871 *þær wearþ micel wælsliht on gehwæþere hond* (the apparent rarity of *wælsliht* and *wælfill* outside the Chronicle making it not possible to determine their potential value as indicators of authorship), while though the victorious side is often (though not always) named, it is never described before 800 as having the victory, or before 833 as getting control of the battlefield.

[2] Outside the section beginning with the annal for 867 the form *gefor* is found only in the entries for 571, 731, and 855. The instance s.a. 571 (found in MSS A, B, and C but altered to *geforþferde* in A) corresponds to MS E *forþfor* (itself exceptional here, though Menner, *MLN* lxiii, p. 6 describes the verb *forþfaran* as 'a WS word that is both early and late') and it is possible that both of these forms are the result of scribal substitution. MS D has a lacuna. The version of annal 731 found in MSS A, B, and C contains features which suggest rewriting and so possibly does annal 855 (see below, p. 280); the corresponding entries in the 'northern recension', which are both rewritten, use the verb *forþferan*. It should be noted that the 'genealogical preface' with which MS A opens and which is now generally believed to be an older document, not necessarily part of the 890 Chronicle, has three instances of *gefaran*.

insertion of new material or scribal alteration.[1] And scribal alteration normally involves an original Anglian *leoran*, *geleoran*, 'pass away'.[2] Of course it could be due purely to chance that all the surviving ninth-century texts other than the Chronicle are of a type that selects one or other of the two forms never both, though this seems unlikely. However, there are other features—and not just features of vocabulary—that appear to distinguish the annals centred on the 870s from those of the 880s. In addition to its selection of *gefaran* not *forþferan* the first group of annals (which I take to extend up to at least 878, the following five annals forming a kind of no man's land, with no significantly distinctive features)[3] is characterized by its use of a variety of words for 'fight' where the second group has only one,[4] its use of *innan* and *into* (each 3×) as well as *on*, *to*, its choice of the collocation *sige niman* (3×), where the second group has *sige habban* (2×), and its fondness for expanded con-

[1] In the Bede I have noted only three instances of *gefaran*, one in MSS O and Ca, ii, 223/42, in the section where someone other than the original translator has filled part of a lacuna by a new translation (see Potter, *Relation*, pp. 30–3, J. J. Campbell, 'The OE Bede: Book III, Chapters 16–20', *MLN* lxvii (1952), pp. 381–6, and D. Whitelock, 'Chapter headings', *Old English Studies*, pp. 263–84). On the two other occasions where this form occurs it is MS C which reads *gefor* for the *geleorde* and *ferde* respectively of the other manuscripts (see Bede 362/3 and 378/1), and it is best explained as a scribal replacement for an original *geleorde*. A similar explanation may be put forward for the solitary instance of *gefor* in MS B of the Martyrology, 188/3, C *gewat*. An instance of *forþferde* beside normal *gefor* in three manuscripts of the West Saxon Genealogy (MSS Cambridge University Library Kk 3. 18, ff. 3v–4r, Cotton Tiberius A iii, f. 178, and Corpus Christi College Cambridge 383, f. 108v) is probably a later addition, BL Additional MS 34652 having *gefor* in a corrupt passage and Chronicle MS A omitting the entry altogether. See *The Genealogical Preface to the Anglo-Saxon Chronicle*, ed. B. Dickins, Cambridge, 1952, also K. Sisam, pp. 153 f. above, and esp. pp. 332–4, and R. I. Page, *Trans. Camb. Bibl. Soc.* vi (1973), pp. 75–9. GD 135/25 *geforon of þysum leohte*, MSS C and H *foron*, is of course not a strictly comparable usage.

After the ninth century the chief user of *gefaran* is the Chronicle. Indeed the only other instances of the verb that I have found in Old English prose are single examples in the Blickling Homilies and *Læceboc*.

[2] See, e.g., Mart 102/17, where MS B *leoran* and *geleorde* appear as *gewitan* and *gewat* respectively in MS C.

[3] It should be noted, however, that the annals 882, 883, and 884 resemble the annals that follow in their use of *up on(long)*. For the suggestion of a new hand at 885 see G. C. Donald, *Zur Entwicklung des Prosastils in der Sachsen-Chronik*, Marburg, 1914, p. 5.

[4] See, e.g., annal 867 *winnende wærun*, 868 *gefuhton*, 870 *feaht*, 871 *onfeohtende wæron*.

structions where the second group has only simple verb forms. The second group, extending from at least 885 up to 890 is further differentiated from the first by its range of verbs of motion,[1] its use of *wiþ þa* as well as *him wiþ gefuhton*, and its freedom from formulae such as *þær wæs micel wæl geslægen* and *ahton wælstowe gewald.*[2] Because of the limited number of forms involved it is not possible to claim that all these choices and preferences are equally significant; however, cumulatively they appear to confirm the difference of authorship suggested by the distribution of *gefaran* and *forþferan* and seem to rule out the possibility of a single author responsible for all the post-Æthelwulfian entries and writing from first-hand knowledge, not taking his information from existing documents.[3]

The question that then arises is whether features, or more particularly combinations of features, typical of either of these two sets of annals[4] are to be found in earlier parts of the Chronicle. As we have seen, the Cynewulf and Cyneheard material in the entry for 755 is distinguished from that of surrounding annals by such features as the use of *adræfan*, *hatan*, and expanded verb forms, a list to which we may add the collocation of *ymb* with *þæs þe*.[5] All these features are found also in the annals

[1] See, e.g., annal 885 *com, eode, gewiton, wendon,* 886 *for. Ferde,* however, is not found in these annals, being confined to a group of early eighth-century annals and to the annals 835, 855, and 868, for which see below, p. 280.

[2] Opportunities for these formulae do, however, occur: see, e.g., the annal for 885.

[3] The annal for 891 reverts to *gefor*, thus possibly lending support to the view that this annal was not part of the compilation circulated in the early 890s. See above, p. 264 n. 3 and below, p. 283 n. 1, and, for the use of *genemnde* in this same annal see below, pp. 291 and 282 n. 2. Separate authorship for the annals 892–7 is indicated by a large number of features.

[4] Single points of agreement are not necessarily significant. Sometimes the forms in question may be due to scribal alteration or partial rewriting (see above, p. 277 n. 2): sometimes they are found in different combinations, suggesting different authors at work (see, e.g., *ferde* in the early eighth-century annals and the discussion above, p. 273).

[5] See above, pp. 274 f. *Ymb þæs þe* and adverbial *þæs ymb* are found nine times between 871 and 878, otherwise appearing only here and in the annals for 606 and 855. The annal for 606 contains a reference to the death of Gregory taken from Bede Epitome 605 (*recte* 604) and the addition *ymb x gear þæs þe he us fulwiht sende* (MSS A, B, and C only) must have been made after the error of date crept in, possibly by someone other than the author of the surrounding annals. We may compare AD 33 and 688 *ymb* and 745 *þa wæs xliii winter agan siþþan*, a single instance of *ymb* occurring alongside

centred on the 870s but are absent from those of the 880s.[1] At the same time, the presence of the expanded forms in the Cynewulf and Cyneheard material links this account with two other entries of the pre-855 section, both of which in their turn have further points of similarity with the annals of the 870s. Thus, in addition to its use of the expanded form, the annal for 835 employs *winnan* and *feran* and disagrees with the annals for the 880s both in these respects and in its use, like the 755 annal, of *feohtan*. The annal for 855 not only has an expanded form and the collocation of *ymb* with *þæs þe*, but employs *gefaran* not *forþferan*, *feran* beside *faran*, and shares with the annal for 878 the expression *þæs/his gefægene wærun* (one of Hodgkin's 'unifying' features), and the preposition *in*, otherwise not found in the Chronicle after the annal for 709. The annal for 855 is of course the entry which contains the notice of King Æthelwulf's death and which is supposed by the supporters of the theory of a two-stage compilation to form the end of the first stage—mainly, though not entirely because of the presence in it of the genealogy of Æthelwulf.[2] However, the fallaciousness of such arguments has been convincingly demonstrated by Kenneth Sisam in an earlier British Academy lecture[3] and, what is more, Professor Whitelock has shown that there are certain inaccuracies in the information given in the annal which appear to imply that it cannot have been recorded (at least in its present form) in any sense of the word contemporaneously.[4] So neither

þæs ymb in annal 878. The annal for 755 also agrees with the annals of the 870s in its use of *swa hwelc swa* and *lytle werode*, the main point of disagreement lying in its use of *nænig*, where the annals centred on the 870s have *nan* (see 868 and 876); however, scribal interference and the influence of the wording of source material cannot be ruled out. In this context note the change from indirect to direct speech in the course of the entry.

[1] Cf. annal 887 *dræfde*.

[2] See, e.g., Wynn, *MÆ* xxv, p. 77. Having commented (n. 28) that 'the last few lines of annal 855 are probably a later continuation', Wynn adds 'In fact with the exception of this one annal there is no evidence of a change of authorship at any point before 891'.

[3] See Sisam, p. 190 above. The pedigree, comments Sisam, reads 'more like additional material, artlessly tacked on, than the studied close of a work ending at 855'.

[4] See *EHD* i, pp. 189 n. 12 and 122 f. As Professor Whitelock points out (private communication) 'If annal 855 is the end of a chronicle written soon after Æthelwulf's death, its author should have known that he did not live *two* years after his return from the continent: he was still in the Frankish kingdom 1 October 856.' Also apparently written some considerable time, not just a handful of years, after the event is the comment, s.a. 851, that the

the presence of the genealogy in this annal nor the nature of the other information in it contradicts the evidence of the vocabulary that its affiliations are with the annals of the time of King Alfred.[1]

It seems reasonable to conjecture, therefore, that the hand of what may for convenience be called the first Alfredian annalist (though the possibility of collaboration cannot be ruled out) may be seen in the final form taken by at least two annals relating to Æthelwulf's reign, possibly more,[2] and in view of the politically sensitive content of one of those annals as well as the reversion to *forþferde* in annal 860, possibly though not necessarily as the result of the rewriting of earlier material.[3] It may well also be seen in the additional material in the annal for 755. However, all the evidence points away from the author being responsible for the translation of Bede Epitome or other Latin material in the early part of the Chronicle, or for general revision of the early Chronicle.[4] The role of the hypothetical author or authors of the second set of Alfredian annals, on the other hand, is less easily determined. Certainly these annals

slaughter inflicted in a battle in that year was the greatest 'that we ever heard of until this present day', while the reference to what the Chronicle describes as the consecration as king of the boy Alfred in 853 (see *EHD* i, p. 123), however we interpret it, has more the ring of a remark made by a chronicler writing in Alfred's reign than that of someone writing under Æthelwulf or indeed under Alfred's rebellious eldest brother Æthelbald.

[1] The affiliations of the two annals (dated 865 and 866) that follow are impossible to determine. However, in view of the use in them of the collocation *friþ (ge)niman wiþ* + dative, where subsequent annals have *friþ niman wiþ* + accusative, it is possible that they may not be the work of the author of the first set of Alfredian annals. See further below, p. 286 n. 1.

[2] See, e.g., annal 853 with *gehwæþere hond* as in annal 871.

[3] Where Asser tells (probably mainly from hearsay) of rebellion by Æthelwulf's eldest son Æthelbald during the king's absence abroad, the 890 Chronicle (MSS A, B, and C) simply reports that Æthelwulf's people rejoiced at his return. Even as diplomatic a comment as this might have been dangerous if made in the period up to Æthelbald's death in 860. Alternative explanations for 860 *forþferde* include a separate source for this annal and a temporary change of authorship. Certainly the vague 'in his day' suggests writing some time after the event.

[4] Apart from the normal use in the earlier part of the Chronicle of *forþferde* not *gefor* and the absence of expanded forms except in the special circumstances already discussed, we may note the use in the first set of Alfredian annals of *adræfan* (874 and 878) and possibly also a syntactical feature, the use of *sio sunne* (879), where the earlier annals normally use *adrifan* and *sunne*.

agree with the early chronicle against the first set of Alfredian annals in their use of *forþferan* not *gefaran*, and of simple not expanded forms. And in other respects, too, the basic vocabulary of the two sections is similar, both showing a preference for *faran*, both employing *todælan*, *bedrifan*, and so on. However, there are a number of differences which, taken together, require us at least to leave open the possibility of more than one author at work. The Bede Epitome entries, for instance, differ from the annals of the 880s in using *swaþeah* not *þeah*, *eac swelce* not *eac*, *adrifan* not *dræfan*, *huerf* not *wende*, *feohtan* not *gefeohtan*, *onfon rice* beside *fon to rice*, and *in* beside *on*.[1] Similar lists of differences can be drawn up for the annals for the 880s and other sections of the early Chronicle, though here, of course, there is a possibility of influence on choice by the usage of vernacular sources.[2]

The distribution of lexical items in the 890 Chronicle, then, appears to rule out the theory of a single compiler writing in or after 890 and drawing on existing oral and written sources (whether Latin or vernacular) for the history of his country up to the death of Æthelwulf, but then himself providing all the information about subsequent events. It does not rule out the possibility of there having been a single compiler for the bulk of the section 60 BC to the early ninth century—working, it

[1] See also the syntactical feature *sunne* not *seo sunne*. None of these is of itself necessarily distinctive; though study of other texts shows that they can be significant in terms of authorship, it can also reveal the dangers of jumping to conclusions. Thus, with the concentration of *in* in the earlier parts of the 890 Chronicle we may compare Or, where the form is similarly confined to the first part of the work only, its last occurrence in MS L being in 85/10, the beginning of Book IV, though in the list of chapter-headings *on* is several times found for the *in* of the text. In contrast to the distribution patterns in Or and the Chronicle, on the other hand, the seven instances of *in* recorded in Sweet's edition of CP occur mostly towards the end of the work, with five between 284/15 and 385/22. Scribal removal of *in* can be clearly seen from a comparison of the manuscripts of Mart (see also D. Yerkes's study of the usage in GD, *Manuscripta*, xxi (1977), pp. 38–41) while for the converse see Pope, *Ælfric Homilies*, ii. xxx, 114 n. However, the very predilection for lack of variation normally shown in the 890 Chronicle makes these differences notable.

[2] See, e.g., 890 *þæs fulluhtnama wæs*, beside 794 *þam wæs oþer noma nemned* and 465 and 508 *þam wæs noma* (also below, p. 123 and n. 2), 885 *hamweard wendon* beside 584 and 813 *hwearf to his agnum*; 885 *herehyþ*, 473 and 584 *herereaf*, 418 *nænig*, 887 *nan*, possibly also 887 *forþæm*, earlier annals *forþon* (658, 661, also, based on BEp., 680), *forþon þe* (694), *þy* (787, 823, 836): see Liggins, *Anglia*, lxxxviii, p. 302. However, for MS A *forþæm* B, C, D, and E read *forþon*.

should be emphasized, at any time between the date of the last annal for which he is responsible up to 890[1]—though if we wish to see his contribution as extending up to 855 or 860 we must, I think, assume the rewriting or expansion of a number of annals between 755 and 855, apparently by the first Alfredian annalist.[2] That the compiler of this early material was not also the author of the annals that conclude the 890 Chronicle may be suspected but not proven. Finally, the evidence of the distribution of lexical items forces us to consider, as an alternative to a single act of compilation by two or more annalists, the possibility that the first Alfredian compilation ended with the annals for the closing years of the 870s (or shortly after), and that the annals for the 880s and 890 which form with it

[1] If he was working around 890, then we would have to assume a team of collaborators. When the annalist responsible for the entries centred on the 870s was working is also an open question: although his use of *gefor* links him with the annal for 891, it should be noted that he never employs the construction *wiþ* + dative following the verb *gefeohtan* whereas the latter does. This construction is indeed very rare in the 890 Chronicle, being confined to annals 495, 710, 722, and 853, though *him wiþ* with *wiþ* preceding the verb occurs four times between 845 and 890. As regards the information provided by this annalist, at least two pieces may indicate writing down some time after the event: thus s.a. 871 only six of nine pitched battles are named, while s.a. 867 Bishop Ealhstan is wrongly given an episcopate of fifty years (see Plummer, *Two Saxon Chronicles*, ii, p. 71). I am indebted to Professor Whitelock for drawing my attention to these details.

[2] Parkes, *ASE* v, p. 154, has drawn attention to the interesting fact that fol. 14 of MS A is a singleton and probably a cancel; noting that the material on the verso has been spread out, while on the recto it is compressed, he suggests that 'either new material has been added on this page or existing material has been rearranged here'. Taken in conjunction with Mr Parkes's earlier comment, p. 153, that the first scribe's booklet was 'probably contemporary with the revision itself', and the fact that the vocabulary of fol. 14 is by and large of a piece with the vocabulary of surrounding leaves but different in a number of essentials from the vocabulary of the final annals of the 890 Chronicle, the implications of this for a study of the compilation of the Chronicle are obvious: if material has been added, rather than just rearranged, then the author of the annals of the 870s could still have been collaborating in 890. However, as an alternative to the theory of the adding of material (perhaps marginalia initially overlooked by the scribe?), I would suggest the possibility of deletion of material, either because the scribe on reading through what he had copied found it (politically?) unacceptable, or simply because of accidental duplication or misplacing (see, e.g., fol. 12ᵛ). The writing on fol. 14ʳ does not seem to me unduly compressed, and the scribe may not have stopped to think till he turned the page that deletion would entail a large blank space on the verso.

the first known circulated version may be, like the annals that follow, a continuation.[1]

This brings us to the much-argued question of the possible association of the 890 Chronicle with King Alfred. As we have seen, some scholars have assumed that the King was intimately associated with the compilation, inspiring it, arranging for its general circulation, and quite possibly dictating some of the material in it.[2] One of the main arguments for this association is based on supposed similarities of usage between the Chronicle and the Old English translation of Orosius.[3] Plummer, for instance, lists a number of correspondences in phraseology between the Chronicle and what he calls Alfred's translation of Orosius: 'No doubt', he says, 'some of these phrases are ordinary phrases which any two historical writers might use; but in many cases the resemblance goes much beyond this, and the total impression is strong that the two works are akin.' Plummer's views are shared by Cornelius Sprockel, who argues that 'the close resemblance in phraseology between the Chronicle and Alfred's Orosius . . . cannot . . . be dismissed as mere correspondences in contemporary works on similar themes'.[4] Kenneth Sisam, too, though not agreeing with the theory of Alfred's authorship of the Orosius, provisionally accepts 'the view now prevalent . . . that [Alfred] encouraged, or planned, or perhaps contributed information to the Chronicle of 892, but did not himself compile it', and gives as one possible explanation of the likeness with Orosius that 'the compiler (or a compiler) of the Chronicle of 892 and the adaptor of Orosius were the same person, whom the king commissioned to do both works'.[5] Sir Frank Stenton, on the other hand, with the support of Dorothy Whitelock, speaks out strongly against an Alfredian connection: 'there is nothing that can be called evidence to connect [the compilers] with the body of learned men who gathered round King Alfred and there are peculiarities of style and syntax

[1] It cannot be emphasized too strongly that a study of the vocabulary does not enable us to decide between the two alternatives. For the possibility that differences in arrangement of material in annal 851 are due to the presence of marginalia in the archetype of surviving manuscripts, see *EHD* i, p. 188 n. 13.

[2] See above, p. 266.

[3] Another argument is that it fits into Alfred's educational plan. See, however, D. Whitelock, 'The Old English Bede', pp. 242–3 above.

[4] See Plummer, *Two Saxon Chronicles*, ii, pp. cvi–cviii, and C. Sprockel, *The Language of the Parker Chronicle*, i, The Hague, 1965, p. xix.

[5] Sisam, p. 193 above.

which place their work apart'.[1] What then can we learn from a comparative study of the vocabulary of the Chronicle and the other texts associated with Alfred and Alfred's reign? And what value as evidence has Plummer's list of resemblances between the Chronicle and the Orosius?

In his list Plummer includes a range of words and more particularly expressions both from the 890 Chronicle and from subsequent annals which for reasons of date have no possible connection with King Alfred. As far as the forms from the 890 Chronicle are concerned—and these are the only ones strictly relevant to this study[2]— the majority are by no means unique to the Chronicle and the Orosius, and most of the resemblances noted need be no more than the result of the handling of similar subjects by authors who were contemporaries and had the same common stock of language to draw on. For example, that both the Chronicle and the Orosius use the same words for 'pitched battle' (*folcgefeoht*), and 'pirate' (*wicing*), is a fact of no special significance given the apparent normality of these terms.[3] The forms *gebære*, *ofstician*, *abrecan*, *bestelan*, *rices beniman*, picked out by Plummer as used by the Chronicle and the Orosius are likewise all part of the common stock, found also in other texts of the period, such as the Old English Bede, Werferth's translation of Gregory's Dialogues, the Martyrology, and Alfred's Cura Pastoralis.[4] As for the larger units of expression cited, some of these actually involve differences as well as similarities, which, to say the least, cancel one another out. For instance, Orosius's statement, *on norðhealfe* [*is*] *Orcadus þæt igland*, which

[1] Stenton, 'South-western element', *PASE*, p. 113.

[2] Forms from other parts of the Chronicle could, of course, be used to show that agreement does not necessarily imply common authorship. It should be noted that although Plummer cites resemblances between the Orosius and the annals for 892–923, the first five of these being the first and only set to use a history layout, these annals too contain a number of features that seem to rule out the possibility of the author of the Orosius being responsible for their composition. See further my edition of *The Old English Orosius*, Introduction, Section VI. 3, pp. lxxxiii–lxxxvi.

[3] A synonym for *folcgefeoht* (*folcgewinn*) is found once in Bo, in verse.

[4] For *gebæru* see, e.g., GD 108/2, Be 328/15, PPs xxxiv. 15; for *ofstician* see, e.g., Mart. 222/7; for (*burg*) *abrecan* see, e.g., Be 42/28, Bo 7/3, and CP 218/17; for *bestelan* see Be 326/21, CP 197/21; for *rices beniman* see Be 168/20, cf. Bo 113/4, 20/26, CP 251/10. The expression quoted by Plummer from annal 891, *on elþiodignesse beon*, is similarly found in Be, Mart, and CP. It should be noted that not all these forms can be said to represent the regular usage of the 890 Chronicle. Thus, for instance, beside 658, 755 *rices beniman* we have 887 *berædde æt þam rice*, 821 *his rices besciered*.

is cited alongside the Chronicle annal 47 (*recte* 46) *Eac swelce Orcadus þa ealond*, not only treats the proper name Orcades as singular where the Chronicle has the correct plural, but uses it with *igland*, the normal word for 'island' in this text, not its synonym *ealond*, which is the only form in the 890 Chronicle. And although Orosius 116/7–8, *he genom friþ wiþ þæt folc*, 7 *hiene siþþan aweg bestæl*, is certainly similar to the Chronicle entry for 865, *genamon friþ wiþ Cantwarum*, and (later in the same annal) *se here hiene on niht up bestæl*, the collocation *friþ geniman*, which is the rule in the Orosius, is the exception in the Chronicle, the normal usage being *friþ niman*, while the Orosius elsewhere uses *nihtes* with the verb *bestelan*, never *on niht*.[1] The resemblances are thus superficial, and do not extend to the 'core of familiar words that recur again and again'. Indeed only one of Plummer's principal resemblances is of real significance:[2] the reference to Titus's saying, that he lost the day on which he did no good act, which is found in both the Chronicle and the Old English Orosius and is without parallel in the latter's source. However, although in this particular instance the Orosius may certainly have derived its comment from the Chronicle, and I have discussed the possibility in detail elsewhere, this need not indicate more than knowledge of the one text by the author of the other.[3]

The similarities in phraseology noted by Plummer do not, then, require us to suppose that the author of the Orosius was

[1] For 'island' see below, p. 287. For the single instance of *friþ geniman* (with *wiþ*+dative) in the 890 Chronicle, see above, p. 281 n. 1; the normal usage, *friþ niman* (with *wiþ* + accusative), is found six times between annals 867 and 876. Or has eleven examples of *friþ geniman*, mostly collocated with *wiþ* + accusative. We may compare CP 353/11 *sibbe niman*. For *nihtes* (found in annal 876) see, e.g., Or 30/18–19 7 *þa nihtes on ungearwe hi on bestæl* and 51/23–4 *hie nihtes on frumslæpe on bestælan*.

[2] The collocation *þær wæs ungemetlic wæl geslægen*, which is found twice in the Orosius and once in the 890 Chronicle, has to be seen, on the one hand, as a modification of the collocation *micel wæl geslean*, which is found not only in the Chronicle and the Orosius but also in the Old English Bede, and, on the other, as utilizing an adjective of quantity found in a wide range of Old English texts. Significantly, on the two occasions where Or has *ungemetlic wæl* (46/32 and 68/15–16) there are respectively three and four other examples of the words *ungemet* and *ungemetlic*(*e*) in the same chapter. *Ungemetlic*(*e*) is found twenty-seven times in all in Or.

[3] See my article in *ASE* viii, pp. 189–92. A second apparently unique correspondence is 60 BC *mid gefeohte cnysede*, Or 52/28–9 *mid gefeohte cnysedan*. However, the Chronicle is merely translating Bede Epitome *bello pulsauit*, using an accepted Old English rendering for Latin *pulsare* which is found also in CP and GD. See also Or 77/3–4 *swa wurdon Romane gecnysede*, for *Roma detrita est*.

also the author of the Chronicle. More significantly, there are a number of differences between the two texts, and also between the Chronicle and the accepted works of King Alfred,[1] which Plummer seems to have overlooked and which appear actually to rule out the possibility of common authorship. Because of the paucity of material provided by the 890 Chronicle, many of these are statistically non-significant.[2] Moreover, certain key concepts are of limited distribution, appearing only in the section of the Chronicle up to 855, or only in one or other of the sections after 855. However, enough occur in significant numbers in the texts to be used as evidence of their authors' normal usage. Among the concepts for which the Chronicle and the Orosius select different terms, for instance, we may cite not only 'island' but also 'Britain', 'the Danes', 'humble', and 'proud', and among the larger units the expressions 'on both sides' and 'subjugate', 'get under one's control'. As we have seen, for 'island' the 890 Chronicle consistently uses the variant *ealand*—though the concept is restricted to the section AD 47–716 (where it occurs seven times), the first instance of *igland* not appearing until the annal for 894. In this it agrees with the Old English Bede and Gregory's Dialogues, where *ealand* is the rule, instances of *igland* in the Bede apparently being the work of later scribes and in the Dialogues of scribes and reviser. The Orosius, however, has only the form *igland* (52×), while in the prose of the Boethius we find *ealand* three times, *igland* and its variants four times. *Igland* is the only form in the verse metres.[3] So too with 'Britain', the Chronicle's forms *Breten*, *Bretene*

[1] CP, Bo, and So. For the possible inclusion of PPs in the Alfredian canon see Bately, *Anglia*, lxxxviii, pp. 454–6.

[2] See, e.g., annal 855 *weorþness*, Or and Alfred *weorþscipe*, *weorþmynd*, with Or also using *weorþfulnes* and CP *weorþung*, etc.; annal 27 *gyming* (transcript of G, erased in MS A), Or (and once CP) *gieme*, CP, Bo, PPs *giemen*, with *gieming* once, CP; annal 584 *herereaf genom*, Or *herefeoh gefon*; annal 853 *geaf his dohtor*, Or *his dohtor sealde* (*giefan* occurring only once in Or, in a different context); annal 871 *getruma* (2×), Or *truma*; 540 *steorran*, Or *tungul*; 501 *monna* (2×), Or only *mon*, *wer*, etc. For *(ge)fultumian* (797, 836, 853, and 868), Or normally *(ge)fylstan*, see Bately, *Anglia*, lxxxviii, p. 445.

[3] Under *igland* I include variants such as *iglond*, *eglond*; under *ealand* I include *ealond*. For scribal alterations see, e.g., Be, where MS B frequently has *igland* for the *ealand* of the other manuscripts; for possible editorial alterations see GD, where H has *igland* for the *ealand* of the other manuscripts. In the 'northern recension' of the Chronicle a preference for *igland* is shown both in the new material and in the old. All but one of the forms in Bo prose are in sections confined to MS B; the exception, 34/29, has *ealonde*, the reading of MS C and the Napier fragment.

(*land*)—found thirteen times from 60 BC to AD 601—have their counterpart in the Martyrology, prose Guthlac, and Bede, while the Orosius regularly uses *Brettania*, *Brittannia* (*þæt lond*) with a single instance of *Bretland*.[1] On the other hand, it is Orosius's form *Dene* that corresponds to the Old English Bede's *Daene*, while the Chronicle annals 833–85 have the alternative *þa Deniscan*.[2] Alfred's usage is in both these cases unknown.

In the case of the concepts 'humble' and 'proud' it is variety of word-formation that is of potential significance, the Chronicle forming the adjectives in *-mod* and *-mede* (828 *eaþmodre*, 750 *ofermedan*), while the Orosius has *-modig* (*eaþmodig*, *ofermodig*). In this the Chronicle differs in part also from Alfred, who normally uses *eaþmod*, *ofermod*, and from the Old English Bede and Gregory's Dialogues where we find *eaþmod* beside *oferhygdig*, *oferhygd*.[3] As for the collocation 'on both sides', in both the Chronicle and the Orosius this occurs in conjunction with the statement 'there was much slaughter', the Orosius's rendering being *þær wæs micel wæl geslægen on ægþere healfe* and the Chronicle's *þær wæs micel wæl geslægen on gehwæþere hond*.[4] Similarly alien to the Orosius's usage is the Chronicle's rendering of 'subjugate', with Bede Epitome 46, *in deditionem recepit* translated *on his geweald onfeng*. Certainly the author of the Orosius uses the collocation *on his geweald*, but with *underfeng* not *onfeng*, while *anweald*, *onweald* is far more common than *geweald*: in any case, the preferred collocation in this text is with *geniedan* or (*ge*)*don*. The equivalent expression in Alfred's Boethius is *in anwald gerehton*[5].

[1] Cf. 787, 836, and 866 *Angelcynnes lond*. Or has only *Brettas*, where the Chronicle uses *Brettas*, *Bretwalas*, and *Walas*; compare Mart with *Brytwalas* and Be with *Brettas*, *Bret* only, also the northern recension with the form *Brytwalas* in the new material. See also annals 650 and 660 *Galwalas* (also Mart), Or *Gallie*, *Gælle*.

[2] *þa Deniscan* is found ten times in this section of the Chronicle beside *Deniscne here* (837 and 845) and *Deniscra monna* (882 and 886). Cf. 787 *Deniscra monna* in a comment obviously made some time after that year.

[3] For a detailed survey of the representation of the concept 'pride' see H. Schabram, *Superbia: Studien zum altenglischen Wortschatz*, i, Munich, 1965. *Eadmod*, *eaþmod* is the normal usage of Mart. CP, however, has a couple of instances of *eaþmodlic* beside normal *eadmod*, *eaþmod*, and also *oferhygd* beside *ofermod*. For a verb never found in Or or Bo see *agan*, s.a. 6, 616, 655 and 745, and cf. Or 35/23–4.

[4] For *on gehwæþere hond* see annals 853 and 871 (2×); *on ægþere healfe* occurs eleven times in Or. See also Or 98/21–2 *þæt him þa geþuhte swelc þæt mæste wæl*, beside annal 839 *Her wæs micel wælsliht* (also 592 *wælfill*).

[5] Bo 7/4. Cf. Be 30/18 *on anweald onfeng*, translating the same Latin expression, also CP 35/15–16 *ðone anwald onfeng ðæs rices*. The construction

A no less significant group of differences between the texts is one where the 890 Chronicle has a greater variety of renderings for a given concept than either the Orosius or indeed the accepted writings of Alfred, with the distribution patterns of these variant forms usually corresponding to major divisions in the compilation. For example, the normal representation of the concept 'die' in the Orosius and in the works of Alfred, including his will, is *gefaran*. As we have seen, however, the most common form in the 890 Chronicle is *forþferan*, occurring seventy-one times, with *gefaran* (6×) restricted to a handful of annals, mainly belonging to the group centred on the 870s. In this use of *forþferan*, in preference to *gefaran*, the 890 Chronicle agrees with the Bede, Gregory's Dialogues, and the Martyrology, though these have as their normal alternative not *gefaran* but *(ge)leoran*, and that apparently originally distributed throughout the texts.[1] And this is not the only area where the 890 Chronicle, in spite of its shortness and lack of variety, has a range of choices not found in Orosius and Alfred. For the concept 'have the victory', for instance, the Chronicle, Alfred, and the Orosius agree in their use of *sige habban* (885, 890, i.e. second set of Alfredian annals only), but the Chronicle's *sige agan* (871, 885) and *sige niman* (used ten times between 800 and 871) are never found in either Alfred or the Orosius. Bede here agrees with the Chronicle in using *sige habban* and *sige agan* but has only one, exceptional, instance of *sige niman*; the Dialogues collocate *agan* and *habban* with *sigor*.[2] Again, in rendering the concept 'succeed to the throne' the Orosius, the Chronicle, and Alfred all employ the formula *fon to rice* with the variant *fon to þæm rice*. These are the only forms in the Orosius, Alfred, and the Chronicle from

in annal 46 (MS A alt. to 47) is also notable for its use of *onfon* + accusative, the preferred usage of this part of the Chronicle and of the Bede but rare in Or and Bo, which normally employ genitive or dative.

[1] *Gefaran* 'die' is found twenty-four times in Or, *forþferan* nearly sixty times in Be. An instance of the verb *geleoran* in PPs cited in Bosworth and Toller's *Anglo-Saxon Dictionary* is in fact an editorial misreading of MS *geteorode* as *geleorode*. Other words for the concept 'die' in the Chronicle are *swealt*, *aswalt*, and *his feorh gesealde* (annals 3, 46, and 855), the first two of general if relatively infrequent occurrence in texts of the period, the last found also in GD and (with *sealde*) Mart. Although both the instances of *(a)sweltan* in the Chronicle refer to evil rulers, the verb was not, as is sometimes claimed, used only of the evil: see, e.g., Mart where it is used of saints.

[2] *Sige habban* occurs thirty-five times in Or, twice in CP, and once each in Bo and PPs. Other verbs collocated with *sige* in these texts are *gefeohtan* (Or 2×, CP 1×), *gefaran* (Or 2×), *geræcan* (Or 3×), *þurhteon* (Or 1×), *gewinnan* (CP 1×).

836. However, up to the annal for 828, including Bede Epitome material, the Chronicle also has the variant *onfon rice*, *onfon rices* (8×, beside *onfon biscopdom*, etc.), a collocation never found in the Orosius and Alfred though it occurs not infrequently in the Old English Bede.

It is, however, not only differences in choice between the texts that are significant, nor the existence of a wider range of expressions in one than in another, but also their preferences, and here again all the major divisions of the Chronicle can be shown to differ in some respect or other from the Orosius and the works of Alfred. For instance, although regnal lengths are sometimes given with the collocation *rice habban* and sometimes with the verb *ricsian* in both the Orosius and the Chronicle, the normal formula in the Orosius, *rice* or *anwald habban*, is the least usual in the Chronicle, where there are only two instances of *rice habban* coupled with a regnal length (626, 716), and the variant *anwald* is completely absent. On the other hand, *rice healdan* (14× in the Chronicle between 611 and 755, including Bede Epitome material) is never found in the Orosius, though *healdan* is used there once in connection with the consulship. *Ricsian*, found sixteen times in the Chronicle between AD 1 and 871 (including Bede Epitome material), occurs only once in the Orosius in association with a regnal length.[1] So, too, with the representations of the concept 'to fight'. In the Chronicle the commonest form is *gefeohtan* (50× in MS A), followed by *feohtan* (22×) and *winnan* (5×) in that order, with single instances of *onfeohtan* and *gewinnan*. Even allowing for disagreements between the surviving manuscripts, *gefeohtan* predominates in every section.[2] No other major text of the Alfredian period has this order of preferences. Alfred and the Orosius both have a preponderance of examples of *winnan*, with the order *winnan*, *gefeohtan*, *feohtan* in the Orosius and *winnan*, *feohtan*, never *gefeohtan* in Alfred.[3] In the Old English Bede the order is

[1] See Or 37/26 and 40/14, and cf. annal 827 where the collocation *rice habban* occurs without regnal length.

[2] See, e.g., annal 455 A, E, F *fuhton*, B, C *gefuhton*, and 552 A *gefeaht*, B, C, E, F *feaht*. In MS A the pattern is *gefeohtan*: *feohtan* roughly in the proportion 6:5 up to the end of the eighth century. Between 800 and 855 there are ten instances of *gefeohtan*; between 860 and 890 there are eighteen, with only two instances of *feohtan* (835 and 870). Of the five instances of *winnan* three occur between 835 and 878, *gewinnan* in the sense 'fight' is found only once, s.a. 741.

[3] Or has over 100 instances of *winnan*, 59 *gefeohtan*, and 35 *feohtan*, and *winnan* is also frequent in Bo (usually metaphorically), with *feohtan* only 2×.

feohtan, *winnan*, with *campian* in third place, followed by *gefeohtan* and *gewinnan*.[1]

Another significant difference of choice between the Chronicle, on the one hand, and Alfred and the Orosius, on the other, involves what may be called the 'naming' formulae. In the pre-855 annals the preference is, as we have seen, for *þe is gecweden* (7×), *þe is (ge)nemned*, *þe mon nemneþ* (8×), and *þam wæs noma* (2×), with *se wæs haten*, *þe hi heton*, and *þæs fulluhtnama wæs* confined to the annals for 755, 878, and 890.[2] In the Orosius and Alfred, on the other hand, it is the constructions with *hatan* that are most common, while Alfred uses not *þam* but *þæs wæs nama* and the Orosius has neither *nama* construction.[3] Finally, we find the Chronicle agreeing with the Orosius against both Alfred and the Mercian texts with invariable *oþiewan*, 'show', where the Bede, the Martyrology, and Gregory's Dialogues normally use *æteowan* and related forms with the prefix *æt-*, and Alfred has a marked preference for *ge-eowian*, *eowan*, etc.[4]

Cf. CP *winnan* (16×), *feohtan* (8×); PPs *winnan* (3×), *feohtan* (3×). See also the Laws of Alfred with *feohtan* (13×), and *gefeohtan* (5×). *Gewinnan* in the sense 'fight' occurs only very exceptionally, in Or (2×) and Be (1×).

[1] I have found no instances of *campian* in early West Saxon prose texts; however, in addition to Be it appears in GD, Mart, and the prose Guthlac, all apparently texts of Mercian origin. For the prose Guthlac see Jane Roberts's unpublished dissertation, *Guthlac: an edition of the Old English prose life together with the poems in the Exeter Book*, ed. J. Crawford, Oxford, 1966.

[2] The instance s.a. 878 occurs in a passage absent from MS A and therefore possibly a later addition. See also 688 *se papa hine heht Petrus*. The construction with *hatan* is favoured by the northern recensionist.

[3] *Nemnan* and *(ge)cweþan* occur only very rarely in Or and the works of Alfred, with *(ge)nemnan*, for instance, only six times in Or and *gecweþan* in the sense 'call', 'describe as' only once. Mart and Be, however, show a preference for these forms. With annal 794 *þam was oþer noma nemned Præn* cf. Or 59/30–1 *þe oðre noman wæs haten Tarcuatus*, etc. (17×) and Bo 43/7 *se wæs oðre naman haten Tullius*; see also GD *þam is nama*.

[4] See annals 540, 678, 729, and 773. *Ætiewdon* in MS A 540 is a correction from original *oðiewdon*, original *ætiewan* first appearing s.a. 892. In other manuscripts of the Chronicle there is a tendency for *oþiewan* to be replaced by a form with *æt-*. In the works of Alfred and associated texts *ætiewan* and related forms occur in significant numbers only in CP and even there they are outnumbered by *(ge)eow(i)an*. *Oþiewan* occurs only once in Bo prose (three times in verse) and once in PPs, with two instances in CP, while *(ge)eow(i)an* is found eight times in Bo prose and twenty-four times in CP. I have noted *ætiewan* and related forms twenty-one times in CP, once in PPs. See also the choice between *adrifan* and *adræfan*, the former occurring five times in the 890 Chronicle between 592 and 823, with *drifan* s.a. 787, the latter being confined in MS A to annals 755 (2×), 874, and 878, with *dræfde* s.a.

From this brief survey it can be seen that although there may be significant disagreements in usage between the various parts of the 890 Chronicle, they all agree in their selection of lexical items alien to the Orosius and the works of Alfred.[1] What then are the affinities of the constituent parts of the Chronicle? It is generally accepted that the dialect in which the 890 Chronicle was written is a West Saxon one,[2] and many would identify what Plummer describes as the 'headquarters' of the compilation with Winchester.[3] However, although Mr Parkes has recently produced highly convincing arguments both for an association of Hand 1 of MS A, the Parker Chronicle, with Winchester and for the putting together there of the various booklets that make up that manuscript,[4] there seems nothing in the evidence currently available that requires us to suppose that the actual composition of the section up to 890 was necessarily undertaken in a Winchester scriptorium.[5] What is more, that the Chronicle

887 (MSS D and E *adræfde*). Although Or uses these two forms with almost equal frequency, with *adrifan* 10×, *adræfan* 11× (unlike the Chronicle, however, employing *ut* only with *adrifan*), the surviving manuscripts of Alfred's works show a marked preference for *adrifan* (Bo 11×, CP 12×, Solil 2×) as do Be and GD, first version. In these texts I have noted *adræfan* only twice—once each in CP and Be, with the instance in Be occurring in the list of chapter-headings—with *todræfed* in the OCa version of Book III ch. 16–20 of Be (Miller, ii, p. 227). For the possible implications of the contexts of the examples in Be see above, p. 263 n. 4.

[1] I have not attempted to assess differences of syntax, though these may well be equally significant in terms of authorship. For the expanded verb forms see G. Nickel, *Die Expanded Form im Altenglischen*, Neumünster, 1966, B. Mitchell, 'Some problems involving OE periphrases with *Beon/Wesan* and the present participle', *Neuphilologische Mitteilungen* lxxvii (1976), pp. 478–91, and *The Old English Orosius*, p. lxxv. Other syntactical variations with potentially significant distribution patterns that might repay detailed investigation include the use of *sunne*, *mona*, and *steorra*, with and without demonstrative and the use of accusative, genitive, and dative with *onfon*.

[2] See, e.g., C. Sprockel, *The Language of the Parker Chronicle*, i.

[3] *Two Saxon Chronicles*, ii, p. cxii.

[4] See Parkes, *ASE* v, pp. 149–71.

[5] There are two separate issues: (i) is there any evidence that the first draft of the 890 Chronicle was either made or kept at Winchester?, and (ii) can the version in MS A be shown to be so close to the first draft that it must be assumed that both necessarily came from the same scriptorium? The answer to (i) appears to be 'no'. The insertion in a tenth-century hand of the annal for 710, apparently accidentally omitted by the first scribe of MS A, certainly suggests the presence in Winchester at that time of a copy of the Chronicle other than MS A, but there is nothing to suggest that this must have been the 'very collection of booklet exemplars' which 'constituted

is silent about at least one important event occurring in the neighbourhood of Winchester but includes a number of 'local' details relating to the south-west, has led both Sir Frank Stenton and Professor R. H. C. Davis to reject a Winchester origin for the compilation and to look instead to the Sherborne area.[1] Unfortunately, we know nothing of the sub-dialects of early West Saxon; we cannot even localize the king's English, that particular form of West Saxon that King Alfred spoke, nor can we be sure how far his written language was influenced by advisers.[2] So we cannot use a study of the vocabulary of the 890 Chronicle to determine the place of origin of its compilers. Indeed, the most we can say of the vocabulary of the extant manuscripts is that by and large it is that associated with West Saxon, with typically Anglian words usually conspicuous for

perhaps the first fair copies on parchment of the original drafts' (see Parkes, p. 165). As Professor Whitelock comments (private communication): 'Winchester may have acquired the version with annal 710 along with one of its bishops or other ecclesiastics.' See further *EHD* i, p. 171 n. 1. My answer to (ii) is also 'no'. MS A does not suggest to me the work of someone necessarily very close to the compiler. It appears to have been at least two removes from the original (see *EHD* i, p. 121) and although changes in its layout probably do reflect decisions by the scribe (see Parkes, p. 154), and we may assume that its exemplar had year numbers in single columns, we cannot guess how long the hypothetically original single column layout may have survived copying. Moreover, there are several possible explanations for the 'new material added or existing material rearranged' on fol. 14 (see above, p. 283 n. 2), while although the inclusion of every single year number from AD 1 on must surely represent an editorial decision (and could well reflect a hope that additional material would be found to fill at least some of the gaps), already in MS A as in the later manuscripts the original function of the annal numbers as part of a piece of historical information seems to have been forgotten: see, e.g., fols. 4^{v} and 11^{r}, and below p. 297 n. 1. Finally, if a number of copies of the 890 Chronicle were produced—as seems to have been the case—the compiler's scriptorium might have needed outside help. See K. Sisam, *Studies in the History of OE Literature*, Oxford, 1953, pp. 140–7, and CP, pp. xvi–xvii.

[1] Thus there is no mention in the Chronicle of the raid on Southampton in 842. See further Stenton, 'South-western element', *PASE*, pp. 107–10, and Davis, *History*, lvi, p. 173. Stenton points out that Winchester was important in the tenth and eleventh centuries, not in the ninth, and also that there is no attempt to give a list of the bishops of Winchester in this period; he also rejects Sherborne as the actual place of compilation (see p. 113). There is of course no reason to suppose that the compiler himself necessarily spoke the dialect of the area where his scriptorium was situated, nor that the scriptorium had developed its own special usage, as Winchester seems to have done later (see Gneuss, *ASE* i, pp. 63–83).

[2] See Sisam, *Studies*, p. 294, 'Alfred's literary language was peculiarly subject to Mercian influence'.

their absence. There are admittedly certain forms in the Chronicle, mostly but not exclusively found in the section up to 855, which are normally associated with Anglian and in particular with Mercian dialects. These are *nænig* (418, 755), *eac swelce* (47, *recte* 46), and the preposition *in* (35–878),[1] a list to which I will venture to add the (non-lexical) use of *mid* with the accusative (189, MSS B, C only), the uncontracted verb form *resteþ* (716), and the reduplicated preterite *heht* (688).[2] However, these words and usages are not confined to indisputably Mercian (or Anglian) texts, all but *heht* being found in the Orosius and the majority also occurring very occasionally in either the works of Alfred or documents intimately associated with the king.[3]

[1] In the Chronicle *in* is found in greatest numbers between annals 35 and 661, including BEp material. It is also apparently favoured by the 'northern recensionist', and the use of *in* in the latter's new material, beside frequent *on* for the *in* of other manuscripts in the 'original' material, suggests that substituted *on* was already present in his exemplar. In MS A *in* is found eighteen times in the section up to 700. After 700 *in* occurs only four times, in annals 709 (2×), 855, and 878. Other manuscripts frequently have *on* for MS A *in*; MS A only once has *on* for their *in*: see annal 501 and see further above, p. 282 n. 1.

[2] For identification of these forms as Mercian or Anglian see, e.g., Vleeskruyer, pp. 27, 30, 32, 142, and 147. For a useful survey of ninth-century Anglian features as found in Mart see C. Sisam, 'A fragment of the Old English Martyrology', *RES*, NS, iv (1953), p. 216.

[3] Isolated instances of *nænig* are found in Alfred's will, the prologue to the Laws of Ine, one manuscript of the Cura Pastoralis, and the Orosius (in the account of Wulfstan's voyages, for which see above, p. 263 n. 4). There are no fewer than twelve instances in the verse metres of Bo. Vleeskruyer sees the appearance of these forms in what he calls archaic West Saxon as 'probably . . . attributable to the influence of Mercian usage' (p. 43 n. 4); however, in view of the tendency of later West Saxon scribes to replace *nænig* by *nan* (see, e.g., Mart 44/12, etc.), no really firm conclusion about the status and distribution of *nænig* in the ninth century can be reached. Of 'Anglian and especially West Mercian *in*' Vleeskruyer remarks that it is 'rare already in eWS, its more frequent occurrence in Orosius being due to the influence of the Latin original . . . possibly also to the somewhat stronger influence of Mercian spelling in this text'. See, however, Or, pp. xxxix ff. and above, p. 282 n. 1. Of the thirty-five instances of *in* in Or only eight in fact correspond to *in* in the Latin 'original'. *In* is also frequent in the first part of the Laws in the mid-tenth-century MS E and occurs seven times in CP, four in Bo. As for *eac swelce*, although the only other early West Saxon text to use this form is Or (where it occurs three times, not once as Vleeskruyer states), it is found also in late WS, in the writings of both Ælfric and Wulfstan, and so its presence in the Chronicle does not necessarily require us to suppose either exceptional Mercian influence or Mercian authorship of the BEp material. Finally *mid* + accusative and third person singular present indicative forms without syncope occur

At the same time, it must be noted that certain words apparently typical of early West Saxon as we know it are either rare or of limited occurrence, and in its choice of terms for a number of concepts where recognized dialectal differences are not involved the Chronicle generally agrees with the three Mercian texts, the Old English Bede, Martyrology, and Gregory's Dialogues, against Orosius and the works of Alfred. The section closest in its usage to these last-named texts is that centred on the 870s, with *gefaran* not *forþferan* and *winnan*[1] as well as *(ge)feohtan*. However, even this section has its differences, with, for instance, a relatively high proportion of forms of the verb *feran* (though not as high a proportion as in the Mercian texts), the rest of the Chronicle sharing the preference of Alfred and the Orosius for *faran*.[2]

I would claim, then, that a detailed examination of the vocabulary of the 890 Chronicle shows Plummer, Hodgkin, and the long line of scholars who have seen affinities between King Alfred's usage and that of the Chronicle, and have interpreted them as due to the king's involvement in that work, to be mistaken—and I would add in passing that none of the arguments for Alfred's involvement takes into account either the absence from the Chronicle of many pieces of information that the king and his officials might be expected to have been able to supply,[3]

occasionally in all the Alfredian texts and Or, while *heht* appears in the (Anglian?) inscription on the Alfred jewel and in CP.

[1] One instance of *winnan* in the pre-855 section, however, links it with GD and Be rather than with the Orosius and Alfred, *feaht 7 won* (597) being a feature of the former never found in the latter; compare the construction (unique in Or) *he winnende wæs 7 feohtende*, Or 62/31.

[2] In Or and the works of Alfred *faran* far outnumbers *feran*. Thus, for instance, Or has nearly 200 examples of intransitive *faran* with *gefaran*, 'go' 34× (six of these being past participles), and *feran* 6×. Bo has *faran* 24× in prose and *feran* 3×, while in CP *faran* outnumbers *feran* more than 5:1. In GD, Mart, and Be, on the other hand, it is *feran* that is the preferred form, though the usage in GD (even in the first version) is approaching the Ælfrician situation, with *faran* present tense and past participle and *feran* preterite. For the appearance of *feran* in the early eighth-century annals see above, and p. 279 n. 1. The figures for the Chronicle, MS A, are *faran* 35×, *feran* 7×.

[3] A strong personal conviction that Alfred's direct involvement is ruled out by the absence from the 890 Chronicle of any traces of the quality of mind and intellectual curiosity displayed by Alfred as author of the Boethius and Soliloquies, and to a lesser extent in the Cura Pastoralis, is of course not evidence. It was in any case not until 887 that, according to Asser, Alfred first began to read and compose. However, Alfred the strategist and Alfred the general had manifested themselves long before. If Alfred had been the

or the presence of certain features that it is hard to reconcile with the theory of his participation.[1] There is nothing in the vocabulary, on the other hand, to refute Sir Frank Stenton's theory that someone commissioned the work quite independently of Alfred, though our present knowledge of West Saxon dialects does not allow us to define the region from which he—or rather his chroniclers—came. Stenton further suggests that the private commissioner of the 890 Chronicle copied Alfred's methods in subsequently circulating the work.[2] This is of course possible, though it raises certain problems of chronology.[3] At the same

inspirer and instigator of the Chronicle, whether the 890 or an earlier version, then one might have expected him to have provided the annalists he commissioned with such information as the location of the sea-battle in 882, or the manner in which the *here on East Englum* broke its peace agreement in 885, or the steps necessary to occupy London in 886. And what about the men of importance in church and state who must have been known personally to King Alfred and played a part in his rebuilding of Wessex—did none of them take up office or die in the period 872–87? We are told of several royal marriages: why are we not told of Alfred's marriage, or of that of his daughter to the ealdorman of Mercia? So too with earlier parts of the Chronicle: King Alfred and his circle would surely have had access to older as well as contemporary archives and had the knowledge to enable them to expand and indeed comment on the significance of the material used here. Even the author of the Orosius is uninhibited in his treatment of world history. See also Stenton, *Anglo-Saxon England*, pp. 692–3, 'when compared with the great Frankish annals of the ninth century, which seem to descend from an official record, the *Chronicle* has definitely the character of private work'. For a detailed discussion of the 'missing material' and a refutation of the theory that the Chronicle was intended as an exercise in propaganda see *The importance of the Battle of Edington,* A.D. *878, A lecture given by Dorothy Whitelock at the Annual Meeting of the Friends of Edington Priory Church, August 27 1977*, Edington, 1978.

[1] Notably the account, s.a. 853, of the boy Alfred's consecration as 'king' (see *EHD* i, p. 123), also perhaps the 'autumn dating of annals from about 850 until just after the reign of Alfred', which Harrison, p. 141, sees as 'idiosyncratic enough to suggest a group of clerks with a secular outlook'.

[2] Stenton, *Anglo-Saxon England*, p. 693, 'The focus of its interest lies in its south-western shires, and it was most probably composed in that country. That in its present form it reflects the example of Alfred's English writings need not be doubted, and it is probable that the despatch of copies to different centres of study, soon after 892, was in imitation of the practice which the king was known to have adopted for the circulation of his own works.' See also P. Hunter Blair, *Roman Britain and Early England*, Edinburgh 1963, p. 12. For doubts as to the possible south-western origin of the Chronicle, see *EHD* i, p. 124.

[3] The only work of Alfred's which is known to have been circulated is CP, and the date of its circulation can only be guessed at from names mentioned in the prefatory letter: see *Sweet's Anglo-Saxon Reader*, revised by Dorothy

time, there is an alternative explanation. That is, that the private commissioner of the work or an associate sent a copy of his chronicle to Alfred and that Alfred then arranged for it to be circulated unmodified, perhaps as the first step in the compilation of a national chronicle, and possibly with the request that recipients should add to it any further information that happened to be available to them. This might help to explain the inclusion in surviving manuscripts of every single year number from AD 1 on, even where there is no entry related to that year, and it might help to account for the presence of additional material in these manuscripts and in the Latin versions of Asser and Æthelweard.[1] This is, of course, pure conjecture: we do not even have incontrovertible proof that there was a deliberate act of circulation.[2] The evidence that a study of vocabulary provides merely suggests that in Alfred's reign at least two chroniclers may have been at work, either simultaneously or separately, one apparently having contributed, rewritten, or revised some of the material relating to the period before Alfred's accession, and that though the 890 Chronicle appears to be a West Saxon compilation, there is nothing in the vocabulary to support the theory of a particularly close connection between the compilers and either King Alfred or the author of the Old English Orosius.

Whitelock, p. 225, 'The preface to the *Cura Pastoralis* cannot have been written before 890, but the translation may be earlier. It was circulated before the death of Swithulf of Rochester'. The date of Swithulf's death Professor Whitelock now puts as 892–5.

[1] For the inclusion of all year numbers—extraordinary, in spite of the precedent of Easter Tables—see above, p. 292 n. 5. We may compare the practice in Bede Epitome and Regino of Prüm, where year numbers are only given where corresponding annals exist. In view of the surprising waste of valuable parchment, with entire leaves consisting of virtually nothing but year numbers (see, e.g., MS A fol. 3^{v}, MS B, ff. 2^{v} and 3^{r}, and MS E, ff. 4^{v} and 5^{r}), it is hard to explain the initial adoption of this practice in any other way.

[2] That is, as opposed to the casual passing on of manuscripts between ecclesiastics from one house to another. Cf. J. M. Wallace-Hadrill, 'The Franks and the English in the ninth century', *History*, xxxv (1950), p. 214, 'Whatever force it was that disseminated manuscripts of the Frankish annals among the *scriptoria* of Northern France in the ninth century also disseminated the *Chronicle* among the English houses.'

ALBERT RECKITT ARCHAEOLOGICAL TRUST LECTURE

THE STUDY OF WINCHESTER: ARCHAEOLOGY AND HISTORY IN A BRITISH TOWN, 1961–1983

By MARTIN BIDDLE

Read 9 March 1983

I

It was Time and Chance, as Dame Joan Evans, the first benefactor of our work, would have said, which led to the start of renewed excavations in Winchester in 1961. Two years before, in his pioneering discussion of 'Winchester Cathedral in the tenth century', Mr Roger Quirk, CB, had set out for the first time the evidence relating to the sites of the Old and New Minsters, and had concluded with a plea for their excavation.[1] In 1960, when working on his second paper dealing with 'Winchester New Minster and its tenth-century tower',[2] Quirk realized that the site then proposed for a new hotel (now The Wessex Hotel), in the centre of Winchester, was precisely that (as he then believed)[3] of the New Minster church itself. Utilizing to the full his knowledge both of the local scene (he was a Wykehamist) and of the Civil Service (in which he was an Under Secretary), Quirk moved rapidly to secure the excavation of the site. With the whole-hearted co-operation of Messrs. Trust Houses Ltd., the Winchester City Council, and the then Ministry of Works, permission was granted and funds were obtained. The Society of Antiquaries, asked to nominate a director, suggested your speaker today, who was then in his final year as an undergraduate at Cambridge.

1 R. N. Quirk, 'Winchester Cathedral in the Tenth Century', *Archaeological Journal*, 114 (1957), 28–68 (published Jan. 1959), see esp. pp. 64–8 and fig. 1.

2 Quirk, 'Winchester New Minister and its Tenth-century Tower', *Journal of the British Archaeological Association*, 3rd. ser. 24 (1961), 16–54.

3 Ibid., pp. 49–54, fig. 6. Quirk revised his views on the site of New Minster in Martin Biddle and R. N. Quirk, 'Excavations near Winchester Cathedral, 1961', *Archaeological Journal*, 119 (1962), 150–94 (= I. Interim: for a list, see below, Appendix A), see esp. pp. 173–82, and fig. 6. The matter was finally settled in 1963 by the discovery of 'Building G' and its identification as New Minster (II. Interim, pp. 210–11, fig. 5; cf. III. Interim, p. 257, fig. 4).

The excavation which followed showed something of the potential of Winchester's buried past. A major public building, probably the forum, a street, and a large town house of the Roman period were overlain by an extensive complex of buildings of several periods related to the New Minster monastery.[1] But the excavation was more important for what it began, for it was impossible in those days to work a long summer in Winchester and not to realize the untapped wealth of the city's archaeology, and the extent to which it was threatened with elimination through the demands of modern development. Building on Quirk's vision of an investigation of the Anglo-Saxon minsters, a broader plan of urban research was conceived and the following spring the Winchester Excavations Committee was formed with this in mind.[2] The chairman from the start was Mrs E. C. Neate, OBE, FSA, who has remained to this day, and to whom much of the success of our work is due.

Such was the *ad hoc* origin of the work of the Committee and its child, the Winchester Research Unit. There had been a number of previous committees of this kind, most recently the Roman and Medieval London Excavation Council,[3] the Canterbury Archaeological Committee, the Cirencester Excavation Committee, and the Verulamium Excavation Committee, but a comparable body founded in Winchester in 1954 was moribund by 1960. Archaeological work in the city had begun in 1949 and between then and 1960 many sites were excavated or recorded during development. The credit for this belongs entirely to the then curator of the Winchester City Museums, Mr Frank Cotrill, FSA, to the City Council, and to the then town clerk, Mr R. H. McCall, CBE. The results of this early work are being published by the City Council in a series of volumes now edited by Dr John Collis, FSA, under the title *Winchester Excavations 1949–60*.[4]

[1] I. Interim.

[2] I. Interim, p. 150; cf. II. Interim, p. 188 and Winchester Studies (for a list, see below, Appendix B), 1, p. vii.

[3] For the origins of the Council, see W. F. Grimes, *The Excavation of Roman and Medieval London* (London, 1968), pp. 1–2, 218–23, 242–51 and the remarks in Martin Biddle and Daphne Hudson, *The Future of London's Past* (Worcester, 1973), pp. 5–7.

[4] Barry Cunliffe, *Winchester Excavations 1949–60*, 1 (Winchester, 1964), dealt mainly with sites within the walls; John Collis, *Winchester Excavations 1949–60*, 2 (Winchester, 1978), with excavations in the suburbs. Volume 3, now in proof, will deal with excavations in St George's Street and High Street (except for those described in Volume 1). Volume 4 will be devoted to the remaining sites of 1949–60 and Volume 5 will deal with post-medieval pottery and other finds. For the history and nature of the work of 1949–60, see Vol. 1, pp. iii–v and Vol. 2, pp. xv–xvi, 1–3.

These excavations carried out up to 1960 were, however, too limited both in scale and approach to make any real impact at the time on the study of Winchester as an urban community. Even the investigation of Roman Winchester (*Venta Belgarum*), which was the focus of much of this work, did not make the advances which were being made in the fifties in a number of other towns of Roman origin.

To a great extent Winchester in 1961 was still *terra incognita*. Nothing certain was known of its origins, almost nothing of its street plan in Roman times, a little of its Roman defences,[1] much less of its cemeteries. As for Winchester after the Romans, it did not even exist as an organized field of archaeological enquiry, except for a few church sites and a large number of pits of every kind containing pottery and other objects which were a rich source for some of the late Dr G. C. Dunning's pioneering studies.[2]

In all this the archaeology of Winchester was little different then from that of most other towns in Britain.[3] But the very contrast between the historical evidence for the importance of early medieval Winchester and the virtual absence of an archaeology of that period, to say nothing of the preceding and following periods, compelled attention.

From the moment of its foundation in 1962, the objectives and approaches of the work of the Winchester Excavations Committee were clearly defined. The city was then passing through a period of intensive rebuilding and development which offered many opportunities for archaeological research. The Assize Courts were to be rebuilt, the offices of the Hampshire County Council greatly extended, some twenty-nine acres of the Brooks area were to be redeveloped and an inner ring road was in the offing. The Second Interim Report, dealing with the Committee's first two seasons in 1962–3, set out the attitudes which were to guide its work:

> With these opportunities in view, the committee was formed to undertake excavations, both in advance of building projects, and on sites not so threatened, aimed at studying the development of Winchester as a town from its earliest origins to the establishment of the

[1] But see Barry Cunliffe, 'The Winchester City Wall', *Proceedings of the Hampshire Field Club*, 22 (2) (1962), 51–81, esp. pp. 79–81.

[2] For studies dealing specifically with finds from Winchester, see the bibliography of Dunning's publications in V. I. Evison, H. Hodges, and J. G. Hurst (eds.), *Medieval Pottery from Excavations: Studies presented to Gerald Clough Dunning* (London, 1974), pp. 17–32, items 141, 179, 202, 207–9, 278.

[3] See my comments on the situation, 'Archaeology and the History of British Towns', *Antiquity*, 42 (1968), 109–116 with the rejoinders ibid. 43 (1969), 42–3.

modern city. The centre of interest is the city itself, not any one period of its past, nor any one part of its remains. But we can hope that this approach will in particular throw light upon the end of the Roman city and on the establishment and development of the Saxon town, problems as vital to our understanding of urban development in this country, as they are difficult to solve. Further it is essential to this approach that the study and interpretation of the documentary evidence should go hand in hand with archaeological research, . . .[1]

By the next season in 1964 the collection and use of evidence derived from a wide range of the natural sciences had been explicitly incorporated in the framework of the project,[2] partly in response to the then still astonishing preservation of organic material in the waterlogged deposits of the Brooks area, partly as the natural result of a Cambridge training under the influence of the Second Albert Reckitt Archaeological Lecturer, Professor Grahame Clark, FBA.[3]

Looking back now over two decades at these aims and approaches, what strikes me is how well they have stood up to the passage of time. They only need translation to appear quite modern: the research strategy was innovative, multidisciplinary, diachronic. In other ways the basic attitudes are perhaps even today ahead of their time: the chance opportunities offered by threatened sites were to be grasped, but were not to become a strait-jacket. 'Rescue' was always subordinate to research, a policy which involved both the excavation of unthreatened sites, and the refusal to excavate threatened sites simply because they were there. All rescue was research, but not all research was rescue.[4] The unifying theme was the urban phenomenon through time and the raw material everything which was potentially grist to this mill. Selection—today we might say sampling—was the key in reducing to manageable proportions the imbalance between the extraordinary potential of Winchester's archaeology and the relatively limited resources available to deal with it.

[1] II. Interim, p. 188.

[2] III. Interim, pp. 245–6; cf. IV. Interim, pp. 318–19. See also Martin Biddle, 'Winchester: the Archaeology of a City', *Science Journal*, Mar. 1965, pp. 55–61, esp. p. 61; and Alan W. Pike and Martin Biddle, 'Parasite Eggs in Medieval Winchester', *Antiquity*, 40 (1966), 243–6.

[3] Grahame Clark, 'The Economic Approach to Prehistory', *Proceedings of the British Academy*, 39 (1953), 215–38.

[4] Cf. the words drafted by the present writer for *Archaeology and Government* (Rescue and the Council for British Archaeology, London, 1974), para. 2.2, which were composed in the light of this Winchester experience, and the surprised reaction to them of F. H. Thompson, 'Rescue Archaeology: Research or Rubbish Collection?', *Antiquity*, 49 (1975), 43–5.

From the very start our intention was not only to look at the changing chances of the city through time, but also to explore contemporary variations between one part of the city and another in successive phases of Winchester's development. At a rather superficial level this study of what some would now call intra-site variation was required as a foil to the study of the great buildings of church and state with which the project was concerned *ab initio*. Only thus could one really appreciate the role such structures played in contemporary society, the relative effort their construction and maintenance involved, and the quality of the achievement they represented.[1] At a more profound level, the study of the urban phenomenon required for the characterization of its successive phases a broadly based exploration of the fabric of the city, across the full range of variation in wealth, class, and occupation. This involved more than gross distinctions between castle, palace, and monastery on the one hand and the 'ordinary' inhabited areas of the city on the other. At an early stage in the Lower Brook Street excavation the problem was defined as distinguishing the typical and the exceptional, among the medieval houses on that site,[2] but it soon developed into a more sophisticated study of variation, both in the archaeology of the Lower Brook Street sites and in the study of the documentary evidence for the city as a whole from the eleventh century onwards.[3]

With many of these requirements in mind a scheme for the development of the Winchester project over a total term of ten years (1961–70) was sketched out in the back of the director's field notebook during the summer of 1964.[4] In the event an extra season was needed in 1971 to complete the necessary objectives, and even so some of the ideas of 1964 had been too ambitious to be practicable.[5] During those years the Iron Age enclosure was

[1] For a contrary view, provoked by the emergence of a truly 'new' medieval archaeology, see Joan Evans, 'Anniversary Address', *Antiquaries Journal*, 41 (1961), 152.

[2] III. Interim, p. 246.

[3] Winchester Studies 1 (*Winchester in the Early Middle Ages*) deals with the period from the late ninth to the late twelfth century on the basis of an edition and discussion of the Winton Domesday. Winchester Studies 2 (*Survey of Medieval Winchester*) by Dr Derek Keene covers essentially the period between the thirteenth and the sixteenth centuries and by tracing the tenure of virtually every tenement in the walled city and its ancient suburbs establishes the base for, and undertakes a comprehensive discussion of, the economic and social geography of medieval Winchester.

[4] Winchester Research Unit, SNB, vol. 61, p. 74.

[5] It envisaged, for example, the complete excavation of New Minster and much more work in Lower Brook Street than actually proved possible.

defined and dated. The Roman defences were investigated in detail at five points, and areas of the Roman town were thoroughly examined for the first time, including several streets, parts of the forum, a temple, five town houses, and a number of other buildings. The Anglo-Saxon cathedral, the Old Minster, was fully excavated except for the part lying below the present cathedral (Pls. 11, 12*a*). The New Minster was identified and its later domestic buildings explored. The royal castle was excavated at its northern end (Pl. 13); the bishop's palace completely explored (Pl. 14); in addition, two parish churches (Pl. 15*a*), three chapels (Pl. 13*b*), and twelve medieval houses (Pl. 15*b*) were uncovered. Most important, perhaps, was the demonstration that the street plan of medieval and modern Winchester derived from a deliberate act of urban refoundation in the later ninth century (Fig. 4).[1] All told, nineteen sites were investigated over eleven years at a total cost of £149,811, with the help of about 3,000 volunteers (no one was paid anything other than daily subsistence), from twenty-four countries.[2] Most of the work took place within the walls, where 11,612 m² (1.16 ha) were excavated to an average depth of 2.5 m. Outside the walls an additional 2,631 m² were investigated, usually to a much shallower depth. The cost of excavation (excluding Lankhills) worked out at £12·17 per m².

By 1966 it was already clear that the great mass of data resulting from the six seasons of excavation so far undertaken, together with that from the four seasons planned for 1967–70, could not be properly analysed and published on a part-time basis by volunteers. A visit to Poland at the invitation of Professor Witold Hensel of the Institute for the History of Material Culture of the Polish Academy of Sciences in September 1966, to see the work being carried on in Polish towns—especially, Wrocław, Poznań,

[1] II. Interim, pp. 215–17; III. Interim, p. 242; VIII. Interim, pp. 285–9; X. Interim, pp. 101–4; Martin Biddle and David Hill, 'Late Saxon Planned Towns', *Antiquaries Journal*, 51 (1971), 70–85; Winchester Studies, 1, pp. 277–82; and see below, pp. 325–32.

[2] For details of the development of the project and its administration, see I–X. Interims; Biddle, 'Winchester 1961–68', *Château Gaillard* iv (1969), 19–30; and idem, *Archaeology in Winchester* (typescript prepared for the new Winchester City District Council following local government reorganization, Apr. 1974). From 1964 to 1970 the University of North Carolina and Duke University in the United States played a vital role in the provision of both student volunteers and funds (£27,761 or 18.5 per cent of the total cost of the excavations), a collaboration pioneered by the late Professor Urban T. Holmes of the University of North Carolina.

Gdańsk, and Szczecin[1]—suggested that the best solution would be the creation for a period of years of a full-time team to undertake the work of preparing the results of the Winchester excavations and associated research for publication. As a result the Winchester Research Unit was set up in October 1968 to produce a series of eleven volumes of Winchester Studies for publication by the Clarendon Press at Oxford.[2] Three volumes have now been published, a fourth is in proof, and others are far advanced, several of them in their final stages of completion. The range of volumes reflects to the full the scope of the Winchester project. In addition to formal excavation reports, there are two volumes on the tenurial, economic, and social history of the medieval city, set firmly in a physical setting derived from documentary, topographical, and archaeological sources. Another volume deals with the production of the Winchester mint, an essential source for the economic and social history of the city between the late ninth century and the middle of the thirteenth, and is of special numismatic importance as only the second such study of a major mint. Other volumes deal with the medieval pottery of Winchester; with its crafts and industries; with its human and animal populations; and with the evidence for the environment of the city from the Roman period to the Middle Ages.

By the time the Winchester Research Unit began work in 1968, there had already been eight seasons of excavation and three more were to come. There was therefore never any real question of publishing in fascicules, although this was already established practice for urban excavations in the classical world, such as the Agora at Athens or Dura-Europos. Instead, we decided to publish the series of substantial, digested, thematic volumes which are now appearing. There is no doubt that this has taken a long time, and that the publication of a series of fascicules might have looked better, but I am reasonably sure that the late start of the Research Unit relative to the excavations themselves will in the end be seen as a blessing in disguise. Because each of the volumes is able to draw on the results of the whole excavation and all the associated research, it can be not only complete in itself, but can be selective

[1] For the Polish achievement, see, for example, Pierre Francastel (ed.), *Les origines des villes polonaises* (Paris, 1960); Witold Hensel, *Słowiańszczyzna wczesnośredniowieczna* (Warsaw, 1965), translated as *Die Slawen im frühen Mittelalter* (Berlin, 1965); idem, *La naissance de la Pologne* (Warsaw, 1966); and the fascicules of *Archaeologia Urbium* published under the auspices of the Union internationale des sciences préhistoriques et protohistoriques (Warsaw), Fasc. 1 (1966) et seqq.

[2] For a list, see Appendix B.

in a way in which a fascicule series published as the work goes along can never be. Moreover, the Winchester volumes, although admittedly expensive in themselves, are actually turning out somewhat cheaper, page for page, than fascicules. If one adds the saving which comes from avoiding unnecessary duplication in publication, a problem which unavoidably affects fascicules, the cost-effectiveness of the substantive volume may be considerable.

The need to be selective in publication, on grounds of both cost and clarity, became clear very early in the Winchester project. The methods of open-area excavation, developed initially as early as 1964–5 to deal with the complexities of medieval house sites continuously occupied for over five centuries in Lower Brook Street,[1] demanded plans as subtle and detailed as the sections, which had long been (and still continue to be) a fundamental element in British archaeological practice. The need to compare the plans of successive surfaces led to the introduction of dimensionally stable transparent drawing film which allowed us to lay one plan over another. A proper record of what our excavations were themselves destroying required the production of plans of a long sequence of successive surfaces. For example, the church of St Mary in Tanner Street required twenty-six plans properly to record the horizontal evidence of its long structural history, a sequence which provided the first-recorded pattern of change in the liturgical planning of an urban church over a period of more than half a millenium.[2] The detail to be recorded, much of it fundamental, also required the use, indeed the introduction, of colour on the drawings. These two factors—the quantity of the records and the use of colour—implied from the start that the days of publishing everything, if indeed they ever existed, were over, and in Winchester we never contemplated doing this.

The complexity of the records arose inevitably from an increasing awareness of the complexity of urban sites and the need to record this complexity as fully as possible if it was to be understood at all. An outline record, in my view, was worse than useless because it was itself a falsification, an oversimplification to the point where the result might be in very fact more misleading than informative. As an example of the kind of detail encountered—none of it to be dismissed as 'trivial'—let us take one trench of

[1] III. Interim, p. 245; IV. Interim, p. 313; Martin Biddle and Birthe Kjølbye-Biddle, 'Metres, Areas and Robbing', *World Archaeology*, 1 (1969–70), 208–19.

[2] VII. Interim, pp. 305–9, fig. 2; X Interim, pp. 312–14, fig. 15. The final publication will be in Winchester Studies 5.

63 m^2 in the excavation of Old Minster (CG 1966–8, Trench XXXIII; Pl. 12*a*): it included four robber-trenches, fourteen walls, twenty-nine pits, seven post-holes, 122 graves, and 893 layers. These required for their recording (and the list is not quite complete), 480 pages of notes in six notebooks; fifty-eight coloured plans of 961 m^2 of deposit at a scale of 1:20; seventy-nine coloured drawings of 209 m of section at a scale of 1:10; 172 photographs (149 in both black and white and colour); and some 5,000 level measurements. The excavation of this trench lasted for thirty-two weeks spread over three seasons, but it was only one of fifty-one trenches on the Cathedral Green between 1962 and 1970. The publication of such a complex in a single volume of Winchester Studies (Volume 4. i) requires the most careful selection and presentation of the evidence if a true and reliable picture is to be given. It also implies the need for adequate time fully to analyse such an archive in the course of preparing the final publication—and this is what the Winchester Research Unit is all about—as well as provision for the long-term public storage of all the detailed evidence upon which the distillation in the published volume is based. Why should we bother to store the evidence, once the final publication is out? Precisely because the record was made in the first place to be reinterrogated at any time in the future, in the light of new knowledge, new ideas, new parallels. Did we make the right deductions from what we thought we saw and recorded? Did we understand what we were recording? The published volumes of Winchester Studies will state our views. The recorded evidence—subjective as it may be—should be available as a primary source for as long as necessary, perhaps for ever, ready to support or disprove alternative interpretations.

This too was fully in mind when the Research Unit was set up in 1968. The indexing of the archive was one of our first concerns, partly to help ourselves, partly because the published volumes will carry references to the excavation archive, comparable to the references to documentary sources in our historical studies, which will enable the reader, however far away he or she may be, to call for copies of the original records to satisfy doubts or to form the base of a new view. The use of colour in the plans and sections caused us some initial concern, but consultation with representatives of IBM and Xerox in 1968 revealed that colour-xerography was on the way, and indeed it was with us ten years later.

Finding a home for the excavation archive—defined as the total information product: records, finds, samples, analyses, reports, computer discs and tapes—was for long a major problem, but after some years of uncertainty the Winchester City Council decided to go ahead with the conversion of Hyde House and Hyde Barn, outside North Gate, into an Historic Resources Centre.[1] This Centre, which is an integral part of the Winchester City Museums under the curator Miss E. R. Lewis, FMA, now houses the total information product of the work of 1961 to 1971 and of the Winchester Research Unit, as well as the results of previous and subsequent excavations in Winchester. It was opened in 1981 and is the first purpose-built archive of the kind in the country. It is the essential companion to the publication of our work in Winchester Studies.

The completion of the Winchester Excavation Committee's eleven-year programme of excavations in 1971 did not mean that the archaeology of Winchester was in any sense done and could now be left to gradual erosion by further development. Quite the reverse: with the knowledge gained from the work of 1961–71 it was now possible to define much more clearly the questions that should be asked. Moreover, the pace of development, far from slackening, was about to increase and an inner ring road seemed at last about to be built.

Although the City Museums had continued throughout the sixties to be responsible for the observation and recording of archaeological discoveries made during building works in the city, all excavations had been undertaken by the Committee. Now some new arrangement was necessary if rescue excavations were to take place in the future. Late in 1971 the City Council accepted the recommendation that a City Rescue Archaeologist should be appointed to take charge of all rescue archaeology in the city, including both the observation and recording of sites in the course of development and the conduct of excavations on threatened sites prior to the start of works. The first holder of the post was appointed early in 1972 and later the same year the current holder, Mr Kenneth Qualmann, was appointed in his stead. Following the reorganization of local government in 1974 the responsibilities of the office were extended to the whole of the new District. Until 1977 the Rescue Archaeologist and his staff were seconded to the Research Unit, which was responsible for the overall conduct and policy of his work, but in 1977, when a start

[1] See the printed proposal *Historic Resources Centre for Winchester* (Winchester City Council, 1976); *Rescue News*, 24 (Dec. 1980), 4; *Architectural Journal*, 14 Oct. 1981, pp. 736–7; Elizabeth Lewis, 'Winchester City Museums', in *Archaeological Storage* (Society of Museum Archaeologists and Yorkshire and Humberside Federation of Museums and Art Galleries, 1981), p. 34.

was made on running down the Research Unit, rescue archaeology reverted to the care of the City Museums where it remains.

In the eleven years since the office was established, rescue archaeology in Winchester has been very much a full-time activity.[1] Partly as a result of deliberate policy, partly because of the geographical concentration of major developments outside the walls, the work has been the perfect complement to that of 1961–71 (Fig. 1). Whereas the Excavation Committee (WEC) conducted fourth-fifths of its work inside the walls, the City Rescue Archaeologist (CRA) has done nine-tenths of his work in the suburbs:

	Years	Inside the walls	In the suburbs	Totals
WEC	1961–71	11,612 m²	2,631 m²	14,243 m²
CRA	1972–83	577 m²	5,263 m²	5,840 m²
Totals		12,189 m²	7,894 m²	20,083 m²

Knowledge of the Iron Age 'Oram's Arbour' enclosure has been considerably extended, particularly with regard to its entrances and subsequent influence on early Roman Winchester (Fig. 3). The Cirencester road has been studied in detail as it approaches North Gate, together with suburban developments along the road and cemeteries of the first to second and fourth to fifth centuries AD. Further information about the eastern and western cemeteries has also been recovered. The early medieval development of the northern and especially the western suburbs has been examined, and within the walls work has been carried out on the castle, on St Mary's Abbey (Nunnaminster), and as a preliminary to large-scale redevelopment of the central car park. The results are being prepared for publication in a series of volumes edited by Mr Kenneth Qualmann under the title *Winchester Excavations since 1972*.[2]

It is vital to stress the value of this work. Far from being an example of diminishing returns, the discoveries of 1972 onwards

[1] Kenneth Qualmann, 'Rescue Archaeology in the City of Winchester', *District Councils Review*, Mar. 1975; and the successive numbers of *Find* (Newsletter of the Winchester Archaeological Rescue Group), 1 (Oct. 1972)–43 (Sept. 1987), continued as *Winchester Museums Service Newsletter*, 1 (June, 1988) onwards.

[2] Vol. 1 will deal with excavations in the western suburbs; Vol. 2 with Wickham Glebe, a site in the District outside the former boundaries of the city; Vol. 3 with excavations in the northern suburbs. In some cases, where convenience or other circumstances dictate, reports or other results of the work of the City Rescue Archaeologist will be found in *Winchester Excavations*

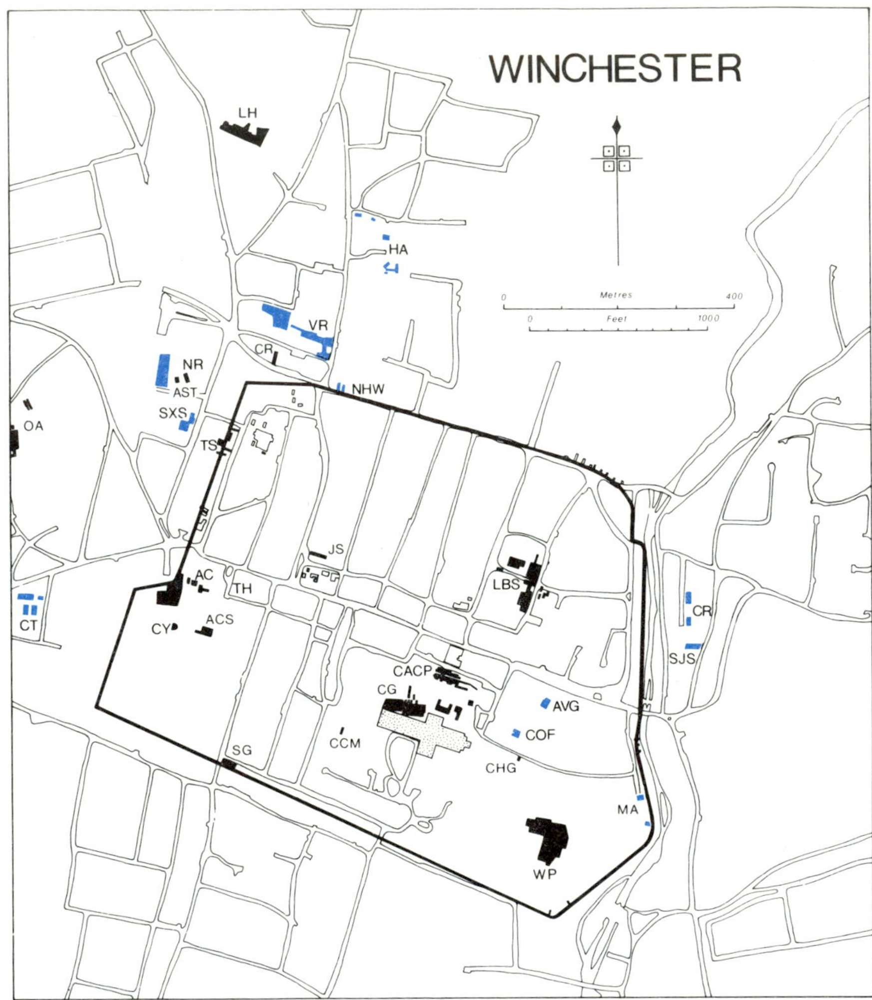

FIG. 1. Excavations in Winchester 1961–83: the continued investment. Sites excavated 1961–71 by the Winchester Excavations Committee (including Lankhills, excavated 1967–72 by the Winchester Schools Archaeological Committee) are shown in black; those excavated 1972–83 by the City Rescue Archaeologist are shown in blue.

have emphasized the importance of building on investment and of continuing work in a place where sufficient has been done to allow questions to be framed with precision and reframed to the degree

1949–1960 (see above, p. 300 n. 4), e.g. 'St. Paul's Church' in ibid. 2 (1978), 264–79 and cf. p. 1; or in Winchester Studies, e.g., the gazetteer of prehistoric and Roman sites in Winchester Studies, 3. i, or the account of the first excavation of part of the Nunnaminster (St Mary's Abbey) in Winchester Studies 4. i. For an especially important discovery, see also David A. Hinton, Suzanne Keene, and Kenneth E. Qualmann, 'The Winchester Reliquary', *Medieval Archaeology* 25 (1981), 45–77.

where reasonably sophisticated answers can be obtained. The City Council and the Department of the Environment are to be congratulated for taking this view and for not accepting the simplistic argument, heard all too often in the stress of funding crisis, that 'it's all been done' or 'there can't be any more to do'. The extent to which the investment of over thirty years of archaeological and historical research into Winchester now allows us to formulate questions for future inquiry is the subject of the next sections of this lecture. Questions such as these will only be answered by the continued activity of the City Rescue Archaeologist and his voluntary support-group WARG (the Winchester Archaeological Rescue Group) in the context of the city as a designated area of archaeological importance under the 1979 Act.[1] The City Council is now proposing to designate the whole of the ancient walled city and suburbs as such an area and is one of the first local authorities attempting to do so under the Act.[2]

II

The excavations of 1961–71 investigated just under 2 per cent of the walled area, a figure which the work of 1972–83 has barely affected. One must ask whether any generalizing statements about the city's past can be justified on so limited a base. The answer is that the sites comprising the 2 per cent were themselves carefully selected with both general and specific problems in mind and that, justified or not, such statements must be made, if only as the starting-points for the next stage of enquiry. But the smallness of the evidential foundation must be kept in mind at all times: it is indeed the reason for some of the more radical questions and ideas I intend to propose. The existence of an increasing body of documentary evidence from the eleventh century onwards provides, of course, a wider context in which ideas derived from the inevitably much more limited archaeological base can be tested, but one must remember that the kinds of interpretation derived from the archaeological evidence may not be testable through the documents and vice versa. For the first thousand years of Winchester's existence, however, the problem scarcely arises, for although almost the entire development of the city belongs to the period of literacy in Britain, its history as a town before the tenth, perhaps even the eleventh century, is unwritten. We are dealing

[1] Ancient Monuments and Archaeological Areas Act 1979.

[2] Qualmann, 'Designation of an "Archaeological Area" at Winchester', *Find*, 32 (Jan. 1984), 11–14.

throughout this early period as regards most aspects of Winchester—certainly its urban aspects—if not with a prehistoric, then at most with a protohistoric community.

Let us look first at the only general interpretation of the origin and development of Winchester published so far (Fig. 2). It appeared in 1965, and was revised in 1968 and again in 1975.[1] This model stressed topographical change, especially increase and contraction in the occupied area. It made the point that in the course of many centuries an urban community could wax and wane, changing, perhaps more than once, from urban to non-urban status and back again. This aspect seemed especially important because discussion of the 'continuity question' was often hampered then—it is even now—by an imprecision of terms. Continuity of urban life is something quite different from continuity of life in former urban places. Until this was clear, the discussion could not (and did not) proceed.

The gross changes revealed in these diagrams have now been plotted for a number of other towns, large and small.[2] The exercise has been useful. It provides several bases for comparison between towns and it brings out many points of both general and detailed change—the establishment of a street plan, the growth of a suburb, the presence or absence of major topographical, social, and economic units, such as a castle or a religious house—but useful as they may be in making comparisons and in calling attention to relationships in time and space, such diagrams are only a very simple tool. What they reflect, like topographical change itself, are profound alterations of function in urban places. The definition of such functional change should be a fundamental goal of urban archaeology and of urban history in general, and it is in the framework of functional change that I want briefly to review our current knowledge of the development of early Winchester.

A good case can be made out for describing the site of Winchester as a preferred location for settlement. This presumably reflects the natural advantages of valley and downland which were exploited from at least the second millennium BC for travel on routes which crossed at the site of Winchester.[3] The Iron Age

[1] *Science Journal*, Mar. 1965, pp. 4–5; VI. Interim, fig. 1; X. Interim, fig. 21.

[2] For example, London, Biddle and Hudson, op. cit. above, p. 300 n. 3, fig. 9; and Saffron Walden, S. R. Bassett, *Saffron Walden: Excavations and Research 1972–80* (Council for British Archaeology, Research Report 45, London, 1982), fig. 4.

[3] Initial discussion in C. F. C. Hawkes, J. N. L. Myres, and C. G. Stevens, *St. Catharine's Hill, Winchester* (Winchester, 1930), pp. 5–6, fig. 3; for Middle and Late Bronze Age sites at and in the immediate vicinity of Winchester, see Sonia Chadwick Hawkes, 'Finds from Two Middle Bronze Age Pits at

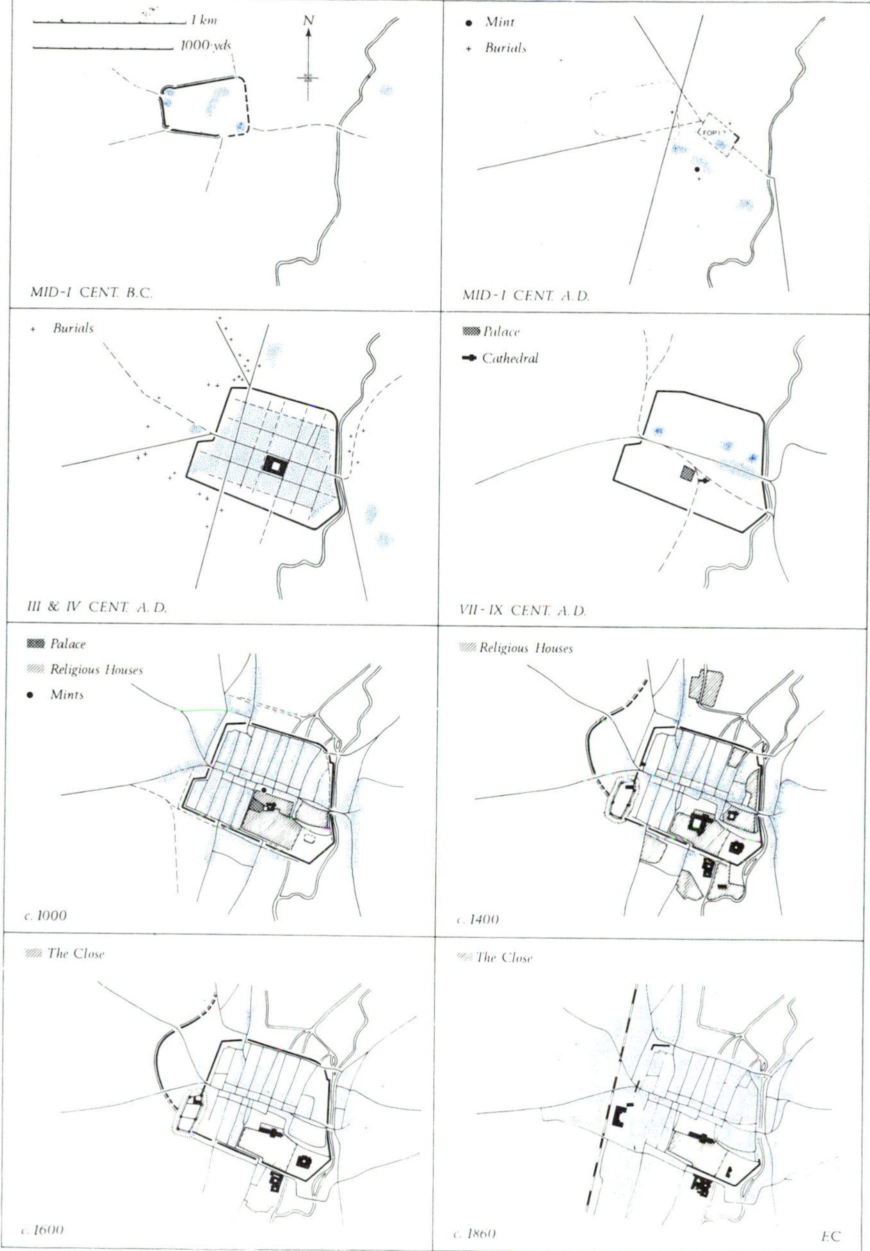

FIG. 2. The development of Winchester. Occupied areas stippled in blue. (Revised to 1983.)

Winnall, Winchester, Hampshire', *Proceedings of the Hampshire Field Club*, 26 (1969), 5–18, esp. fig. 1; Collis, *Winchester Excavations 1949–60*, 2 (1978), 109, 121, 161, 200 (*pace* Collis, p. 4, the evidence clearly shows that Bronze Age activity was *relatively* intense in the area); and, for the latest (1982) discoveries at Easton Lane, Richard Whinney in *Find*, 29 (Jan. 1983), 5–10.

hillfort on St Catharine's Hill, preceded from perhaps the fifth century BC by an unenclosed settlement on that dominating and isolated down, reflects the growing centrality of the Winchester area in the third century.[1]

On the opposite side of the valley, on the site of the later walled city, a local concentration of settlement is characterized by the same kind of pottery (the 'St Catharine's Hill Group') as is found in the later phases on St Catharine's Hill.[2] Enclosed settlement on the Hill and unenclosed settlement at Winchester are probably in part contemporary, but at Winchester the pottery tradition seems to develop further than on the Hill, where the entrance to the hillfort was burnt and the site abandoned perhaps about 100 BC.

During the currency of pottery types of the St Catharine's Hill Group an area of 16 ha (41 acres) on the Winchester site was enclosed by a line of bank and ditch (Fig. 3). The enclosure lies on the hill slope, partly below the north-west corner of the Roman town, but mostly without and to the west of the walled area. Entrances have been excavated at Oram's Arbour on the west and tentatively identified at the point where Romsey Road now crosses the ditch to the south-west, at Trafalgar House to the south, and at the site of the later North Gate.[3]

Three major questions remain unsettled: the status of this enclosed settlement; the period during which it was in use; and its relationship to the Roman town.

Collis considers that the Oram's Arbour enclosed settlement did not cross 'the threshold of urbanisation',[4] but there is much to support the opposite view. The scale of the public works involved in making the bank and ditch (1.7 km, 1.06 miles, in length); the area enclosed (16.5 ha, 84 per cent larger than the area enclosed on St Catharine's Hill); the multiple entrances with their evident relationship to the long-distance routes of the area; the presence of imported amphorae of Dressel Type I (from the lower, but not the lowest, fill of the ditch);[5] and the remarkable concentration of native and imported coins, Ptolemaic, Massiliot, and Gaulish;[6] all

[1] Christopher Hawkes, 'St. Catharine's Hill, Winchester: the Report of 1930 Re-assessed', in D. W. Harding (ed.), *Hillforts* (London, New York, San Francisco, 1976), pp. 59–74.

[2] Cunliffe, *Winchester Excavations 1949–60*, 1 (1964), 1–6; Collis, *Winchester Excavations 1949–60*, 2 (1978), 3–6.

[3] X. Interim, pp. 98–100, fig. 1.

[4] *Winchester Excavations 1949–60*, 2 (1978), 6.

[5] X. Interim, pp. 99–100.

[6] Biddle, 'Ptolemaic Coins from Winchester, *Antiquity*, 49 (1975), 213–15, fig. 1, based on the work of the late Mr Derek Allen to be published in Winchester Studies 3. i.

these make a case for a pre-Roman oppidum at Winchester albeit not in the immediate pre-Roman period.

The chronological problems are indeed formidable: not only the fine chronology involved in deciding which components of this settlement belong together (for example, which of the coins derives instead from the earliest Roman activity on the site),[1] but also the chronology of the enclosed settlement itself. The defences were certainly constructed after, perhaps long after, the first appearance of pottery of the St Catharine's Hill Group on the site; they were probably constructed after, perhaps well after, the abandonment of St Catharine's Hill itself. But how long do they continue to define an associated settlement? Pottery of what might be a later, even an immediately pre-Roman, phase occurs in the latest pre-Roman filling of the Iron Age ditch on the Assize Courts site. Its significance is quite unclear. Does it represent continued use of the enclosure, or its disuse and the shift of settlement south and east into areas of Winchester which have never been archaeologically examined (cf. Fig. 1)? How long, if at all, was the site deserted before the Roman arrival? And to what extent do we mean 'desertion' as an absolute or a relative description?

The problem is of particular importance in relation to the role played by the Oram's Arbour earthwork in the emergence of Roman Winchester. It has been clear for some time that the presence of the Iron Age earthworks had a considerable topographical effect—but that could be due simply to their bulk, to their role as relict features and 'morphological frames' long after they had gone out of use. As work goes on, however, the closeness of the mesh between the earthworks and the earliest Roman roads becomes ever more striking (Fig. 3): it now looks as if the Cirencester and Silchester roads are making for an Iron Age entrance on the site of North Gate, and the Old Sarum road for an entrance at the south-west corner of the Iron Age enclosure. The entrance excavated at Oram's Arbour in 1967 was likewise occupied by a Roman road, albeit a late and minor one.

The significance of these observations will only become clear with further work on the Iron Age earthworks themselves, on the settlement they enclose, and on the early Roman long-distance

[1] On this problem, and for the differing views of Collis and Cunliffe on the status of pre-Roman Winchester, see Cunliffe (ed.), *Coinage and Society in Britain and Gaul: Some Current Problems* (Council for British Archaeology, Research Report 38, 1981), p. 54, cf. fig. 15, and see the review by P. H. Robinson, *British Numismatic Journal*, 51 (1981), 204–5.

roads. Enough has been said, however, to indicate how twenty years of intermittent observation and excavation have only served to stress and to define, but not to solve the problems of Iron Age Winchester and of the beginnings of urbanization in the Itchen valley.

This short consideration of pre-Roman Winchester has already served to define a brief florescence—whether urban or not—which probably died away before the Roman arrival. It has also shown how very incomplete our evidence is. When we turn to the origins and subsequent fortunes of the walled city of 58.2 ha (143.8 acres), we must always remember that only 1.22 ha (3.01 acres) has been excavated within the walls in the last twenty-two years (1961–83): a mere 2.1 per cent. Obviously something can be added to this for the excavations of 1949–60, and to allow for the sites which have been observed in the course of building work, but in both these categories the quality of the evidence is less than satisfactory. This very small percentage—2.1 per cent—means not only that we must be cautious in putting forward general views (or at least cautious in how much weight we put upon them), but also that we must be very careful indeed in arguing from negative evidence. In urban archaeology as a whole, not least in Winchester, negative evidence is at best a dangerous and often, perhaps usually, a misleading guide.

Roman Winchester (*Venta Belgarum*) was the fifth largest city of Roman Britain in terms of walled area and, as its name implies, the principal town of the *civitas* of the Belgae. Like many of the other towns of Roman Britain, the Roman origins of *Venta* may be with the establishment of a military fort,[1] intended here, as elsewhere, to control important routes and a centre of British settlement (dispersed settlement, perhaps, if the Oram's Arbour enclosure was by then abandoned). The earliest phases of Roman Winchester are extremely difficult to reach: over nearly half the walled area they are waterlogged and everywhere they are covered by deep medieval deposits of the greatest complexity and interest. There are hints, however, that the earliest stages of Roman Winchester are anything but simple: the course and early date of the Silchester–Bitterne road;[2] its route to the west of the supposed

[1] X. Interim, pp. 296–7, figs. 10, 11, and 21. No further discoveries relating to the possible fort have been made since 1971.

[2] At South Gate (X. Interim, p. 110) this road precedes the early Flavian timber gate and runs north to North Gate on a line which appears unrelated to the possible fort in the flood-plain to the east (cf. here fig. 2, mid first century AD).

fort and its relationship to the Iron Age earthwork (Fig. 2); the early and unexplained salient at the south-west angle of the later first-century defences; and the gradual realization that there is a street layout in and outside the north-west corner of the walled area on a different alignment to the rest of the street grid[1]—all these suggest that our knowledge of early *Venta* is a sketch, and possibly a misleading one at that.

We are perhaps on slightly safer ground from the Flavian period onwards. Whatever went before, the evidence from all over the town suggests a massive intensification of activity. Defences of earth and timber were thrown up to south, west, and north on the line that was to be followed by all subsequent walls; the main street grid was laid out; and thoroughly Romanized timber buildings with tiled roofs, painted walls, glazed windows, and the occasional mosaic floor were constructed. This marks the first phase of full urbanization. Whether the previous Roman phases were urban, or simply the surviving *vici* of an earlier military occupation, we do not yet know, but there is no doubt that the establishment of full urban status was sudden and that it took place in the seventies of the first century AD. The immediate reasons for this change may be in part political or dynastic, as has been suggested,[2] but the change would have been stillborn had it not responded to underlying processes which fostered the existence of an economic, social, and administrative centre at *Venta*.

III

It is not possible to trace here the development of *Venta* in the second, third, and earlier fourth centuries.[3] In the sequence of its defences, public buildings and town houses, it seems, so far as we can see, to have followed a pattern common to the Roman towns of south-central Britain. Shortly after AD 350 the character of the town changed, perhaps quite suddenly. All seven of the town houses of which sufficient is known went out of use at this time.[4] In most cases they were demolished and their sites cleared and

[1] I am grateful to Mr K. Qualmann for this information.

[2] Anthony A. Barrett, 'The Career of Tiberius Claudius Cogidubnus', *Britannia*, 10 (1979), 227–42, esp. 240; cf. J. E. Bogaers, 'King Cogidubnus in Chichester: Another Reading of *RIB* 91', ibid., pp. 243–54, esp. pp. 252–4.

[3] Winchester Studies, 3. i will include a full discussion, together with a gazetteer of all previous discoveries relating to prehistoric and Roman Winchester.

[4] Cathedral Car Park, Building 1 (S.E.): I. Interim, pp. 155–6 (demolition redated to *c*.350); Wolvesey Palace, Buildings West 1, East 1A, 1B, 2, 3: X. Interim, pp. 321–4, fig. 17; and houses in Middle Brook Street and St George's Street.

fenced. In some cases industrial activity, or a kind of domestic use very different from what had gone before, took over. In one case a small, rectangular, two-roomed structure was built alongside a street over part of a demolished house. This two-roomed building cannot have been built before the second half of the fourth century; in its date and situation it recalls a comparable structure found by Professor Frere in Dorchester on Thames in 1962.[1] At the same time occupation, as reflected in the distribution of pottery and coins, seems to have spread for the first time over the whole walled area of Winchester, the western third of which, at least, had until then been only lightly used. This extended occupation is characterized by the 'dark earth' layer which is found all over the walled area on top of the Roman deposits,[2] and also by the presence for the first time in the Roman period of relatively large quantities of iron-working residues.[3]

The disuse of houses and the presence of the 'dark earth' have usually been taken as evidence of 'decline' or 'decay'. It is doubtful, however, if this view can be maintained. The town's defences were strengthened in the second half of the fourth century by the addition of bastions, one of which has been partly excavated at South Gate and a second tentatively identified to the south of West Gate.[4] Outside the walls, although the suburbs may be smaller, there appears to be a remarkable increase in the size of the cemeteries.[5] Kenneth Qualmann has estimated that, of the

[1] X. Interim, pp. 324–6; cf. Sheppard Frere, 'Excavations at Dorchester on Thames, 1962', *Archaeological Journal*, 119 (1962), 120–3, figs. 5 and 6, and idem, 'The End of Towns in Roman Britain', in J. S. Wacher (ed.), *The Civitas Capitals of Roman Britain* (Leicester, 1966), p. 94. For a rural building of the same type and date, see D. S. Neal, *The Excavation of the Roman Villa in Gadebridge Park, Hemel Hempstead, 1963–8* (Society of Antiquaries, Research Report 31, London 1974), pp. 57–8, fig. 32, pl. xix*a* (Building E).

[2] R. I. Macphail, 'Soil and Botanical Studies of the Dark Earth', in M. Jones and G. W. Dimbleby (eds.), *The Environment of Man* (British Archaeological Reports, British Series 87, Oxford 1981), pp. 309–31; and idem., 'The Micromorphology of Dark Earth from Gloucester, London and Norwich: an Analysis of Urban Anthropogenic Deposits from the Late Roman to Early Medieval Periods in England', in P. Bullock and C. Murphy (eds.), *Soil Micromorphology*, i (Proceedings of the International Working-Meeting on Soil Micromorphology, Aug. 1981, Oxford, 1983), 245–52.

[3] Identified by R. F. Tylecote and quantified by R. Davies and D. L. Long for publication in Winchester Studies, 3. i and 7. ii.

[4] For the bastion at South Gate, see X. Interim, pp. 115–16; the possible bastion south of West Gate is reported (pers. comm.) by Mr K. Qualmann as a result of his excavations against the outside of the Roman city wall at the south end of Castle Avenue.

[5] See Winchester Studies, 3. ii, pp. 5–7, figs. 1 and 2.

approximately 1,300 graves so far recorded, over a thousand belong to the third and fourth centuries, and most of these to the fourth century. Nor is there any indication of any marked decrease in burial in the second half of the fourth century.[1]

All this suggests that *Venta* underwent a considerable change in the later fourth century, but not that it was necessarily in decline or decay.[2] To the contrary, one could argue from the size and density of the occupied area, from the evidence of industrial activity and from the cemeteries, that late Roman Winchester was more urban than it had ever been. The closest parallel might be a densely occupied, industrially and commercially active, pre-Roman oppidum,[3] or its post-Roman analogue, a maritime trading and industrial settlement such as Anglo-Saxon Southampton.[4]

Late Roman *Venta* was clearly different from what had gone before. The city was not kept clean and the roads were no longer swept and regravelled, but it was occupied and it was defended. What sort of place was it? A useful analogy may perhaps be provided in reverse by the changes which took place in late medieval and early modern Winchester.[5] The textile industry and commercial functions of medieval Winchester finally collapsed in the sixteenth and early seventeenth centuries to be replaced in the later seventeenth century by the rise of the city as a centre for county society, characterized by large town houses and an expanding retail market serving both the specialized needs of the gentry and the increased purchasing power of those dependent on them. The administrative role of the city as an ecclesiastical and legal centre continued throughout, but it is interesting to observe

[1] For example, at Lankhills in the northern cemetery, Winchester Studies, 3. ii, pp. 113–22; or at Chester Road in the eastern, *Find*, 21 (May 1980), 3–4, and phased plans. At Victoria Road, outside North Gate, a new cemetery came into use *c.*350, *Find*, 11 (winter 1975), 5–7.

[2] Cf. Susan Reynolds, 'Decline and Decay in Late Medieval Towns: a Look at some of the Concepts and Arguments', *Urban History Yearbook 1980*, pp. 76–8. For another view of late Romano-British towns, see Richard Reece, 'Town and Country: the end of Roman Britain', *World Archaeology*, 12 (1980), 77–92.

[3] See Barry Cunliffe and Trevor Rowley, *Oppida in Barbarian Europe* (British Archaeological Reports, Supplementary Series 11, Oxford, 1976).

[4] See now Philip Holdsworth, *Excavations at Melbourne Street, Southampton, 1971–76* (Southampton Archaeological Research Committee, Report 1; Council for British Archaeology, Research Report 33, London, 1980) with full bibliography; see also idem, 'Saxon Southampton; a New Review', *Medieval Archaeology*, 20 (1976), 26–61.

[5] Adrienne Rosen, 'Winchester in Transition, 1580–1700', in Peter Clark (ed.), *Country Towns in Pre-industrial England* (Leicester, 1981), pp. 143–95.

that when that administrative role also faltered, for example in the 1540s after the Dissolution and in the 1640s during the Civil War, Winchester's fortunes reached their lowest ebb.

The analogy between Roman *Venta* of the late first to mid fourth centuries and later seventeenth-century Winchester is clear: both were administrative centres with a special attraction for the gentry and retail markets to suit their needs. The difference may be that, whereas in the sixteenth century Winchester was abandoning its industrial function, in the later fourth century *Venta* changed rather rapidly, perhaps very suddenly, in the reverse direction, facilities for the gentry, such as town houses, being removed in favour of something very different.

The very small area examined within the walls must counsel caution: change in one area, even in several areas of the walled town, might not apply to other areas, but the functional change suggested here as a model for the later fourth century can be tested as further sites become available.

Was Winchester in the later fourth century urban, or was it simply a military or industrial centre, or all three? They are, after all, not necessarily exclusive functions. We cannot yet answer this question, but the place-name may provide a clue.[1] In common with most other Romano-British *civitas* capitals, the tribal element in the name *Venta Belgarum* was lost. Subsequently *Venta* acquired the Old English suffix *ceaster*. The usual view would see the element *ceaster* as a generalized Old English description for a Roman walled town or ruin, derived from Latin *castrum*, but without specific military meaning.[2] The stages by which *Venta Belgarum* became *Wintanceaster* seem, however, to merit further and comparative study, to establish whether the sequence might have included the usage *Castrum Venta* or *Venta castrum* in the military sense. Late Roman *Venta* with its refurbished defences, plentiful population, industrial activity, and internal compounds, might after all have had an important military function, if not as a fortress, then as a defended administrative base and supply centre dealing with the *annona militaris*.[3] The *gynaeceum* at *Venta* mentioned

[1] For the importance of place-names in general for the study of early Winchester, see Winchester Studies, 1, pp. 231–9.

[2] See the valuable discussion, stressing the need for further work on this place-name element, by Margaret Gelling, *Signposts to the Past* (London, 1979), pp. 151–3.

[3] For the *annona* itself, see Walter Goffart, *Caput and Colonate: towards a History of Late Roman Taxation* (Toronto, 1974), pp. 31–54; and for the suggestion that the defended towns were important for the protection of the *annona*, see Derek A. Welsby, *The Roman Military Defence of the British Provinces in its Later*

in the *Notitia Dignitatum* would be entirely at home in such a base and might even be its *raison d'être*.[1] The production of textiles in a *gynaeceum* would leave archaeological traces, but conditions for the recovery and correct interpretation of the fulling and dyeing vats, the weaving and drying sheds, would be difficult to fulfil in a town where the later Roman levels have been so damaged by subsequent activity.[2] The search for such traces remains nevertheless a high priority. The possibility of a textile industry of this date stresses the aptness of the analogy drawn earlier between late Roman and later medieval Winchester. The closing down of a *gynaeceum* in 407 might also account for the sudden collapse of later Roman Winchester seen so vividly in the abandonment of organized burial in the cemeteries which until that collapse provide some of the best evidence for the city's continued existence.[3]

IV

If this view can be maintained, it emphasizes that the explanation of urban change in Winchester is closely related to change in function imposed by external requirements. The long period on which Winchester now enters, covering at least four centuries, from the fifth to the ninth, is both initiated and terminated by such a response to external process; in the one case, the economic and social dislocation attendant on the end of empire; in the other, the growing productive capability and consequently enhanced internal and external trade of the emerging English kingdoms.

During this long period Winchester was not an urban place, if the essential elements of urbanism include the presence of a relatively large and concentrated population engaged in

Phases (British Archaeological Reports, British Series 101, Oxford, 1982), pp. 146–56, esp. p. 153.

[1] J. P. Wild, 'The *Gynaeceum* at *Venta* and its Context', *Latomus*, 26 (1967), 648–76, concludes that of the three possibilities 'Winchester on the face of it appears to be the best choice for the site of the *gynaeceum*' (p. 676). W. H. Manning in *Antiquity*, 40 (1966), 60–2 argued that Caistor-by-Norwich (*Venta Icenorum*) could not be excluded. Cf. Sheppard Frere, *Britannia* (London, 1967), p. 300, and Peter Salway, *Roman Britain* (Oxford, 1981), p. 656.

[2] Cf., for example, the damage done to the Romano-Celtic temple in Lower Brook Street by medieval pits and foundation trenches: X. Interim, pl. L, cf. fig. 10.

[3] An abandonment never so clearly seen as in the rapid fading out of burials at the edge of the Lankhills cemetery: Winchester Studies, 3. ii, pl. ii, cf. fig. 105; see here Pl. 12*b*.

industrial and commercial activities which set it off from the surrounding countryside.

I have long argued, however, that the former city remained of considerable importance throughout this period as a centre from which authority was traditionally exercised.[1] The authority hypothesis was developed from the work of Carl-Richard Brühl on the Gallic *civitates*[2] and was a response to the need to produce a coherent explanation of the focal role apparently played by former Romano-British towns far into the early Middle Ages.[3] In the case of Winchester, the need was to find a general theory which would explain the relative concentration of sixth-century pagan Anglo-Saxon cemeteries around the city as well as the selection of Winchester in the seventh century as the site of a bishopric. The development of the argument need not be gone into again. The basic suggestion is that authority over the late Roman town, together with its *territorium* and perhaps a large part of its *civitas*, passed into the hands of those who had been entrusted with its defence. In whatever ways this group was formed and modified by external influences—and there is no space here to deal with the complex interaction of British and Germanic elements in the rise of Wessex[4]—it exercised its authority from the original seat of that authority in the former *civitas* capital, and more precisely from a site in or adjacent to the basilica of the forum, just to the west and north of the present cathedral.[5]

Does the theory stand up? A recent attempt to refute it has nothing to put in its place other than the old view—unhelpful in

[1] First argued in Biddle, 'Archaeology and the Beginnings of English Society', in P. Clemoes and K. Hughes (eds.), *England Before the Conquest* (Cambridge, 1971), pp. 393–6, and taken further in idem, 'The Development of the Anglo-Saxon Town', in *Topografia urbana e vita cittadina nell'alto medioevo in occidente* i (Settimane di studio xxi, Spoleto, 1974), 203–30, esp. 206–12; idem, 'Winchester: the Development of an Early Capital', op. cit. in p. 326 n. 1 below, pp. 237–41; and idem, 'Towns' in Wilson (ed.), op. cit. in p. 325 n. 1 below, pp. 105–6.

[2] Carl-Richard Brühl, *Palatium und civitas*, i, *Gallien* (Cologne, 1975); idem, 'Die Stätten der Herrschaftsausübung in der frühmittelalterlichen Stadt', in *Topografia urbana e vita cittadina nell'alto medioevo in occidente*, ii, (Settimane di studio, xxi, Spoleto, 1974), 621–40.

[3] Biddle, 'Towns', in Wilson (ed.), op. cit. in p. 325 n. 1 below, pp. 103–12.

[4] Biddle, 'Hampshire and the Origins of Wessex', in G. de G. Sieveking *et al.* (eds.), *Problems in Economic and Social Archaeology* (London, 1976), pp. 323–42.

[5] For the Anglo-Saxon royal palace in Winchester, see Winchester Studies, 1, pp. 289–92; and for its site and possible antiquity, see Biddle, 'The Development of an Early Capital', op. cit. in p. 326 n. 1 below, pp. 237–40 and fig. 2. The whole question will be reviewed in Winchester Studies 4. i.

the wider context of Winchester's urban history—that the re-emergence of Winchester in the seventh century was because it 'was probably chosen as the site of the new see in accordance with the wishes of the West Saxon clergy'.[1] This statement fails to account for the concentration of pre-Christian settlements reflected in the presence of fifth- to seventh-century cemeteries near the city, and ignores the need to explain the function and functioning of a missionary see distant, *ex argumento*, from a royal residence, granted that such a residence would only be occupied intermittently as one in a series of royal estates between which the king was constantly on the move. More important, this rejection of the authority hypothesis dismisses the generalizing character of the proposition. In addition, evidence is accumulating, for example from York[2] and Lincoln,[3] for just that continued use of central administrative buildings long into the post-Roman period which the theory suggests and which Brühl's original work in Gaul found so compelling.

In Winchester the authority hypothesis can finally be tested only by excavation of the site of the Anglo-Saxon royal palace. This lies immediately west of Old Minster and is either on or beside the basilica of the Roman forum. Investigation of this key area may lie far in the future, but evidence relevant to the nature of fifth- to ninth-century Winchester may come from any site in or near the town. Germanic pottery of fifth-century date was first recorded in Winchester on the Lower Brook Street site in 1970, in the tenth year of our excavations.[4] It is worth stressing this point, for it emphasizes how valueless negative evidence can be. By 1970 there had been twenty years of excavation and recording in Winchester, yet no pagan Anglo-Saxon pottery had previously been recognized. In 1970 and 1971 it was recorded on seven sites

[1] Barbara Yorke, 'The Foundation of the Old Minster and the Status of Winchester in the Seventh and Eighth Centuries', *Proceedings of the Hampshire Field Club*, 38 (1982), 75–83.

[2] B. Hope-Taylor, *Under York Minster: Archaeological Discoveries, 1966–1971* (York, 1971); A. D. Phillips, 'Excavations at York Minster, 1967–73', *Friends of York Minster, Annual Report*, 46 (1975).

[3] M. J. Jones and B. J. J. Gilmour, 'Lincoln, Principia and Forum: a Preliminary Report', *Britannia*, 11 (1980), 61–72; B. J. J. Gilmour, 'The Anglo-Saxon Church at St Paul-in-the-Bail, Lincoln', *Medieval Archaeology*, 23 (1979), 214–18. The Roman forum and the seventh-century church have been brought together in a striking diagrammatic reconstruction by Warwick Rodwell, *The Archaeology of the English Church* (London, 1981), p. 144, fig. 69, which shows that the church was constructed in the forum courtyard in a formal architectural relationship to the surrounding colonnade.

[4] IX. Interim, pp. 101–2, fig. 3.

scattered all over the walled area and has since been found in the suburbs.[1]

While some of this pottery is certainly of fifth-century date, the majority probably belongs to the sixth century or later.[2] Its discovery[3] at several different points in the city probably indicates the location of a number of discrete settlement areas of this date, the high social status of which is indicated by the residence excavated in Lower Brook Street in 1971.[4] An early stage was marked by a small cemetery, one burial in which contained a necklace with gold and garnet pendants and a collar of silver rings.[5] At a later stage this complex included timber buildings, a stone building, perhaps of two storeys (Pl. 15*a*), and evidence for the assaying and working of gold and for bone working.[6] At present I would see such complexes as residential enclosures of thegn-status scattered here and there in the walled area, comparable in all essentials to the postulated royal residence, and perhaps only occupied intermittently by their owners, probably when the king was also in residence in the city.

The threads of continuity between Roman *Venta* and Anglo-Saxon Winchester can thus with some degree of probability be explained by the continuing exercise of authority from a traditional centre. With the advent of Christianity in the mid seventh century these threads become clearer, but the archaeological evidence continues with increasing precision to indicate that they stretch

[1] X. Interim, pp. 117, 303, 326. Study of the pottery from the excavations of 1961–71 has subsequently shown that grass- or chaff-tempered pottery, some with distinctive early Anglo-Saxon decorative features, occurs in small quantities on most of the sites. Mr K. Qualmann tells me that it has since been found during rescue excavations in the suburbs.

[2] Dr. Helena Hamerow has examined the decorated sherds and Miss Katherine Barclay the grass-tempered material. I am grateful to them for their comments which will be pbulished in Winchester Studies, 7.i, forthcoming.

[3] In the previously published version of this paper reference was made to 'imported glass of the fifth to seventh centuries'. Re-examination of this material has shown that some if not most of this glass could equally well be of late Roman date. The whole problem will be discussed in the light of scientific analyses in Winchester Studies, 3.i, forthcoming.

[4] X. Interim, pp. 303–10. Other units of this kind are probably indicated by Ealhswith's estate (see below, p. 325 and n. 3) and by the place-name *Coiteburi* (see Winchester Studies, 1, p. 236), to the south and north of the eastern end of High Street respectively.

[5] Ibid., pp. 303–5, fig. 13; see also Sonia Chadwick Hawkes in Winchester Studies, 7. ii, forthcoming.

[6] X. Interim, p. 309; for the gold and bone working, see Winchester Studies, 7. ii, forthcoming.

back into the days when *Venta* was a centre of regional administration in Roman Britain.

V

This long period was brought to an end in the ninth century by a new movement of urban foundation in Wessex.[1] One of the major results of the excavations of 1961–71 was to show that the street plan of medieval Winchester was created in a single action at some time in the late ninth century and certainly before 901–3 when some of the streets were used as boundaries in defining the site of New Minster at the time of its foundation.[2]

Of the four elements of which the street plan is composed (Fig. 4)—High Street, the back streets flanking High Street to either side, the north–south streets, and the wall or intramural street which runs round immediately inside the city wall—two are used in the New Minster bounds: north–south streets and the back street south of High Street. The other two elements appear for the first time in the bounds of Ealhswith's tenement, which became the site of Nunnaminster. These bounds, which are no later than Ealhswith's death in 902, refer specifically to *ceapstræt* (High Street), and in mentioning the two double fords (i.e. four fords) on the course of the boundary from north to south just inside the east wall of the city imply the existence of the wall street by this date.[3]

The wall street brought the street layout and the defensive circuit into an integrated system, exactly in the manner of Roman military planning, allowing the defenders to concentrate quickly using interior lines at any threatened point of the defences. The date of the refurbishing of the defences should therefore be that of the laying out of the new street system; the streets should at least be no older. On this basis the street system has been dated to the years

[1] Biddle, 'Towns', in David M. Wilson (ed.), *The Archaeology of Anglo-Saxon England* (London, 1976), pp. 124–34.

[2] P. H. Sawyer, *Anglo-Saxon Charters: an Annotated List and Bibliography* (London, 1968), no. 1443. For a new edition, see Winchester Studies, 4. iii, no. ii. The significance of this charter for the topography and date of the Winchester street plan has been recognized since Martin Biddle and David Hill, 'Late Saxon Planned Towns', *Antiquaries Journal*, 51 (1971), 76, but the information could not be fully utilized until it was realized that the streets used as bounds could be identified with now vanished streets which formed part of the original street plan in the south-eastern quarter of the city (see Winchester Studies, 1, p. 278 n. 1). The matter will be fully discussed in Winchester Studies, 4. i.

[3] Sawyer 1560. For a new edition, see Winchester Studies, 4. iii, no. i and discussion ibid. 4. i.

between *c*.880 and 886, that is, to the period after the Battle of Edington and before the 'restoration' of London.[1] This has seemed the latest probable date on the evidence of the Winchester charters, and it cannot be much earlier if it is dependent on the assumption that the defences of Winchester were restored by Alfred as part of his 'burghal system' in the years before 892.[2]

We may well ask whether that was a fair assumption, and for an answer can look to the relationship between Winchester and Southampton in the middle years of the ninth century. During the eighth and earlier part of the ninth century Hamwic was a thriving commercial and industrial centre. Winchester during this period was something very different, not an urban place, but rather a traditional and ceremonial centre, seat of a bishop, occasional, perhaps seasonal, residence of itinerant Wessex kings.[3] By the end of the ninth century, Hamwic was virtually abandoned and Winchester once again an urban place. In the chronology of this reversal may lie the key to urban change in ninth-century Wessex.

The decline of Hamwic may have begun before the middle of the ninth century, perhaps even before the Viking raids on the settlement in 840 and 842.[4] There seems no good reason to suppose, however, that the commercial needs fulfilled by Hamwic disappeared, least of all in the period following Egbert's (802–39) great expansion of the power of Wessex, consolidated by his son Æthelwulf (839–55).[5] Wider European movements may have led to a decrease in international trade,[6] but manufacture and internal trade will not have ceased.

If we now turn to Winchester, we see perhaps the other side of this coin. In 859, according to a tenth-century poem, Bishop

[1] For successive stages in the refinement of this date, see II. Interim, pp. 215–17; III. Interim, p. 242; Biddle and Hill, op. cit. in p. 325 n. 2 above, pp. 70–85, esp. pp. 76–8; Biddle, 'Winchester: the Development of an Early Capital', in H. Jankuhn *et al.* (eds.), *Vor- und Frühformen der europäischen Stadt im Mittelalter*, i (Göttingen, 1973), 229–61, esp. 248–50; and Winchester Studies, 1, p. 273, esp. n. 7, and pp. 277–9.

[2] F. M. Stenton, *Anglo-Saxon England* (3rd edn., Oxford, 1971), pp. 264–5.

[3] For the characterization of this relationship, see Biddle, 'Winchester: the Development of an Early Capital', op. cit. in n. 1 above, pp. 242–7.

[4] John F. Cherry and Richard Hodges, 'The Dating of Hamwih: Saxon Southampton Reconsidered', *Antiquaries Journal*, 58 (1978), 299–309. Mr Mark Brisbane (pers. comm.) tells me that he would now put the beginning of the decline in the 840s with virtual abandonment by 880.

[5] Stenton, op. cit. in n. 2 above, pp. 232–5, 244–5.

[6] For a recent view, see Richard Hodges and David Whitehouse, *Mohammed, Charlemagne and the Origins of Europe* (London, 1983), pp. 158–68.

Swithun (852–62) built a bridge over the river Itchen, immediately outside East Gate.[1] The road which led over this bridge was the principal, possibly at this time the only, route through the walled town, and by 902 at the latest it was the *ceapstræt* of the city. But the blocking of South Gate (Pl. 16) had already ensured as early as the sixth or seventh century that all through traffic would follow this east–west line.[2] Swithun's reported action in providing a permanent bridge to carry this road over the Itchen may thus suggest that traffic had increased to such an extent on the approach to Winchester that a bridge had become an urgent requirement. A year later in 860 Winchester was stormed by the Vikings.[3]

It was during the reign of Æthelbald (855–60) that the triple duty of service in the army, bridge building, and fortress construction was first regularly reserved in the diplomas of a king of Wessex.[4] This does not mean that these burdens were not owed before his reign, nor does their reservation under Æthelbald necessarily mean that this king levied these duties to a greater extent than his predecessors, although it must indicate his concern that they should be leviable when needed and not eroded in their yield.

Hamwic seems never to have had defences, although the 1982 excavations at Six Dials showed that the area of intense settlement was defined to the west by a boundary ditch of less than defensive scale.[5] Winchester on the other hand lay within its Roman wall, and the blocking of South Gate by a cross-ditch in the sixth or seventh century, replaced by a stone blocking *c.*700 (Pl. 16), shows that the Roman wall had remained an effective barrier, even if it was not defensible. Swithun's probable construction of the

[1] Winchester Studies, 1, pp. 271–2. For a new edition of the poem, see Winchester Studies, 4. ii. In the late eleventh century the bridge was *arcubus lapideis opere non leviter ruituro* (E. P. Sauvage, *Analecta Bollandiana*, 7 (1888), 378, ll. 16–18). Whether this stone bridge was the same as the one said by the poem to have been built by Swithun, and described there simply as *operatio pulchra*, is unknown.

[2] X. Interim, pp. 117–18; cf. Winchester Studies, 1, pp. 261–3, 276, 278.

[3] C. Plummer (ed.), *Two of the Saxon Chronicles Parallel*, i (Oxford, rev. imp. 1965), 67–8.

[4] Nicholas Brooks, 'The Development of Military Obligations in Eighth- and Ninth-Century England', in P. Clemoes and K. Hughes (eds.), *England Before the Conquest. Studies in Primary Sources Presented to Dorothy Whitelock* (Cambridge, 1971), pp. 69–84, esp. pp. 81–2.

[5] I am indebted to Mr Mark Brisbane for showing me his excavations at Six Dials and for discussing many points of Hamwic archaeology in advance of publication.

Itchen bridge at East Gate in 859 may well reflect a period of renewed attention to the defences at just the time when Æthelbald was first reserving, presumably under the threat of Viking attack, the triple duty of bridge work, fortification, and army service. The use of the word *abræcan* in the annal for 860,[1] describing the Viking attack on Winchester, implies that there were defences to be breached, and although we cannot necessarily assume that these were other than the decayed Roman wall, it looks as if this had to be forced and was thus defended. It may also be of some significance that Æthelweard in recording this event describes Winchester as *urbs regia*, a phrase not found in the Chronicle.[2]

If the urban revival of Winchester belongs to the 880s, there seems to be an uncomfortable gap opening in the provision of urban functions in Wessex between the decline of Hamwic and the rise of Winchester. The extraordinary wealth of Hamwic, its considerable population, and the services of exchange and production which it provided, cannot in the general context of the advance of Wessex in the ninth century have vanished. They can only have moved elsewhere. If, however, it was Æthelbald who started the process of re-urbanization at Winchester (perhaps with the collaboration of Swithun whose concern for his episcopal city was often recalled in later years),[3] the shift from the undefended port to the walled city may have been one continuous process.

This suggestion would allow the laying of the new grid of streets to either side of High Street, together with the wall street, to be dated earlier than *c.*880–6. This would fit better with the evidence for the high value of inherited land in the centre of the city which had to be purchased by Edward the Elder in 901–3 for the site of New Minster from those *circummanentibus iure haereditatis*,[4] but it is still impossible on archaeological grounds alone to date the use of the earliest excavated streets more accurately than to *c.*900 with a considerable margin of error.[5] One should always remember that

[1] Plummer, loc. cit. in p. 327 n. 3 above. Æthelweard used *fregerunt*: A. Campbell (ed.), *The Chronicle of Æthelweard* (London, 1962), p. 35. *brecan*, *abrecan* is the normal Old English word used in the Chronicle for successful attacks on *fortified* places: see, for example, Canterbury and London (s.a. 851 ADE, 853 C), York (s.a. 867 ADE, 868 C), the unfinished fortification, ? Newenden, Kent (s.a. 892 AE, 893 CD; cf. B. K. Davison in *Medieval Archaeology*, 16 (1972), 123–7); Benfleet (s.a. 893 AE, 894 CD).

[2] Campbell (ed.), loc. cit. in n. 1 above, p. 35.

[3] For the historical Swithun and his cult, see Winchester Studies, 4. ii.

[4] Winchester Studies, 1, p. 314.

[5] Gar Street (III. Interim, p. 242); north–south street below the castle (VIII. Interim, pp. 285–9; for an uncalibrated radiocarbon date of a.d. 880 ± 60

the laying out of the streets not only organized the interior space in relation to the defences, but also reflects the division and apportionment of the area for permanent settlement. Whether in Winchester this definitive act should still be regarded as belonging to the 880s, whether indeed it is Alfredian at all, rather than the work of one of his elder brothers, must be a matter for future investigation.

The dating of the beginning of the decline of Hamwic to the 840s, and the possibility that the urban revival of Winchester began earlier than *c.*880–6 (even if only in an initial stage expressed mainly in the refurbishing of the defences), appear to fit very well the postulated existence of a mint at Southampton until early in the reign of Æthelwulf (839–58), followed by break in the operation of a mint or mints in Wessex until the opening of the Winchester mint at the very end of the century.[1]

The sequence suggested here may also bear on another problem: the source of the population of the renewed urban community in Winchester. For if the shift from Hamwic to Winchester was a continuous process, it seems reasonable to suppose that some at least of the new Wintonians had previously been among the 5,000 or so inhabitants of Hamwic.[2] Nor, apparently, did all the newcomers settle within the walls. The evidence for occupation as early as the late ninth century in the western suburb of Winchester, along Sussex Street to the north of West Gate, is striking and requires further investigation.[3] What the attraction of extramural living might be at just the moment when defence must have seemed the paramount concern is not obvious. What advantages can an extramural tenement have enjoyed that were

(calibrated AD 902 ± 60) for material on the lowest surface of this street, see X. Interim, p. 103); wall-street below the castle (X. Interim, p. 103).

[1] Michael Dolley, 'The Location of the pre-Ælfredian Mint(s) of Wessex', *Proceedings of the Hampshire Field Club*, 27 (1970), 57–61.

[2] The figure is based on the density of buildings on the Six Dials site which suggests a population of *c.* 200 persons to the hectare or *c.* 9,000 for the *c.* 45-hectare settlement as a whole. Since all sites so far examined seem to show the same density of features, this seems a reasonable extrapolation, but it has been halved to allow for possible variations in population density over the area as a whole. I am grateful to Mr Mark Brisbane for this information: the halving is my responsibility.

[3] David A. Hinton, Suzanne Keene, and Kenneth E. Qualmann, 'The Winchester Reliquary', *Medieval Archaeology*, 25 (1981), 48–9. If the refurbishing of the defences is to be dated earlier than *c.*880–6, as suggested here, the Sussex Street occupation, which overlies what may be upcast from the newly dug ditch system, may also be dated earlier than was previously thought. This would seem to be quite consistent with the evidence of the pottery.

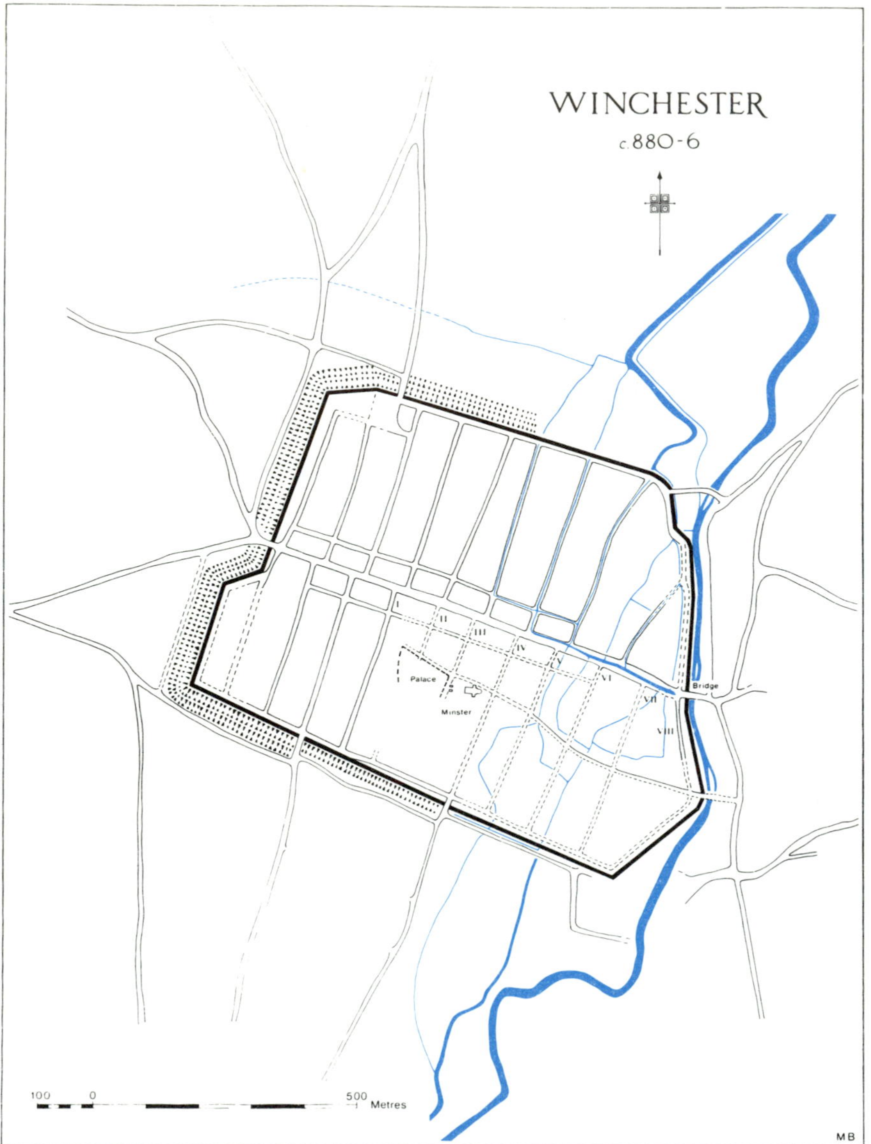

Fig. 4. Winchester in the later ninth century. Revised to show the extension of the northern back street west to the wall street (discovered in 1984 at Staple Gardens), and the stretch of the southern back street between II and III (found in 1988 at 31 A–B, The Square).

denied to someone who dwelt within the walls? It cannot be irrelevant to this enquiry that the western suburb formed an important part of the king's fief in Winchester, and by 1148 was (next to High Street) the most intensively developed area of the city and showed signs that this development had been in progress for a long time.[1]

[1] Winchester Studies, 1, pp. 350–1, 380–1, 453.

To turn lastly to one specific aspect of Winchester's ninth-century urban renewal: the street plan itself. Not all scholars have accepted that the regular arrangement of the streets (Fig. 4) is necessarily the result of deliberate planning. Some have preferred rather to regard the regularity as the inevitable result of laying out properties to either side of the pre-existing axis of High Street, and within the rectangular frame provided by the Roman defences.[1] To my mind there have so far been three substantial arguments in favour of deliberate planning: first, the similarity in construction of the first street surface wherever it has been seen in Winchester;[2] second, the use of plans of 'Winchester type', involving the same components of axial street, back streets, side streets, and wall streets, in a series of other burhs, many of them on new sites; and third, the predictability of the pattern in Winchester itself. This predictability allowed one to suggest the original layout over much of the south-eastern quarter of the city, where it was subsequently lost by the creation and extension of the sites of the three minsters and the royal palace, but where it has now been shown to have existed (Fig. 4), both by excavation and by fresh topographical analysis, especially of the relevant Anglo-Saxon charters.[3]

The reality of deliberate planning (and the reason for the predictability of the system where it had vanished) has now received strong support from Philip Crummy's analysis of the layout of the street systems of parts of Colchester and London, and that of Winchester itself.[4] He has effectively demonstrated that the

[1] Hinton, *Alfred's Kingdom: Wessex and the South 800–1500* (London, 1977), pp. 60–5, accepts that the Winchester plan was 'new, an act of deliberate creation' (p. 61), but seems to regard other plans of the same type as more probably the result of piecemeal growth conditioned by rectilinear defences and the position of gates, whether of Roman or 'Alfredian' date. See also Helen Clarke, reviewing Winchester Studies 1, in the *Bulletin of the Institute of Archaeology of the University of London*, 15 (1978), 255.

[2] VIII. Interim, p. 287; X. Interim, p. 103; Winchester Studies, 1, p. 450.

[3] Winchester Studies, 1, p. 278 n. 1. The matter will be discussed in detail in Winchester Studies, 4. i.

[4] Philip Crummy, 'The System of Measurement used in Town Planning from the Ninth to the Thirteenth Centuries', *Anglo-Saxon Studies in Archaeology and History*, 1 (1979) [= British Archaeological Reports, British Series, 72], 149–64; idem, 'Colchester Between the Roman and Norman Conquests', in D. G. Buckley (ed.), *Archaeology in Essex to AD 1500* (Council for British Archaeology, Research Report 34, London, 1980), pp. 76–81; and idem, *Aspects of Anglo-Saxon and Norman Colchester* (Council for British Archaeology, Research Report 39, London, 1981), pp. 50–1, 71–4. Crummy has suggested in these papers that the Winchester street plan may be earlier than the 880s. He

module used was a 4-pole unit ($4 \times 16\frac{1}{2}$ feet) of 66 feet or 1 chain, now enshrined in English hearts as the length of a cricket pitch, but already used in seventh-century Winchester for the length of the original nave of Old Minster. This demonstration of conscious order underlying the regularity of the street systems of pre-Conquest England provides not only a powerful proof that they were deliberately planned, but also an insight which may well be called archaeological into the minds of Anglo-Saxon men.[1]

VI

This is as far as I intend to go on this occasion in reviewing current knowledge of the development of early Winchester. Similar re-evaluations are taking place in the other phases of Winchester's past, in the long second cycle of urbanization from the tenth to the fifteenth century,[2] in the crisis of the sixteenth and seventeenth centuries, and in the third cycle which sees the emergence of the county town from the later seventeenth century onwards.[3] My purpose here has been to show something of the kind of work and rethinking which is possible when the evidential base is broad and full of detail.

If I have concentrated on the urban phenomenon and its change through time, that is because it was the theme with which our work at Winchester began twenty-two years ago, and because in a paper such as this one can only offer an adequate discussion of a few themes. This emphasis on the urban phenomenon, on aspects of social and cultural archaeology, should not obscure the broader character of the work of the Excavations Committee and the Research Unit, much of which has been concerned with

also suggests, however, that it might be as early as the period immediately after the Viking raid of 860 (see above, p. 327) and was possible because of the supposed extent of the devastation on that occasion. There is, I think, as yet no good evidence for dating the street plan so early, and no evidence at all for any devastation in the mid ninth century. The laying out of the street plan over virtually the whole of the walled area was possible in the later ninth century, not because the town was cleared by fire or otherwise devastated, but because the walled area was then to a great extent not built up due to the special character of early medieval Winchester up to this time as a ceremonial and ecclesiastical centre (cf. Biddle, 'Winchester: the Development of an Early Capital', op. cit. in p. 326 n. 1 above, pp. 239–49).

[1] Colin Renfrew, *Towards an Archaeology of Mind* (Inaugural Lecture, Cambridge, 1982), p. 21.

[2] See now especially the *Survey of Medieval Winchester* by Derek Keene (Winchester Studies 2, Oxford, 1984).

[3] Rosen, op. cit. in p. 319 n. 5 above.

buildings, with architectural archaeology, and with the attempt to put back into architectural history, as well as into the evolving fabric of Winchester, the great creations of the built past such as the Old Minster, Wolvesey, and Winchester Castle, or the lesser houses and churches which composed the foil to these greater structures across the wider part of the city. There are many archaeologies, of art, of architecture, of culture, society, and mind, and the house of archaeology is large enough to contain them all.

The lessons learnt and the needs now

This attempt to explain some of the premisses which lay behind our work in Winchester, and to illustrate our approach by a consideration of a few of the larger problems, should not end without some statement of the general lessons learnt and the principal needs for the future.

First, is the absolute importance of general and specific model building, or if you wish hypothesis formation. Without such hypotheses our work would have been without form and direction from the start. Thus, while I would not accept Hugh Thompson's view that much of urban rescue archaeology can be characterized as rubbish collection rather than research,[1] urban archaeology without the direction provided by the formation and testing of hypotheses results in mere data collection. It is because simple hypotheses about the development of Winchester in general and aspects of its fabric in particular—such as the roles played by Old Minster or Wolvesey Palace, and the interrelation of the various components of the city across the social classes—guided our work from the beginning, that the 2 per cent of the walled area which we excavated can be relied upon in further theory building to a greater extent than such a small proportion of the walled area might otherwise allow.

Second, one must stress the need for quantification and conceptual interpretation if we are to proceed to the next stage of comparative studies, and eventually to explanation. It is an irony of our knowledge of eleventh- and twelfth-century Winchester that precisely because it is so detailed, it is difficult to evaluate, for there is little with which to compare it.

Only in a few fields, notably in the study of the mint, are we yet able to evaluate the status of Winchester in relation to other towns. Without such comparison we cannot accurately understand the role and character of the city itself.

[1] See above, p. 302 n. 4.

The concept of functional change which I have stressed in this lecture may also be useful in comparative studies, not only between one town and another, but also diachronically within a single town (as between Roman and early modern Winchester) and cross-culturally between different societies (as between trading places or ceremonial centres in different cultures). Diachronic and cross-cultural studies demand, however, accurate chronological definition and scrupulous cultural description. Without a body of data which is well-founded and sufficiently extensive to carry the weight of such definition and description, diachronic and cross-cultural comparisons and all attempts at the explanation of cultural process must fail. I hope to have shown in this paper that the establishment of an adequate body of data comes only with long-continued investment which builds on strength and which operates on a scale commensurate with the opportunities offered and above all with the questions being asked. There is, unfortunately, rarely any point in small-scale excavations on urban sites.

My third point is that one cannot in urban archaeology separate research objectives and their achievement from the practical considerations of working within the pressures of a living town. Never was research conducted further from an ivory tower. These considerations almost inevitably involve high costs which have led some to question the heavy expenditure on urban archaeology by comparison with other areas of archaeological activity. I hope to have shown, however, that even in a town where much has been spent, with reasonably well-defined objectives, as much or even more remains to be learnt, principally because we can now define more closely what the real problems are, where the gaps in our knowledge lie, and what we must do to fill them. It is precisely the long continuance of work in Winchester which is yielding results that are more than superficial sketches of the city's development and changing character. Only the further continuation of work in Winchester, York, Southampton, Lincoln, London, Canterbury, and other cities large and small will eventually teach us something worth knowing about the development of the British town. The archaeology of a town must be backed with long-continued resources if the value of an initial investment is to be realized to the full. It is also too important to be left to rescue work alone. Research considerations, in urban as in other archaeology, should be the guide to future work.

Lastly, one must stress that a long-term archaeological presence is necessary in our major towns for the foreseeable future. The sudden introduction of outside teams into the complex research framework of a town's archaeology is intellectually and financially ineffective. The kind of technician's archaeology now on the increase, competent but conducted without understanding of the problems involved, is no answer to the problems of archaeology in British towns, or indeed of British archaeology. The role of local authorities in supporting active, continuing, professional archaeology in our towns is essential. It may also perhaps offer the best hope that research objectives rather than rescue requirements may come to dominate the field. An informed local authority is, after all, more likely to be concerned with the excitement and value of knowledge about its town than simply with the need to rescue sites before they are destroyed.

It is the good fortune of Winchester that it has for long had such a local authority, whose good will was the basis of our work and ensured for us so much support and not least that of this Academy.

Felix urbs Winthonia

Acknowledgements: I am most grateful to colleagues who have helped in the preparation of this paper, especially Katherine Barclay, Mark Brisbane, Birthe Kjølbye-Biddle, and Kenneth Qualmann, but they should not be held responsible for the opinions it contains and any errors which may remain. The line-drawings and photographs are the copyright of the Winchester Excavations Committee.

The work at Winchester since 1961 would not have been possible without the generous financial support of the Department of the Environment, the Hampshire County Council, the Winchester City Council, and many other public and private bodies: The American Council of Learned Societies (USA), The Avenue Trust, Barclays Bank, The Mary Duke Biddle Foundation (USA), The British Academy, the British Museum, The Calouste Gulbenkian Foundation, Duke University (USA), The Grocer's Charitable Trust, The Haverfield Trust, The Robert Kiln Charitable Trust, the Leverhulme Trust, The National Endowment for the Humanities (USA), The Nuffield Trust, The Old Dominion Foundation (USA), The Pilgrim Trust, The Rank Foundation, The Jean Sainsbury Charitable Trust, The Social Science Research Council, The Society of Antiquaries of London, The University of North Carolina (USA), The Fellows of Winchester College, The Wolfson Foundation, and many private donors. The Hayward Foundation has provided the subsidy needed for the publication of Winchester Studies.

APPENDIX A

Interim reports on the excavations of 1961–71 were published annually. The short titles shown here are used in the footnotes to the present article and in Winchester Studies.

I. Interim	Martin Biddle and R. N. Quirk, 'Excavations near Winchester Cathedral, 1961', *Archaeological Journal*, 119 (1962), 150–94, with appendices on the documentary evidence relating to the three Saxon minsters and on selected finds.
II. Interim	Martin Biddle, 'Excavations at Winchester 1962-63, Second Interim Report', *Antiquaries Journal*, 44 (1964), 188–219, with an appendix on 'Guenta' by Frank Barlow, pp. 217–19.
III. Interim	Idem, 'Excavations at Winchester 1964, Third Interim Report', ibid. 45 (1965), 230–64, with an appendix on 'Late Saxon Metalwork from the Old Minster, 1964', by David M. Wilson, pp. 262–4.
IV. Interim	Idem, 'Excavations at Winchester 1965, Fourth Interim Report', ibid. 46 (1966), 308–32, with an appendix on 'A Late Saxon Frieze Sculpture from the Old Minster', by Martin Biddle, pp. 329–32.
V. Interim	Idem, 'Excavations at Winchester 1966, Fifth Interim Report', ibid. 47 (1967), 251–79, with an appendix on 'A Late Ninth-century Wall Painting from the Site of New Minster', by Martin Biddle, pp. 277–9; see also Francis Wormald, ibid. pp. 162–5.
VI. Interim	Idem, 'Excavations at Winchester 1967, Sixth Interim Report', ibid. 48 (1968), 250–84.
VII. Interim	Idem, 'Excavations at Winchester 1968, Seventh Interim Report', ibid. 49 (1969), 295–328, with an appendix on 'A Late Anglo-Saxon Strap-end', by David M. Wilson, pp. 326–8.
VIII. Interim	Idem, 'Excavations at Winchester 1969, Eighth Interim Report', ibid. 50 (1970), 277–326.
IX. Interim	Idem, 'Excavations at Winchester 1970, Ninth Interim Report', ibid. 52 (1972), 93–131.
X. Interim	Idem, 'Excavations at Winchester 1971, Tenth Interim Report', ibid. 55 (1975), 96–126, 295–337, with an appendix on 'A Wooden Statuette from *Venta Belgarum*', by Anne Ross, pp. 335–6.

APPENDIX B

The final reports on the excavations of 1961–71 are appearing, together with the results of allied research carried out by the Winchester Research Unit, in a series entitled 'Winchester Studies' which is being published at the Clarendon Press, Oxford. The excavations of 1949–60 and those carried out since 1972 are being published in two series entitled *Winchester Excavations 1949–60* and *Winchester Excavations since 1972*, for which see above, p. 300 n. 4 and p. 309 n. 2.

The list of Winchester Studies which follows has been revised up to 1984. Volumes 1, 2, and 3. ii have already been published.

WINCHESTER STUDIES

1 *Winchester in the Early Middle Ages: an Edition and Discussion of the Winton Domesday*, by Frank Barlow, Martin Biddle, Olof von Feilitzen, and D. J. Keene, with contributions by T. J. Brown, H. M. Nixon, and Francis Wormald (published January 1976), xxxiv. 612.

2 *Survey of Medieval Winchester* (in two parts) by D. J. Keene, with a contribution by Alexander R. Rumble (published December 1985), xxxviii. 1490.

3 *Pre-Roman and Roman Winchester*:

Part I *Venta Belgarum*, by Martin Biddle and others, and including a gazetteer of pre-Roman and Roman discoveries by Kenneth Qualmann.

Part II *The Roman Cemetery at Lankhills*, by Giles Clarke with contributions by J. L. Macdonald and others (published January 1980), xlii. 468.

4 *The Anglo-Saxon Minsters of Winchester*:

Part I *The Anglo-Saxon Minsters*, by Martin Biddle, Birthe Kjølbye-Biddle, and others, and including a gazetteer of early and middle Saxon discoveries and of all other discoveries from the area of the Close by Kenneth Qualmann.

Part II *The Cult of St. Swithun*, by Michael Lapidge, with contributions by Robert Deshman and Susan Rankine.

Part III *Anglo-Saxon and Early Norman Charters Relating to the Topography of Winchester*, by Alexander R. Rumble.

5 *The Brooks and Other Town Sites of Medieval Winchester*, by Martin Biddle and others, including a gazetteer of late Saxon and medieval discoveries, other than from the Close, by Kenneth Qualmann, and

an analysis of the radiocarbon and dendrochronology dating project by R. Otlet and A. C. Barefoot.

6 *Winchester Castle and Wolvesey Palace*:

Part I *Winchester Castle*, by Martin Biddle and Beatrice Clayre.

Part II *Wolvesey Palace*, by Martin Biddle and Henri Galinié.

7 *The Crafts and Industries of Medieval Winchester*:

Part I *The Pottery of Medieval Winchester*, by Katherine Barclay and others.

Part II *The Arts, Crafts, Industries, and Daily Life of Medieval Winchester*, by Martin Biddle and others (published 1989).

8 *The Winchester Mint and Other Medieval Numismatic Studies*, by Yvonne Harvey and others, edited by Martin Biddle.

9 *Human and Animal Biology*:

Part I *The People of Early Winchester*, by D. R. Brothwell, Theya Molleson, and Caroline Stuckert.

Part II *The Animals of Early Winchester*, by Pauline Sheppard, Gina Adams, and others.

10 *The Environment, Agriculture, and Gardens in Early Winchester*, edited by Jane M. Renfrew, with contributions by F. Green, M. Monk, P. R. Murphy, J. Z. Titow, and others.

11 *The Origins and Development of Winchester: a General Survey*, by Martin Biddle, including a bibliography of writing on Winchester and a general index.

APPENDIX C

A selective bibliography of articles on, preparatory to, or resulting from, the excavations of 1961–71, the work of the Winchester Research Unit since 1968, and the activity of the Winchester City Archaeologist since 1972. For interim reports 1961–71, see Appendix A. For interim reports since 1972, see *Find* (the Newsletter of the Winchester Archaeological Rescue Group). For final reports 1949–60, 1961–71, and 1972 onwards, see Appendix B.

Barefoot, A. C., Woodhouse, Lewis B., Hafley, William L., and Wilson, E. H., 'Developing a Dendrochronology for Winchester, England', *Journal of the Institute of Wood Science*, 6 (5) (June 1974), 34–40.

——'A Winchester Dendrochronology for 1635–1972 AD: its Validity and Possible Extension', ibid. 7 (1) (May 1975), 25–32.

——Hafley, W. L., and Hughes, J. F., 'Dendrochronology and the Winchester Excavation', in Fletcher, J. (ed.), *Dendrochronology in*

Europe (British Archaeological Reports, International Series 51, Oxford, 1978), pp. 162–72.

Biddle, Martin, 'Winchester: the Archaeology of a City', *Science Journal* 1 (i) (March 1965), 55-61.

——'Health in Medieval Winchester: the Evidence from Excavations', in Cockburn, Aidan (ed.), *Infectious Diseases: their Evolution and Eradication* (Springfield, Illinois, 1967), pp. 58–60.

——'Two Burials of the First Century AD from Winchester', *Antiquaries Journal*, 47 (1967), 224–50.

——'Wolvesey: the *domus quasi palatium* of Henry de Blois in Winchester', *Château Gaillard*, 3 (1969), 28–36.

——'Winchester 1961-68', ibid. 4 (1969), 19–30.

——'Winchester: the Development of an Early Capital', in Jankuhn, H., Schlesinger, W., and Steuer, H. (eds.), *Vor- und Frühformen der europäischen Stadt im Mittelalter*, i (Abhandlungen der Akademie der Wissenschaften, Philologisch-Historische Klasse, 3te Folge, Nr. 83, Göttingen, 1973), 229–61.

——'The Archaeology of Winchester', *Scientific American* (May 1974), pp. 32–43.

——'The Evolution of Towns: Planned Towns before 1066', in Barley, M. W. (ed.), *The Plans and Topography of Medieval Towns in England and Wales* (Council for British Archaeology, Research Report 14, London, 1975), pp. 19–32.

——'Ptolemaic Coins from Winchester', *Antiquity*, 49 (1975), 213–15.

——'Felix urbs Winthonia: Winchester in the Age of Monastic Reform', in Parsons, D. (ed.), *Tenth-century Studies* (Chichester and London, 1975), pp. 123–40.

——'Venta Belgarum (Winchester)', in Stillwell, Richard (ed.), *The Princeton Encyclopedia of Classical Sites* (Princeton, 1976), pp. 964–5.

——'Hampshire and the Origins of Wessex', in Sieveking, G. de G., Longworth, I. H., and Wilson, K. E. (eds.), *Problems in Economic and Social Archaeology* (London, 1976), pp. 323–42.

——*Wolvesey: the Old Bishop's Palace* (English Heritage, London, 1986).

——*King Arthur's Round Table: an Archaeological Investigation* (London, 1989).

——'Archaeology, Architecture, and the Cult of Saints in Anglo-Saxon England', in Butler, L. A. S., and Morris, R. K. (eds.), *The Anglo-Saxon Church. Papers on History, Architecture, and Archaeology in Honour of Dr. H. M. Taylor* (Council for British Archaeology Research Report 60, London, 1986), pp. 1–31.

——'Seasonal Festivals and Residence: Winchester, Westminster and Gloucester in the Tenth to Twelfth Centuries', *Anglo-Norman Studies* 8 (1986), 51–72.

——'Early Norman Winchester', in Holt, J. C. (ed.), *Domesday Studies* (Woodbridge, 1987), pp. 311–31.

——'Winchester: The Rise of an Early Capital', in Ford, Boris (ed.), *The Cambridge Guide to the Arts in Britain* 1 (Cambridge, 1988), pp. 194–205.

——and Barclay, Katherine, 'Winchester Ware', in Evison, Vera I., Hodges, H., and Hurst, J. G. (eds.), *Medieval Pottery from Excavations: Studies Presented to Gerald Clough Dunning* (London, 1974), pp. 137–65.

——and Clayre, Beatrice, *Winchester Castle and the Great Hall* (Winchester, 1983).

——and Collis, John, 'A New Type of 9th and 10th-century Pottery from Winchester', *Medieval Archaeology*, 22 (1978), 133–5.

——and Hill, David, 'Late Saxon Planned Towns', *Antiquaries Journal*, 51 (1971), 70–85.

Biddle, Martin, and Kjølbye-Biddle, Birthe, 'Metres, Areas and Robbing', *World Archaeology*, 1 (1969), 208–19.

——*Winchester: Saxon and Norman art* (Catalogue of an exhibition in Winchester Cathedral Treasury, revised edition with illustrations, Winchester, 1973).

Collis, John and Kjølbye-Biddle, Birthe, 'Early Medieval Bone Spoons from Winchester', *Antiquaries Journal*, 59 (1979), 375–91.

Dolley, R. H. M., 'A Recent Find of Long Cross Pennies of Henry III from Winchester', *Numismatic Chronicle*, 7th ser. 1 (1961), 185–9.

Dolley, Michael and Blunt, C. E., 'Coins from the Winchester Excavations 1961–1973', *British Numismatic Journal*, 47 (1978), 135–8.

Hinton, David A., Keene, Suzanne, and Qualmann, Kenneth E., 'The Winchester Reliquary', *Medieval Archaeology*, 25 (1981), 45–77.

Keene, Derek, 'Suburban Growth', in Barley, M. W. (ed.), *The Plans and Topography of Medieval Towns in England and Wales* (Council for British Archaeology, Research Report 14, London, 1975), pp. 71–82.

——'Medieval Winchester: its Spatial Organization', in Burnham, Barry C. and Kingsbury, John (eds.), *Space, Hierarchy and Society: Interdisciplinary Studies in Social Area Analysis* (British Archaeological Reports, International Series 59, 1979), pp. 149–59.

——'Rubbish in Medieval Towns', in Hall, A. R. and Kenward, H. K. (eds.), *Environmental Archaeology in the Urban Context* (Council for British Archaeology, Research Report 43, London, 1982), pp. 26–30.

——'Town into Gown: the Site of the College and other College Lands in Winchester before the Reformation', in Custance, R. (ed.), *Winchester College Sixth-centenary Essays* (Oxford, 1982), pp. 37–75.

——'The Medieval Urban Environment in Written Records', *Archives*, 16 (1983), 137–44.

——'Introduction to the Parish Churches of Medieval Winchester', *Bulletin of the CBA Churches Committee*, 23 (Winter, 1983), 1–9.

Keene, Suzanne, 'An Approach to the Sampling and Storage of Waterlogged Timbers from Excavations', *The Conservator*, 1 (1977), 8–11.

Kjølbye-Biddle, Birthe, 'A Cathedral Cemetery: Problems in Excavation and Interpretation', *World Archaeology*, 7 (1) (1975), 87–108.

——'The Seventh-Century Minster Church at Winchester Interpreted', in Butler, L. A. S. and Morris, R. K. (eds.), *The Anglo-Saxon Church. Studies on History, Architecture, and Archaeology in Honour of Dr. H. M. Taylor* (Council for British Archaeology, Research Report 60, London, 1986) pp. 196–209.

——'The Winchester "Weather Vane" Reconsidered' in Lind, Birgit *et al.* (eds.), *Mindeskrift til Ole Klindt-Jensen* (=*Hikuin* 10 (1984)), pp. 307–14.

——and Page, R. I., 'A Scandinavian Rune Stone from Winchester', *Antiquaries Journal*, 55 (1975), 389–94.

Laurent, V., 'Byzance et l'Angleterre au lendemain de la conquête normande: à propos d'un sceau byzantin trouvé à Winchester', *Numismatic Circular*, 71 (1963), 93–6.

——'Un sceau inédit du patriarche de Jérusalem Sophrone II trouvé à Winchester', ibid. 72 (1964), 49–50.

Pike, A. W. and Biddle, Martin, 'Parasite Eggs in Medieval Winchester', *Antiquity*, 40 (1966), 293–6.

Qualmann, Kenneth E., 'Rescue Archaeology in the City of Winchester', *District Councils Review*, March 1975, 64–7.

——'A Late-Roman Cemetery at West Hill, Winchester', *Britannia*, 12 (1981), 295–7.

Quirk, R. N., 'Winchester Cathedral in the Tenth Century', *Archaeological Journal*, 114 (1957), 28–68.

——'Winchester New Minster and its Tenth-century Tower', *Journal of the British Archaeological Association*, 3rd ser. 24 (1961), 16–54.

Rance, Adrian, *A Prospect of Winchester: a Guide to the City Museum* (Winchester, 1978).

Schadla-Hall, R. T., *Winchester District: the Archaeological Potential* (Winchester, 1977).

Sheerin, D. J., 'The Dedication of the Old Minster, Winchester, in 980', *Revue Bénédictine*, 88 (1978), 261–72.

INDEX